Community Builders Handbook Series

SHOPPING CENTER DEVELOPMENT HANDBOOK

Sponsored by the

Executive Group

of the

Commercial and Office Development Council

of

ULI–the Urban Land Institute

1977

ULI–the Urban Land Institute, Washington, D.C.

About ULI–the Urban Land Institute

ULI–the Urban Land Institute is an independent, nonprofit research and educational organization incorporated in 1936 to improve the quality and standards of land use and development.

The Institute is committed to conducting practical research in the various fields of real estate knowledge; identifying and interpreting land use trends in relation to the changing economic, social, and civic needs of the people; and disseminating pertinent information leading to the orderly and more efficient use and development of land.

ULI receives its financial support from membership dues, sale of publications, and contributions for research and panel services.

ULI Staff for Shopping Center Development Handbook

Managing Editor	Frank H. Spink, Jr.
Associate Editor	Nathaniel M. Griffin
Manuscript Editor	Mark Schlotterbeck
Production Manager	Robert L. Helms
Production Assistant	Sarah V. Lantz
Art Director	Carolyn E. Noe
Graphic Consultant	Ken Fuller
	Scott-Fuller Communications, Inc.

Second book in a new series of publications based on the
philosophy of The Community Builders Handbook
First Edition and First Printing 1947
Revised Printing 1948
Second or J. C. Nichols Memorial Edition and Second Revised Printing 1950
Third or The Members Edition and Third Revised Printing 1954
Fourth Revised Printing 1956
Fourth or The Executive Edition and Fifth Revised Printing 1960
Sixth Printing 1965
Fifth or Anniversary Edition and Seventh Revised Printing 1968

Other books in the series:
Industrial Development Handbook, 1975
Residential Development Handbook, 1978

Recommended bibliographic listing:
Urban Land Institute. *Shopping Center Development Handbook.*
Washington: Urban Land Institute, 1977.

© 1977 by ULI–the Urban Land Institute
1200 18th Street, N.W.
Washington, D.C. 20036

Second Printing 1978
Third Printing 1979

Library of Congress Catalog Card Number 77-79326
Printed in the United States of America

Authors

Principal Authors

J. Ross McKeever
Nathaniel M. Griffin

Contributing Author

Frank H. Spink, Jr.

with
The Commercial and Office Development Council
of
ULI–the Urban Land Institute

Acknowledgments

The two principal authors each had primary responsibility for major portions of the text. J. Ross McKeever, editor and principal author of the predecessor work, *The Community Builders Handbook*, prepared the initial drafts for Chapters 1 through 5 and for Chapter 7. Nathaniel M. Griffin developed the case studies presented in Chapter 6 and was responsible for compiling and selecting all illustrative materials presented in the book. As managing editor, Frank H. Spink, Jr., was responsible for overall coordination of the authors' work, incorporation of the council's suggestions, and final preparation of the manuscript for publication.

In assembling any book of this magnitude an author must call upon many people for advice and assistance. To list all those who helped would be impossible; to list a few is to run the risk of leaving out someone who should receive credit. Nevertheless, an added note of thanks is due to Donald Blair, Philip Duffy, Robert Grossman, Ede Kean, Keith Peterson, William Parlee, Richard Roti, Robert Schout, Gerald Schwartz, and Michael Was for the extra effort they made.

Special thanks must also be given to Roy P. Drachman, past president of both the Urban Land Institute and the International Council of Shopping Centers, for his review of the initial manuscript and his suggestions for expansion and modification; and to Michael F. Kelly, under whose term as chairman of the Commercial and Office Development Council this book was started, for devoting many hours to a final, galley-by-galley review.

The members of the Commercial and Office Development Council provided continuing review as the manuscript proceeded from the first through the final drafts. Council members also provided an important service by identifying the principal future trends presented in Chapter 7.

About ULI Councils

Within the Urban Land Institute there are six councils: Commercial and Office Development, Industrial, New Communities, Recreational Development, Residential, and Urban Redevelopment. Each council is composed of 40 active members drawn from the ULI Sustaining membership. Council appointment is based on knowledge, experience, and a willingness to share. Developers, consultants, public officials, and academicians are included on each of the councils to provide a broad perspective and to encourage interaction among various disciplines.

Executive Group of the
Commercial and Office Development Council, 1976-1977

Chairman:

N. S. Ridgway, Jr.
Vice President
Fritz B. Burns & Associates
Los Angeles

Vice Chairmen:

Donald R. Riehl
President
D. R. Riehl, Inc.
San Francisco

Marion G. Smith, Jr.
President, Intereal Company
National Life and Accident Insurance Company
Nashville

Donald R. Waugh, Jr.
Vice President, Mortgages
The Equitable Life Assurance Society
New York

John R. White
President and Chief Executive Officer
James D. Landauer Associates, Inc.
New York

Paul D. Ambrose*
Ambrose & Company
Denver

Claude M. Ballard, Jr.
Vice President
The Prudential Insurance Company of America
Newark

Boyd T. Barnard**
Counselor
Jackson-Cross Company
Philadelphia

Robert B. Barrows
Senior Vice President, Investments
The Northwestern Mutual Life Insurance Company
Milwaukee

David D. Bohannon**
President
David D. Bohannon Organization
San Mateo, California

Temple H. Buell
President
Buell & Company
Denver

James L. Burke, Jr.
Palos Verdes Estates, California

James H. Coker
James H. Coker & Associates
Dallas

U. A. Denker*
Real Estate Broker and Consultant
Wichita

George A. Devlin
President
National Planning, Inc.
Detroit

David Dodge
Alliance Properties, Inc.
Atlanta

James B. Douglas*
Seattle

Roy P. Drachman**
Roy Drachman Realty Company
Tucson

Hubert D. Eller
Real Estate Consultant
San Francisco

Michael A. Feiner
Vice President
U.S. Realty Investment
Cleveland

Douglas M. Godine
Godine & Company
Baltimore

Gerald D. Hines
Gerald D. Hines Interests
Houston

Hunter A. Hogan, Jr.**
Chairman of the Board
Goodman Segar Hogan, Inc.
Norfolk

Alander F. Hogland
Partner
Hogland, Bogart & Bertero
San Francisco

Earl D. Hollinshead**
Bethel Park, Pennsylvania

R. E. Hughes
President
Hughes Real Estate
Greenville, South Carolina

Harold R. Imus
President
Development Control Corporation
Northfield, Illinois

Eugene Johnson
Senior Vice President
Security Pacific National Bank
Los Angeles

Keith Kelly
Vice President, Development
Crown Center Redevelopment Corporation
Kansas City, Missouri

Michael F. Kelly
President
Dayton Hudson Properties
Minneapolis

Contents

List of Illustrations

A Brief History of the Community Builders Handbook Series

The Community Builders Handbook Series came into being when the *Industrial Development Handbook* was published in 1975. This new series expands and replaces *The Community Builders Handbook*, first published in 1947.

The objective of the original handbook was to share the experience and knowledge of developers and to encourage the improvement of land use and development practices. The handbook was sponsored by the Community Builders Council (now the Residential Council), which had been formed in 1944. The first edition contained 205 pages and was sparsely illustrated, but it was a major accomplishment since, for the first time, a book was made available which described the development of residential communities and shopping centers.

The second edition, the J. C. Nichols Memorial Edition, was published in 1950. It incorporated a modest revision and updating of the original text. In 1954 the third or Members edition, with 315 pages, significantly expanded the scope of the work. The fourth or Executive edition of 1960 continued this expansion in response to the increasing complexity of development practices. By this time the handbook had grown to 476 pages, but it continued to focus on residential and shopping center development. The fifth or Anniversary edition was published in 1968. The handbook had now grown to 526 pages and had been broadened once more in coverage. In addition to sections on residential and shopping center development, new material discussing a variety of special types of land development was included. Also added was a section on industrial development, drawing on the experience of ULI's Industrial Council, which had been formed in 1951. The Industrial Council had sponsored other ULI publications but was now represented for the first time in the handbook.

The Community Builders Handbook became widely recognized as a major reference source and textbook on land use and development practice based on the practical experience and accumulated knowledge of leading practitioners in the field. In 1965, as work on the 1968 edition was beginning, ULI was growing rapidly in membership and in areas of interest. The development industry was maturing and new directions for the Institute were being examined. By 1970 a decision had been made to publish future editions of *The Community Builders Handbook* in separate volumes, in order to provide the expanded and more comprehensive coverage not possible in a single text.

In 1972 the three original councils of the Institute—the Community Builders, Central City, and Industrial Councils—were reorganized into six councils in order to accommodate the new diversity in development activities and in ULI's membership. Members of the Community Builders Council and the Central City Council formed the nucleus of the Commercial and Office Development Council, under whose aegis this volume was developed. The reorganization itself was one of the events that led to a multivolume Community Builders Handbook Series.

The *Shopping Center Development Handbook* is the second volume of the new series, having followed the *Industrial Development Handbook*. The *Residential Development Handbook*, which will follow shortly, will complete the basic replacement of the 1968 edition of *The Community Builders Handbook*. Other volumes, each focusing on a specific land use type, will be added to the series in the future.

Frank H. Spink, Jr.
Managing Editor
Community Builders Handbook Series

Foreword

Shopping center development has reached a level of maturity and sophistication that would have been hard to imagine when the first edition of *The Community Builders Handbook* was prepared in 1947. An even earlier ULI publication, *Mistakes We Have Made in Developing Shopping Centers*, written by J. C. Nichols and published in 1945, was the first to develop a body of practical knowledge about the evolving concept of shopping centers. The projects discussed were the pioneering efforts out of which the contemporary shopping center evolved. The significance of these publications, however, lies as much in their approach as in their content. By emphasizing the recording and sharing of practical experience of leading shopping center developers, rather than dealing primarily with theoretical concepts, *Mistakes We Have Made* became the guiding principle for *The Community Builders Handbook* in its first and all subsequent editions. This practical approach has likewise guided the creation of the present work. Throughout, the discussion focuses on recommended practices and standards of excellence.

As shopping centers have developed, several clearly identifiable types have been defined. We now see three major categories: the neighborhood, community, and regional centers. The super-regional center can reasonably be considered a fourth category, although it differs from the regional center only in magnitude. These categories are not precise, and patterns are still evolving. Typical tenant compositions for each of the basic types have changed: stores that might once have been found most often in one kind of center might now be found mostly in another. The sizes of centers, as well, have changed greatly: a center that might have been considered one of the giants ten years ago is now just another regional center, having been replaced in stature by the super-regional center with as many as six department stores.

Special markets have stimulated the development of a variety of special kinds of shopping centers that do not quite fit traditional definitions. The most glamorous of these are now being referred to simply as *theme centers* or *specialty centers*. The search for the shopping center of strikingly unusual character has also led to the adaptive reuse of existing buildings as shopping centers, adding another facet to the complexities of analysis and description. This complexity is perhaps most clearly seen if we look at the community center. At first, the anchor tenant was either a variety store or junior department store. But the junior department store has been replaced by the discount department store, and the variety store has been replaced to a large extent by the super-drug, whose pharmacy is now only an adjunct to its much larger array of other merchandise.

It was this kind of evolution that suggested the need to develop this handbook as a replacement for the shopping center section of *The Community Builders Handbook*. The Urban Land Institute has always attempted to provide leadership in recommending new and better development practices; a present need for such leadership was perceived if the developer, planner, public official, and various other professionals were to continue to be able to make decisions concerning shopping centers that would be responsive to present and future community needs. For this reason, the development of this volume has been a major commitment of the Commercial and Office Development Council for a little over two years.

When the first draft of Chapters 1 through 5 was completed in November 1975, the review and revision process began. During a full-council review of the material, it became clear that a series of case studies—covering each of the major types of centers and including as well some of the emerging subtypes—was needed to fully address current practices in shopping center development. In addition, even though the real estate industry was then experiencing an economic recession, council reviewers felt that a modest effort at identifying future trends should be incorporated. This was consistent with the approach taken by the Industrial Council, which was just finishing its review of the *Industrial Development Handbook*. After a second draft was prepared, individual sections were sent to various members of the council for further review and comment. Finally, the many comments and suggestions were themselves reviewed, consolidated, and incorporated into the final version.

As a consequence of this review process, the *Shopping Center Development Handbook* represents an attempt by ULI to distill the knowledge and experience of its members in the shopping center development industry. We of the Commercial and Office Development Council offer this book in the hopes it can contribute to the understanding of shopping centers as one of the most important land use elements in community development.

Michael F. Kelly
Council Chairman, 1973-76

N. S. Ridgway, Jr.
Council Chairman, 1976-77

1.
Introduction

Definitions
The Shopping Center

The shopping center is a specialized, commercial land use and building type commonly found in suburban areas. Shopping centers are found throughout the country, but the term *shopping center* is often used rather loosely, even though its definition and those of related terms have been standardized. When used accurately, the term *shopping center* refers to:

A group of architecturally unified commercial establishments built on a site which is planned, developed, owned, and managed as an operating unit related in its location, size, and type of shops to the trade area that the unit serves. The unit provides on-site parking in definite relationship to the types and total size of the stores.

This definition was originated by the Community Builders Council of ULI–the Urban Land Institute. The council, established in 1944, formulated many planning and development principles and terms for the shopping center that are basic in the industry today.

In 1947, under the chairmanship of Jesse Clyde Nichols of Kansas City, the council produced its first major publication, *The Community Builders Handbook*, which was divided into two sections—one on residential development, the other on shopping center development. The original *Community Builders Handbook* and its later editions were the forerunners of the present Community Builders Handbook Series, of which this book is a part.

The Community Builders Council existed under the same name until 1972, when ULI reorganized its council structure. Some of the definitions developed by the council are the *shopping center*, given above; the *standard types* of shopping centers; *gross leasable area* (GLA), for uniform measurement of the size of a shopping center; and the *parking index*, a measurement of the parking space provision within a site.

Each of these terms arose from a need to communicate precisely about the shopping center. The definition given above for shopping center, for example, distinguishes this land use and building type from miscellaneous collections of individual stores which stand on separate lot parcels along streets and highways or which are clustered as a concentrated business district, with or without incidental off-street parking. These are retail *shopping areas* or *shopping districts*. Shopping centers, because of their preplanned layout and unified operation, differ from shopping districts even though both are commercial use areas for retail selling and the operation of other businesses.

1

The following elements characterize the shopping center and set it apart as a building type and planned commercial land use:

- Unified architectural treatment for the building or buildings that provide space for commercial establishments which are selected and then managed as a unit for the benefit of all tenants. A shopping center is not a miscellaneous or unplanned assemblage of separate or common-wall structures.
- Unified site, suited to the type of center called for by the market. The site may permit building and parking expansion if trade area and other growth factors demand. In addition, the site is located for easy access from the trade area and is arranged to distribute customer pedestrian traffic so as to maximize retail merchandising.
- On-site parking, arranged to provide adequate entrance and exit and acceptable walking distances from the parked car to the stores.
- Service facility for goods delivery, separated from customer awareness.
- Tenant grouping that provides merchandising interplay among stores and the widest possible range and depth of merchandise appropriate for the trade area.
- Agreeable surroundings for shopping in comfort (including weather protection), convenience, safety, and quality of design—including signs and their placement.

These characteristics are not associated with the usual commercial district. An important point about shopping centers is that they create an image for the unit through *single ownership and management* and through joint promotional efforts by tenants and owners.

Each element in a shopping center must be adapted to fit the circumstances peculiar to the site and its environs. Innovations and various interpretations of the basic features must be considered in planning, developing, and operating a successful shopping center. To be successful, the center must be not only profitable but also an asset to the community within which it is located.

Other Terms

Within the commercial land uses which are properly called shopping centers, there are several major, identifiable types—neighborhood, community, and regional shopping centers—and a number of distinct variations of these major categories.

To discuss these types, however, we must first look at several other terms necessary for the delineation of the major kinds of centers, and necessary as well for any discussion of shopping centers. These include the terms *GLA, parking index,* and *trade area,* and the names for the classes of goods a store or center may offer.

- *GLA.* In the shopping center industry, sizes of centers and tenant spaces are expressed in terms of *gross leasable area,* or *GLA.* Gross leasable area is the measurement to use for uniform comparison and accurate measurement. Its use avoids misunderstandings in statistical analyses and other descriptions.

  GLA is the total floor area designed for the tenants' occupancy and exclusive use—including basements, mezzanines, and upper floors—expressed in square feet and measured from the centerline of joint partitions and from outside wall faces. It is all that area on which tenants pay rent, including sales areas and integral stock areas.

  The difference between gross floor area and gross leasable area is the common area not leasable to individual tenants. Gross leasable area does not include public or common areas such as public toilets, corridors, stairwells, elevators, machine and equipment rooms, lobbies, or mall areas, whether open or enclosed. *Gross floor area* would include these and other areas integral to the building function. Except for community rooms and management offices, common areas and storage areas in shopping centers do not generate demand for customer parking. Enclosed common area is typically 10 to 30 percent of the total area in the regional or community center; in office building terminology, enclosed common area is essentially the difference between gross building area and net rentable area.

- *Parking index.* GLA is also a useful measurement for determining the appropriate number of parking spaces for a shopping center, because it affords a comparison between the shopping area and the parking demand of shoppers. In defining the relationship between parking and structure, the shopping center industry has arrived at the acceptable level of parking provision and has developed the standards of measurement of this provision. The unit of measurement is the *parking index,* which is the number of parking spaces per 1,000 square feet

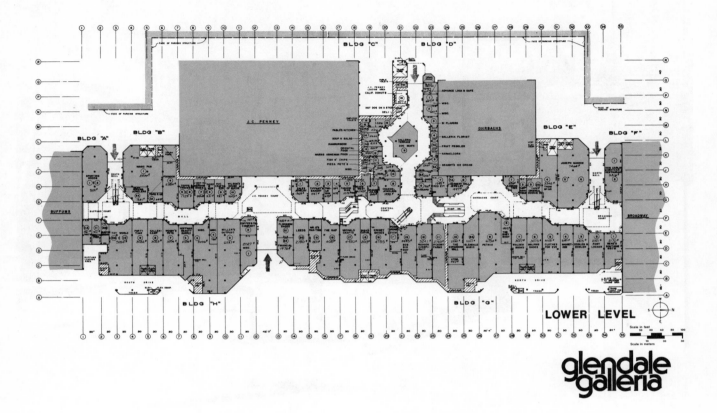

1-1   Lease plan of Glendale Galleria in Glendale, California. Shown in color is the center's gross leasable area.

of GLA. The commonly accepted standard index for shopping centers, based on research and experience, is 5.5—in other words, 5.5 spaces per 1,000 square feet of GLA. The parking index is discussed further in Chapter 3.

- *Trade area* is that area containing people who are likely to purchase a given class of goods or services from a particular firm or group of firms.
- *Convenience goods* are those which are needed immediately and often and which are purchased where it is most convenient for the shopper.
- *Specialty goods* are those which shoppers will take more care and spend greater effort to purchase.
- *Shopping goods* are those which draw forth the utmost in time, effort, and the desire for comparison shopping.
- *Impulse goods* are those which are not actively sought by shoppers. Impulse goods have an

indefinite trade area and are placed so as to get them into the customer flow created by other businesses or within a store where people are passing by on their way to find a definitely sought-for item.

The Key Types of Shopping Centers

As mentioned earlier, the shopping center has evolved into three distinct types, but with some variations on these. The three key types are the neighborhood, community, and regional centers. Each is different in its function.

In all cases, even within the variations, the *major tenant classification* determines the type of shopping center. Tenant classifications and auxiliary facilities are in keeping with the territory from which the center draws customers. *Neither the site area nor the building size determines the type of center.*

1-2 Country Club Corners, in Colorado Springs, is an innovative neighborhood shopping center with 43,350 square feet of GLA, including 14,100 square feet of office space. A series of interconnected buildings, designed for compatibility with an adjacent residential area, are oriented toward an open courtyard with a clock tower.

The *neighborhood center* provides for the sale of convenience goods (food, drugs, and sundries) and personal services, those which meet the daily needs of an immediate neighborhood trade area.

A supermarket is the principal tenant in the neighborhood center. Consumer shopping patterns show that geographical convenience is the most important factor in the shopper's choice of supermarkets. The customer usually chooses such stores from among those most conveniently located, usually those nearest the shopper's home. Only as a secondary consideration does wide selection of merchandise or service come into play.

The neighborhood center has a *typical* gross leasable area of about 50,000 square feet but may range from 30,000 to 100,000 square feet. For its site area, the neighborhood center needs from 3 to 10 acres. It normally serves a trade area population of 2,500 to 40,000 people within a 6-minute drive.

The neighborhood center, sometimes called a convenience center, is the smallest type of shopping center.

The *community center* is built around a junior department store or variety store as the major tenant, in addition to the supermarket. *Such a center does not have a full-line department store,* although it may have a strong specialty or discount store as an anchor tenant.

The community center offers shoppers greater depth and range of merchandise—assortments in clothing sizes, styles, colors, and prices—than does a neighborhood or convenience center.

The community center has a *typical* gross leasable area of about 150,000 square feet but may range from 100,000 to 300,000 square feet. For its site area, the community center needs from 10 to 30 acres. It normally serves a trade area population of 40,000 to 150,000 people.

1-3 Pomerado Village shopping center in Rancho Bernardo, the new community near San Diego, California. The Spanish-style center accommodates a variety of community-scale shopping needs and includes a bank, a grocery, beauty shops, barber shops, a furniture store, and many other retail shops.

If population increases in the trade area can be predicted reliably, the prudent developer of a community center will plan to have adequate land available for expansion. When the growth in sales volume warrants and the drawing power justifies, the community center can often be increased in status to that of a small regional by the introduction of a full-line department store and additional shops, offices, and services.

In the metropolitan area, a community center is vulnerable to competition. It is too big to thrive from its immediate neighborhood trade area and too weak to make a strong impact on the whole community, except in smaller cities, those with populations of 50,000 to 100,000. The development of a strong regional center, with the pulling power of one or more department stores, may impinge on a community center's trade area. But in a normally strong market area, both can succeed, even if they are within several miles of one another, because of the difference in the types of merchandise offered and because of the community center's convenience to the shopper, particularly the convenient vehicle travel distance.

In cities with populations of 50,000 to 100,000, the community center may actually take on the stature of a regional center because of the center's local dominance and pulling power, even though the array of tenants does not include a full-line department store. A popular price or discount store may substitute locally in customer acceptance and in function as the leading tenant.

A community shopping center is the type whose size and pulling power are the most difficult to estimate. Because some shopping goods are made available, shoppers are less predictable in their shopping habits for clothes and appliances but will customarily go to their favorite supermarket for their household's daily needs.

1-4 Sherway Gardens, a twin-anchor regional shopping center with a strategic freeway location in the southwestern suburbs of metropolitan Toronto.

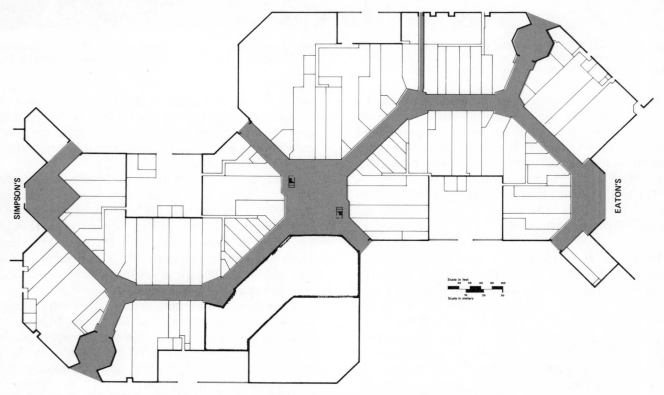

1-5 The S-shaped pedestrian mall at Sherway Gardens was recently expanded into a figure eight.

CHARACTERISTICS OF SHOPPING CENTERS

CENTER TYPE	LEADING TENANT (BASIS FOR CLASSIFICATION)	TYPICAL GLA	GENERAL RANGE IN GLA	USUAL MINIMUM SITE AREA	MINIMUM SUPPORT REQUIRED
NEIGHBORHOOD CENTER	Supermarket or drugstore	50,000 sq. ft.	30,000–100,000 sq. ft.	3 acres	2,500–40,000 people
COMMUNITY CENTER	Variety, discount, or junior department store	150,000 sq. ft.	100,000–300,000 sq. ft.	10 acres or more	40,000–150,000 people
REGIONAL CENTER	One or more full-line department stores of at least 100,000 sq. ft. of GLA*	400,000 sq. ft.	300,000–1,000,000 sq. ft. or more*	30–50 acres or more	150,000 or more people

*Centers with more than 750,000 sq. ft. GLA usually include three or more department stores and hence are super-regionals.

The community center is the in-between or intermediate type of shopping center.

The *regional center* provides shopping goods, general merchandise, apparel, furniture, and home furnishings in full depth and variety. It is built around the full-line department store, with a minimum GLA of 100,000 square feet, as the major drawing power. For even greater comparative shopping, two department stores—even three or more—are being included among the tenantry. The normal design uses the pedestrian mall, either open or enclosed, as a connector between the major anchor stores. The mall also establishes a basic pattern for directing customer flow past supplementary tenant stores which are placed between the purposely separated majors.

The regional center has a *typical* gross leasable area of 400,000 square feet. Regional centers range from 300,000 to more than 1,000,000 square feet. *When the regional center exceeds 750,000 square feet in GLA and includes three or more department stores, it becomes a super-regional center.*

Regional and super-regional centers establish their customer drawing power from their ability to offer full ranges of shopping facilities and goods. This attraction extends their trade areas by 10 to 15 miles or more, modified by such factors as competitive facilities and travel time over access highways. There is no difference in function between regionals and super-regionals—only strength and range in their customer drawing power.

The regional and super-regional are the largest types of shopping center. They are also the glamour centers. They come closest to reproducing shopping facilities and customer attraction once available only in central business districts.

Figure 1-6 compares the characteristics of the three major types of shopping centers. Numbers shown in the table must be regarded only as convenient indicators for defining the various types of centers; the basic elements of any center may change because of the need to adapt to the characteristics of the trade area, including the nature of the competition, population density, and income levels. The number of people needed to support a shopping center of any type, for example, cannot be fixed, because income level, disposable income, dilution by competition, and changing methods of merchandising and changing store sizes all enter into the calculations. Obviously, no rigid standard for size would be realistic. Local conditions within a trade area (number of households, income levels, existing retail outlets) are more important than any standard population figure in estimating purchasing power needed to support a center.

Once more, it is emphasized that tenant composition and the characteristics of the leading tenant define a shopping center type. Building area, site size, and population do not.

Variations of the Major Types

The seventies has begun an era of consumer and citizen awareness, energy and environmental controls, and heightened levels of public taste and sophistication. Established behavioral patterns are shifting under social and economic pressures and because of the liberalized lifestyles among families and young people.

Design criteria change rapidly. Merchandisers readily gear to change. Pants stores quickly become jean or unisex shops. But the shopping center development industry, in responding to the changing demands of the market, must also work with externally imposed constraints on concepts with which approval authorities may not yet have become familiar. Yet despite the difficulty of achieving general acceptance of new concepts, developers are proceeding with improvements and variations of the conventional types of shopping centers.

The original variation of the strip-type pattern was the pedestrian mall. Two facing strips were separated by introducing a pedestrian street. Later, the open garden space between the facing structures was enclosed, heated, and air-conditioned. The innovation of weatherproofing for pedestrian appeal and shopper comfort was readily adapted to regional centers.

The predominant pattern in today's regional shopping center building design is the enclosed mall, an air-conditioned pedestrian concourse to which tenant stores have direct access. The enclosed mall pattern has also been adapted to community centers. An enclosed mall is unusual in a neighborhood center, though not impractical. *The enclosed mall building pattern does not change a center's regional, community, or neighborhood classification.*

What follows is a discussion of several other variations of the conventional shopping center types.

1-7 A dramatic light sculpture highlights Queens Center, a four-level vertical shopping mall in Elmhurst, New York. Two major department stores, 80 retail shops, and parking spaces for almost 1,500 cars are accommodated on the 5-acre site. A conventional center would have required about 10 times as much land.

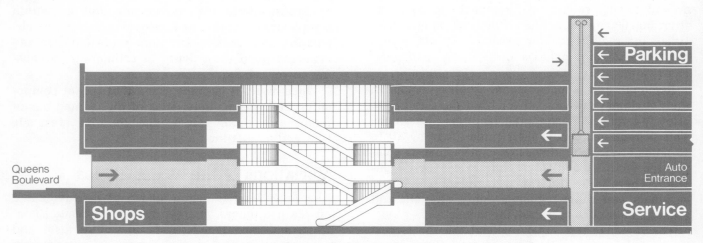

1-8 Cross section of Queens Center showing parking, pedestrian, and retail area relationships.

8

The *vertical center* is an emerging trend. The enclosed regional mall has become multilevel, with interior vertical movement provided by stairways, escalators, or ramps. The multilevel variation has been introduced to reduce horizontal walking distances and to reduce building site coverage.

Even though multilevel centers offer shorter walking distances and prospective savings in land costs, there are several disadvantages that the developer must carefully evaluate:

- Vertical transportation for customers adds to the capital cost, as do exit stairs and freight elevators.
- Having two levels reduces the developer's options for heating, air conditioning, and ventilating. In general, a more expensive system is required.
- Wasted space and extra stairs, elevators, and service corridors add about 5 percent to the gross area, involving additional cost but without producing additional income.
- Merchandising problems are compounded for tenant location and mix. Leasing problems, such as which level and what store size to offer, may be more complicated.
- Customers may be confused by the choice of levels.

Still, the vast, horizontal center is no longer being built. Instead, the vertical concept of development is being spurred both by the need to reduce customer walking distances and by economic circumstances, particularly land cost and the need to conserve land and protect the environment. The vertical concept also allows special, interesting architectural forms.

The *mini-mall* center has come into prominence during the seventies.[1] The mini-mall, with a typical gross leasable area between 80,000 and 150,000 square feet on a corresponding site of 8 to 15 acres, emerges as an enclosed mall mostly adapted to community-type shopping facilities in areas of extreme climatic variations.

The key in these mini-malls is consumer convenience. They offer little ostentation, are wholly utilitarian, and economize on site area, building cost, and tenant mix. The idea is convenience of location for selected goods and services, with savings in energy consumption and vehicle miles.

Key tenants in the mini-mall are a junior department store, variety, food, or drug store; the remaining tenants consist of specialties and services. Typical key store sizes would be: food store or

supermarket, 25,000 square feet; drugstore, 6,000 to 10,000 square feet; specialty or junior department store, 30,000 to 40,000 square feet, with small units of personal services and other retailing making up the remainder.

The *small regional mall* center, with approximately 300,000 square feet of GLA, is another form of the seventies which has evolved from the pressure for economical development, from the need to serve smaller mid-markets, and from the need to use smaller, suitably located but bypassed sites. Zoning and environmental requirements can be met more readily with the smaller mall. The small regional allows shorter design and construction time and a wider choice of contractors. Development entails fewer tenant demands and reduced financing and mortgage commitment time. Although the tenantry of smaller regionals is similar to that of larger regionals, the smaller mall can attract tenants who desire new outlets in smaller centers and who, for various reasons, do not choose to become tenants in a large regional center.

The scaled-down regional center with an enclosed mall requires care in planning for amenities, which will include narrower malls, smaller courts and sitting areas, reduced lighting, and windowless storefronts, with unlighted but controlled signage, both inside and out. Building materials are those which are economical but durable—such as precast panels of concrete aggregate or stone—and which can help make the structure pleasing with their color and texture. Scarcity of good sites, along with spiraling inflation in construction costs, land costs, and interest rates, dictates such innovations.

Small regional malls offer retailers an atmosphere in which one or two tenants in the major retail categories provide a selection of goods but not a full range of competitive outlets. The developer has lower maintenance costs and a shorter start-up time between building commitment and tenant occupancy.

With a smaller market and with amenities scaled down from those customary in larger regional centers, the developer must take care to negotiate an acceptable rent structure. This income structure influences the financial success or failure of the project. The smaller mall, because of its scale and concept, may have a financing advantage over larger regional centers, since it is easier to find mortgage sources who will lend within the smaller

---

[1] See Willard Thorsen, "Mini Malls," *Urban Land*, Vol. 33, No. 9 (October 1974).

regional's income and capital cost structure.

The *mini-mart* is a version of small neighborhood convenience merchandising. The mini-mart is a store of 3,000 to 5,000 square feet with parking for 15 to 20 cars. It offers packaged groceries and token selections of all types of sundries. These centers typically operate with long hours—opening early in the morning and closing late, or running 24 hours. In addition to serving as freestanding units such facilities are sometimes operated as adjuncts to neighborhood and community centers. Such convenience marketing can also serve a locality until population growth justifies the construction of a regular neighborhood center. The mini-mart, as a convenience facility, can also be introduced into a secondary location such as a basement area within a large-scale, multifamily, high density complex in an urban core.

The *superstore* is at the other end of the scale in single-unit convenience marketing. The concept sprang up in Europe, where such outlets are known as *hyper-marchés*. Their adaptation in this country has been rare.

The superstore requires a metropolitan area for its trade and generally contains between 60,000 and 150,000 square feet, although some have been built with as much as 250,000 square feet. The superstore, or "super supermarket," offers a warehouse atmosphere, with everything under one roof and one bank of checkout stands. It offers a huge variety of foodstuffs, general merchandise, and hard lines. Its discount merchandising technique is premised on piling goods high to pull down prices and operating costs. The technique involves saving on service costs while allowing as much shopping as possible to be done at lower prices in one trip.

The *specialty or theme center* is another shopping center variation. These centers cater to unusual market segments, either wide or limited. Development of such centers follows the principles of planning, design, and operation of the standard

1-9   Royal Palm Plaza in Boca Raton caters to the specialty shopping needs of retirees and visitors in this affluent southern Florida community. The center contains 95 retail stores and offices in 166,000 square feet of GLA.

1-10 Five of a projected six department stores are either complete or under construction at Lakeside, a super-regional shopping center in the northern suburbs of Detroit. Parcels outside the ring road have been planned to accommodate compatible land uses, including office buildings and ancillary retail facilities. The development concept is predicated on substantial growth in this section of the metropolitan area.

types of shopping centers. The theme center is adaptable to historical structures worthy of interior renovation and preservation as shopping centers.

The *fashion center*, another variation, is a concentration of apparel shops, boutiques, and handcraft shops carrying selected merchandise, usually of high quality and high price. Although not a necessary criterion, a fashion center may include one or more small specialty department stores. Gourmet food and food service could be included, but a supermarket would not. Fashion centers are most suitable for high-income areas. A high-fashion complex, like the theme center, can also be adapted readily to mixed use developments, as well as to space within an architecturally historical structure which is being renovated for preservation and re-use. High-fashion specialty centers draw on very wide rather than limited trade areas, frequently

supplemented by impulse buying by tourists. Based on gross leasable area, such centers fall into the neighborhood, community, or smaller regional range.

Super-regional centers are enlargements of regional centers. The creation of larger regional centers involves including three to six department stores at a strong and unique location within the largest metropolitan markets.

Super-regional centers evolve or are introduced not only where retailing is growing rapidly, but also where a new regional centralized place or suburban "downtown" needs to emerge within the orbit of the large metropolitan city. Here, with rising land costs and a scarcity of suitable sites, this new kind of commercial community becomes a multilevel center built and owned under the principle of single entity control.

The arrangement of the complex may incorporate mixed use land planning and zoning, with several land uses combined under one planned development package. Depending on the intensity and number of uses, the complex may become a *mixed use development, or MXD.*[2]

Centers with multiple shopping levels have been brought about by developer response to a new era of land use. These centers have found a place in a multiuse form, the MXD, under a planned arrangement of land use. In a central city urban redevelopment project, the multilevel center becomes a high-rise of three or more levels surrounding an atrium, with circulation provided by vertical people-mover equipment—elevators and escalators.

In current planning and urban development, the shopping center does not necessarily depend on vast site area. Innovative planning and the development of multiuse projects enable more intensive land use, thereby achieving a critical land savings and protection of the environment.

There is a healthy acknowledgment that shopping centers must become more than pure retail service centers. They need encouragement to fill other community needs. One example is the shopping center which provides a downtown mix. For larger regional centers, this mix would include business and medical office buildings, libraries, theaters, hotels, recreational facilities, and any number of other public or quasi-public uses. Day-care centers, religious facilities, and senior citizen centers are but a few examples. Such elements can often be placed in fringe or nonoverlapping, underused parking areas conveniently linked to the center for protection of the pedestrian from the weather. Basement areas, if included in the center design, may also provide suitable locations. Of course, the introduction of these uses will lead to management problems, but the logic of their inclusion should overcome any objections.

As can be seen from the above discussion of variations, the basic concept is simple while the variations are many. It is reasonable to assume that new variations will continue to emerge and that those we have now defined will be modified to the point that recognition may be difficult. For example, the community center has been changing dramatically. The decline of the junior department store and variety store and the rise of the discount department store, home improvement center, super drugstore, and super supermarket have all muddied the definition.

Evolution of the Shopping Center
Importance of the Automobile

The rise of the automobile, the rise of the suburbs, and the rise of the shopping center are parts of a single phenomenon. When cities spread beyond established transportation lines, automobiles came into use to meet a great variety of transportation needs. Retailing also moved into the suburbs, in pursuit of the shifting purchasing power; the present-day shopping complex necessarily began as an innovation in retail location.

As travel patterns and buying habits shifted with the rise of the suburbs and the custom of shopping by car, new concentrations of shopping facilities arose away from established downtowns and business corridors. But these were also new *kinds* of shopping areas: the narrow and shallow strip commercial lots in business districts and along major streets could not readily accommodate the new concept of shopping with on-site parking. Beginning in the twenties, provision for parking became a necessary adjunct of retail facilities.

Private enterprise responded to this need by devising a complete marketplace with its own built-in customer parking. Through a process of growth and innovation in response to the shifting nature of the market, early development on vacant sites unfolded from a strip of stores fronting on a street into the compact shopping center complex of today, identifiable by its planning principles, array of tenants, development procedures, and operational practices.

Early Experiments and Patterns

The shopping center grew out of early, freestanding Sears and Ward's stores and out of the innovative grocery outlets that were first built in locations outside of downtown, on plots large enough to accommodate both the store and customer car parking spaces. Under developer enterprise, these experiments were soon scaled to a unified row of stores with display windows fronting on traffic streets and on-lot parking for the customers at the rear or side of the strip; the tenantry usually comprised a food store, a drugstore, and several service shops. Gradually, the concept of grouping

---

[2] See Robert E. Witherspoon, Jon P. Abbett, and Robert M. Gladstone, *Mixed-Use Developments: New Ways of Land Use,* ULI Technical Bulletin 71 (Washington, D.C.: ULI–the Urban Land Institute, 1976).

stores acquired the sophistication of site design, location, tenant selection, and operation found in today's shopping center.

The earliest "shopping center" venture, however, predated even the advent of the large grocery markets which provided some on-lot customer parking. In 1907, Edward H. Bouton, president of the Roland Park Company, constructed an architecturally unified building for stores, set back from the street, at Roland Avenue and Upland Road in Baltimore. The Roland Park shopping site also provided space for horse-drawn carriages, and the conversion of this space to the parking of automobiles required only paving the front grass and the carriage drive. (It is interesting to note that in September 1975, when the Roland Park Company filed for a permit to tear down the building, local residents protested the action, viewing the potential demolition as the destruction of a historic landmark.)

Bouton, the developer of the prestige residential community of Roland Park, pioneered in many other ways. He initiated the use of protective covenants, "zoning" for a specific use, setback requirements, architectural control, flexible restrictions, wider lots, homeowners' maintenance funds, extensive landscaping, and civic responsibility on the part of the developer. He also gathered other developers at his Roland Park home to discuss these advances in subdividing land and the drawing together and integration of commercial facilities to serve nearby residential areas. At Bouton's

1-11   Country Club Plaza, in Kansas City, Missouri, has adopted an architectural style reminiscent of Seville, Spain. Shops front on the public thoroughfares which traverse the 40-acre retail district. This pioneering commercial development has been under active development for half a century.

home, such community builders as J. C. Nichols of Kansas City and Hugh Potter of Houston received inspiration and guidance. There, too, were sown the seeds that ultimately blossomed in 1944 as the Community Builders Council of the Urban Land Institute.

In the early twenties, such unified commercial ventures were often identified with high-quality residential communities fostered by forward-looking developers. J. C. Nichols led the way. It was during this period that he began his Country Club Plaza in what was then the outlying area of Kansas City. Nichols inaugurated stylized architecture, unified management policies, sign control, and landscaping amenities. As a developer, he provided for customer parking in "parking stations." In the strictest sense, Country Club Plaza is not a shopping center but a shopping district; parking spaces are provided along public streets that traverse the district and in parking garages. Still, the principles of a shopping center exist at Country Club Plaza in such areas as quality of management, tenant mix, and merchandising operations.

In 1931 in Dallas, Hugh Prather pioneered with the first unified commercial development in which stores were turned inward, away from the surrounding streets. Highland Park Shopping Village in the Dallas area can accurately be called the prototype for the present-day planned shopping center —the site all in one piece, not bisected by public streets, with individual stores built and managed as a unit with a unified image, under single ownership control and with the amount of on-site parking determined by parking demand.

In 1937, Hugh Potter, once ULI president and later chairman of the Community Builders Council, started a shopping center as an adjunct to his renowned residential community, River Oaks, in Houston. Potter used a contemporary style of architecture but added cantilevered canopies along the storefronts. He violated a major present-day shopping principle—his center was bisected by a major public street—but even so, River Oaks initiated many operational practices, such as percentage leases and merchants associations, which are now standards in the industry.

These pioneers of the thirties, each working to meet the needs of a particular area but without significant precedent to guide them, established the patterns of development which ultimately determined the merchandising concept of today's shopping center.

After World War II there was a surge in construction. A wave of residential and commercial development swept through the country, centering in dormitory suburbs in the form of tract sub-

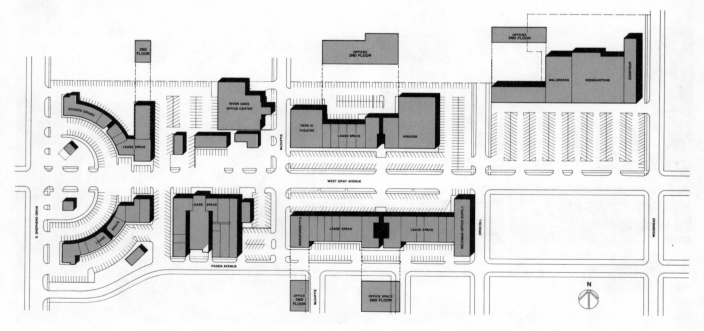

1-12   Site plan of River Oaks Shopping Center, Houston. The original portion, built in the thirties and forties, is located between Driscoll Street and South Shepherd Drive. The eastern block, containing a grocery, drugstore, and several other shops, was added in 1972.

14

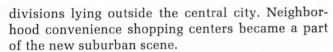

1-13   Truck tunnel at Northgate Shopping Center, Seattle.

1-14   Roofed mall at Northgate. The mall, originally open, was later roofed over, as shown in this 1963 photograph. The center has since been completely remodeled and enclosed. Note the use of asphalt paving in the pedestrian mall.

divisions lying outside the central city. Neighborhood convenience shopping centers became a part of the new suburban scene.

In 1950, the next great innovation took place. That year, on behalf of the Allied Stores Corporation of New York, James B. Douglas opened Northgate in Seattle as the first suburban regional shopping center built with a major full-line branch department store as the leading tenant. Northgate was the first to feature the central pedestrian mall with service truck tunnel below. The open pedestrian mall and underground truck tunnel became an early building pattern for regional centers, although the truck tunnel soon proved to be too expensive. (Today, Northgate has an enclosed, weather-conditioned mall, three department stores, and over a million square feet of GLA. Douglas, who was president of Northgate Shopping Centers, Inc., was also a trustee of ULI, a member of the Community Builders Council, and later a member of the Commercial and Office Development Council of ULI.)

During the fifties, the further spread of the suburbs and the increased use of the automobile gradually induced the construction of shopping centers as a new merchandising plant to serve the new market. The fifties produced successful practices and innovations that led to tested procedures for shopping center planning, and the shopping center became recognized as a distinct building and land use type.[3]

[3] The following works discuss shopping center development during this period:

J. C. Nichols, *Mistakes We Have Made in Developing Shopping Centers*, ULI Technical Bulletin 4 (Washington, D.C.: ULI–the Urban Land Institute, 1945).

Seward H. Mott and Max S. Wehrly, eds., *Shopping Centers: An Analysis*, ULI Technical Bulletin 11 (Washington, D.C.: ULI–the Urban Land Institute, 1949).

J. Ross McKeever, *Shopping Centers: Planning Principles and Tested Policies*, ULI Technical Bulletin 20 (Washington, D.C.: ULI–the Urban Land Institute, 1953).

J. Ross McKeever, *Shopping Centers Re-Studied: Part One—Emerging Patterns; Part Two—Practical Experiences*, ULI Technical Bulletin 30 (Washington, D.C.: ULI–the Urban Land Institute, 1957).

1-15 Southdale Center in Edina, Minnesota, initiated the multilevel enclosed mall concept. The center also includes a truck tunnel, which serves individual stores. This photograph was taken shortly after Southdale opened in 1956.

Innovations proceeded apace. The first enclosed mall regional shopping center was planned in 1953 and opened in 1956. Southdale, near Minneapolis, instituted weatherproofed shopping on two levels surrounding a "garden court," all enclosed and under one roof.

In 1957, the shopping center as a new industry came of age. That year the International Council of Shopping Centers (ICSC), headquartered in New York City, was founded as a trade association for fostering interest and improving operating practices among shopping center developers, owners, managers, and tenants.

The sixties produced a great increase in shopping center development activity. Planning and operating principles were tested and refined. Adjustments took place in response to changing conditions in financing, leasing, location, construction, and operational aspects of expanding markets. Variations in standard types began to appear.

The enclosed, heated, and air-conditioned mall became the dominant building form for regional centers. Two, three, and four full-line department stores added to a regional complex led such merchandising representation to a position of strength in customer attraction. Such ranges in shopping goods and other retail classifications had once been found only in downtowns. By the second half of the sixties, open mall centers began converting to covered mall operations.

Shopping Centers in the Economy

As an industry, shopping centers play an important role in the economy. More significant than numbers are the role that centers play in the community and the practices that lead to the centers' success.

No official nationwide census of shopping centers exists, although there are a few such tabu-

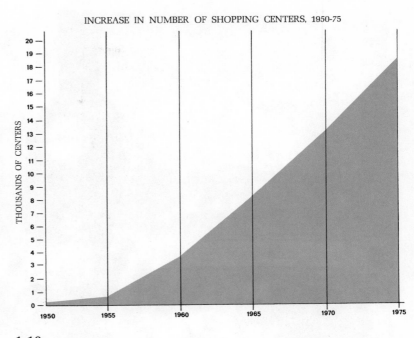

1-16

lations for particular metropolitan areas.[4] An actual numerical count is not vital. But the present edition of the *Shopping Center Directory*[5] lists approximately 18,500 centers in the United States in operation, under construction, or in planning.

In 1950, according to ULI records, there were only 100 centers, mostly of the neighborhood or community categories. By 1953 the number had tripled. But consider the scale and rate of growth in the next 20 years: by 1973, there were an estimated 16,000 centers. And ICSC estimates show that of the total number today, 90 percent are less than 15 years old and 40 percent are less than 5 years old; major growth obviously took place in the late sixties and early seventies.

For reasons of nondisclosure of individual businesses, the *U.S. Census of Business* counts and reports retail sales volumes only by broad retail classification for central areas and for business concentrations outside the central business district. Hence, shopping center retail volume can only be interpolated. Furthermore, in interpolating census data, it is necessary to exclude the non-shopping-center type of retail goods—lumber, building materials, farm equipment, hay, grain and feed, and automobile sales.

On the basis of shopping goods, U.S. shopping centers capture an annual retail sales volume in excess of $140 billion, or 45 percent of the total for the general merchandise and apparel categories of retail business. Shopping centers also include over 1.2 billion square feet of gross leasable area. Centers constructed since 1970 represent about 7 percent of all nonresidential construction volume.[6]

The Seventies

The present decade began with a bright prospect for the shopping center industry. But at mid-decade, a general economic softening showed that the period would be one of adjustments to new sets of conditions, particularly for the land development industry. Restrictions and regulations of an unexpected severity surfaced. Environment, ecology, and energy became labels for three sets of limita-

[4] A notable exception to the lack of comprehensive shopping center data is *Massachusetts Shopping Centers*, published in 1973 by the Department of Commerce and Development of the Commonwealth of Massachusetts. See also *Shopping Center Guide*, a complete summary of shopping centers in metropolitan San Jose, published by the San Jose *Mercury-News*, 1973–74; and *Shopping Centers*, published by the Nassau County (New York) Planning Commission (Carle Place, New York). Also see local market guides published by newspapers, such as *Buffalo Shopping Plazas*, a marketing service of the *Buffalo News*.

[5] Published annually by the National Research Bureau, Inc., Burlington, Iowa. The 17th edition (1976) lists 18,540 centers of all types in the United States, 1,259 in Canada, and 247 in other countries.

[6] Estimate made in 1974 by ICSC's California Environmental Action Committee.

1-17 One of the new large centers is Puente Hills Mall, completed in 1974 and located in City of Industry, a Los Angeles suburb. This multilevel retail complex has a cruciform design, 1.4 million square feet of GLA, and four anchor tenants: J. C. Penney, Sears, The Broadway, and J. W. Robinson. Shown is a view of Puente Hills' massive central court.

tions that sprang up to alter the pace of land development in all its forms.

Shopping center developers are not alone in having to face new constraints. Inflation has complicated the general economic picture and has contributed to high levels of unemployment and overall economic conditions which can be described as recessionary.

The corollaries of undirected, rampant, nationwide urbanization have been land spoilage, ecological infringement, water pollution, landscape pollution, and lower air quality. Public reaction to flagrant abuses generated by uncontrolled urban growth set in at the beginning of the seventies. Reactive measures are evidenced by attempts at national land use policy legislation and by national and state enactments governing sensitive ecological areas such as wetlands, scenic areas, and coastal zones.[7]

An example of such reactive measures are the EPA regulations promulgated under the Clean Air Act of 1970. These regulations focused sharply on shopping centers as an "indirect source" of air quality deterioration. Although shopping centers themselves are not air pollution sources, shopping centers were considered for examination by EPA because of the necessary parking areas for automobiles. Since direct regulation of the automobile and its proven level of air pollution was postponed or weakened, the brunt of regulation was placed indirectly on shopping centers with parking spaces for 1,000 or more cars. Regulations based on evidence that parking concentrations induce air quality deterioration proved to be impractical, however, and on July 3, 1975, EPA indefinitely suspended those portions of its indirect source regulations governing parking-related facilities.

In 1974, environmental considerations became complicated by supply shortages—the unprepared-for "energy crisis"—in organic fuels, particularly natural gas, oil, and gasoline.

In the long run, energy may have a more crucial influence on the shopping center industry than will environmental controls. The prospect shows strong emphasis on smaller centers to serve shortened travel distances from built-up residential areas. The developers of new regional centers in markets suitable for such service will be confronted with two major considerations—environmental protection and energy conservation.

The requirement of energy conservation will mean certain alterations in planning criteria and daily operations. Smaller cars with greater fuel efficiency mean smaller spaces for parking. With gasoline use curtailment, travel habits and shopping habits shift. Customer travel to several centers for comparison shopping is hampered. Single-purpose trips for convenience or "total needs" buying will be a more dominant consumer practice than will comparison shopping and will encourage existing shopping centers to provide greater public services.

Any long-term curtailment in travel will mean that existing centers of all types will be strengthened by their one-stop convenience for retail buying. In addition, new centers being planned are confronted with new sets of conditions for construction permit approval:

> The shopping center project of the present and the future requires the ability to deal not only with complex mechanical and financial considerations, but also with the emerging problems attendant to various facets of governmental regulation. In the past, developers could get their permit for a shopping center after satisfying zoning authorities and presenting the appropriate traffic studies and sewer and water plans. Today and tomorrow the bureaucratic web may well require several additional equivalent procedures. Transportation regulations, land use legislation, pollution control and a range of indirect source regulations will face the developer.[8]

Nevertheless, good planning produces good environment. Guidelines and standards designed to assist shopping centers in meeting principles and practices of good land use planning and operation will be even more important in the future than they have been in the past. Hence this reissuing of a text on the principles and practices of shopping center development.

---

[7] See J. Ross McKeever, *Shopping Center Zoning*, ULI Technical Bulletin 69 (Washington, D.C.: ULI–the Urban Land Institute, 1973). Discussed in the report are the Clean Air Act of 1970, establishment of the Environmental Protection Agency, and state and regional land use controls. *Environmental Comment*, a monthly publication of ULI, has also featured a number of articles on these and related issues.

[8] From "Shopping Centers: Recent Problems and Development Trends," a seminar prospectus prepared in 1974 by the Practicing Law Institute.

2.
Development Preliminaries

The shopping center is a distinct commercial land use type. As such, it is vastly more than a real estate venture. It is a retail merchandising complex that generates supplementary land uses and influences community values. In each of its several standard forms and variations, the shopping center is built on the concept of planned arrangement and development and unified management control. The whole undertaking goes through certain essential stages before arriving at the day when the project opens for business.

The development process is a series of complicated decisions. It is based on more than high hopes and good intentions. The procedure has moved from that of a few simple steps in site and tenant selection to one involving intricate studies in feasibility. Market analysis, environmental impact evaluation, site planning, traffic handling, lease negotiations, financial processing, structural designing, and public relations—all of these areas require input from a team of experts under the guidance of an astute developer.

To solve the complexity of development problems, the developer draws on the teamwork of a group of professionals. Technical experts usually called upon, particularly for a complicated regional center, include such professionals as the market analyst, site planner-architect, landscape designer-environmentalist, lawyer, engineering and construction specialist, financial advisor, and leasing agent. For a less complicated community or neighborhood center, the developer may use fewer team members; for example, only a market analyst, an architect-planner, and a leasing agent may be required. There are also cases where several or all of the disciplines are represented within the developer's own staff organization.

Team members cannot work independently of one another. They must act together, meeting with the developer regularly to learn about collaborative assignments and the accomplishments and progress of each team member. The experienced developer knows that in decision making there is no substitute for informed judgment—his own, backed by the work of his development team.

In the emerging era of environmental protection and energy conservation, the team approach is necessary to coordinate and expedite the clearance and approval procedures in environmental impact and zoning matters as required by new regulations at the state, regional, or local level.

In putting together any shopping center project, there are a number of essential preliminaries. At each stage, the development team makes a series of studies to aid in the decision process while proceeding along the critical path toward construction. The precise order of evaluations will vary. Each melds into and overlaps with another. Each determination is part of an exercise that assembles the basis for answering the ultimate question: Will it work? The series of steps which make up the feasibility study must eventually provide the developer with his go or no-go decision.

The timetable for completion of tasks will shift, usually by lengthening. Snags invariably arise from local conditions and such contingencies as key tenant negotiations, financing commitments, permit approvals, and clearances.

Essential preliminaries which are part of the feasibility study include:

- Market and economic analysis, including an evaluation of existing competition as well as potential future competition.
- Site selection, evaluation, and control.
- Key tenant commitments.
- Zoning and environmental approvals.
- Financial negotiations.
- Capital costs.

The steps are detailed and are dependent on many variables and uncertainties. No precise how-to-do-it formula holds. Domino-like preliminaries precede any final decision. Ultimate site acquisition, for example, depends on zoning approval. In turn, leasing depends on site approvals and on the securing of key tenants, while financing rests on leasing. The full development decision requires clearing a series of hurdles before arriving at the construction stage.

Under provisions of the Clean Air Act Amendments of 1970 and the subsequent enactments of California, Florida, Vermont, Maine, and other states, an environmental impact statement (EIS) has also become a regular part of the land use process. An EIS and its related analyses can be useful to the developer in a land use development proposal at the market strategy planning, site selection, prepurchase planning, and project site planning stages.

Market and Economic Analysis

Before embarking on any shopping center project, a developer must identify and evaluate the community, then calculate its potential patronage of commercial outlets. This step should be taken before prospecting for suitable sites. A new shopping center may be equivalent to adding the retail space of a small city to the community's shopping facilities. Where there has been no great popula-

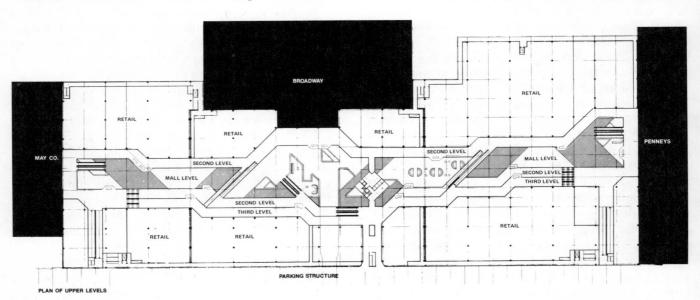

Foxhill Mall
Culver City, California

Developer
Ernest W. Hahn, Inc.; Broadway-Hale Stores, Inc.
Architect
Gruen Associates
Leasing Agent
Coldwell, Banker & Co.
Traffic Engineers
Donald Frischer & Associates

Description
Two level shopping center with three major department stores and 80 tenant stores on a 49 acre site.
Gross Area: 997,544 square feet.
Parking: Four level parking structure accommodating 2,050 cars plus surface parking for 2,110 cars. Total 4,160 parking spaces.

2-1   The development team for Foxhill Mall includes the financial partners, architect, leasing agent, and traffic engineer.

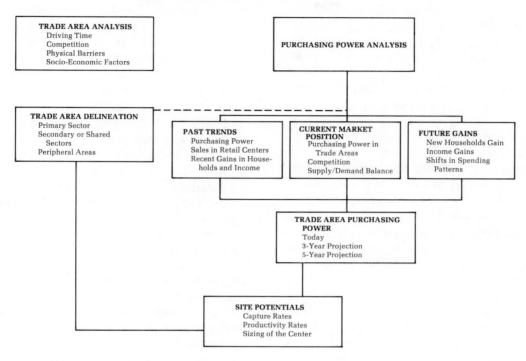

SALES POTENTIALS FOR A RETAIL CENTER
ANALYTIC PROCESS IN OVERVIEW

TRADE AREA ANALYSIS
Driving Time
Competition
Physical Barriers
Socio-Economic Factors

PURCHASING POWER ANALYSIS

TRADE AREA DELINEATION
Primary Sector
Secondary or Shared
Sectors
Peripheral Areas

PAST TRENDS
Purchasing Power
Sales in Retail Centers
Recent Gains in House-
holds and Income

CURRENT MARKET POSITION
Purchasing Power in
Trade Areas
Competition
Supply/Demand Balance

FUTURE GAINS
New Households Gain
Income Gains
Shifts in Spending
Patterns

TRADE AREA PURCHASING POWER
Today
3-Year Projection
5-Year Projection

SITE POTENTIALS
Capture Rates
Productivity Rates
Sizing of the Center

Source: Gladstone Associates

2-2

tion growth, the existing retail space is probably fairly adequate, at least on a quantitative basis. In such situations, the entrepreneur must be sure the community can absorb the proposed increment in retail selling space with a new merchandising mix.

A seasoned developer will have clear ideas about the characteristics of a trade area that suit the type of center he hopes to build. His point of departure from this ideal is the key tenant that may be obtainable. Until that vital element is uncovered, the developer can only surmise the type or size of center that may be feasible.

Assume a neighborhood center is under consideration. Then, as James B. Douglas of Northgate once explained:

> If the top-volume supermarket operating in the area is not represented within the vicinity for which your center is proposed, and if that supermarket chain is in a mood for expansion of its outlets, if its management traditionally makes commitments with land developers that developers can live with, and if your real estate broker has a history of accomplishing successful negotiations, *then* a certain pattern of success can be projected. On the other hand, if the major volume-producing chains are already located, thus leaving only the poorer producers available for a site in question, then the size of the center, its success, and other factors will be evaluated differently. Only the person well-versed in leasing will be able to resolve the matter of key tenant selection.

> For a regional shopping center proposal, the strength of the major tenant or key tenants that may be interested in the site selected is the determining factor for the size, character, and success of the center, and even the price that can be paid for the land.

The type of center and its site character, drawing power, and ultimate success hinge strongly on this investigation. The developer will have a hunch about what is feasible. But he must be equipped with hard data to interest prospective tenants, to identify the site, to sketch the proposed plan, to satisfy the community, to obtain zoning approval, and to secure financing.

Measurement of a project's possibilities becomes the first exploratory step in determining the feasibility of development:

> The developer's principal aim is to match the location, size and composition of the center to the needs of the trade area. To attain that goal he usually attempts to obtain an accurate economic analysis of the

23

trade area, based on a market survey, from which he can derive a tentative plan for a shopping center.[1]

The market analysis is a problem like that of the chicken and the egg: you cannot interest a key tenant until a market analysis is made, and you cannot detail the market until you know what kind of key tenant the trade area will appeal to. As a consequence, two types of analyses must be made simultaneously: one analysis is made to interest the key tenant in anchoring the prospective center; second, an economic analysis is made to determine the number and types of customers who may be brought to the center. In turn, the customer draw influences the volume of business that can be expected by other major and supplementary tenants.

The economic market analysis is a job for a specialist in the field. The analysis does not take the place of a developer's sound judgement, but its measurements show on paper whether or not the new center is justified. With strong competition in the retail field, plus complications of high land development and building construction costs and heightened financing and operating charges, a developer faces a risk that leaves little room for miscalculations, including miscalculations about the general tenor of community attitudes toward growth and development activity at the site or in its surroundings.

The market study is the developer's prime sales kit for approaching major tenants, local governments, and financial institutions. The analysis is used to discover how the project will serve the prospective market. The economic part of that discovery must determine whether a great enough sales volume can be generated by the contemplated project to justify its development.

The analysis tells the investor-developer whether there is a demand for shopping facilities. Study will show whether new facilities will answer a need growing out of increased population and purchasing power, and whether new outlets are needed to replace worn-out facilities.

It is very important to understand that *a shopping center cannot generate new business or create new buying power; it can only attract customers from existing businesses, which may be obsolete, or capture the increase in purchasing power that accrues with population growth. It can cause a redistribution of business outlets and consumer patronage, but it cannot create new consumers.* Each new center must be justified by gauging the purchasing power available to it and the nature of

the competition. Without fully taking competition, both existing and potential, into consideration, a new center may find itself struggling against retail facilities presently serving the population, and struggling as well against any facility built later to serve the same trade area.

The required scope and degree of the market investigation is suggested by population, income, purchasing power, competitive facilities, site access, proposed major tenants, and shoppers' buying habits and preferences. The number of potential customers living in a projected trade area will be counted. The territory to be drawn from will be indicated by a study of access roads, with limits set by distance, travel time, and competition. The type of retail outlets needed or wanted in the market area is determined by a study of the supporting population's income and composition. The age groups and other characteristics of the trade area population have a strong bearing on the tenant composition. Are major segments blue-collar workers, college-educated young people, or retirees? Changes in composition of the population are a vital consideration. Accurately analyzing the population factor is of paramount importance in evaluating the feasibility of any retail location. The number, composition, density, growth rate, income, expenditures, and buying habits of the population can be translated into market potential. Much of this information can be extracted from census tract data, including metropolitan area supplements.

The total spendable income measured against the total volume of business done in existing retail areas shows whether there is excess purchasing power available. Trade that escapes existing establishments because of their shortcomings indicates prospects for new offerings. The proportion of this spending power to be drawn to a new center depends on the customer pull to be created. This estimation points to the size and type of the operation which should be planned. The character of the prospective trade area indicates the quality level at which to aim the tone of the project.

The developer makes his market analysis to find out whether the area can support a new center. Secondarily, the study is needed to convince pros-

---

[1] S. O. Kaylin, "Selecting the Best Site for a Shopping Center," *Shopping Center World*, Vol. 2, No. 5 (June 1973), p. 38; excerpted from *How to Create a Shopping Center* by S. O. Kaylin (New York: Communication Channels, Inc., 1973).

pective tenants that the trade area needs and can afford the center. When he goes further with the market analysis, the developer tries to determine who might be his key tenants. Obtaining a commitment from the major tenant or tenants is basic to determining project type and size and is necessary for estimating project costs and framing leasing arrangements with other tenants.

Tenant negotiations and commitments between landlord and prospective tenants provide an outline of the developer's whole investment feasibility picture. In a developer's economic planning, there will not be a shopping center until there is a key tenant. This is true whether the center is a small neighborhood cluster or a regional giant.

Trade Area

The term *trade area*, already defined in Chapter 1, can also be considered to mean the geographic area from which is obtained the major portion of the continuing patronage necessary for steady support of the shopping center.

As stated earlier, new shopping centers do not create new buying power; rather, they attract customers from existing districts or capture a portion of new purchasing power in a growing area. Hence, it is necessary to determine first the extent of the area from which the center can be expected to draw customers. This trade area naturally varies, as do the types and qualities of merchandise to be offered.

To a great extent, families buy food and sundries within their immediate neighborhoods. They go considerable distances to buy "big ticket" items such as furniture, major appliances, and clothing. Boundaries for a trade area are estimated by carefully accounting for shoppers' habits, location of competition, drawing power of the tenants, and access by highway and public transportation.

Within a shopping center's trade area, the strongest influence will be exerted closest to the site, with influence diminishing gradually as the distance increases. Trade area is initially a judgement matter. To take account of this condition, any trade area (for a regional shopping center, for example) is usually divided into three categories or zones of influence:

- The *primary trade area* is composed of the nearby walk-in area plus the area which has no daily convenience stores closer than the site under investigation. For convenience items, such as food and personal services, it is likely

that 60 to 70 percent of the ultimate sales volume will represent the population within 5 minutes driving time. For a regional center, the primary trade area will extend, at the least, to an area within 10 minutes driving time of the center.

- The *secondary trade area* is the area which may have local convenience stores but with no important soft line (apparel), hard line (hardware, appliances, etc.), or shopping goods (furniture, high-ticket clothing) stores. It may have some of these stores, but they would be less conveniently accessible than the prospective site. Driving limits can be set at 15 to 20 minutes or 3 to 5 miles. This wider territory may generate 15 to 20 percent of all sales.

- The *tertiary or fringe trade area* is the broadest area from which customers may be drawn because of easier access, greater parking convenience, and better merchandise, even though other shopping goods stores or general merchandise stores may be available within the territory. Driving time from this area to the site can be set at roughly 25 to 30 minutes.

It is important to differentiate between geographic distance and travel time. The movement of shoppers in an urban area is largely controlled by the *competitive relationships* of retail areas. Hence the use of distance is not reliable as the only criterion for establishing the extent of a trade area. It has been found, however, that the average person will travel 1½ miles for food, 3 to 5 miles for apparel and household items when selection is not important, and 8 to 10 miles when ranges of selection and price are important.[2] The late Larry Smith, eminent analyst and real estate consultant, felt that the population within 7 to 8 miles of the center is likely to account for 80 percent of the sales volume of a large regional center, and that a limited amount of business can be expected from a more distant population (within 15 to 18 miles of the center) which may have access to an expressway by which the center can be reached in 20 minutes.

Thus, the trade area may extend farther in one direction than in another. Natural barriers, such as lakes, rivers, hills, and parks that will remain as open space or undevelopable land for residential use, also act as trade area limits.

[2] See Alan M. Voorhees, Gordon B. Sharpe, and J. T. Stegmaier, *Shopping Habits and Travel Patterns*, ULI Technical Bulletin 24 (Washington, D.C.: ULI–the Urban Land Institute, 1955).

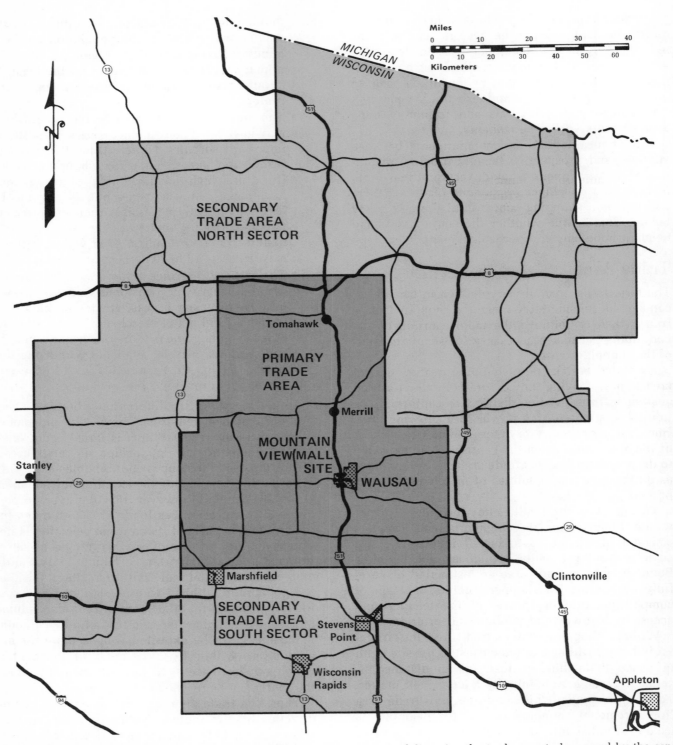

2-3 Projected trade area for Mountain View Mall, Wausau, Wisconsin. In delineating the trade area to be served by the center, four major factors were considered: location of major competitive shopping centers, natural or physical barriers, driving time from the site, and socioeconomic character of the various surrounding population sectors. The primary trade area was defined as the area in which the center could expect to capture approximately 90 to 95 percent of retail sales, with only minor sales loss to other regional centers. Secondary trade area was then defined as the area in which Mountain View Mall would share sales with other centers; in other words, the secondary trade area was considered to be the portion of Mountain View Mall's trade area that overlapped the trade areas of other major retail centers. Mountain View can expect to capture a substantially smaller portion of secondary trade area sales. Source: Gladstone Associates.

Travel times should be set by actual trial runs over access routes, the runs made at off-peak times and under weather conditions typical of the area. The following are *rules of thumb* for theoretical trade area distances:

- Neighborhood center—draws from a radius of 1½ miles, depending on character of residential use.
- Community center—draws from a radius of 3 to 5 miles.
- Regional center—draws from a radius of 8 miles or more. Driving time would ordinarily be 20 minutes, but this may be 2 or 20 miles.

The areas from which customers will drive to the site are related to the ease of access by streets and highways. Driving times, traffic lights, roadside hazards, and barriers such as steep slopes, stream valleys, parks, and railroads are all factors in the measurement of access. Allowance must be made for any proposed changes in existing routes. Access by mass transit will also affect the size of the trade area.

The type of streets and thoroughfares which serve a prospective site also affect accessibility. For example, a car driven on an expressway for a given time will travel perhaps three times the distance covered by a car on a congested, signal-impeded street. A trade area is shaped by the various zones of accessibility, population, buying power, and competition. Because of these factors, the trade area will not assume a regular size or form.

After looking at geographic factors, a map of the trade area can be plotted. This map or a series of diagrams is needed to visualize present and proposed access routes, population density of developed areas, commercial locations and competitive facilities, and topography and land use features.

Types of base maps useful for the purpose include ordinary route maps, such as those issued by service stations, topographic maps published by the U.S. Geological Survey, and aerial photos available from or specially prepared by commercial air mapping services.[3]

Population Data

Within the limits of the trade area as delineated through the above process, characteristics of the population must be studied. These include such things as present population and future growth possibilities, and composition by age, income level, and family and household unit sizes.

The U.S. Census of Population and Housing (taken each decade) and the latest Census of Retail Trade (conducted every 5 years as part of the economic censuses) offer basic statistics. In mid-decade periods, such as between 1975 and 1980, population figures can be updated by special sample enumerations or by recourse to other survey sources. (See Figure 2-4, "Market Data Sources," for specific reference works and sources.) Of course, current plans to conduct a mid-decade census will eventually lead to more current data than has been available to date.

If aerial photography is available for a census base year, current photography will allow identification of growth activity and may even allow housing counts. Another source is building permit records, which will show the number of new dwelling units constructed in each census tract since the census year. Many metropolitan newspapers maintain updated census tract maps and regularly conduct buyer surveys. A further check can be made with utility companies for new meter installations; these increase in direct proportion to the increase in new dwelling units. Adjustments can be made to allow for known absorption of vacancies or demolitions. By such devices, fairly accurate estimates for population and households can be made in post-census years. In areas of rapid growth, state or local governments often conduct special censuses, since allocation of funds for roads, schools, health and welfare, etc., may be tied to population or to growth rates.

Buying Power

The income level within the trade area is important, not only in terms of total dollars available but also in relation to expendable income by retail categories. Income figures for households in the trade area can be derived from the census. In addi-

---

[3] USGS maps can be purchased at public inquiry offices in Anchorage, Dallas, Denver, Los Angeles, Salt Lake City, San Francisco, Spokane, Washington, D.C., and Reston, Virginia. The two major public inquiry offices are located in Washington, D.C. (202/343-8073) and Reston (703/860-6167).

For more information about sources and uses of USGS maps and commercial field instrument surveys and aerial surveys, see Donald C. Lochmoeller et al., *Industrial Development Handbook*, Community Builders Handbook Series (Washington, D.C.: ULI–the Urban Land Institute, 1975), pp. 98–99.

MARKET DATA SOURCES

Mini-Guide to the Economic Censuses, prepared by the Bureau of the Census, U.S. Department of Commerce. Publications Distribution Section, Social and Economic Statistics Administration, Washington, D.C. 20233.

1972 Census of Retail Trade. Separate reports for the United States, states, SMSAs, and non-SMSAs where feasible.
- Vol. I—Summary Statistics Series RC72S-1 and 2—reports on number of establishments, sales, payroll, employment, proprietors.
- Vol. II—Area Statistics Series RC72A-1 to 52
- Vol. III—Major Retail Centers, Series PC72-C-1 to 50
- Vol. IV—Retail Merchandise Line Sales Series RC72-L-1 to 52—U.S. summary and individual reports for each state. Data provided in tables by kind of business for employer establishments on the number and total sales by 27 broad merchandise lines.

Market Data Yearbooks—estimated disposable income by states, SMSAs, counties, and cities.
- *Survey of Buying Power.* Offers buying income by total and by household, and proportion of households in each of five income groups; issued quarterly and annually. Sales Management, 630 Third Avenue, New York, N.Y. 10017.
- *Market Guide.* Gives total individual income. Editor and Publisher Company, Inc., 850 Third Avenue, New York, N.Y. 10022.

1970 Census of Population and Housing
- PC Reports: Population
  Series PC(1)A: Number of inhabitants
    PC(1)B: General population characteristics
    PC(1)C: General social and economic characteristics
    PC(1)D: Detailed characteristics
  Series PC(2): Subject reports. Detailed cross-relationships for the United States and four regions for national origin, race, migration, employment, etc.
  Series PC(3): Selected area reports. Selected characteristics of the population for SMSAs and state economic areas.
- HC Reports: Housing
  Series HC(1): States and small areas
  Series HC(2): Metropolitan housing
  Series HC(3): City blocks
- PHC Reports: Census Tracts
  Series PHC(2)1: U.S. summary. General demographic trends for metropolitan areas, 1960 to 1970.

An outline of the publication program for the 1970 Census of Population and Housing can be obtained free of charge from the Bureau of the Census, Washington, D.C. 20233, or from any U.S. Department of Commerce field office.

In general, census publications may be purchased from the Superintendent of Documents, U.S. Government Printing Office, Washington, D.C. 20402, or from the Publications Distribution Section, Bureau of the Census, Washington, D.C. 20233, or from field offices maintained by the U.S. Department of Commerce in 42 large cities.

Bureau of Labor Statistics, U.S. Department of Labor, publishes sample surveys, *Consumer Expenditures and Income.*

---

tion, the Bureau of Labor Statistics indicates how much is spent by family income ranges for categories of goods and services—such as food, general merchandise, apparel, furniture and home furnishings, and automotive parts and accessories. From purchasing power in each of the segments of the trade area, consumer expenditures can be esti-

mated. To obtain an approximation of total buying or purchasing power in the trade area, multiply the number of people by the average per capita expenditure for general merchandise and apparel. When the number of expected customers is multiplied by average annual expenditures for consumer items, the sales potential of the trade area comes into focus. Another factor, the variation in expenditures of the different income groups, should also be applied.[4]

Income can be estimated by using the normal ratio of income to home value. There is a fairly close relationship between value of the owned home and family income. (A usual ratio is 2 to 2.5 times the amount of annual income for what can be afforded for a house.) In the U.S. Census of Housing, the values (and rentals) of houses are available for every block in cities with a population of 50,000 or more. For suburban areas, the U.S. Bureau of the Census will furnish, on request and at a reasonable cost, photostat sheets of unpublished data for census years, showing home values and rentals by enumeration districts. Where there is a state income tax, it may be possible to learn the distribution of families by income groups in a city or county. State income tax returns can indicate a prevalence of high-income families in the trade area.

The proportion of total family income spent for food increases rapidly as income declines. As a result, in a trade area with a lower average family income as compared with the average for the city as a whole, the proportion of total expenditures available for nonfood stores is much less than that in an area of medium-income or high-income families. Where all families within a given trade area have similar average incomes, the store composition will be quite different from that in a trade area with the same average income but with a large proportion of high-income families counterbalanced by a large proportion of low-income families.

Buying power and the number of families needed to support any shopping center are variables, particularly in a new development area. Developers of new communities in isolated areas must provide shopping facilities in advance of market justification in order to provide limited goods for families who move into the area.

Competition

A new shopping center will not, of course, attract all the business in its trade area. Basically, it will draw on three sources: new population growth, patronage from existing stores in the trade area, and patronage for outlets of goods and services desired but not already offered in the area.

A new center will not generate more purchasing power than already exists within the trade area.

Instead, it will bring about a redistribution of expenditures by way of transfer and new appeals. For these reasons, an important step in the market analysis is a study of the retail facilities that are or are not already present. It is necessary to determine what portion of the spendable income is unsatisfied by local offerings. Often it will be found that potential sales are escaping to other communities.

With one exception, no formula exists for estimating the share of the buying power that can be attracted to a new center. The single exception is Reilly's Law of Retail Gravitation, formulated nearly 50 years ago:

> When two cities compete for retail trade from the immediate rural areas, the breaking point for the attraction of such trade will be more or less in direct proportion to the population of the two cities and in inverse proportion to the square of the distance from the immediate area of each city.

Reilly's Law cannot be used as the sole method of determining a shopping center's pull. As the late Richard L. Nelson said, "All this law says is that people normally will get to the biggest place they can get to easiest." In addition, it is a mistake to apply this tool to market analyses for neighborhood centers. First employed to measure retail attraction between the central business districts of two cities, it was later adopted by a few analysts of early regional shopping centers to measure local attraction between different department stores. Each case, however, depends on its own circumstances. Estimates for a contemplated shopping center must allow for composite pulls of retail shopping areas. According to some analysts, there is a breaking point between competing retail districts where the natural pull of one is equal to that of the other. Proponents of a formula-judgement method sometimes find a revision of Reilly's Law useful in predicting sales potential, particularly for shopping goods presentations such as those found in a regional center.

---

[4] See *Survey of Consumer Expenditures*, report supplements issued periodically for total U.S. and urban and rural regions, with cross-classification of family characteristics; and the catalogue *Publications of the Bureau of Labor Statistics*, issued semiannually. Both are available from the U.S. Department of Labor, Bureau of Labor Statistics, Washington, D.C. 20212.

Also see *Statistical Abstract of the United States* and *Country and City Data Book: A Statistical Abstract Supplement*, both issued annually by the U.S. Bureau of the Census and available from the U.S. Government Printing Office, Washington, D.C. 20402.

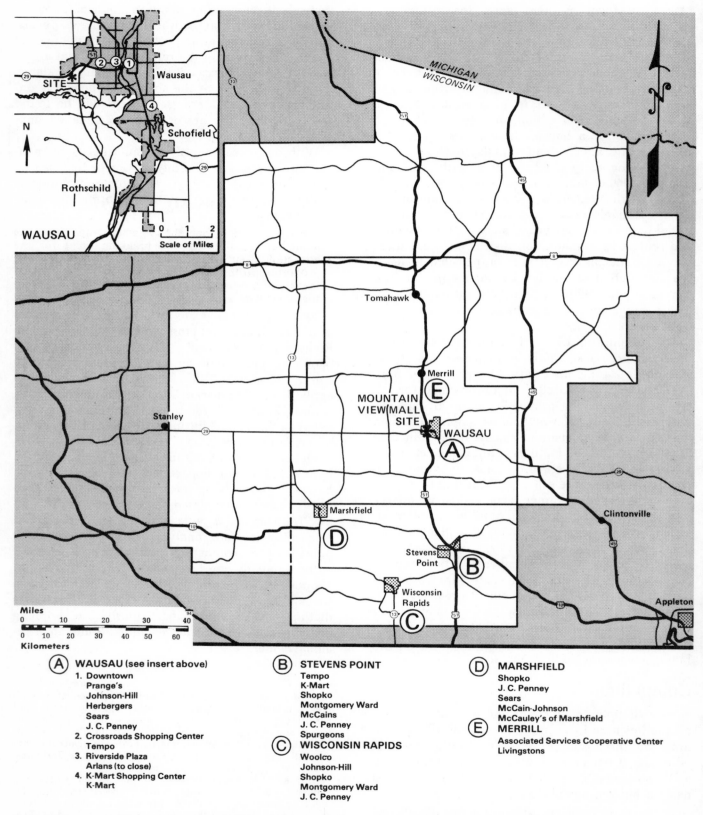

2-5 Major competitive retail centers in Mountain View Mall's market area. Source: Gladstone Associates.

Ⓐ **WAUSAU (see insert above)**
1. **Downtown**
   Prange's
   Johnson-Hill
   Herbergers
   Sears
   J. C. Penney
2. **Crossroads Shopping Center**
   Tempo
3. **Riverside Plaza**
   Arlans (to close)
4. **K-Mart Shopping Center**
   K-Mart

Ⓑ **STEVENS POINT**
   Tempo
   K-Mart
   Shopko
   Montgomery Ward
   McCains
   J. C. Penney
   Spurgeons

Ⓒ **WISCONSIN RAPIDS**
   Woolco
   Johnson-Hill
   Shopko
   Montgomery Ward
   J. C. Penney

Ⓓ **MARSHFIELD**
   Shopko
   J. C. Penney
   Sears
   McCain-Johnson
   McCauley's of Marshfield

Ⓔ **MERRILL**
   Associated Services Cooperative Center
   Livingstons

Customers' shopping preferences are based on convenience. Customers want the best shopping place that is close to home. They do not want to drive great distances for convenience goods to meet their day-to-day needs.

In evaluating the pulling power of a new center, consideration must be given to the strength and effectiveness of other retail shopping facilities—both existing and proposed—with which the center will have to compete. The competition that will influence the potential sales volume of a location consists of three separate types: other existing suburban shopping facilities within and beyond the trade area; the central business district, which may exercise a strong though varying influence on residents throughout the metropolitan area; and shopping facilities that are likely to be built in the future.

Accordingly, having determined the income of each segment of the trade area population, it is possible to calculate how much the families in the trade area spend at all shopping areas that comprise the center's present competition. The surplus in buying power is the figure that may be assignable to the new center.

It is necessary to take into account any future growth and its potential. Two basic types of analysis are needed: a study of the direction that future growth may take, and a study of the community's economic base.

The anticipated volume of business and the appropriate types of merchandise for the new center can be calculated on the assumption that the center will capture a reasonable percentage of buying power in its trade area. What this volume and merchandise mix may be is determined by evaluating known data on the proportion of family income spent in each major category, such as food, clothing, furniture, and other retail. The unknown quantity is the weight to be given to the new center because of its attraction as a convenient shopping place with easy parking and with customer appeal provided by the array of merchandise that the center will offer. Proper tenant mix increases the pulling power of any shopping center. The function of tenant mix is to provide the greatest depth of selection across a wide range of consumer goods.

Kind of Center

With the trade area and a sales potential outlined, the kind of center that can be built begins to emerge, particularly when leading or key tenants

are known. Exploitation of this knowledge then depends on site selection and skillful arrangement, plus the choice of good merchandisers as other tenants and the creation of strong customer attractions. These decisions call for skilled judgements.

At the time a market survey is made, the names of probable tenants are compiled. In most places there is a strong or weak merchandising position occupied by local merchants. For example, most customers prefer one supermarket over another; hence, the relative local standing of a merchant should be considered because preferred merchants will draw more patronage to a new center and should be represented to strengthen customer appeal.

From the sales volume estimate of the market analysis, the store types and the approximate square footage of building can be determined, in a preliminary way, to meet the merchandising potential. With store size roughed out, cost and income factors can be set up. From the building area and the types of stores, parking needs can be estimated in relation to the gross leasable area. With the parking demand gauged, the total area required for the site can be measured. This determination allows site evaluation, tenant provisions, and plans for the site layout to be put into sketch form.

Summary — Market and Economic Analysis

Market evaluation is a job for an expert in the field, but the developer should be familiar with the items listed below. The developer's judgement and common sense will temper the analysis, which should be prepared in terms that are understandable. The market analysis is a tool to assist in making judgement; it should not be taken as a substitute for judgement itself.

To recapitulate, the rudiments of market analyses include:

- Determination of the trade area tributary to the the shopping center. Analysis of the area's population changes, both numerically and in percentages for present and future growth, translated onto maps and displayed graphically. Analysis of the area's basic employment and economy. Analysis of access—present and future highway patterns, traffic counts, street capacities, travel times—translated onto maps and other data displays.

- Purchasing power for primary, secondary, and

remote trade areas. Disposable income in amounts or percentages after standard deductions have been estimated for federal income and local taxes, housing costs (mortgage or rental payments), insurance, savings, and transportation costs. The remaining dollars constitute *net spendable income,* the really important component.

- Measurement of competition—discount for composite pull of other competing retail outlets.
- Retail sales potential—deductions from analysis in the two above items. Includes investigation of total retail expenditures, sales capacity for existing stores by types of merchandise, and surplus available to the center.

Above all, caution must be used to obtain a clear understanding of the assumptions employed in completing any market study. The assumptions are critical to the validity of the study, which should reflect realizable achievements.

At this point, market analysis becomes economic analysis. The economic survey, in addition to being one of the principal tools for determining the feasibility of the center, serves the very important function of telling the developer how much space he should allocate to the various types of merchandise.[5]

Estimates and computations such as the following begin to show the kind of center that may be planned:

- Total retail space, with assignment to key tenants and supplementary stores.
- Projections of rental income by minimum guarantee, per annum sales volume, and rate of percentage rent.
- Parking index for the entire center.

Estimates are then developed into an economic feasibility and profitability study. A performance projection must be prepared showing:

- The estimated capital costs of development.
- The costs of carrying the investment during the period of market absorption.
- The estimated annual gross revenues.
- The estimated annual expenses related to operating costs.

Estimated expenses of operation are the final deduction before the net income can be determined. Amortization, depreciation, and income taxes, if any, are then calculated. In these estimates, the developer must also anticipate and pay careful attention to possible increases in the costs of labor, materials, and money from the levels current at the time of the initial estimates. Finally, when all of these calculations are carried out, the performance projection thus derived will indicate the return on capital costs in developing the center.

Roy Drachman, a past president of ULI and past president of the International Council of Shopping Centers, has addressed the area of economic analysis and the importance of the person who conducts such an analysis:

The experience of a knowledgeable economic analyst is of great importance in relating the information in the survey to the merchandising plan for the center. In other words, he must correctly "analyze the market analysis" and interpret the "nose count" to create the end result . . . a shopping center containing stores offering the kind of merchandise at the proper prices and in sufficient amount to satisfy the demand from the trade area.

A qualified economist will be able to advise the developer that in the trade area, for example, there is an unsatisfied purchasing demand for shoes approximating $800,000 per year. This, as a potential volume, may include $300,000 for medium priced women's shoes; $150,000 in medium priced men's shoes, and the balance in miscellaneous footwear.

To continue with this example, an analyst will further state that the center may contain a shoe store of 4,000 square feet offering medium priced women's shoes; a shoe department of approximately 1,000 square feet within a high fashion apparel store; a family shoe store of 3,500 to 4,000 square feet; and a store of approximately 2,000 square feet selling medium priced men's shoes.

This same type of analysis and store size recommendation can be applied to the other lines of merchandise. The end result will be a meaningful picture of what the tenant size and mix could be for all the stores in the center. A tabulation might be:

Shoe Type	Sales Volume	Store Size in Sq. Ft.
Women's medium priced	$300,000	4,000
Women's high priced	100,000	1,000
Family	200,000	3,500–4,000
Men's	150,000	2,000
Miscellaneous	50,000	—
	$800,000	10,500–11,000

A final word about the market analysis: too many developers have made an economic survey in order to convince prospective tenants that the trading area needs and can afford the center. Instead, the survey should be made to find out *whether* the area can support a new shopping center.

[5] See *Dollars and Cents of Shopping Centers: 1975* (Washington, D.C.: ULI–the Urban Land Institute). Updated and reissued triennially.

2-6　A corollary of Reilly's Law is that other factors being equal, shoppers will patronize the larger shopping center. This presumption provides the rationale for developing very large retail complexes, such as Northridge Fashion Center in Los Angeles' San Fernando Valley. Opened in 1971, Northridge is anchored by four department stores and has structured parking.

Site Selection and Evaluation

With a good market analysis that substantiates the project, the next preliminary stage in development can move forward—site selection and evaluation. Care must be taken to assure that a prospective location is the best from all points of view for the type of center proposed. Findings from the market analysis must be tied in closely. Site selection is a crucial determination.

Suitable sites for shopping center development are hard to find. In all probability, when a site is discovered, either the location is not zoned for commercial use or there will be complications in acquiring the property.

In site selection and evaluation, whether for a small neighborhood center or a regional giant, and whether or not the developer already owns the site, he must make sure that it has the best possible combination of characteristics such as the following:

- Location and access
- Size
- Shape
- Topography
- Drainage
- Minimal subsoil complications
- Surroundings
- Utilities
- Zoning
- Environmental impact feasibility

If a site is already owned, the problem is to evaluate it and to justify its use for the proposed shopping center. Too often a developer will plan to build a shopping center simply because he owns a tract of land with highway frontage. His decision to build must be based on proof that the site quali-

33

fies by reason of the market and site analyses. A shopping center should be developed on the owned site only if it is suitable for shopping center purposes. If the developer does not own *the best site,* he should acquire it—or forget the development. It is emphasized that any site, even if it is available and owned by the developer, should not be developed as a shopping center if it is not the best site. Otherwise, the best site will also be developed. The result will be overdevelopment, and the center on the less desirable site is likely to suffer from overcompetition.

Location

Site location is of paramount importance in the success of all shopping center types. The site must qualify by its trade area characteristics, the income level of the area households, competition, highway access, and visual exposure.

Location and access are interrelated but separate. The site must be convenient to reach over roads with enough unused traffic capacity to avoid a high level of congestion. The site must be both easy to enter and safe to leave, for both customers and employees, or must be capable of modification to make it so.

From the standpoint of location, the site should represent an impregnable economic position. The site's superior access, greater convenience, better merchant array, and improved services should make it impractical for another project, *similar in type,* to later be introduced nearby.

Necessary distances between shopping centers cannot be stated precisely. After all, it is not distance between centers that counts in drawing power but convenience for the customer and availability of merchandise. For example, a convenience type of center can operate successfully next to or across the road from a regional center. The reason

2-7 Glendale Galleria occupies a 28-acre site two blocks west of Glendale, California's main shopping street, Brand Boulevard. The two areas are presently separated by secondary commercial uses and parking lots, and further redevelopment will be required to fully integrate the new center with the city's established retail district. Glendale's financial district is the cluster of high-rise buildings outlined in the upper portion of the picture.

2-8 Pedestrian access can be particularly important for neighborhood centers, whose primary market generally lies within 1½ miles. This walkway underpass at Tall Oaks Village Center in Reston, Virginia, provides pedestrian access from townhouses and a recreation center separated from the shopping center by a major thoroughfare.

such coexistence is possible is that the two types of centers offer different ranges of merchandise. Shoppers at a neighborhood center want convenience for buying everyday goods and services. Customers of the regional center are primarily "shoppers" who are looking for and comparing general merchandise by range in price, quality, size, color, and style.

But if one needs theoretical distances for site location, the indicators mentioned earlier in this chapter may be used as very general guidelines:

- Neighborhood centers draw from a distance of approximately 1½ miles, depending on density and character of the residential area. Walking distance is not a valid criterion, particularly in suburban locations. A mile and a half is too far to carry groceries. But in built-up areas where high-density, multifamily housing and mixed use are part of the general development pattern, walking distance plus mass transportation and relation to other commercial areas are considerations.

- Community centers draw from the area within 3 to 5 miles of the site.
- Regional centers draw from distances of 8 miles or more. Driving time, however, is a better determinant than distance for delineating areas of attraction. While the maximum driving time might be 20 minutes, this may actually be a distance of 2 to 20 miles, depending on traffic conditions and type of highway travel to a site. Drawing power for regional centers in metropolitan areas suggests 5 to 10 miles between competing locations.

Neighborhood centers are located for access from collector streets. The location must avoid having minor residential service streets as its principal access for automobile traffic.

Where a neighborhood convenience type of center is justified in a new planned unit or residential cluster development, the center should be placed at an outer edge of the property, where a major artery can serve the center, the outside territory,

SHOPPING CENTER TRADE AREAS--THEORETICAL TRAVEL DISTANCES

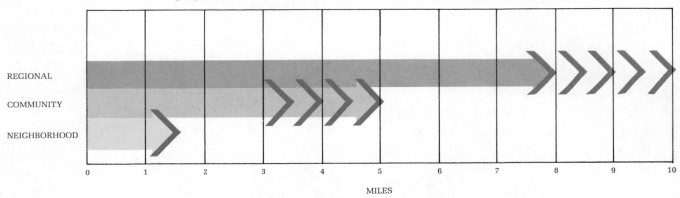

REGIONAL

COMMUNITY

NEIGHBORHOOD

0   1   2   3   4   5   6   7   8   9   10

MILES

2-9

and the interior residential areas of the development.[6]

Within an all-new, large-scale residential development such as a satellite community or new town on several thousand acres of land, the hierarchy of shopping center locations will be determined by land use allocation on the master development plan while the project is in its site planning stage. In these cases, site selection becomes part of the overall planning process. The developer and his planning team have the opportunity of choosing the most advantageous shopping center sites in accordance with principles of site selection. The major commercial center can also incorporate civic facilities—offices, library, auditorium, and police and fire stations—as the planned center for the new community.

Community centers are located for access from major thoroughfares. Because the array of stores represents limited lines of shopping goods plus convenience goods and services, accessibility from an extended trade area via high-speed freeways is not needed in order for the location to qualify as suitable for development.

Regional centers are customarily located where the site is easily accessible from interchange points between expressways and freeways. Under energy use constraints, easy access to mass transit may become equally or more important in regional centers. *Easily reached* implies short travel distances and ease of driving for customers, employees, and service vehicles. *Short distance* from an inter-

change may range from one-half mile to a mile, depending on local circumstances.

When high-activity centers, such as busy regional shopping centers, have site access points too close to freeway interchanges, traffic is likely to be severely congested under occasional peak hour conditions. Shopper traffic interferes with the flow of through traffic, and the resultant congestion is intensified if the stacking lanes, where cars wait to enter or exit from high-speed freeways, are too short.

In theory, a cloverleaf-type grade separation between two intersecting traffic routes creates a strong locational pull, because of high visibility and because of the center's nearness to exchanges in travel direction. But in reality, a site at a cloverleaf grade separation offers poor access. The grade separation treatment is complicated, confusing, and subject to traffic backups and accident hazards.

At directional interchanges, travel speeds are such that distance factors prevent ready separation of through traffic from off-route destination traffic. Even explicit directional signing does not substitute for providing the distance needed for safe lane changes and free traffic flow.

Site frontage on a restricted access highway is good only as visual exposure. Entrance and exit points to the site require special local access lanes

[6] See Maxwell C. Huntoon, Jr., *PUD: A Better Way for the Suburbs* (Washington, D.C.: ULI–the Urban Land Institute, 1971).

for avoiding left turns and other traffic movement which may interfere with smooth traffic flow and control. These considerations suggest a site location about a mile from freeway interchanges.

If there is a choice, the site for a regional center should offer ease of access and should be a reasonable distance from a radial highway leading to the city and from a circumferential highway that taps the urbanized residential periphery of the metropolitan area.

The ideal site for a regional center is ringed by major traffic routes which have access points and traffic control devices carefully designed to dis-

perse traffic over a major street system and to handle the peak loads generated by such centers.[7]

---

[7] See *Special Traffic Generator Study*, Commercial Generations Report 4 (State of Delaware Department of Highways and Transportation, 1975). The study measures average daily one-way trips to and from commercial centers for each day of the week, including Saturday and Sunday. Extensive tabulated data in such areas as gross floor area and total number of employees are presented to evaluate the impact of the three standard types of shopping centers as well as the freestanding establishment.

Also see *Guidelines for Planning and Designing Access Systems for Shopping Centers*, prepared by Technical Council Committee 5-DD, Institute of Traffic Engineers (Arlington, Va., 1976).

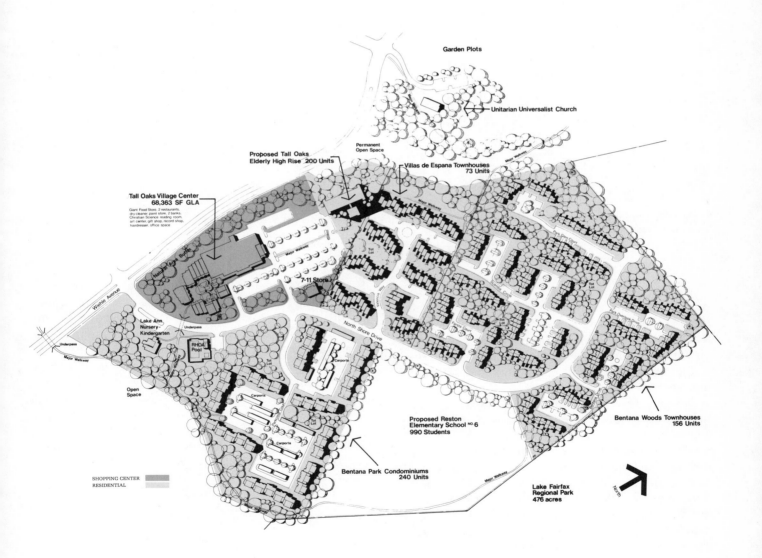

2-10   Tall Oaks Village in Reston, Virginia, is served by a neighborhood shopping center.

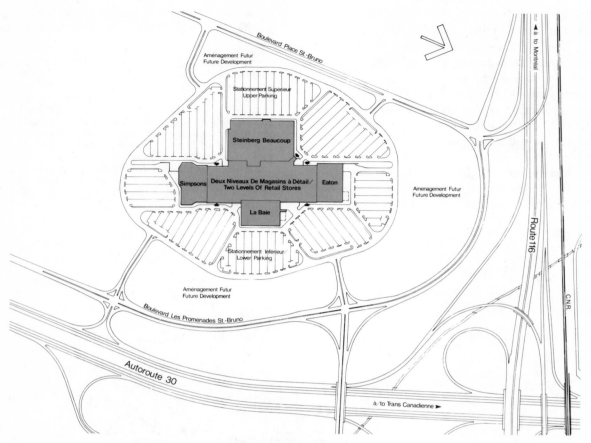

2-11   The site plan of Les Promenades–Saint Bruno illustrates the complexities of vehicular access. The center, near Montreal, is scheduled to open in the fall of 1978.

Access

Access is an integral part of site location. As mentioned, a site must be easy to enter and safe to leave or must be able to be made so. Easy access also means that a driver experiences free-flowing traffic conditions while driving toward and entering the site.

Designing or redesigning traffic flow at entrances to centers requires cooperation with traffic engineers and local highway departments. If the access road design cannot carry the additional traffic and turning movements generated by the center, the cost of any necessary improvements and signalization must be investigated. This includes determining whether costs will be borne by the highway construction authorities, by the developer, or shared—and in what proportion.

Left turns require specially constructed lanes, or an "island" for turning movements. Right turns on a heavy trafficway require deceleration lanes for easy entrance and acceleration lanes for easy exit. If cars moving into or out of a center create traffic bottlenecks, resentment arises. Congestion at entrances and backups on major traffic routes can lead to customer and driver annoyance.

Visibility is another factor of accessibility. A shopping center has poor visbility when it is not seen until local traffic speeds (35 miles per hour) carry the driver past the parking area entrance. Even though traffic flow attracts retail business, a site that fronts on a highway heavily built up with strings of competing distractions, including signs, has a decreased level of accessibility.[8]

To achieve the optimum in traffic access to any site, particularly to community and regional centers, the service of a professional traffic engineer is essential in the early site analysis stage.

[8] See William Applebaum, *Guide to Store Location Research: With Emphasis on Supermarkets* (Reading, Mass.: Addisonian Press, 1968).

2-12   This ramp was constructed by the developer to ease traffic movement to and from Landmark Shopping Center, Alexandria, Virginia. Built after the center opened, the ramp was necessary to avoid traffic jams: primary access to the center is provided by a freeway exit a quarter mile away, and the original design required the driver to cross three lanes of traffic and then make a left turn across three more lanes of oncoming traffic in order to enter the shopping center.

As stated earlier, high-activity centers should be planned so that traffic originating at or destined for the center is separated from regional traffic. This can be accomplished by locating major center sites with their access and exit points about a mile away from regional freeways. Then cars can disperse by proper directional signing in different directions onto arterial streets before feeding onto the freeway, rather than having all traffic feed onto one freeway at one interchange.[9]

Shape

The shape of the site normally should be regular, all in one piece, undivided by highways or dedicated streets, with sufficient site area for the intended size of center.

A few successful centers exist where the property is divided by dedicated streets; Hillsdale, in San Mateo, California, is one example. A block plan was typical of early shopping centers. The block arrangement used dedicated streets with parking perpendicular to the curb on both sides. The arrangement placed parking directly in front of the canopied storefronts. This provided a convenient walk from the parked car to the store, but the movement of cars jockeying for and changing preferred positions prevented the pattern from becoming widespread. Notable examples of the block pattern of site design are Country Club Plaza in Kansas City, Missouri, the prototype; Cameron Village in Raleigh; and Utica Square in Tulsa. In the latter two cases, the streets are private. As recently as 10 years ago, the concept of the block pattern was revived in a few centers, notably Town and Country Village in Houston, the Town and Country Villages in Palo Alto and San Jose, California, and Old Town Village in Dallas.

Exceptions such as these should remind us that viable changes can be made in long-accepted stand-

9 Ibid.

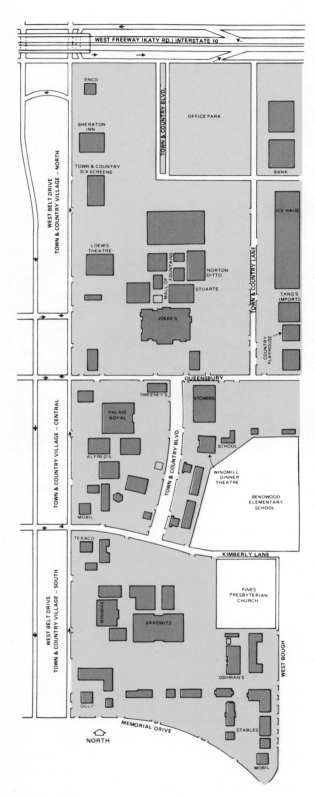

Map labels:
WEST FREEWAY (KATY RD.) INTERSTATE 10
ENCO
OFFICE PARK
TOWN & COUNTRY BLVD.
SHERATON INN
WEST BELT DRIVE TOWN & COUNTRY VILLAGE — NORTH
TOWN & COUNTRY SIX SCREENS
BANK
LOEW'S THEATRE
ICE HAUS
MALL OF FOUNTAINS
NORTON DITTO
STUARTS
TOWN & COUNTRY LANE
TANG'S IMPORTS
JOSKE'S
COUNTRY PLAYHOUSE
QUEENSBURY
SWEENEY'S
STOWERS
PALAIS ROYAL
SCHOOL
WEST BELT DRIVE TOWN & COUNTRY VILLAGE — CENTRAL
ALFRED'S
TOWN & COUNTRY BLVD.
WINDMILL DINNER THEATRE
BENDWOOD ELEMENTARY SCHOOL
MOBIL
KIMBERLY LANE
TEXACO
PINES PRESBYTERIAN CHURCH
MINIMAX
WEST BELT DRIVE TOWN & COUNTRY VILLAGE — SOUTH
SAKOWITZ
WEST BOUGH
GULF
OSHMAN'S
MEMORIAL DRIVE
STABLES
NORTH
MOBIL

2-13 Town and Country Village, Houston. This pre-planned grouping of freestanding retail and office buildings occupies a site of more than 150 acres. Developers rarely use such an arrangement today.

2-14 Colonnades have been used throughout Town and Country Village.

40

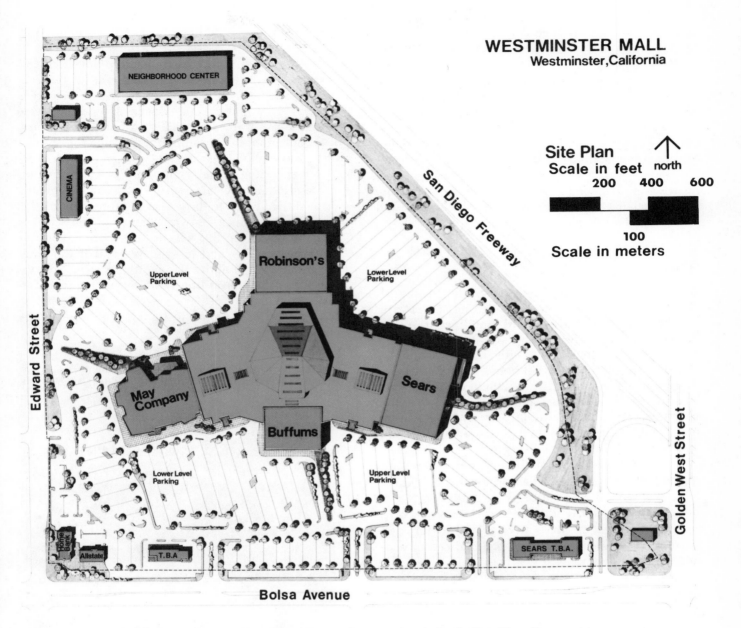

WESTMINSTER MALL
Westminster, California

NEIGHBORHOOD CENTER

CINEMA

Robinson's

Upper Level Parking

Lower Level Parking

San Diego Freeway

Site Plan
Scale in feet   north
200   400   600

100
Scale in meters

May Company

Sears

Buffums

Edward Street

Golden West Street

Lower Level Parking

Upper Level Parking

Home Bank
Allstate
T.B.A.

SEARS T.B.A.

Bolsa Avenue

2-15   Westminster Mall has a 93-acre triangular site, bounded on one side by the San Diego Freeway.

ards and principles of procedure. Normally, however, trafficways through a site impede the flow of pedestrians, complicate customer car movement within the parking area, and contradict the basic principle of unity in the shopping facility. For an enclosed mall, a divided site is unworkable. Do not deliberately set out to create a suburban shopping center on a site which is split or otherwise interrupted by a route for outside traffic.

Site depths cannot be suggested in any standardized way. Depths of perhaps 400 feet or more distinguish shopping centers from the old standard

strip commercial areas, which were usually platted only 100 or 150 feet in depth. The type of center to be built and the total acreage involved affect the site depth. The standard strip commercial areas of the past are no longer appropriate models of design for commercial developments. Requirements for parking access and circulation in shopping centers dictate much greater depth than was required by the out-of-date strip patterns.

A regularly shaped property without acute angles, odd projections, or indentations is best for efficient layout, even though an irregular shape can be used. But without adequate frontage, the center cannot enjoy the advantages of visibility from access thoroughfares.

Any awkwardly or very irregularly shaped property should be avoided, even though the total site area may be sufficient, because portions of the site may be unusable or, if used, may result in excessive site consumption, although this is an exception. Freestanding auxiliary features—such as auto service centers, various types of convenience facilities or drive-in, fast-food restaurants, and dry cleaning establishments or financial institutions—can be placed to advantage in odd-shaped parcels of shopping center property.

Size

As a rule of thumb for checking the adequacy of site area for a shopping center, one can figure roughly 10,000 square feet of building area and 30,000 square feet of parking area for each 40,000 square feet (about 1 acre) of site area. For example, a site of 10 acres for conventional shopping center development will readily accommodate 100,000 square feet of building area in the center. Such rough calculation is useful only for gauging a shopping center site proposal in an outlying location and would not be applicable elsewhere.

In today's planning, shopping centers are not dependent on vast site areas. Innovative planning for development of multiple uses within a single project enables more intensive land use and a consequent savings of land. Rising land costs may make a sprawling, single-level regional center economically unjustifiable.

Future land parcels will tend to be smaller, not only because of limited locations but also because of zoning restrictions which arise from environmental concerns and because of changing dimensions for car parking. When a horizontal center spreads itself over vast acreage, the benefit of shopper convenience is negated. With structured parking and multilevel shopping surrounding an enclosed mall, the design concept changes from horizontal to vertical development, thus saving on site area.[10]

Where there is a strong possibility of growth within the trade area, the size of the site should provide for the initial development plus space for growth. In suburban locations, the initial price of land will normally be low enough to permit acquisition of sufficient site area to provide for addi-

tional facilities, including shops, offices, and parking spaces.

A site too large for the immediate development possesses the advantage of having land in reserve for expansion and strengthening of the center. However, no more retail space should be constructed than is needed initially. Much of the future will depend on the strength of the original location, its access, and the original site area.

If a shopping center achieves a full measure of success, reaching its projected sales volume through its ability to draw a high proportion of the available purchasing power, then someone will inevitably try to tap this success by building competition nearby—if land is available and if the zoning situation will allow the additional use. Always present is the possibility that open land zoned for residential use across the street from a shopping center may be changed to permit additional commercial use.

[10] See Leonard Berg, "Eight Reasons Shopping Centers Have to Go Vertical," *MCA Real Estate Reporter*, October 1973.

2-16   THEORETICAL SHOPPING CENTER SITE AREAS

Neighborhood	5-7 acres
Community	10-30 acres
Regional	35-80 acres
Super-Regional	80-125 acres

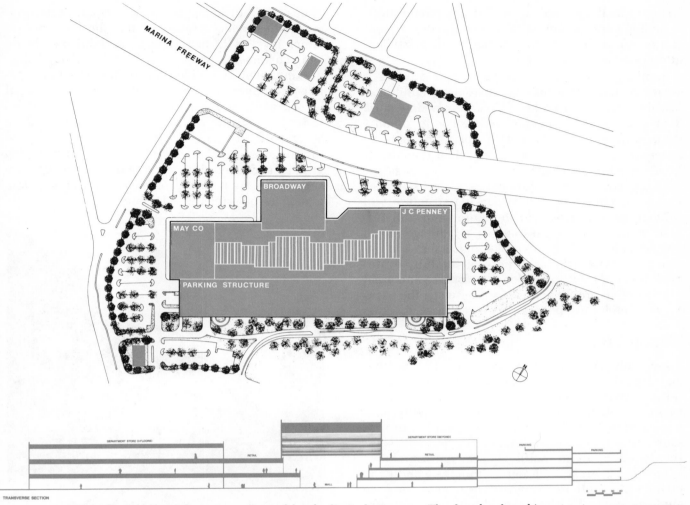

2-17 Foxhill Mall's multilevel design was dictated by the limited site area. The four-level parking structure can accommodate 2,400 vehicles.

This possibility should be kept in mind by the initial developer. Often the developer can afford to buy extra land in order to protect his location from subsequent undesirable encroachment. The center and its operation should be so well conceived and so successful that it would be unwise for anyone to establish competition close by. In other words, build a center to fit its trade area and its potential.

Land purchased when the center is first conceived but not used at the outset is very likely to increase in value. This land can be planned for compatible uses, such as freestanding banks, restaurants, motels, and office and medical buildings, and should prove to be a feasible investment. However, developers are finding that, because of high interest rates, taxes, and other carrying costs, the practice of holding land for extended periods is not

as feasible or as profitable as it once may have been.

As land costs keep rising, site costs can become a dominant factor in site selection and development. For coping with very high site acquisition costs, two-level merchandising arrangements may offer a means of reducing site costs and of getting parking and pedestrian walking distances within comfortable ranges. Where enclosed regional mall centers are to be built with about 350,000 square feet of GLA, not including department stores, two-level merchandising can be a solution for these problems. Where two-level merchandising is used, walking distances between tenant stores are reduced; and with two-level parking, walking distances between parking areas and stores are also reduced. In two-level schemes, it is important to provide structurally well-placed escalators in the enclosed mall area and to have strong tenant pulls, including parking and entrances to the department stores, on each level for customer interplay and attraction among the stores.

Similarly, as a center matures and attracts a greater volume of sales and customers, additional leasable area may be added. To accommodate store area expansion, it may be necessary to double-deck parking areas instead of spreading parking spaces over additional site area. When the cost of land for additional parking equals or exceeds the cost of construction for parking decks, decks should be constructed. The parking structure will provide parking closer to the stores and will furnish some covered parking, an advantage in all but the mildest of climates. The placement and design of parking structures must be carefully evaluated; this requires professional assistance and great sensitivity to proper connections between the parking deck and the mall area.

Topography

Topography is an important factor in site selection and layout, building design, and construction. A fairly level or gently sloping piece of ground is easily adaptable for shopping centers. With skill, a more steeply sloping site can be adapted to provide customer access at different levels. (This solution would apply to multilevel regional centers.)

Low-lying areas and poor drainage conditions create complications in subsurface construction for any center. Ideally a site should have minimal subsoil complications and neither solid rock nor a high water table, although such sites are now hard to find. Surface topography is best when the gradient across the property is slight—under 5 percent. A steeper slope, if used for surface parking, will require site preparation work for cut and fill and may require sedimentation and detention ponds for control of surface water runoff.

If the slope across the site corresponds to grades on surrounding roads, an opportunity for a two-level arrangement of buildings and parking may exist. Sloping site conditions offer the possibility of innovative two-level solutions in large projects. Smaller neighborhood and community projects are more readily arranged on a single level.

In a regional shopping center, the developer can more easily take advantage of sloping site conditions. To obtain satisfactory merchandising on two levels, however, customer attractions and circulation opportunities for each level must be equalized.

Shops on both levels must have equal access opportunities; concentration of the "best" stores on either level is a disadvantage to both merchants and customers. With two-level merchandising, parking must be divided to provide equal accessibility to upper and lower mall areas. No principal level should result from the merchandising solution.

Sensitive use of a site's topography can produce a compatibility between the shopping center and the site's natural characteristics. A site with sloping ground and specimen trees that need to be preserved can be skillfully reshaped to accommodate a stepped but single-level center.

2-18 Sites for multilevel shopping centers usually incorporate a change in grade to provide entrances of equal attractiveness to both levels of the center. At Santa Anita Fashion Park in Arcadia, California, the slopes are attractively landscaped.

Drainage

The proper handling of stormwater runoff has become a major issue in shopping center design. The strategy that will be used to handle this water should be developed in the preliminary stage of development planning. Coverage of part of the site by buildings and parking areas results in a dramatic rise in the post-development pattern of peak stormwater flows and total runoff. Reducing or delaying

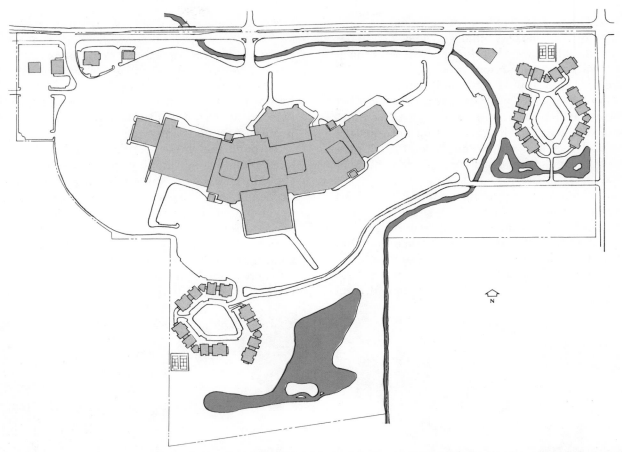

2-19   The site plan for Northbrook Court, Northbrook, Illinois, includes retention basins for flood control. A drainage canal parallels the inner loop street and feeds into ponds in the development's residential sections. Source: Homart Development Company.

this runoff is an important design issue with significant cost implications. Communities which do not have excess storm system capacities—and few do—are or will be looking at such concepts as rooftop ponding, temporary detention basins (in portions of the parking area, for example), detention ponds, and other mechanisms for reducing the runoff rate and total runoff after development. Likewise, potential water pollution may be another problem that needs to be addressed.

Utilities

Availability of utilities at or near the site is an asset to be considered in site selection. Off-site improvements are a critical element in capital cost, and a location close or easily accessible to utilities —water, sewer, gas, and electricity—cuts down on the costs of these improvements. Off-site development costs usually can be shared with the municipality and the utility company. To minimize time-consuming negotiations with officials, make sure

that the site is at least within easy reach of the required water supply and sewage disposal facilities.

Surroundings

Rarely can a site be found that is ideally surrounded by major streets or trafficways. Land use adjacent to or across the road from any site is important in evaluating the site's suitability for development. If the adjacent site is already built up, there is one set of circumstances; if the area nearby consists of raw land, open for development, there are different factors to consider.

In either case, the local political climate may be opposed to development in any form, with a prevailing resentment against "intrusion" by a shopping center. The developer must explore the local temper before he goes too far in site selection.

The public is not well-versed in shopping center design. Where the site, particularly for a neighborhood center, is adjacent to residential areas, it will be necessary to offset any adverse impact on the livability of the nearby houses. The developer must be doubly sure that his project will meet the criteria for good shopping center design. He must be prepared to prevent visual, noise, or traffic "pollution." Failure to provide site access by other than local residential streets or to provide permanent and effective physical separation between the commercial use and single-family detached residences may spell the death of the development proposal.

Local objections to shopping centers can be dealt with by explaining the concept of a shopping center operation—not a miscellaneous aggregation of stores, but an architecturally harmonious unit that uses less fuel energy than would separate stores, produces minimal air pollution, offers integrated, privately policed parking for public benefit, and

has controlled truck delivery, signing, lighting, and landscaping. Where there are residences across the street, a border of hardy evergreens and landscaped berms can minimize the effects of noise and night lighting. Architectural walls, solid fences, berms, or narrow but dense plantings of hedges or evergreens can be introduced as buffers at appropriate property lines.

Through the formulation and implementation of local planning and zoning policy, public agencies should express their interest in protecting the public benefit derived from comprehensively planned development by discouraging the tendency for parasitic commercial uses to spring up in strips near major shopping centers. In general, enlightened municipal planning bodies tend to look favorably on planned developments, such as shopping centers. Because of the shopping center's planned

2-20   The area around Fairview Mall, one of metropolitan Toronto's largest shopping centers, includes a freeway interchange and numerous multistory apartment buildings. Local zoning policy encourages high-density development near suburban focal points such as regional shopping centers.

site arrangement, including buffer provisions and screening, approval authorities find that the effect on streets, highways, and adjacent property is much less adverse than it is with the strip type of development.[11]

In converting from residential to commercial use allocation, authorities should recognize that the total cost of providing such public services as police and fire protection, schools, streets, and utilities is much less for commercial facilities than for residential development. Commercial developments produce a sizable return in real estate and sales taxes. Such revenue might well be lost, or received by another municipality, if commercial use were disallowed for the location proposed for the center.

Properly located, the center produces net income to the community far in excess of that produced by land uses resulting from single-family residential development. The tax advantages available to to the community should overcome many objections that may arise.[12]

The comprehensively planned shopping center development unquestionably increases the value of land adjacent to the center. It is logical that the developer should benefit directly from the increase in value, provided he controls the land so positioned. The developer himself may not control all adjacent land development. It is important to encourage development of compatible fringe uses, such as apartments, planned office parks, medical clinics, motels, restaurants, and other nonretail commercial uses which do not affect peak hour traffic flow to the center. Such fringe development will also concentrate shopper traffic within the area approximate to the center, rather than diluting and diverting that buying power to areas beyond the center's influence.

The shopping center can very likely be encouraged to become a center of community life, with library, community center, and other public facilities located within the complex. Impending energy shortages, which may cause the public to seek ways to reduce driving, will also contribute to this centralization of community activity.

Apartments or office uses developed adjacent to a shopping center site are an excellent transition zone between a shopping center location and a single-family residential area. A site adjacent to high-density apartment developments has the additional prospective benefit of receiving greater walk-in trade.

Acquisition

A site must be acquirable through reasonable negotiation. Adequate sites in single ownership are not often found at ideal shopping center locations. A higher land cost for a good location is preferable to a lower land cost for a less desirable property. It is impossible to generalize about land cost, except to point out that this cost factor is an important part of the initial economic calculations.

The following data, taken from the 1975 edition of *Dollars and Cents of Shopping Centers,* show the land costs for shopping centers opened in 1974, expressed in dollars per square foot of GLA:

2-21

LAND COSTS FOR NEW CENTERS, 1974

	Median	Bottom of range	Top of range	Number in sample
Regional and super-regional centers	$2.56	$1.10	$22.39	12
Community centers	5.55	.98	10.17	17
Neighborhood centers	3.70	.96	8.21	19

Naturally, the cost of land is important no matter what use is planned for a site. But land cost is particularly important in a shopping center, regardless of type, because approximately 4 square feet of land must be acquired for each square foot of building desired. This relationship allows 1 square foot of ground under the building and 3 square feet for roadways, parking spaces, malls, landscaping, and other nonbuilding uses. This means that if land is selling for $1 per square foot and if 4 square feet of land are required for each square foot of building (assuming a single-level structure), then $4 per square foot must be added to the project cost for each square foot of building. Such land cost could prove to be excessive, but the economics for the project will determine what land cost can be supported.

Since site location for the shopping center is of great importance, it is also important to remember that in areas where the land cost is extremely high,

[11] See J. Ross McKeever, *Shopping Center Zoning,* ULI Technical Bulletin 69 (Washington, D.C.: ULI–the Urban Land Institute, 1973).

[12] See Michael S. Levin, *Measuring the Fiscal Impact of a Shopping Center on Its Community* (New York: International Council of Shopping Centers, 1975).

Also see Darwin G. Stuart and Robert B. Teska, "Who Pays for What: A Cost-Revenue Analysis of Suburban Land Use Alternatives," *Urban Land,* Vol. 30, No. 3 (March 1971).

2-22 This eight-square-block section of Hawthorne, California, was platted in 1905 by the Hawthorne Development Company. The curving blocks, boulevards, and landscaped parks are now the site of an 840,000-square-foot regional shopping center. Redevelopment was accomplished through the mechanism of tax increment financing. In all, 167 separate parcels were acquired by the city.

multilevel or vertical centers may result in a more economic land-to-building cost ratio. Where mixed use and multifloor structures for parking are incorporated into the center, the cost of the land must be compatible with the overall economics of the development.

Land costs, building costs, and volume of sales vary so widely from one section of the country to another that any standard set of figures can be misleading for a particular site. The fact that land cost is low in a certain location should not lead to a false assumption that a shopping center placed there will yield the best overall project economics. At a higher price for land, a strategic location may enable a center to draw the maximum sales volume potential of the trade area, thus spelling the difference between success and failure.

In most cases, compromises will have to be weighed by balancing advantages with shortcomings. If more than one site is being analyzed for suitability, each site should be checked carefully, as one will undoubtedly offer more advantages than the others. However, site evaluation must finally show that the site selected is the best one, the strongest location for the project under analysis.

Summary — Site Selection and Evaluation

Three principal factors are weighed heavily in evaluating a location: size of the market; key tenant availability for the selected site; and site characteristics, including access, size and shape, costs of land, site preparation, utilities, and drainage, and favorable zoning and environmental considerations. Characteristics and availability of adjacent vacant land for later compatible use are also factors that can sway the site selection.

An accurate comparison of several alternative sites depends on an accurate economic appraisal of the project's income possibilities and potential, measured against the costs of site acquisition, building construction, parking areas, landscaping, maintenance, and operation.

For a neighborhood center, the site must be selected for its ready access from the supporting residential area. In the case of an entirely new community, the neighborhood shopping center site selection must avoid adverse impact on adjacent residential property, and must assure future accessibility to the site.

For a community center, the site evaluation will be similar to that for a regional center, including the considerations of physical factors and surroundings.

For a regional center, a few more minutes of driving may not make too much difference in accessibility; or perhaps the acquisition of a few more acres of land will make the site measure up to standards of suitability.

Key Tenant Commitment

There will not be a shopping center until there is a key tenant; this is true whether the center is a small neighborhood facility or a regional giant. Key tenants are determining elements in site design, design and layout considerations, and financial negotiation. And as already noted, it is the key tenant or tenants, not the size of either the site or the center, that determines the type of center.

As stated earlier, the key or anchor tenants are the supermarket in a neighborhood center, with a drugstore almost equally necessary; the junior department store, variety store, or popular price or discount operation in a community center; and the department store (of at least 100,000 square feet) in a regional center. Few really successful regionals have been developed with only one such anchor tenant; most include at least two department stores.

The developer's first test on the way to realizing his hopes comes from his negotiations for key tenant commitments to the project. The key tenants also determine the image that the center will offer, and any major efforts in site design will be wasted unless who the major tenants will be, and where they will probably be located in the center, are first considered.

The developer will find that key tenants have firm ideas about the general arrangement of the center and where they want to be. They will require certain conditions to be met if they are to occupy space in the center.

The key tenant commitment is a form of partnership between the major store and the developer; for this reason, the key tenant, whether a supermarket, discount store, or department store, should

2-23   Lord and Taylor is a key tenant at The Galleria, Houston.

be tied in very closely with the developer in his land and building planning. The key tenant's requirements will influence the developer's decisions on leasing, financial negotiations, building treatment, architectural style, parking provisions, signing, and landscaping. Furthermore, at this point—before site planning or further leasing—the key tenant should be committed to agreements for ultimate centerwide operations, such as tax participation, membership in the merchants association and its advertising and publicity programs, and the tenant's "fair share" of the common area upkeep, including cost escalations. *(Fair share* for the key tenant does not generally imply a pro rata share, but a negotiated sum determined by the tenant's size and importance to the center.)

In this stage, the project's form begins to adapt to the characteristics of the site and the potential of the trade area. In a high-income area, for example, two high-fashion stores may sign as tenants, thus creating a quality image for a proposed center. It is the quality of the market here that determines the type of center suitable to the area. The image of the leading tenant in turn determines the type of satellite tenants that are suitable to the particular center. If a popular price store were the key tenant, then all factors in tenant planning would be different. The wrong key tenant can complicate the satellite tenant problem. Nevertheless, a too homogeneous tenant mix, even in high-income areas, has proven to be a mistake in leasing.

The important role of the key tenants' image requires that in the very early development preliminaries the owner-developer or his leasing agent must determine what key tenants may be available and must start the negotiations with these tenants.

A competent real estate leasing agent will know the characteristics of major key tenants in the area. He will know what their expansion philosophy is and what lease or occupancy provisions can be negotiated, because he will have had some experience in dealing with such major stores. Likewise, he will know of other commitments that have been made by the key tenant prospects, and he will know under what conditions these tenants will be available or unavailable, as well as what arrangements may make the key tenants strong attractors of other tenants.

Because of the need to deal with these tenant selection subtleties, the leasing agent or real estate expert must be on the development team from the start and must work with the market analyst and guide the developer and his architect, engineer,

and planner. Some developers have in-house leasing expertise. Those successful developers who use outside broker-agents know enough about the field that they are not forced to rely entirely on outside advice for resolving critical questions.

After the key tenants have been tied down—preferably through a "letter of intent" or clear expression of interest, if not an actual lease or occupancy agreement—then a building and site layout can be roughed out. Based on data from the market and economic analyses, supplementary tenant classifications can be used to produce a leasing plan.

In the discussion that follows, we will most often use the term *lease*. It should be recognized that in many cases the key tenant will own his own site, rather than lease; for the purposes of general discussion, however, *lease* is used where *occupancy agreement* might be more accurate for some tenants.

In *How to Create a Shopping Center,* S. O. Kaylin outlines the elements of a leasing plan as follows:

Type of tenant (by retail line); names of prospective tenants in each category; GLA assignable on basis of market study; the economic analysis, footnoted by characteristics of the prospects in each category; tentative location of each tenant on the building plan; and rate of percentage rent applicable to the tenant's sales in excess of a breakpoint computed as

$$\text{breakpoint} = \frac{\text{minimum rent}}{\text{percentage rent}}$$

Thus, if minimum rent is \$20,000 per year and the rent percentage is 5 percent, then

$$\text{breakpoint} = \frac{\$20,000}{.05} = \$400,000$$

The tenant would pay an annual rent of \$20,000 until sales reached \$400,000. He would then pay 5 percent of all sales in excess of \$400,000. If his sales totaled \$500,000, he would pay \$20,000 plus 5 percent of \$100,000 (or \$5,000) as *overage* rent, so that his total rent would reach \$25,000. The list of tenants in the leasing plan shows each prospective tenant's breakpoint in total dollars and in dollars per square foot of GLA. Other listed data would include credit rating and length of lease.[13]

Leasing negotiations for supplementary tenants follow along after major leases have been signed or committed. While negotiations for key tenants

---

[13] Kaylin, *How to Create a Shopping Center* (footnote 1 above), ch. 5.

are not susceptible to rules of procedure, getting commitments or expressions of interest from supplementary or satellite tenants precedes the firming up of the financing plan and any preparation of construction details. In addition, developers do not start final plans or even finalize site acquisition procedures before zoning approval is concluded, because economically unfeasible conditions may be imposed. Final commitment of major tenants will generally be subject to zoning approval.

A prospectus in attractive brochure form makes a useful exhibit in explaining market findings, site advantages, and the tentative arrangement of building and site to prospective tenants. A rendering of the architectural treatment, showing as well whether a mall will be open, or enclosed and air-conditioned, can work as another very useful presentation for tenant negotiations.

At this point, the developer should have a form lease to present to satellite tenants. Basic economic provisions should be made known to tenants early in the process so that matters such as the tenant's tax participation, public area maintenance contribution, merchants association membership, rental scale, and promotion are discussed and resolved at the outset. Otherwise, misunderstandings can arise over such matters as the distribution of tenant and owner responsibilities, creating dissension and damaging the later operation of the center.

During the negotiation stage, a firm commitment rather than a precise lease is called for from the lead tenants. Whether the key tenant is to lease space in a building owned by the developer or construct his own building, the commitment should be made before proceeding too far with site planning. After key tenants have been tied down, it is logical to go ahead with the building layout. The placing of supplementary tenants must encourage good distribution of pedestrian traffic in order to induce impulse buying:

> . . . the best layout would be a supermarket at one end and a discounter or general merchandise store on the other. If one of the anchors were in the middle of the center, "it would seriously affect the traffic at the far end and the little fellow there can be hurt." [14]

While it is desirable to have a key tenant committed to the project early in the development process, it is not always possible. In major regional centers, for example, certain planning efforts, such as obtaining zoning clearance, must often proceed at the developer's risk while final negotiations are proceeding with department stores.

Zoning and Land Use

Favorable zoning is needed for any site. *Favorable* in this sense refers to provisions that grant approval of a workable plan before development takes place.

In many local jurisdictions, suitable shopping center sites are not zoned for commercial or mixed use prior to development, nor should they be. But a community's master plan may indicate general locations for various types of shopping centers and may include community planning policies that will assist the developer in identifying areas where development would be consistent with community objectives. Prezoned, mapped commercial strips are usually not suitable locations for shopping centers.

With any site, the zoning provisions in effect must be studied before site purchase is finalized. If a site is zoned for other than shopping center use, a change of use or modification of the provisions obviously must be applied for. Part of the early study must be an exploration of the attitudes of the local residents, zoning staff, and approval body toward a shopping center proposal.

Even though zoning provisions in some jurisdictions may not yet have been revised to automatically provide for the planned unit concept (and the shopping center is a planned unit), zoning authorities generally recognize the shopping center as a legitimate form of planned land use.

Conventional elements of ordinance provisions, such as strict specifications for floor area ratio, building height, lot coverage, and setbacks, are modified by the concept of planned unit development and the provisions for comprehensive site plan review and approval. Under the planned unit shopping center concept, retail uses are compatible with the trade area, and on-site parking is provided in relation to the commercial use. Hence, site area and parking for the shopping center require parcel shapes with depth and breadth, not long, narrow strips of land. In many jurisdictions, the shopping center concept and its development have advanced despite standard zoning procedures. It is important that zoning ordinances be updated to provide for *planned shopping center districts,* not through arbitrary map indication but through planning commission review (based on locational and site attribute

---

[14] From "Small Center Needs Draw Top Interest at Convention," *Shopping Center World,* Vol. 1, No. 6 (July 1972), p. 35.

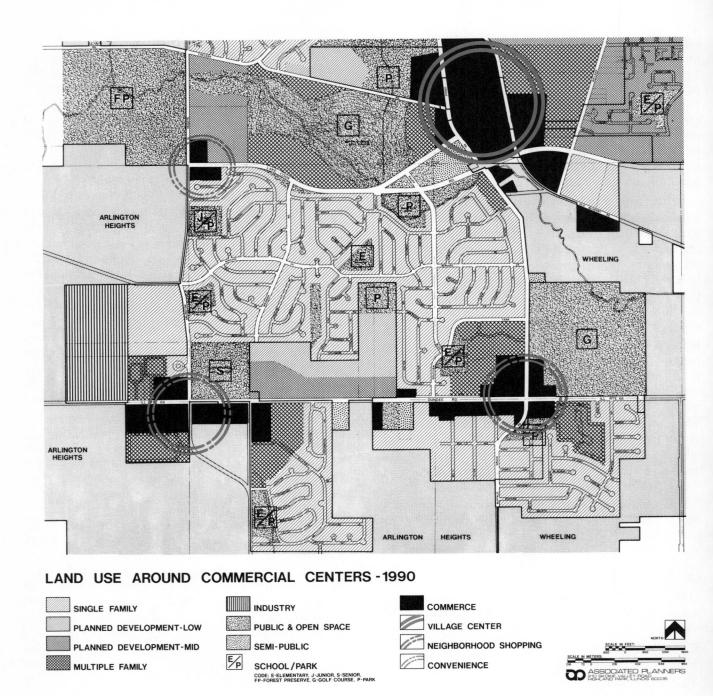

LAND USE AROUND COMMERCIAL CENTERS - 1990

SINGLE FAMILY	INDUSTRY
PLANNED DEVELOPMENT-LOW	PUBLIC & OPEN SPACE
PLANNED DEVELOPMENT-MID	SEMI-PUBLIC
MULTIPLE FAMILY	SCHOOL/PARK

COMMERCE
VILLAGE CENTER
NEIGHBORHOOD SHOPPING
CONVENIENCE

CODE: E-ELEMENTARY, J-JUNIOR, S-SENIOR,
FP-FOREST PRESERVE, G-GOLF COURSE, P-PARK

NORTH

SCALE IN FEET:
SCALE IN METERS:

ASSOCIATED PLANNERS
210 SKOKIE VALLEY ROAD
HIGHLAND PARK, ILLINOIS 60035

2-24 Comprehensive planning for the suburban community of Buffalo Grove, Illinois. Community boundaries are contiguous with those of neighboring municipalities. Single-family neighborhoods, focusing on school park sites, are the prevailing land use. Multifamily areas are located near large open spaces, golf courses, or forest preserve lands or are placed as support for the commercial centers.

Two existing neighborhood shopping centers, with a total of 385,000 square feet of retail space, are located along Dundee Road, an east-west arterial. A village center is planned near the geographical center of the town, where three major streets converge. An 80-acre site will be required to accommodate a community commercial center of 456,000 square feet, recreational uses totaling 90,000 square feet, office uses totaling 172,000 square feet, and public uses totaling 125,000 square feet. Additional supportive uses include 135 mid-density housing units occupying 147,000 square feet of land.

Uses planned for the village center are expected to total 990,000 square feet. Buffalo Grove's population is projected to reach 30,000 by 1990, and a need for about 1.5 million square feet of retail floor area in convenience, neighborhood, and community-scale shopping centers is projected.

criteria), public hearings, and board of appeals procedures.[15]

There are valid reasons in the public interest for favorable shopping center zoning. The community at large is relieved of the need to provide and maintain parking facilities. The center produces a net income from real estate and sales taxes in excess of the demands for public services that would result from residential zoning. The center is an employment generator. However, it is also a traffic generator that must be handled properly to minimize its effects on the community around it. The poor management of a center may also, in effect, encourage an increase in theft and vandalism.

Informing the community of the economic benefit it can receive from a shopping center can help overcome objections to a change in land use, particularly where the inherent general-welfare-related aspects of the land use are considered. Planned site and building arrangement is integral to the shopping center. By design, elements are placed in a planned relationship to one another, and in a planned relationship to the surroundings and the highways which furnish access to the property.

The developer must provide sound reasons for project approval. He must justify the increase in the community's shopping outlets and the increase in the array of goods and services. He can show that the community at large is relieved of underwriting the center's maintenance, policing, and operation. He must convince doubters that the center is architecturally tasteful; that lighting within the property is necessary for security and safety; that identification signing is not blatant or offensive and that it will not cause an inconvenience or nuisance to adjacent properties.

Planning and zoning approval bodies must avoid entering into the private business aspects of shopping centers. Any other approach is likely to result in ordinance provisions which are both onerous and —even worse—quickly outdated. Variations in arbitrary standards of shopping center types, sizes, and design can be made necessary by special tenant leasing needs and developer innovations. Similarly, tenant selection and placement, parking area layout, and arrangement of service areas are internal matters. The developer's site itself incorporates the proper building setbacks, building heights, and lot coverage. On-site parking and off-street loading are well-established principles of the shopping center concept and are provided as essential adjuncts to the commercial space for the convenience of customers and tenants. In short, approval authorities should weigh only those elements of shopping centers that pertain to general welfare and broad community concern. The approval authority must avoid injecting specifications for approval that prohibit design latitude and impose excessive costs or unusual burdens on the development. Yet all too often one finds approval bodies entering into non-zoning matters because of insufficient expertise.

At one time, zoning was virtually the only approval required before submission of plans for a building permit. Today, however, zoning approval is only a preliminary step in the shopping center development process. A fundamental change in attitudes and practices across the country can be seen just in the fact that an overwhelming number of communities have established planning boards with the authority, established under zoning provisions, to review site plans for approvals prior to the submission of other plans for building permits. The same forces that have produced sophisticated consumers have created concerned citizen groups who are ecologically aware and aesthetically responsible. The developer must be attuned to the community throughout the approval process.

Community attitudes are demanding. They are apt to be fraught with political intrigue and occasional bad judgement. The developer must offer the best design for his project that his leasing agent, architect, and site planner can produce under the circumstance of location, access, topography, adjacent land use, and economic goals. He must recognize the importance of environmental sensitivity and be aware that environmental and ecological issues are important, both technically and aesthetically, to every community. Landscaping and the preservation or planting of trees must be considered, to an extent never before recognized, as major project concerns. The need to preserve natural features of the site should be apparent to developers and private officials.

The passage of the National Environmental Policy Act by Congress in 1969 ushered in a new era of development regulation. That act, and the Clean Air Act Amendments of 1970, the Federal Water Pollution Control Act Amendments of 1972, and the Noise Control Act of 1972 were the result of a growing nationwide concern about the impact that man was having on the environment.

---

[15] See *Shopping Center Zoning* (footnote 11 above). This report offers guidelines for applying the general welfare purpose of zoning to the concept of site plan approval. In essence, the guidelines identify realistic controls for external features of the overall development.

Of these pieces of federal legislation, the Clean Air Act Amendments have had a significant impact on the shopping center developer. Because shopping centers attract large numbers of automobiles, which correspondingly have a negative impact on air quality, the federal legislation and the state-administered air quality programs approved under it have begun to seriously examine shopping center location, size, and design in an attempt to discover ways in which the adverse impact on air quality can be mitigated.

To date, the federal government itself has refrained from reviewing shopping center proposals. A number of states, however, now require a permit for centers as "indirect" sources of air pollution, and some states have also included large centers, because of their "regional impact," in another review process.

There is no ideal checklist or procedure for obtaining zoning and other approvals. Each case, each community, each area is different and must be approached in a different way. In an atmosphere of resentment against intrusion by a new shopping center, the developer is faced with the task of convincing the community and the authorities that his proposal is worthwhile. He must judge the local temper before he goes too far in firming his plans. In advance of a public hearing or before going to various city officials, the developer should meet with local residents and citizens associations to explain his proposal. Communication with the citizens is important early in the process, preferably before any announcement of the project is made.

When a public hearing is held, the developer must make his presentation understandable, possibly with the use of visual aids. A zoning change becomes a public relations problem. Photographs, statistical charts, drawings, and models help make an explanation comprehensible. Prior meetings with neighbors and civic groups can be informative for both the community and the developer.

The developer, in his preparations, must take pains to see that the project resolves as many local anxieties as possible. Because he is asking for a change, the developer must be able to overcome people's natural preference to keep things as they are.

If a tone of resentment continues, even before the project is started, the developer must be doubly sure that he meets all the criteria of good shopping

2-25 Evergreen Plaza, in the Chicago suburb of Evergreen Park, has grown from community to regional in scale over more than 20 years of continuous development. This model shows the second major expansion, which included a Carson Pirie Scott department store, mall shops, and 11 acres of structured parking. Outlined area indicates the original center. More recent components include a TBA store, mall enclosure, a nine-story office building, and a freestanding cinema. In 1974, the center's interior was completely renovated.

2-26   The original section of Evergreen Plaza, photographed about 1956.

center development. If the site is adjacent to residential areas, buffer planting strips and landscaped berms, protective screening, or well-designed walls or fences and controlled night lighting are necessary to insulate the homes against potential adverse effects.

In summary, the developer must learn what the community's problems are. In today's community climate, the developer must be prepared to answer questions about his project by supplying straightforward answers that allay community fears. Even so, the merchandising mix is the responsibility and privilege of the developer; he must be free to pick and choose his tenants and determine their arrangement on the site and within structures.

A characteristic of all types of centers is contemplated eventual expansion. Too many shopping centers are prevented from expanding because their site area is fixed. The center may have sufficient sales and trade area buying power to justify expansion but insufficient site area to provide for additional parking. A ready solution to the problem is construction of a parking structure on the property in lieu of acquiring additional land.

The goal should be to encourage clustering and to require shopping-center-like standards of design while discouraging the unrestricted strip-type commercial zoning that leads to cluttered highways with their customary pattern of random commercial land uses scattered throughout the community. In a planned unit residential development, where a developer reserves a shopping center tract for later development, then obtains commercial zoning, and then proceeds to develop the residential portion

of his community in accordance with his master street and lot plan, the residents know in advance that there may be a shopping center in the community. In such cases, the developer can easily design the shopping center to prevent any adverse effect on the residential property.

It may prove difficult for the shopping center to provide a balance of convenience store outlets suited to the market, because the trade available to these outlets will be diluted by competition from nearby strip developments. Yet a store in a planned shopping center normally can better withstand competition than can a freestanding store. In only a few urban fringe areas is the planning function adequately developed or strong enough to keep a newly urbanized area free from highway strip-type commercial establishments.

Whether land use control can be made flexible enough to provide for improved planning and zoning techniques—whereby preplanned and large scale projects can be offered the flexibility of approval by site plan and review, while still providing for safeguards intended by zoning—depends on how well local planning approval authorities and legislative bodies understand and appreciate the development process and the characteristics of the planned development that a developer wishes to create. The solution to the dilemma is the elimination of the idea that development must be controlled by preestablished rules to such an extent that nothing is left to administrative judgement or developer innovation. As matters now stand, many people suspect that part of the communication gap between zoning and development is attributable to

2-27　Enclosing the mall at Evergreen Plaza.

a misplaced—and probably overemphasized—effort to achieve new community values by using an old framework for land use controls.

Financial Planning and Negotiation

Shopping center success depends on a combination of things. Among these are a good site plan; a location that market and traffic studies show as being well suited to the shopping center purpose; strong key tenants and leases; careful attention to cost control before and during construction; and expert managerial operations.

Like good physical planning, careful financial planning is critical to making the development a successful venture. Basically, financing is the art of leverage. Leverage, as referred to in the financial world, entails using someone else's money with what one already has to make more money. The other half of leverage relates to the term *cash flow,* or the money left in one's account when all is said and done in a shopping center.[16]

Circumstances for shopping center proposals are never exactly alike. In nearly all cases, however, guidelines exist for the patterns of financing that should be considered. The common ingredient in any center's financial planning and negotiation is the projected income stream from high-credit-rated retail tenants and seasoned merchandisers, a projection which is based on minimum guaranteed rents, with cushions provided by rental income over and above the guaranteed rent. As discussed earier, the cushion is rental overage, based on a percentage of sales volume. Even so, more and more lending institutions are recognizing the importance of the local merchants and are deemphasizing the need for a high percentage of rated tenants.

By estimating earning power carefully, the developer can realistically establish his pro forma analysis. However, the developer's financial planning depends not only on the rental income to be produced by the center, but also on the lender and the money market at the time of project planning. Furthermore, financial planning must include protection against increasing taxes and provide for operating cost escalations.

At the outset, an experienced developer should avail himself of the services of a financial consultant or qualified mortgage broker. Mortgage consultants are becoming more and more important because of the complexities and the various methods of financing that have been created by the vagaries of the money market. "When the developer is looking at a piece of land with his architect, that is when the mortgage broker should be involved," advises a prominent lender. The financial consultant or broker, if involved in the first stages of financial planning, can help prevent problems in later negotiations. The techniques of shopping center financing are limited only by the versatility, imagination, and ingenuity of the developer, his financial representative, and the lending institutions.

The financing to be sought should be part of the financial plan, which in turn includes pro forma statements for such financing components as capital cost, income and expenses, and cash flow.

The developer's primary initial outlays are for control of the site and "front" or development money to carry out such development preliminaries as market analysis; site acquisition, selection, and negotiations; preliminary designs and sketches;

16 The following works discuss shopping center financing: *Dollars and Cents of Shopping Centers.*

Paul B. Farrell, Jr., "Basic Real Estate Financing," *AIA Journal,* Vol. 57, No. 4 (April 1972).

Robert L. Garrett, Hunter A. Hogan, Jr., and Robert M. Stratton, *The Valuation of Shopping Centers* (Philadelphia: Ballinger Publishing Company, 1976).

Kaylin, *How to Create a Shopping Center.*

Norman B. Kransdorf, "Financing the Shopping Center," *National Real Estate Investor,* Vol. 12, No. 5 (May 1970).

Canaler S. Rogers and James J. Brown, "Shopping Center Financing," *Kansas City Law Review,* Vol. 43 (Fall 1974).

zoning approval procedures and environmental impact clearances; legal matters; and key tenant solicitations.[17]

In shopping center development, unlike most other forms of real estate development, substantial site work is usually not started until key tenant leases or other binding agreements have been completed. When key tenants are committed and the certainty of a "deal" is apparent, a permanent financing commitment can be sought. As with lease negotiations, this search for permanent financing can precede any construction.

The developer's objective is to meet conditions of the permanent lender's letter of commitment. He can then shop for satisfactory interim or construction financing. Once the conditions have been met, the construction loan can be activated and construction begun. It makes sense to have a permanent loan package before getting a construction loan, because the permanent loan then pays off the construction loan.

In essence, the financing of shopping centers incorporates five major elements: land acquisition, equity investment, front money, construction money, and permanent or long-term financing. Once the site is controlled and the anchor tenant is set, with a leasing plan prepared, financing may take a variety of forms.

Land Control

Land control, or site acquisition, is part of the financial plan. The site must qualify as being suitable for the shopping center. It must be buildable, and it must have attributes which will attract shoppers for the goods and services that the center will offer.

There are several methods of land control. Each offers varying advantages in financing and "leverage."

- Historic ownership—where the site has been owned and held for a number of years. Under long-term past ownership, land prices as capital outlay may be minimal, even nonexistent as a percentage of total cost outlay. In such situations, the owner-developer must be sure that his site qualifies in all respects as a good shopping center location.
- Outright purchase—the least attractive, most costly method. Outright purchase entails heavy initial investment of equity or front-end funds. This method is unattractive if there are development uncertainties, restricted money markets, or high interest rates, unless a subse-

quent sale and leaseback or land loan is contemplated.
- Purchase contract with options—a favored method, since it allows the developer to run the hurdles of zoning and approval procedures without jeopardizing the bulk of his investment. The contract to purchase should provide other options subject to such pertinent current conditions as land title report; accurate property survey; zoning approval with declarations of land use acceptance; investigation of on-site and off-site easements, if any; site conditions; stormwater runoff; site plan clearance; and any environmental clearances. The option period should allow from 9 months to 2 years before the developer must commit himself to purchase the land.

The developer should try not to let the purchase be concluded before building permits have been obtained. His option should allow a price which will remain fixed during the option period. With the potential of a number of adverse factors facing the developer, the degree of risk in a land investment depends on the length of time the property can be controlled by option.
- Deferred purchase with simultaneous sale and leaseback—an advantageous and commonly used technique, and one which avoids heavy financial commitments by the developer. In effect, the developer induces the lender to buy the land and provide the money to build the center. The developer then leases the project from the lender but retains the option to buy the development back from the lending instituton at a later date.
- Ground lease—eliminates a major initial investment in land. The financial arrangements of a ground lease are flexible and are well suited to shopping centers and other urban building types; the income tax laws have contributed to the popularity of this method of land control. A landowner who sells land that has increased in value is placed in a high capital gains tax position. By offering a long-term lease (40-year minimum with option to extend is common; 50 to 59 years is better), the owner can spread the return to reduce the tax consequences. By

---

[17] For benchmarks in front money aspects of overhead and development costs as a percentage of total capital costs, including land and on-site improvements, see the "Supplementary Information" chapter in *Dollars and Cents of Shopping Centers.*

using a ground lease, the owner can retain fee ownership while receiving, in effect, an annuity over the term of the lease. Inheritors or long-time owners of land can be interested in ground leasing, although there are many dangers in the arrangement. As inflation occurs over the years, the fixed ground rent causes a fixed or reduced sale value of the property until the lease term is expired. Rent escalation provisions are difficult to acquire and rarely provide a proper return on investment. On the other hand, the lessee benefits because the amount of capital required for land control is reduced. The annual ground rent payment is a deductible business expense. In order to maximize his possibilities for financing, the developer should insist on his right to place a mortgage on the fee title to the land he leases.

Under a ground lease, the developer becomes the middleman between the actual fee owner and the tenants who produce the income through rent payments in the developed project. The principle of land leasing offers the landowner an alternative to direct sale and frees the developer from an initial investment in land. The annual ground rent is equivalent to a payment on a loan, assuming the loan money would be used to purchase land, except that the developer does not own the land at the expiration of the lease.

The ground rent is usually determined by negotiation. The contract can provide for readjustment of the ground rental at predetermined intervals. In addition, it is not uncommon for lessors to have equity participation in projects developed on their land. Annual rents run from 6 to 9 percent of the initial value of the land, plus anti-inflation benefits from tenant rent increases or even a participation in percentage rent payments of the tenants in lieu of other equity participation or escalation in ground rent.[18]

There are two types of land leases:

- Subordinated—the preferred arrangement for the developer. The landowner submits the land as collateral for part of the total mortgage commitment on the developed property, including land and buildings. In effect, subordinated land is collateral against default in mortgage payment by the developer. Lenders usually insist on subordination.
- Unsubordinated—the landowner does not agree to the condition wherein the land becomes collateral for the mortgage. A subsequent mortgage loan is difficult to secure. Financing with an unsubordinated ground lease, if available, usually costs at least half a percent more per year than a subordinated ground lease. An absolute right of purchase can substitute for subordination, although the mortgagee may deduct the price of the land from the loan.

Ground leasing frees capital and permits the developer to raise more capital through the mortgage medium. For example, if the land is worth $1 million and the owner can be persuaded to lease it, then that $1 million need not be invested in land. When the land is leased with the right to mortgage the fee, then another half million or more is gained by borrowing on the land. Without the right to subordinate the fee on the land to a mortgage, the developer may not succeed in his subsequent steps in financing. When the developer has obtained a ground lease which permits a mortgage on the fee, the financing takes the form of a straight first mortgage on land and building.

Permanent Financing

Depending on the method by which land control is obtained, the developer has several options for subsequent financing of his projects:

- Conventional—the most straightforward program, particularly when the developer controls the land. Conventional financing in shopping centers generally follows the pattern of conventional financing of any other type of real estate. In a first mortgage on land and building, the amount of the loan will depend on the capitalized value of the project, which in turn is based on the funds after operating costs.

The mortgage on the project is likely to equal approximately 75 percent of the capitalized value of the funds after operating costs. There may or may not be a stipulation that the total amount of the mortgage cannot exceed actual development cost.

Mortgage financing depends on the value of the property involved. In shopping centers, capital cost does not necessarily equal value. The income stream from tenants is the primary basis for value. According to theory, lenders loan at 75 percent of appraised value. It is

---

[18]See Neil Underberg, "Ground Leasing Makes Dollars and Sense for Developers," *Real Estate Review*, Summer, 1971.

to the developer's advantage to maximize appraisal value. Appraised value may be determined in three ways: by the income and expense or income stream approach; by comparable sales; and by development cost (or by a combination of two or all three approaches).

Depending on the quality of the project, the key tenants, and the terms of the key leases, the term of the mortgage may be as long as 35 years. In periods of tight money and depending on the ratio of loan to developer's investment and the need for protection against inflation, some lenders have insisted on participation in gross or overage rents.

- Sale and leaseback—various methods are used. Sale and leasebacks are sophisticated devices where a high level of financing is both needed and justified by the project. Lenders and developers have worked out patterns that involve ownership of the land by the lending institution with a ground leaseback to the developer and then a leasehold mortgage. Or the arrangement may involve ownership of the entire asset by the financing institution with a leaseback to the developer with an option to purchase at a later date. Another variation may involve ownership by the lender of part of the stock in the developer's corporation.

The general feeling on the part of lenders is that if they are expected to assume all or most of the equity risk, they should have, in addition to interest and principal return, a substantial stake in the equity rewards that flow from a successful enterprise. Insurance companies are the primary source of long-term financing, but other sources include savings and loan associations, thrift institutions, banks, real estate investment trusts, and pension funds. In general, the more experienced the lender, the more flexible his attitudes and the less rigid his dependence on high-credit tenants will be, provided other tenants are satisfactory.

- Component financing—useful under certain special conditions in a large center. The arrangement involves financing of component parts of the center. A central heating and air conditioning plant, built as a total energy system, can be "spun out" and financed separately. The system is subordinate to the first mortgage; a mortgagee has a first lien on a component of the center, and a company operates it under contract. Legal complications about repairs and insurance must be worked out, but component

financing can reduce the developer's investment equity by as much as 10 to 20 percent in a high-quality project. However, the arrangement may be very difficult to work out.

- Construction or interim financing—short-term funds advanced for construction and preopening costs. Funds for costs that come due during construction and preliminary costs, other than construction, are normally advanced by short-term lenders, such as commercial banks and real estate investment trusts. These lending institutions make such arrangements on the condition that their investment in the project will be refunded by the permanent lender at project completion. Construction funds are normally advanced only if the developer has received a permanent mortgage commitment from a long-term lender, although there have been exceptions to this pattern during periods of rapid economic expansion. The construction loan thus relies primarily on the credit of the ultimate mortgage lender.
- Sophisticated forms of financing—other arrangements of real estate financing available for special situations. These carry such names as gap financing, standby commitments, installment sales contracts, bonded lease financing, wraparound mortgages, secondary financing, purchase money mortgages, and development loans. Other elaborate devices are joint ventures, partnerships, and refinancing.

Whatever the form of financing, the developer should not overlook the cost of arranging it. At the time the commitment is accepted, the correspondent or branch office of the lender will normally expect to be paid about 1 percent for services. The borrower also bears all costs of legal services, surveys, independent appraisal fees, and other related work. A standby fee, perhaps 0.1 percent per month, may be charged for holding money aside for "takedown" when construction is finished. These costs are usually negotiable.

While some long-term lending institutions will also handle the interim or construction financing, most prefer to see this handled by a commercial bank. Many lenders, however, like to cooperate with the borrower and the commercial bank through early agreement on use of a single set of loan documents which can be transferred upon completion from the bank to the permanent lender, thus reducing both the cost of financing to the borrower and the risk to the bank of being stuck with the loan. Such agreements, if properly drawn, also tend to reduce the risk to the long-term lender of loss from the loan due to material change in money market conditions.

From the developer's standpoint, the importance of the skill, experience, and reputation of both the permanent lender and the construction lender should not be underestimated. Just as the experienced lender is normally not interested in doing business with the amateur developer, the experienced developer is normally not interested in doing business with a financial institution inexperienced in shopping center loans. Shopping center financing, at best, is complex, time-consuming, costly to arrange, and full of pitfalls. Inexperience and lack of know-how on the part of either party in the financial arrangement will only add to the problems and costs.

Leasing Plan

A clear-cut cost and income pro forma statement is essential at the start of financial planning, regardless of the means by which site control is obtained and later financing is to be arranged.

The leasing plan is the crux of the investment potential. The following elements of the plan should be determined early in the development process:[19]

- The basic building plan for the entire center must recognize customer pull and include a tenant placement that draws the maximum pedestrian shopper flow past as much frontage as possible.
- Building depths should normally not exceed 150 feet for mall shops or stores in a strip center in order to avoid excessive overall store depths not suitable for tenant sales. Neighborhood centers run 40 to 60 feet in depth for small tenants. Malls should be no wider than 40 feet, except for courts and promotional areas. A balanced tenant mix should provide for both strong, credit-rated national firms and good local merchants in order to meet the financial credit requirements of lenders.
- Distribution of tenants should be predetermined by the merchandising plan, although not all goals of the original plan can be met. Tenant preferences and resistances will result in a number of compromises. But repositioning will require constant attention if the merchandising plan is to direct the leasing.
- Each store space should be "priced" on the basis of tenant size, tenant classification,

amount of tenant allowance, and location in the project. These prices should be constantly updated as the project moves from an essentially speculative paper exercise to a finalized program.
- Detailed rent schedules are needed to clearly indicate tenant classification and type, tenant name, square footage allocation, guaranteed rent, and rate of percentage for overage rent. Tenant allowance allocation and heating, ventilation, and air conditioning (HVAC) charges should be projected as a guide to those leasing the project. This schedule too should be continually updated.
- Shell plus an allowance system is a preferred method of handling tenant finish, because it defines the limits of owner capital costs. It is best adhered to in all cases, even if a greater allowance is sometimes necessary to produce a turnkey solution for a particular tenant.
- A good lease form should be prepared, requiring a minimum of processing, with exhibits attached indicating landlord's work, tenant's work, HVAC rate schedules, other rate schedules if applicable, and other related matters, including the site plan. Lease modification, often necessary, can most conveniently be handled through an addendum to the basic lease document itself. The addendum aids in administration by providing a single location for changes applicable to specific tenants.
- Tax stops should be provided for in the lease. This can sometimes be accomplished by net leasing, with the lease amount being determined by the strength of the store location. (Most centers are leased net after real estate taxes.) Tax stops can also be provided by a landlord agreement to a fixed tenant contribution, expressed in a certain amount per square foot; or the landlord can agree to use real estate taxes for the first full year as the basis for the tenant contribution, with an escalation provision included for later contributions. Open-ended landlord tax obligations are to be avoided.
- Tenant payment provisions should also be included in the lease for the costs of common area operation, including mall maintenance, insurance, and mall HVAC costs. Leases should

---

[19] This list is taken from "The Developer's View of Shopping Center Finance," a paper presented by Harold R. Imus to ULI's Commercial and Office Development Council on October 20, 1972.

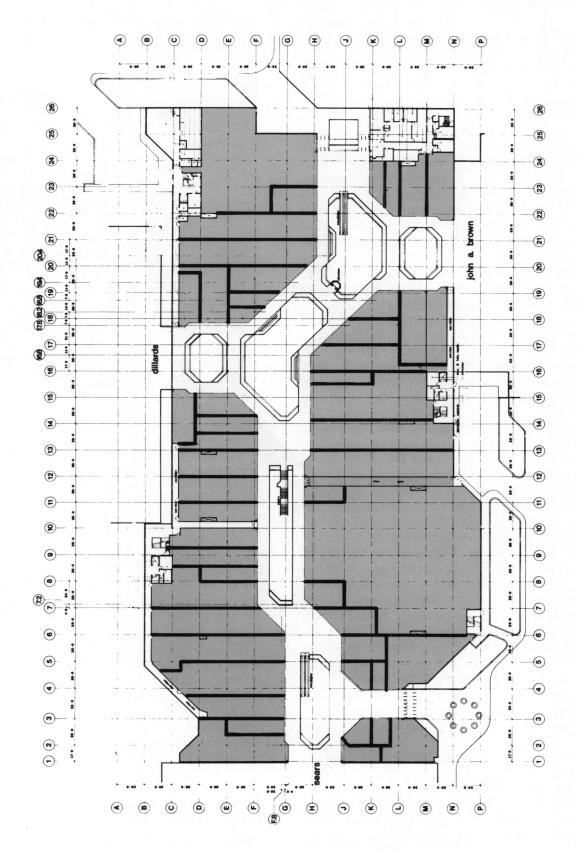

2-28 Upper level lease plan of Woodland Hills Mall, Tulsa. Source: Dayton Hudson Properties.

also provide that common area charges will include real estate taxes on common area and mall facilities. These charges should be prorated to GLA, with the common exception of key tenants, who are on other prearranged payment bases.

- Responsibility for payment of HVAC charges and gas and electricity costs should be clearly defined, with escalators provided to accommodate increased costs of labor, energy, administration, and replacement of parts.

All such lease provisions permit an early definition of the landlord's fiscal obligations. These provisions are well known to national tenants; lease provisions, as well as rent provisions, are resisted more by local tenants, who may not be accustomed to them because of the limited scope of the local tenant's operations, but this resistance should not prevent the developer from negotiating these costs and explaining why their inclusion is essential. Obviously, stronger properties are able to insist on reducing the fiscal uncertainty they must face, but the principles set forth above are useful in structuring any present-day shopping center.

In a regional shopping center, the department store is treated differently from other tenants. The key department stores may build their own stores on land bought or leased from the developer, and they contribute to required parking. They usually do not build their own parking areas, but a contribution to the developer is necessary; otherwise, the developer will be subsidizing the store and diluting his financial return. The developer must have satisfactory reciprocal operating agreements which provide for handling of on-site and off-site construction costs, easements, operating costs for common areas, merchants association, common mall wall, and other areas of expense. Long-term cross-easements and agreements are extremely important to the permanent lender, the tenants, and the developer. Reciprocal easement agreements, or REAs, are necessary in any center with separate legal ownership or any type of site-sharing uses, such as freestanding banks, service stations, or restaurants.

To encourage the department stores to enter the project on a buy-build basis, land can be sold to them at an appraised value, or it can be sold at or below cost, or—if all else fails—it can be given to the stores. The amount of money involved, while substantial, represents a smaller subsidy problem than would result from even a fairly favorable

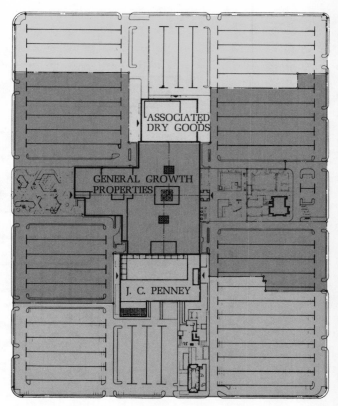

2-29   Citadel Shopping Center, in Colorado Springs, is owned by three parties.

gross lease. Typically, the developer will sell to the department store not only a building pad but necessary improved parking as well. The sale price will, of course, be negotiated, but it generally reflects the pro rata off-site and on-site improvement costs attributed to the land area sold.

Presentation Package

Once the site is controlled and the key tenant negotiations and the pro forma leasing plans are nearing satisfactory completion, permanent financing can be actively sought. As mentioned earlier in this chapter, the developer must decide whether to employ the services of a mortgage broker or to seek the financing himself. The size and type of the project, the experience of the developer, his willingness to face the realities of dealing with prospective lenders, and the willingness of lenders to deal with individuals as contrasted with the use of correspondents all influence the developer's decision. An experienced real estate attorney is essential for avoiding the hazards of major financing.

Making a loan application to a lender requires a complete presentation package. What follows is an outline of the items which must be included in such a package.

DEPARTMENT STORES—A SPECIAL CASE

Bruce P. Hayden, real estate counselor, explains the special leasing position held by department stores:

Some lenders will require that all operating costs plus interest expense be covered. The requirement on the part of major lenders that developers fill most of their space with the category of tenant that does the least business and pays the least rent may seem questionable to some and deplorable to others, but this continues to be the situation. It should be added that the more experienced the lender, the less insistence there is likely to be on such an arrangement.

Since in most instances the availability of financing to the developer is contingent upon the number or dollar amount of triple-A leases he is able to sign, and since major chains are fully aware of this fact, the developer is usually at a negotiating disadvantage in trying to work out reasonable lease terms with this type of tenant. However, more experienced lenders will generally take a dim view of financing centers where the developer has had to make too favorable lease terms available to his key tenants. "Subsidy situations," in which a key tenant does not guarantee enough rent to cover the developer's cash out-of-pocket costs, are looked on with particular disfavor by lenders.

A hypothetical but fairly common subsidy situation might involve a 150,000-square-foot department store which would agree to pay a minimum rental of $1.25 per square foot versus, say, 2 percent of sales. The tenant requires a turnkey job. Here the best available cost indication is that the landlord will have to spend $18 or more per square foot in order to finish the space to the tenant's specifications. The landlord is hopeful of getting a loan of $15 per square foot. The lease term is 25 years. (Many of these dollar amounts are not realistic in current dollars and are used only for the purpose of illustration.)

In such a situation, debt service on a $15 per square foot loan at 8 percent constant will amount to $1.20 per square foot per year. A minimum allowance for operating expenses and taxes might be an additional $0.55 per square foot. Thus, the developer, without any regard to return on his own investment of $3 per square foot, must collect $1.75 per square foot per year in *cash*, simply to pay his bills. His tenant has agreed to pay $1.25. The landlord is committed to subsidizing the operation to the extent of $0.50 per square foot per year, which for 150,000 square feet is $75,000 per year, or $1,875,000 for 25 years. This is the measure of the potential subsidy which the landlord must make to have this particular tenant. The strain that this subsidy puts on the financial health of the full enterprise is obvious, and more sophisticated lenders in the shopping center field prefer to have no part in such leasing.

There are a number of possible ways for the developer to work around such a subsidy situation, even in instances where he is unable to persuade his key tenant to pay an adequate rental. The most common way is to give, or sell, or lease to the tenant the ground on which the store is to be located, let the tenant arrange his own financing and do his own building, but then tie the tenant back into the center for operating purposes through the operating agreements, cross-easements, and other mechanisms. Most major lenders today will approve of such arrangements, although they will review the collateral agreements very carefully.

- The developer must prepare a complete discussion of the property characteristics with plot of survey, developer's plan, parking layout, type of HVAC system, amenities to be provided, service systems for deliveries and trash handling, and, above all, lease or purchase arrangements for key tenants in the composition. These materials can be accompanied by sketches, models, and other illustrative material which the mortgage officer can present to his own committee, should he feel that the project is worthy of consideration.

- A market study, prepared by a recognized economic consulting firm, accompanies the presentation. It should detail the characteristics of the trade area, including population and growth characteristics, arterial roadways, economic base of the community, directions of growth, and other factors.

- A traffic survey should be included. The developer's plans should substantially conform to the recommendations of the traffic consultant. Negotiations with governmental bodies controlling access should have been concluded, or at least strong affirmations obtained of the practicality of proposed solutions.

- A financial pro forma statement is important. It should contain the leasing plan with its detailed anticipated rent schedule for both major and minor tenants, as well as space allocation, terms of leases, guaranteed and percentage rents, HVAC charges, common area maintenance program, and other income matters. The statement should include operating expenses, especially taxes, insurance, maintenance, management, anticipated assessments, and other areas of expense. Construction costs and other development expenses should be supported by estimates from an architect or general contractor. The closer the developer comes to an appraisal of the investment value of the property the better, although the lender will prepare a separate appraisal in order to confirm the validity of the developer's presentation.

- Material indicating the developer's experience, integrity, and financial responsibility should accompany the presentation portfolio.
- The lender will be interested in the lease form and its attached exhibits and in the proposed operating agreement to be worked out with key tenants. Completion and signing of an operating agreement largely confirms the validity of the developer's initial concept but is not a prerequisite for obtaining a permanent commitment.
- The developer should also prepare a statement as to what he will accept in the financial agreement—terms, rates, etc.—and what he will not accept, such as sales clauses, personal guarantees, etc. Such a statement places some vital issues on a negotiating basis more favorable to the developer.

Many problems of implementation remain, and the developer will be obligated to adhere closely to his projections, but if he has made the proper appraisal of the market and has obtained the key tenants, and if the balance of his pro forma indicates recognition of development risk, the most frustrating part of the work is completed.

Capital Cost

Capital cost estimates are the final phase in planning preliminaries. A continuing spiral of inflation in construction and related costs, along with scarcity in money markets, is uppermost among the problems developers face.

Capital cost is the total investment in the project. It includes the initial cost (not depreciated) of all items and may be broken down into the following three major categories:

- Land and land improvements.
- Building and equipment.
- Overhead and development costs incurred prior to opening.

These items are so variable in their dollar amounts that citing figures for total costs or per square foot would not be very helpful and could be misleading. On the other hand, items that must be taken into account are well documented for arriving at a valid estimate of the capital investment against which the arithmetic of anticipated rental income can be applied to measure whether the project is feasible. Composite items in capital cost are:

- Land cost—the basic land cost plus carrying charges to the date of completed construction.
- Off-site improvements, such as bringing utilities to the site, and road or traffic access improvements.
- On-site improvements, including grading, underground utilities, storm drainage, parking lot paving, marking and lighting and—of major importance—landscaping.
- Building costs for construction of the basic building itself plus the cost of tenant improvements paid for by the landlord.
- Professional fees, including legal fees and fees for economic surveys, land planning, architecture, interior and graphic design, engineering, landscape architecture, and preparation of environmental impact statements and zoning approval applications.
- Lending commissions and financing fees.
- Carrying charges during construction. These include interest and fees for construction financing, as well as taxes and insurance costs incurred during the construction period. Preopening expenses for publicity, public relations work, and the grand opening activities should also be provided for.[20]

The developer must be certain that the return on the investment can justify his expenditures. In these days of high construction costs, high money costs, increased competition, and occasional no-growth philosophies, it is important to evaluate the economics of shopping centers very carefully.[21]

A mortgage is normally based on the sum of the minimum rent schedules as set up by the leases. The total income guaranteed in minimum rents by financially strong tenants, rather than the construction cost, establishes the amount of the loan. Because of this, the budget for construction cost becomes geared to expected income from guaran-

---

[20] For a more detailed list of shopping center items included in capital cost, see p. 280 of *Dollars and Cents of Shopping Centers: 1975.*

[21] See the section entitled "Operating Results in Relation to Capital Costs" in *Dollars and Cents of Shopping Centers.*

teed rents. By gauging the earning power of the project, the developer can establish a realistic construction budget. Without the assistance of such analysis, the careful planning for stores, malls, parking, and planting can produce another project of great hopes but little demonstrable assurance of success.

Summary — Financial Planning and Negotiation

There obviously are a great number of variations and details in forms of financing. No two projects are alike, and requirements vary. Much creative thought can be offered by intelligent lenders, schooled in shopping center financing, or by skilled and imaginative financial consultants, mortgage brokers, and developers. The proper basis for any program is sound financial planning at the outset and careful attention to the implementation of that planning during all phases of development. Naturally, the sophisticated elements in lease clauses and financing methods pertain primarily to community and regional centers. Developers of small neighborhood centers, however, need to be aware of present-day practices.

Thus far, this discussion has dwelt on the preliminaries of shopping center development, even though capital costs and financing are essentially parts of the planning process. Any mistakes made in the planning and leasing of a center can be rectified, if only painfully. Little can be done, however, if the mistakes are poor site selection or overestimation of the market.

3.
Planning

Once the feasibility of development has been determined and the go-ahead decision has been made, serious site planning and architectural and structural design can begin.

Planning the shopping center calls for care in combining elements—tenant mix and placement, convenience for the customer, inducements to impulse buying—to ensure that the merchandising complex serves its function as a marketplace and successful economic venture. The planning of the site layout is, therefore, a process of dealing with problems and needs by formulating physical solutions for merchandising, architecture, and engineering. Shopping center planning has to be approached from many angles—proper structures for tenant operations, customer appeal, and services; parking for customers and employees; means of ingress and egress; and landscaping and other aesthetics. All these parts are brought together in a suitable and affordable design solution.

A second generation of shopping centers began in the seventies. At mid-decade, new projects must contend with new social and economic forces. New requirements in the areas of environmental approval, energy use, and financing place new limitations on land use. Developers must respond to the new dimensions in development by taking greater care than ever before in market analysis, site selection, and financial planning. Since shopping centers must meet new levels of public taste and discernment, planning and design take on greater importance.

Convenience and environmental harmony will be major considerations in centers planned and built after 1975. There is a trend toward smaller, innovative, weather-controlled centers in smaller regional markets, designed for convenience to the supporting trade area and attention to environmental concerns. Amenities and energy savings are being emphasized in interior and exterior planning and design.

Good planning is functional as well as practical. Good planning can overcome faults in the size, shape, and topography of a site. A site too expensive for horizontal merchandising may be suitable for multilevel retailing and for parking structures. A site too large for retailing alone may be suitable for multiple uses.

The best planning, of course, is no substitute for careful tenant selection and leasing, sound construction, and expert management. With the best of these ingredients, plus good planning for site design and tenant placement, most physical problems (other than a mistake in site selection, or gross overbuilding) can be satisfactorily overcome.

Tenants

It is the retail tenants of a shopping center who make it viable. The developer merely melds the components of tenantry, structure, and site attributes into the particular ambience of the development.

Despite all that can be said about preliminaries in planning for the type and size of the center, site and building construction cannot begin until the anchor tenants are identified, selected, and committed. The importance of securing key tenants cannot be overemphasized. At the beginning, reliable commitments rather than precise lease contracts are called for. This means that whether the key tenant is to lease space in a shell or in a finished building or is to independently lease or own land, a binding commitment should be obtained before building and final site layouts are begun.

The key tenant—whether a supermarket, discount store, or full-line department store—should be tied in closely with the development team in the building and site planning. The key tenant will influence the developer's decisions on building treatment and architectural style and even parking, lighting, signing, and landscaping. Furthermore, at this point in the planning, the key tenant should be committed to agreements for ultimate centerwide operations, such as common area maintenance, tax participation, membership in the merchants association, and participation in the association's promotional programs.

Key Tenants

A standard for tenant composition cannot be set forward; each community and each shopping center are different. Any list of the tenant classifications most frequently found in a given type of center can serve only as a selection guide. A shopping cen-

3-1   A grocery store is the key tenant in a neighborhood shopping center.

3-2 A variety, discount, or junior department store is the key tenant in a community shopping center.

ter's composition will be determined by negotiation and search, based on the market and feasibility studies, and will obviously also depend on the type of center to be built. Once the developer knows the characteristics of the market his center will serve, he can decide on the anchor tenant classifications, then on the supplementary array.

The following is an outline of the key tenants for the various types of centers, as discussed in Chapter 1.

In neighborhood centers, the supermarket is the key. The drugstore is equally necessary. Personal services and convenience goods normally comprise the balance of the tenantry.

In community centers, the variety store, the junior department store, and the popular price (low margin) or discount store make up the anchor classifications. Supplementary tenants include those of the neighborhood center, with added shopping goods representation, particularly of the apparel and home furnishings categories.

In regional centers, at least one full-line department store of 100,000 square feet GLA is essential. A majority of regional centers include two or more such department stores. For the supplementary tenant roster, all tenant classifications are drawn upon. Representation by several stores of the same category is customary, allowing the final tenant composition to represent as closely as possible the ranges in price and merchandise once found only in downtowns.

In super-regional centers, three or more full-line department stores and a total center GLA of at least 750,000 square feet are required by definition for this type of center.

In specialty centers, a key tenant of the traditional categories need not be present. The grouping of tenants is determined by the special nature of the trade area or according to the tenants' suitability to a unique structure, such as a rehabilitated historic structure.

A wide range in gross leasable area may be expected for specialty centers; between 40,000 and 300,000 square feet GLA may be feasible. A variety of tenants—boutiques, import shops, high-fashion or specialty apparel shops, arts and crafts stores, hobby shops or other specialty stores, food stores, and food service outlets—may be considered for their suitability to the character, quality, and drawing power of the location.

Any specialty center, whether located in a new structure or in a landmark structure or other building newly converted for retail use, must have at least one prime or anchor tenant. Such a key tenant could be either a specialty retail store or a restaurant.

In mini-malls (a variation of the community shopping center), a junior department store or supermarket performs the function of anchor tenant. Mini-malls are enclosed and weather-conditioned and have between 80,000 and 150,000 square feet of GLA. Other tenants will usually include food

3-3   A department store is the key tenant in a regional shopping center.

service stores, apparel stores, independent local specialty merchants, and specialty chain stores.

In all types of centers, tenant selection and negotiation require flexibility rather than adherence to fixed or standard listings. Numerous adjustments will take place in interior arrangements and tenant placement as space becomes identified with tenant leases. Under normal conditions, a shopping center will have a substantial percentage of the planned GLA—represented by key tenants—committed before final construction drawings are made; otherwise, the development takes on aspects of a speculative enterprise.

Classification

Tenants are classified in several ways: by lines of business in which they are principally engaged; by overall credit rating; and by ownership. Some definitions adopted by ULI are useful for describing prospective tenants by ownership classification:

- *National chain store*: a business operating in four or more metropolitan areas in three or more states.

- *Independent store*: a business operating in not more than two outlets in only one metropolitan area.
- *Local chain store*: a business that does not fall into either of the preceding categories.

The tenant classifications by lines of business, as presented in Figure 3-4, are those established for *Dollars and Cents of Shopping Centers: 1975*. The principal groupings are generally related to major Standard Industrial Classification (SIC) codes.[1] A number of *Dollars and Cents* categories, however, do not have exactly equivalent SIC designations. As shown in Appendix B, the 1978 edition of *Dollars and Cents* will regroup the categories to remove most of these inconsistencies.

---

[1] The two works in which these codes are set forth are *Dollars and Cents of Shopping Centers: 1975* (Washington, D.C.: ULI–the Urban Land Institute); and *The Standard Industrial Classification Manual 1972*, prepared by the Statistical Policy Division of the Executive Office of the President–Office of Management and Budget. Definitions and classifications found in the SIC manual are used by government, industry, and trade associations in gathering statistics.

TENANT CLASSIFICATIONS

Categories from *Dollars and Cents of Shopping Centers,* and
comparable categories from the *Standard Industrial Classification (SIC) Manual*

DOLLARS AND CENTS CODE AND CATEGORY	SIC CODE AND CATEGORY	DOLLARS AND CENTS CODE AND CATEGORY	SIC CODE AND CATEGORY
FOOD		115 Flowers	5992 Florists
011 Supermarket	5411 Grocery stores	116 Tobacco	5993 Cigar stores and stands
012 Meat, poultry, fish	5423 Meat and fish markets	117 Drugs	5912 Drug stores and proprietary stores
013 Specialty food	5499 Miscellaneous food stores		
014 Delicatessen	5411 Grocery stores	118 Sporting goods	5941 Sporting goods and bicycle shops
015 Bakery	5463 Retail bakeries—selling only	119 Credit jewelry	5944 Jewelry stores
016 Hot bakery	5462 Retail bakeries—baking and selling	121 Costume jewelry	5999 Miscellaneous retail stores not elsewhere classified
017 Candy, nuts	5441 Candy, nut, and confectionery stores	122 Jewelry	5944 Jewelry stores
018 Dairy products	5451 Dairy products stores	124 Sewing machines	5722 Household appliance stores
019 Health food	5499 Miscellaneous food stores	125 Key shop	7699 Repair services not elsewhere classified
FOOD SERVICE		126 Cosmetics	5999 Miscellaneous retail stores not elsewhere classified
031 Restaurant without liquor	5812 Eating places	127 Cards and gifts	5947 Gift, novelty, and souvenir shops
032 Cafeteria	5812 Eating places	128 Toys	5945 Hobby, toy, and game shops
033 Fast-food/carryout	5812 Eating places	129 Cameras	5946 Camera and photographic supply stores
034 Restaurant with liquor	5812 Eating places	130 Liquor and wine	5921 Liquor stores
035 Cocktail lounge	5813 Drinking places	131 Wine only	5921 Liquor stores
036 Doughnut shop	5812 Eating places	132 Wine and cheese	5921 Liquor stores
037 Ice cream parlor	5812 Eating places		5451 Dairy products stores
GENERAL MERCHANDISE		133 Trading stamp redemption	7396 Trading stamp services
041 Department store	5311 Department stores	139 Other retail	5999 Miscellaneous retail stores not elsewhere classified
042 Junior department store	5311 Department stores		
043 Variety store	5331 Variety stores	**FINANCIAL**	
044 Department store—discount	5311 Department stores	141 Bank	602 Commercial and stock savings banks
045 Catalog store	5399 Miscellaneous general merchandise stores	142 Savings and loan	612 Savings and loan associations
CLOTHING AND SHOES		143 Finance company	6145 Licensed small loan lenders
051 Ladies' specialty	5631 Women's accessory and specialty stores	144 Small loans	6145 Licensed small loan lenders
052 Ladies' ready-to-wear	5621 Women's ready-to-wear stores	145 Post office	7399 Business services not elsewhere classified
053 Bridal shop	5621 Women's ready-to-wear stores	146 Insurance	63 Insurance carriers
054 Maternity	5621 Women's ready-to-wear stores	147 Brokerage	6211 Security brokers and dealers (and flotation companies)
055 Hosiery	5631 Women's accessory and specialty stores		
056 Millinery	5631 Women's accessory and specialty stores	**OFFICE**	
057 Children's wear	5641 Children's and infants' wear stores	151 Medical and dental	8011 Offices of physicians
058 Menswear	5611 Men's and boys' clothing and furnishings		8021 Offices of dentists
059 Family wear	5651 Family clothing stores		8031 Offices of osteopathic physicians
061 Family shoe	5661 Shoe stores	152 Legal	8111 Legal services
062 Ladies' shoe	5661 Shoe stores	153 Accounting	8931 Accounting, auditing, and bookkeeping
063 Men's and boys' shoe	5661 Shoe stores	154 Architect	8911 Engineering and architectural services
064 Children's shoe	5661 Shoe stores	155 Real estate	6531 Real estate agents and managers
065 Furs	5681 Furriers and fur shops	156 Contractor	15 General building contractors
066 Formal wear rental	7299 Miscellaneous personal services	157 Employment agency	7361 Employment agencies
067 Unisex/jean shop	5699 Miscellaneous apparel and accessories	159 Other office	— no classification
DRY GOODS		**SERVICE**	
071 Yard goods and fabrics	5949 Sewing, needlework, and piece goods	161 Beauty shop	7231 Beauty shops
072 Curtains and drapes	5714 Drapery and upholstery stores	162 Barber shop	7241 Barber shops
075 Imports	5999 Miscellaneous retail stores not elsewhere classified	163 Watch repair	7631 Watch, clock, and jewelry repair
		164 Shoe repair	7251 Shoe repair and hat cleaning shops
076 Luggage, leather goods	5948 Luggage and leather goods stores	165 Cleaner and dyer	7212 Garment pressing and cleaners' agents
FURNITURE		166 Laundry	7212 Garment pressing and cleaners' agents
081 Furniture	5712 Furniture stores	167 Travel agents	4722 Passenger transportation arrangement
082 Lamps	5719 Miscellaneous home furnishings stores	168 Music studios and dance	7911 Dance halls, studios, and schools
083 Appliances	5722 Household appliance stores		8299 Schools and educational services not elsewhere classified
084 Floor coverings	5713 Floor covering stores		
085 Radio, TV, hi-fi	5732 Radio and television stores	171 Coin-operated laundry	7215 Coin-operated laundries and cleaning
087 Interior decorator	7399 Business services not elsewhere classified	172 Photographer	7221 Photographic studios, portrait
088 Upholstering	5714 Drapery and upholstery stores	173 Optometrist	8042 Offices of optometrists
089 China and glassware	5719 Miscellaneous home furnishings stores	174 Figure salon	7299 Miscellaneous personal services
OTHER RETAIL		179 Other service	7299 Miscellaneous personal services
101 Hardware	5251 Hardware stores	**OTHER**	
102 Home improvements	5211 Lumber and other building materials	191 Service station	5541 Gasoline service stations
103 Automotive (TBA)	5531 Auto and home supply stores	192 Bowling alley	7933 Bowling alleys
104 Auto dealer	5511 New and used car dealers	193 Cinema	7832 Motion picture theaters except drive-in
105 Paint and wallpaper	5231 Paint, glass, and wallpaper stores	194 Ice skating rink	7999 Amusement and recreation not elsewhere classified
106 Garden shop	5261 Retail nurseries and garden stores		
107 Hobby shop	5945 Hobby, toy, and game shops	195 Community hall	— no classification
108 Art gallery	5999 Miscellaneous retail stores not elsewhere classified	196 Warehouse or storage	4225 General warehousing and storage
109 Arts and crafts	5999 Miscellaneous retail stores not elsewhere classified	**SPECIAL**	
		197 Arcade, amusement center	7993 Coin-operated amusement devices
110 Candle shop	5999 Miscellaneous retail stores not elsewhere classified	198 Car wash	7542 Car washes
		201 Vacant space	— no classification
111 Records and tapes	5733 Music stores	202 Miscellaneous income	— no classification
112 Musical instruments	5733 Music stores		
113 Pet shop	5999 Miscellaneous retail stores not elsewhere classified		
114 Books and stationery	5942 Book stores		
	5943 Stationery stores		

Source: see footnote 1 in this chapter.

3-4

Placement

Tenant placement follows a simple rule: locate major or anchor tenants so that as much of the pedestrian shopper traffic as possible flows past the storefronts of supplementary tenants. Separate the principal key tenants. Place a key tenant at each end of a strip or mall, for example, rather than side by side near the center of the building. Arrange the parking and the major entrances and exits of the building so that the movement of customers to and from the key tenants is convenient but also exposes the customer to as many other tenants as possible.

Tenants may have strong and sometimes apparently arbitrary views about where they will or will not go within a center. Such views must obviously receive serious consideration if the developer wishes to have a particular tenant in the center.

A location that is good for one type of business can be entirely wrong for another. Placement within the tenant composition is important and complex. Grouping of tenants in the center may follow either the "mix" or "match" principle as long as customer interest is maintained throughout. Stores can be placed in affinity groupings, but mixing is desirable. Logical clusters may include service and repair shops; food and food services; and variety, hardware, appliance, and home furnishings stores. The "merchandising" principles involved in determining tenant array in a shopping center are similar to those used by successful full-line department stores to determine locations for their various departments within the store.

Another principle of store location is that convenience goods stores should be placed for ready access from the parking area. In fact, developers of regional mall centers often find it preferabe to locate supermarkets and certain pickup personal service stores, such as dry cleaners, laundries, and carryouts, in a separate building at the edge of a parking area, allowing immediate access for quick, in-and-out parking. A long walk into a mall to reach a convenience store will be neither comfortable for the customer nor appropriate for such a tenant. In addition, a buying trip to the supermarket serves a purpose far different from that of a shopping trip for general merchandise and apparel, and the rent structure of a regional center may be difficult for a supermarket or other low margin tenant. Finally, the trade area for a supermarket is so narrow that the supermarket may not belong in the regional center.

The following is a list of general considerations for tenant location, not necessarily in order of importance:

- Suitability of the tenant for the location.
- Pulling power or customer acceptance by reason of local preference for the merchant.
- Compatibility and complementary status with adjoining stores.
- Tenant's merchandising policy.
- Parking needs generated by the tenant.

Composition

Tenant classifications by kind of center are listed only to suggest a common tenant composition. The tenant mix will naturally be affected by circumstances of leasing, financing, and tenant availability for an individual trade area. In addition, a tenant appropriate for one center could be a mistake in another. Selection of store types must be left to the individual developer because of the greatly varying income ranges and other characteristics of the tributary population, inducements to impulse buying, local buying habits, store sizes, and merchandising practices in different site conditions and various geographic areas. There is, however, a distinct pattern of prevalence of certain store types, apart from the definition of center type by key tenant classification. Nearly every neighborhood center, for example, except for the new specialty or high-fashion center, will contain a drugstore as well as a food service store or supermarket.

Seasoned leasing brokers, appraisers, landlords, and shopping center operators have learned many things about grouping certain kinds of businesses:

- Men's stores—shoes, clothing and haberdashery, sporting goods—tend to swell each other's volume.
- Similarly, women's apparel, shoes, and millinery and children's clothes and toys—the soft lines—prosper in proximity to one another.
- Food products do well when grouped together —groceries, meat and fish markets, delicatessens, bakeries, doughnut shops, and confectioners.
- Stores which sell personal services and conveniences naturally go together, but in shopping centers they should be as close as possible to the parking area, as mentioned earlier.

Other considerations in store placement include convenience to the customer and the tenant's rent-paying ability.

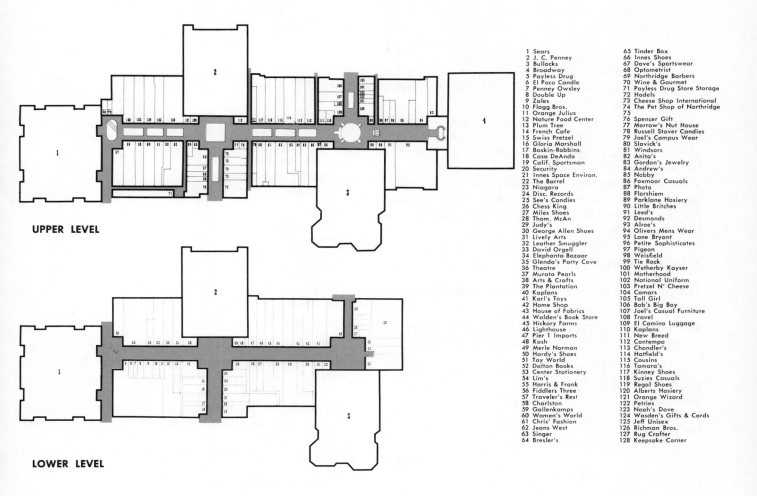

UPPER LEVEL

LOWER LEVEL

1 Sears	65 Tinder Box
2 J. C. Penney	66 Innes Shoes
3 Bullocks	67 Dave's Sportswear
4 Broadway	68 Optometrist
5 Payless Drug	69 Northridge Barbers
6 El Poco Candle	70 Wine & Gourmet
7 Penney Owsley	71 Payless Drug Store Storage
8 Double Up	72 Hodels
9 Zales	73 Cheese Shop International
10 Flagg Bros.	74 The Pet Shop of Northridge
11 Orange Julius	75
12 Nature Food Center	76 Spencer Gift
13 Plum Tree	77 Morrow's Nut House
14 French Cafe	78 Russell Stover Candies
15 Swiss Pretzel	79 Joel's Campus Wear
16 Gloria Marshall	80 Slavick's
17 Baskin-Robbins	81 Windsors
18 Casa DeAnda	82 Anita's
19 Calif. Sportsman	83 Gordon's Jewelry
20 Security	84 Andrew's
21 Innes Space Environ.	85 Nobby
22 The Barrel	86 Foxmoor Casuals
23 Niagara	87 Photo
24 Disc. Records	88 Florsheim
25 See's Candies	89 Parklane Hosiery
26 Chess King	90 Little Britches
27 Miles Shoes	91 Leed's
28 Thom. McAn	92 Desmonds
29 Judy's	93 Alroe's
30 George Allen Shoes	94 Olivers Mens Wear
31 Lively Arts	95 Lane Bryant
32 Leather Smuggler	96 Petite Sophisticates
33 David Orgell	97 Pigeon
34 Elephanta Bazaar	98 Weisfield
35 Glenda's Party Cove	99 Tie Rack
36 Theatre	100 Wetherby Kayser
37 Murata Pearls	101 Motherhood
38 Arts & Crafts	102 National Uniform
39 The Plantation	103 Pretzel N' Cheese
40 Kaplans	104 Comars
41 Karl's Toys	105 Tall Girl
42 Home Shop	106 Bob's Big Boy
43 House of Fabrics	107 Joel's Casual Furniture
44 Walden's Book Store	108 Travel
45 Hickory Farms	109 El Camino Luggage
46 Lighthouse	110 Kaplans
47 Pier 1 Imports	111 New Breed
48 Kosh	112 Contempo
49 Merle Norman	113 Chandler's
50 Hardy's Shoes	114 Hatfield's
51 Toy World	115 Cousins
52 Dalton Books	116 Tamara's
53 Center Stationery	117 Kinney Shoes
54 Lim's	118 Suzies Casuals
55 Harris & Frank	119 Regal Shoes
56 Fiddlers Three	120 Alberts Hosiery
57 Traveler's Rest	121 Orange Wizard
58 Charlston	122 Petries
59 Gallenkamps	123 Noah's Dove
60 Women's World	124 Wasden's Gifts & Cards
61 Chris' Fashion	125 Jeff Unisex
62 Jeans West	126 Richman Bros.
63 Singer	127 Rug Crafter
64 Bresler's	128 Keepsake Corner

3-5   The tenant mix at Northridge Fashion Center, Northridge, California.

Even though surveys have been made of the store types and groupings suitable for shopping centers,[2] a missing ingredient in locational studies is the effect of proper groupings on the prosperity of the whole center. Another immeasurable factor is the ability of a particular merchant to work as a member of the merchandising team—the team which ultimately becomes the shopping center.

In a well laid out shopping center, there will be no poor locations. Each tenant's location carries equal advantage for high-volume retailing. The long-established retail theory of the "100 percent location" that was once applied to downtowns should not be reflected in well-designed shopping

centers. Certain types of tenants produce their own draw and do not in fact require locations on a main mall. They will be sought out. Banks, travel agencies, restaurants, and service shops are suited to side malls or other locations which have a lower volume of foot traffic.

In choosing stores for a center in a new growth area, the developer must secure shops which can

---

[2] For a discussion of the principles of compatibility among retail businesses in selecting tenants, see Richard L. Nelson, *The Selection of Retail Locations* (New York: McGraw-Hill, 1966).

render a service to the trade area and which have the financial stamina to weather a pioneering period. Other special points to consider are the tenant's credit rating, his profit and loss experience, his advertising policy, his type of merchandise, his class of customers, his housekeeping practices, his long-term operational record and merchandising policy, and his integrity.

Certain axioms about store grouping have grown out of shopping center experience: arrange the tenants to provide the greatest amount of interplay between the stores. Be careful where you put the supermarket because of its heavy demand for parking spaces; if you do not have convenient parking for the supermarket, or for a theater, you will not have customers.

Neighborhood Centers

The following lists are offered as a guide for tenant composition:[3]

3-6 TWENTY MOST FREQUENTLY FOUND TENANTS IN NEIGHBORHOOD CENTERS

TENANT CLASSIFICATION	RANK
FOOD AND FOOD SERVICE	
Supermarket	2
Restaurant without liquor	8
Ice cream parlor	20
GENERAL MERCHANDISE	
Variety store	14
CLOTHING AND SHOES	
Ladies' specialty	15
Ladies' ready-to-wear	7
DRY GOODS	
Yard goods	18
FURNITURE	
Radio, TV, hi-fi	19
OTHER RETAIL	
Hardware	16
Drugs	4
Cards and gifts	10
Liquor and wine	12
FINANCIAL	
Banks	13
OFFICES	
Medical and dental	3
Real estate	9
SERVICES	
Beauty shop	1
Barber shop	6
Cleaners and dyers	5
Coin laundries	11
Service station	17

3-7 NEIGHBORHOOD CENTER COMPOSITION BY TENANT CLASSIFICATION

TENANT GROUP	PERCENT GLA	PERCENT SALES	PERCENT TOTAL CHARGES (INCOME FROM TENANTS)
Food	26.5	43.8	21.4
Food service	5.1	3.2	6.7
General merchandise	16.3	8.9	12.2
Clothing and shoes	5.5	4.2	7.7
Dry goods	3.8	1.6	4.3
Furniture	4.8	1.7	5.2
Other retail	16.9	13.4	17.6
Financial	3.0	0	3.7
Offices	4.7	0	5.0
Services	5.6	2.5	7.8
Other	4.7	20.7	8.4
Vacant	3.1	0	0
Total	100.0	100.0	100.0

The neighborhood center has its major tenants in the food group; those tenants represent 26 percent of GLA, 44 percent of sales, and 21 percent of total revenue. The "other retail" category (drugs, liquor, hardware, etc.) comprises the second major tenant group and represents about 18 percent of total charges. (*Total charges* includes minimum rent, overage rent, and common area charges.)

Community Centers

Community centers, the "in-between" centers, provide a greater array of tenant classifications than do neighborhood centers.

3-8 TWENTY MOST FREQUENTLY FOUND TENANTS IN COMMUNITY CENTERS

TENANT CLASSIFICATION	RANK
FOOD AND FOOD SERVICE	
Supermarket	2
Restaurant without liquor	17
Restaurant with liquor	20
GENERAL MERCHANDISE	
Junior department store	6
Variety store	13

[3] These lists of tenants in neighborhood centers, as well as the lists which follow for community, regional, and super-regional centers, are taken from *Dollars and Cents of Shopping Centers: 1975*, cited in footnote 1 above. The ranking shown in the lists, as well as the percentages shown for GLA, sales, and landlord income, were current in 1975 but obviously will change.

CLOTHING AND SHOES
Ladies' specialty	14
Ladies' ready-to-wear	1
Men's wear	7
Family shoe	5

DRY GOODS
Yard goods	11

FURNITURE
Radio, TV, hi-fi	19

OTHER RETAIL
Drugs	8
Jewelry	12
Cards and gifts	10

FINANCIAL
Bank	16
Insurance	18

OTHER OFFICES
Medical and dental	3

SERVICES
Beauty shop	4
Barber shop	9
Cleaners and dyers	15

3-9 COMMUNITY CENTER COMPOSITION BY TENANT CLASSIFICATION

TENANT GROUP	PERCENT GLA	PERCENT SALES	PERCENT TOTAL CHARGES
Food	15.7	33.2	13.1
Food service	3.7	3.8	6.0
General merchandise	35.8	30.1	27.0
Clothing and shoes	7.8	7.6	10.6
Dry goods	3.0	2.0	3.6
Furniture	3.7	3.6	3.6
Other retail	14.5	15.5	18.2
Financial	2.5	0	3.6
Offices	2.2	0	3.0
Services	3.6	1.8	5.0
Other	4.3	2.4	6.3
Vacant	3.3	0	0
Total	100.0	100.0	100.0

The community center is typified by a tenant mix which lies between the arrays offered by regional and neighborhood centers. General merchandise represents the second greatest portion (about 16 percent). However, food tenants represent 33 percent of total sales, and general merchandise represents 30 percent of sales. General merchandise represents 27 percent of total charges, and "other retail" represents 18 percent of total charges.

Regional and Super-Regional Centers

Tenant classifications depend somewhat on lease negotiations with the department stores. As mentioned before, there must be at least one full-line department store in order to have a regional center.

Proper tenant location in a regional center is complicated but essential. In supercenters, the merchandising plan requires even greater care to place small tenants in the path of pedestrian circulation between the larger magnets—department stores, junior department stores, specialty stores, and quality restaurants.

A regional center must be all-inclusive and self-sufficient. These characteristics suggest the importance of store grouping. To create self-sufficiency means that in addition to the stores with big drawing power there must be a full range of merchandise available to the shopper, including nearly every retail offering (with the growing exception of the variety store) once found downtown.

Completeness also means competition within the center. Competition between merchants is good for the center and good for the merchants. It keeps merchants aggressive and gives customers the comparison shopping they want. As one developer has said, "Put in two markets, two dress shops, two drugstores—because a single tenant may get too arrogant."

It is important that the amount of selling space be based on the estimated sales volume determined in the market analysis. It is also important to remember how many people it takes to support a center of the proposed size.

3-10 TWENTY MOST FREQUENTLY FOUND TENANTS IN REGIONAL CENTERS

TENANT CLASSIFICATION	RANK
FOOD AND FOOD SERVICE	
Candy and nuts	9
Restaurant without liquor	12
Fast-food/carryout	17
GENERAL MERCHANDISE	
Department store	14
Variety store	18
CLOTHING AND SHOES	
Ladies' specialty	6
Ladies' ready-to-wear	1
Men's wear	2
Family wear	11
Family shoe	3
Ladies' shoe	7
Men's and boys' shoe	20

DRY GOODS
Yard goods   13

OTHER RETAIL
Books and stationery   8
Drugs   19
Jewelry   5
Cards and gifts   4

FINANCIAL
Banks   15

OFFICES
Medical and dental   16

SERVICES
Beauty shop   10

3-11 REGIONAL CENTER COMPOSITION BY TENANT CLASSIFICATION

TENANT GROUP	PERCENT GLA	PERCENT SALES	PERCENT TOTAL CHARGES
Food	5.5	7.9	6.0
Food service	2.9	3.6	5.2
General merchandise	53.4	48.5	32.0
Clothing and shoes	16.9	20.4	26.3
Dry goods	1.4	1.5	2.5
Furniture	1.4	1.7	1.8
Other retail	10.1	13.3	16.6
Financial	1.6	0	2.7
Offices	.4	1.1	.6
Services	1.2	1.1	2.7
Other	3.0	2.0	3.6
Vacant	2.2	0	0
Total	100.0	100.0	100.0

General merchandise represents 53 percent of the GLA of regional centers, clothing stores about 17 percent. The typical regional shopping center has 48 percent of the sales in general merchandise and 20 percent in clothing and shoes. General merchandise represents 32 percent of the total charges, clothing and shoes about 26 percent.

3-12 TWENTY MOST FREQUENTLY FOUND TENANTS IN SUPER-REGIONAL CENTERS

TENANT CLASSIFICATION	RANK
FOOD AND FOOD SERVICE	
Candy and nuts	10
Restaurant without liquor	13
Fast-food/carryout	9
Restaurant with liquor	19
GENERAL MERCHANDISE	
Department store	18
CLOTHING AND SHOES	
Ladies' specialty	3
Ladies' ready-to-wear	1
Men's wear	2
Family wear	15
Family shoe	6
Ladies' shoe	5
Men's and boys' shoe	8
Unisex/jean shop	17
DRY GOODS	
Yard goods	11
OTHER RETAIL	
Books and stationery	12
Jewelry	7
Cosmetics	4
FINANCIAL	
Bank	14
SERVICES	
Beauty shop	16
Optometrist	20

3-13 SUPER-REGIONAL CENTER COMPOSITION BY TENANT CLASSIFICATION

TENANT GROUP	PERCENT GLA	PERCENT SALES	PERCENT TOTAL CHARGES
Food	4.7	6.6	4.2
Food service	4.6	6.4	6.8
General merchandise	38.0	25.5	22.7
Clothing and shoes	26.0	33.8	34.0
Dry goods	1.9	2.3	2.2
Furniture	1.8	1.8	2.1
Other retail	12.7	20.7	20.0
Financial	1.9	0	2.2
Offices	.5	0	.7
Services	1.4	1.7	2.3
Other	3.9	1.2	3.9
Vacant	2.6	0	0
Total	100.0	100.0	100.0

The typical super-regional center has 38 percent of the GLA in general merchandise and 26 percent in clothing and shoes. The general merchandise group represents 25 percent of sales and 22 percent of total charges. Clothing and shoes represent about 34 percent of sales and 34 percent of total charges.

Tenant Evaluation

Tenant evaluation is important to the productivity and merchandise offerings in any center. Shopping center operators watch tenant performance carefully. Any weaknesses are corrected through tenant replacement, provided a short-term lease is in effect, or otherwise through negotiation. Operators of new centers must monitor and encourage tenant performance, particularly the performance of any tenants which are first-time entrants into a shopping center.

There is a trend to reduce dependence on and the proportion of triple-A credit-rated national chains and to increase the representation of local chain and independent merchants who have built-in customer appeal, merchandising expertise, and operational performance capabilities. These independent merchants may require more continuous performance evaluation and merchandising assistance than national or local chains.

In enclosed mall centers, from the viewpoints of both developers and tenants, an ability to pull customer traffic into and along the mall may be a greater test of productivity than are the clauses of a lease. An anchor tenant, particularly, is expected to deliver a significant share of the customer count to the rest of the tenants.

At this stage in the planning procedures, it is well to point out that some shifts in tenant locations will undoubtedly be needed in any center; some tenants will outgrow their original space and others will require smaller spaces. Some tenants may need to be shifted to strengthen the whole center's operations.

Many merchants fail because of an initial burden of excess space, with its additional overhead. The need for the flexibility to fit space to changing

3-14 Most modern regional centers feature an enclosed pedestrian mall. At Hillcrest Mall in Richmond Hill, Ontario, pedestrian areas are highlighted by a two-toned quarry tile floor, formed sprayed-plastic bulkheads, metal-strip ceiling, and decorative banners. This 566,000-square-foot center has two department stores, a discount store, and 85 mall tenants.

needs of tenants cannot be overemphasized. There is a continuing trend toward smaller tenant spaces to encourage higher productivity and greater use of the space.

Developers who are seeking tenants must consider not only the service the center is to offer a community but also the current trends in tenant classifications and merchandising. Developers must avoid fads, yet they must take into account the effects of current economic conditions.

Current surveys can help determine these conditions. In September 1974, for example, a survey showed that the number of gasoline stations had dropped 9.1 percent. Apparel stores showed a gain, including a 6.5 percent increase in the number of discount department stores. Eating and drinking places, including drive-ins with fast-food carryout, had expanded in number of outlets. Furnishings supply houses were up slightly, with radio, television, and stereo outlets showing the greatest advance. A slow and steady decline in hardware and building supply stores reflected in part the continuing decline in housing starts brought on by tight mortgage money.[4]

In calculating the rental income stream to be achieved, the developer must remember that all types of stores cannot and should not pay the same rental per square foot. The tenant should be aware that this rent is based on the probable volume and profit level in his particular business. Certain types of service establishments may pay comparatively low rentals and may even be loss leaders for the center. Such tenants, however, are valuable to high-rent tenants for their drawing power and for rounding out the center's services to the community—an essential ingredient in maintaining continued patronage and goodwill.

The following discussion is intended to help in these and other areas of tenant evaluation.[5]

Food and Food Service
Supermarkets

The supermarket is the anchor tenant in traditional neighborhood centers; a key tenant in community centers; and an optional tenant in regionals, not now customary unless placed in a special structure to which customers drive directly.

A supermarket is defined by the Super Market Institute, Inc., as a "complete, departmentalized food store with a minimum sales volume of one million dollars a year and at least the grocery department fully self-service." A superstore is defined

as one with 25,000 or more square feet of *selling area*. A "superette" is a similar type of store which has a weekly sales volume of $10,000 to $20,000.

The developer may have a choice of whether to have one or more than one supermarket in a strong location. A typical supermarket now contains approximately 30,000 square feet of GLA. A larger supermarket would be likely to carry an unnecessary proportion of nonfood items, a practice that may be detrimental to the other tenant mix desired in a shopping center. Rates for percentage rents on food items are between 1 and 1½ percent of sales, whereas rates on nonfood items could be 4 to 6 percent if sold by stores other than the supermarket. Because of the differences between percentage rates for various classes of merchandise, it is important to have a clear understanding of the specific internal characteristics of a supermarket. The proportion of nonfood sales to total GLA varies widely and changes somewhat each year.[6]

The degree of the supermarket's departure into nonfoods has a bearing on the lease negotiations. Two approaches to the percentage rent problem can be taken:

- Limit the supermarket to food items and items normally associated with food sales. In some cases this could be accomplished by limiting the lessee to the sale of those items which he is merchandising in other stores; such an approach would obviously be effective only where the prospective tenant is presently limiting his merchandising to conventional food items and has not already branched out into a series of nonfood departments.
- Limit the floor area devoted to nonfood items to a percentage of the total sales area or to a specific maximum. Ten percent of the total sales area may be a reasonable limit for nonfood sales.

---

[4] Survey by Audits and Surveys, Inc., a New York marketing firm, as reported by United Press International, September 26, 1974.

[5] For performance information for specific tenant classifications and types of centers, see *Dollars and Cents of Shopping Centers* (footnote 1 above).

[6] For complete information about supermarket sales volume, store size, extent of competition, lease terms, customer count, departments within the store, etc., including information about supermarkets which are part of discount stores, see *Facts About New Super Markets Opened in* —— (current year), prepared by the Super Market Institute, Inc., Chicago; and its companion report, *The Super Market Industry Speaks* —— (current year), also prepared by SMI.

Unless a clear understanding is reached with the supermarket, the store may sell a significant quantity of nonfood items at a percentage markup far lower than that for which the same items would be sold in other stores in the center; such a situation may or may not be acceptable to the developer.

Supermarkets need adequate parking for heavy customer turnover; they also require direct entrance from the parking areas for normal, off-hour, and Sunday selling. They require loading docks for over-the-road trucks. Special trash storage and pickup spaces are required in addition to the loading dock and truck turning area. For the delivery, pickup, and storage areas, the best architectural treatment is a court, screened from customer awareness.

In general, supermarkets are not big customer attractions within the large regional or super-regional center. In fact, their importance to a center varies inversely with the size of the center. In those centers where the supermarket is a preferred tenant, it is the supermarket's *draw* which is its greatest contribution to the center as a whole.

Other Food Stores

Small food specialty shops—delicatessens, and stores which offer meats, fish and poultry, candy and nuts, baked goods, or dairy products—when effectively merchandised, are valued tenants in any shopping center.

Restaurants

Every shopping center needs eating facilities. Even a small neighborhood center should have at least a counter or fountain operation. In a regional center, eating places of every type are important. A quality restaurant operation can draw patronage from throughout the trade area. The good restaurant takes a skillful operator and top management technique. Any restaurant business takes special know-how.

A freestanding location on the shopping center site permits drive-to service and specially assigned parking spaces. Since a good restaurant may do much of its business on Sundays, or during evening hours, direct access, ready identification, and adequate parking are important site placement considerations. A restaurant may also be located for access from a mall or plaza in order to draw traffic to an otherwise light pedestrian traffic area.

Restaurants cover a wide variety of classifications and types of operation—independent, local, or national chain. They range from the small, quick-order, limited-menu counter or table service operation to the distinctively decorated, high-quality, high-price gourmet table service establishment with or without liquor.

All types have succeeded in regional, community, and specialty centers; all types have failed. Care in selection of the operator is essential. The wise developer will limit his investment to good restaurant operations.

All regional centers need at least one *quality* restaurant and, if the law allows, liquor service. If the developer can lease restaurant space only by providing fixtures and furniture, he should select the best locally known successful proprietor and advance necessary funds on a basis of an eventual recovery of his investment.

Gourmet Food Marts

The gourmet food mart is an innovation in placement and arrangement of food specialties and eating services that produces a high volume of sales and customer traffic for a regional center.[7] The mart generally has food specialties and fast-food outlets arranged in clusters or around the edge of a large, commonly used dining area that may include tables and chairs, stand-up counters, or other eating arrangements. Customers may carry selected food items from one or more food purveyors to a table on the premises. Such spaces are really just a restaurant for self-service, made more attractive by variety in food offerings and by interior design style and treatment. Bordering stalls are leased to tenants who offer food specialties—sandwiches, meats, fruits, candies, exotic foods—usually on very short leases in order to assure a high quality of products. Such bazaars or markets need food preparation, washing, and cold storage facilities. All stall tenants are on separate percentage leases, resulting in a higher overall rent than would be paid by a single tenant restaurant. Problems in maintenance, cleanliness, and placement within the center should be carefully evaluated. There are also problems of achieving an overall design which avoids a hodgepodge appearance. Other details to be worked out include whether china, silverware, and glasses are to be used or whether the operation will rely on disposable items; whether these items will be separately or commonly owned by the food service tenants; what the practical and financial

[7] See "Gourmet Fair at Sherway Gardens," *Project Reference File*, Vol. 2, No. 14 (July–September 1972).

3-15   Diners at the International Café, in Kansas City's Crown Center Shops, select their food from seven different counters surrounding a central dining arcade that seats 600 persons. Customers have a choice of Italian, Mexican, and Oriental cuisines, hamburgers and steak sandwiches from an American broiler, Jewish and German favorites from a New York-style delicatessen, barbecued chicken and ribs, or seafood from an oyster bar. The seven-in-one restaurant is a part of Crown Center's two-block, trilevel retail and entertainment complex.

arrangements will be for procurement, stocking, and washing or disposal of these items; what the arrangements will be for providing condiments and paying cleanup costs; and so forth.

Fast-Food Outlets

In a regional center the chain fast-food outlet will most likely be treated like any other mall tenant. In community and neighborhood centers, however, this use is another matter. This book has already recommended the elimination or reduction of strip commercial development; and in the absence of new strip development, the likely location for fast-food stores is the community center or, in some cases, the larger neighborhood center. Most fast-

food chains have distinctive building designs and specific on-site circulation and parking patterns, related to their method of operation. While the building design of such outlets has improved considerably over the prevalent design of the fifties and early sixties, the general appearance of fast-food stores is still the target of public criticism. A shopping center developer planning to include such tenants should apply the same standards of design control he would apply to any other freestanding tenant. The developer's ability and willingness to help the community modify the unacceptable characteristics of these uses will be an important aid to the developer in obtaining necessary public approvals.

General Merchandise and Apparel
Department Stores

The full-line department store of a least 100,000 square feet of GLA is the key or anchor tenant and a must in regional centers. Two such stores are common. With three or more department stores and at least 750,000 square feet of GLA, the center becomes a super-regional.

As the dominent tenants of regional shopping centers, department stores are the main generators of customer traffic. With more than one department store, placement becomes a matter of finding a building pattern that separates these anchor tenants. The location of the stores determines the composition and placement of supplementary tenants, who must benefit from the flow of customers between the anchors. The department stores want balanced parking directly accessible to them. Resolving the dilemma of providing for a safe and convenient customer flow between the parking area and the building entrances, while inducing pedestrian flow through the mall, is the crux of site planning and building design in community and regional centers.

In negotiating for a department store tenant, the developer should be aware of customer loyalties, the segment of the market the tenant serves, the store's policies in price lines, and its merchandising image. Each market area is generally served by one or more department stores; these will be the primary prospects for any new development. The success of any regional center development may depend on the ability to interest these already operating stores in the new development. Other department stores, those who are seeking a new market entry, will generally prefer to be associated with established stores.

Before adding another department store to increase an *existing* center's drawing power and customer convenience, the developer must be sure of the deal he works out and its effect on his investment. Generally, such an addition would be beneficial.

The usual practice in regional centers today is an arrangement whereby the department store (including appropriate parking area) is owned by the store itself and not by the shopping center developer-owner. In such cases, the department store customarily becomes an integral part of the shopping center through an elaborate, detailed set of easement and operating agreements (REAs). Thus, the customer sees no physical evidence of a difference

3-16   A department store's china and glass display.

in ownership between the department store and the rest of the center. In smaller markets, a gross lease is the preferred method of department store participation.

The design quality and architectural treatment of a department store must be closely related to the character of the trade area. Since the full-line store is such a major attractor, the department store will be a prominent feature. The department store, with its own standards in merchandising techniques and quality, will complement the other stores but will also set the tone for the entire center.

Junior Department Stores

In a community center, the variety, junior department, or popular price store is a key tenant. The term *junior department store* is not capable of close definition but generally refers to a store that does not carry the full lines customary in department stores, and that is smaller than a department store, as measured in GLA. The junior department store usually carries clothing and token representations of such lines as glassware, linens, other home accessories, luggage and leather goods, and sports equipment. Typical GLA is 40,000 to 100,000 square feet.

The junior department store category was originally associated with small outlets of the major national chains, such as Sears, Penney's, and Ward's. These chains have withdrawn from this approach, but there are still a great number of locally owned stores and regional chains in the junior department store category. In addition, other store classifications are evolving toward the role of the junior department store.

A junior department store or specialty store of 10,000 or more square feet GLA would be unusual in a neighborhood center.

Variety Stores

Variety stores contribute to the merchandise completeness of neighborhood or community centers. The five-and-ten format for variety stores is fading from prominence in merchandising. The variety store's image has changed extensively through the widening of ranges of general merchandise and furnishings and the addition of self-service and checkout stands.

Self-Service or Discount Stores

Once an anathema to the shopping center, the self-service or discount store is now becoming an acceptable tenant. The discount operator has softened his merchandising and advertising practices so that they are now more in keeping with the style of a conventional business cluster.

The discount house grew up as a retail store that sold well-known brand merchandise or substitute house brands of lesser quality at less than customary prices. The discount concept provided little customer service and, originally, a less convenient location. Then certain discount stores were upgraded to offer credit and higher grade merchandise. They became self-service, low margin department stores.

With good interior decor and attractive fixturing now found in many discount stores, the major difference of the store type is its self-service operation, which permits lower prices to the consumer—often discounts of 10 to 20 percent for nationally advertised products. Cost reduction is made possible by minimum service, volume buying, lower profit margins, direct receipt of merchandise from manufacturers, and the use of sales areas as storage areas, thus reducing storage space to as little as 10 percent of the gross leasable area. In contrast, traditional department stores generally use from 20 to 40 percent of the floor area for storage and other nonselling purposes.

If a discount store is to be a key tenant in a community center, its practices of merchandising, advertising, and sign control must be compatible with those of satellite tenants and the shopping center management.

3-17   Apparel stores are the largest space users at many shopping centers.

Apparel Stores

Tenants in the apparel category cover a full range of store types, quality, style, and price. In the neighborhood center, an apparel store usually presents goods that serve as a convenience to the local market. Apparel stores are the lifeblood of community and regional centers. Men's, women's, children's, and family clothing lines provide a strong attraction for comparison shopping. Independent merchants, local chains, national chains, customized shops, ready-to-wear outlets, and accessories are all represented. Store area, sales, and rent-paying productivity are important factors to the developer who is seeking such tenantry.

Community and regional centers can have groups of selected high-price, high-fashion, and other specialized apparel stores. In the right trade area, such stores strengthen the merchandise pull to the center. Women's stores with attractive styles and prices have a strong attraction for special-purpose shopping trips.

Men's stores with complete clothing lines are becoming more important in the regional center, less important in the community and neighborhood centers. A selected range of haberdashery can be an appropriate offering in a neighborhood center.

Shoe Stores

While a neighborhood center may or may not have a shoe store, community and regional centers include a number of them, usually of the chain variety. It is entirely possible to include a number of women's and family shoe stores in a center; competition within the lines keeps productivity at a high level. The stores must, of course, be carefully selected. There should be fewer shoe stores for men than for women and children, because men buy fewer pairs per season.

Furniture and Home Furnishings

A furniture store produces little traffic and a low sales volume per square foot of GLA. The average household purchases furniture infrequently and only after a special trip. Furniture stores fit into suburban locations and the pattern of evening shopping. But they usually require large display and storage areas while returning low rentals per square foot.

3-18   Specialty furniture stores and decorator shops are tenants in some shopping centers.

Full-line furniture stores are more suitable to freestanding locations than to the shopping center itself. If a furniture store is to be placed in the actual center, an easily merchandised basement or other location out of the main traffic area of the principle shopping level is the preferred arrangement. A full-line furniture store is not usually found in a neighborhood center.

An interior decorator shop can function as a substitute for the full-line furniture store in any center. The decorator shop can offer a token selection of home furnishings in the form of a specialized boutique. Like the furniture store, however, the decorator shop does not need to be placed in a high-traffic location.

Sizes of furniture stores range from 400 square feet upward. A freestanding, full-line furniture store can occupy 50,000 square feet or more.

Other Retail and Services
Hardware and Home Repair Centers

These stores have taken up supermarket ways with self-service and ranges of selected household wares. Furthermore, the do-it-yourself market has changed the traditional hardware store into a building equipment and materials and home repair center. Display racks occupy space once used by the clerk's aisle. The hardware store appears most often in neighborhood and community centers. The large home improvement center has become a major tenant in the community center. In regional centers, such home centers can be placed in a fringe area of the property, similar to the treatment of a freestanding supermarket.

Wallpaper and Paint Stores

Wallpaper and paint stores are a special version of the hardware store classification and can be found in every type of center.

Garden Shops and Plant Stores

These stores similarly fall within a home furnishings and hobby shop category of "other retail and service" establishments. Garden shops require space for outdoor selling and display. The display must be adjacent to the store itself, necessitating special attention in site arrangement. During certain seasons, department stores may add a special garden shop which is converted to other uses during the rest of the year.

Auto Supply Stores

Auto accessory stores generally do not belong in the main unit of a shopping center, except as required as an associated unit of a department store.

The tire, battery, and accessory (TBA) store should be placed in a secondary or freestanding location, where parking and car service will not

3-19   Freestanding tire, battery, and accessory (TBA) stores usually occupy a secondary location.

interfere with the center's general customer parking.

Most chain department stores now desire their own TBA store as a customer service supplement. These TBA stores can either be placed in a freestanding building, as suggested above, or attached to the department store. Most department stores have a firm preference for one approach or the other.

Drugstores

A good drugstore is a key tenant in the neighborhood center. It is also a desirable tenant in any other type of center, except a high-fashion or other specialty center. Community and regional centers may have two drugstores; these may be prescription pharmacies, traditional drugstores with or without fountain service, or the super or merchandising drugstore, usually of the chain type.

Prescription pharmacies generally have 650 to 1,200 square feet GLA; the traditional drugstore, 3,000 to 5,000 square feet; and the superdrug, 7,000 to 12,000 square feet. The developer usually is faced with a choice between a chain drugstore and a strong independent merchant. Drugstore sizes have increased to the point that a super-drugstore may fill the center's variety store needs. Some may even have a size and a range of goods that begin to make these stores a substitute for a junior department store.

Service Shops

Personal service tenants are common to all types and sizes of shopping centers. These tenants occupy a much higher percentage of total GLA in neighborhood centers than they do in regionals, as was shown earlier.

Barber shops or men's hair stylists, beauty salons, laundries and dry cleaning services, shoe repair shops, key makers, and other service shops are all important elements in the shopping center's convenience function. Service tenants are usually independent merchants who yield high rentals per square foot of store area. Since service shops are difficult to check for their gross sales, a higher minimum guaranteed rent per square foot can be substituted for the arrangement of sales percentage.

Service shops are traffic builders in the neighborhood center and traffic users in the large center. They need a location that provides direct access to customer parking, because much of their trade is the "run-in, run-out" kind. In an enclosed mall

3-20 Most regional shopping centers have one or two bookstores.

center, most of the service shops are usually placed in a secondary location or apart from the mall in a freestanding building or other separate convenience center within the property.

Community Rooms

These facilities aid in the public relations efforts of a regional center. The community room is usually placed in a secondary location. As a center becomes the focal point in a suburban community, the community room can become a place for civic-type meetings, club gatherings, and social affairs. If a community room can be located next to a restaurant, the room can be used for banquets, luncheon meetings, and receptions.

Kiddielands and Nurseries

These were once considered a valuable attraction for shopping mothers who could benefit from a place for supervised children's activities. Because liability insurance requirements and the public attitude toward child care have changed, nurseries need be considered only as an adjunct of a large-scale multiuse development.

Amusement Centers

The amusement center is the current version of the penny arcade. Such tenants have been successfully introduced in regional centers when given special architectural treatment and placed in a secondary location. Care should be taken to select tenants who demonstrate an ability to control and police their premises.

3-21   Georgetown Marketplace, a neighborhood center in Overland Park, Kansas, features an unusual building configuration designed to encourage pedestrian circulation throughout the center. The principal tenant, a supermarket, occupies a central location, and the 27 smaller tenants face outward on three sides.

Buildings

Building Patterns

Determining the building configuration is an important part of the site planning process for both developer and tenant. In contemplating the building pattern, the developer's main consideration should be placement of the key or anchor tenants. These tenants must be placed in such a way that they will draw customers between them and past the intervening tenants, as mentioned previously.

A steady design evolution has taken place in building patterns. The original shopping center concept started as a strip with parking in the rear, at the sides, or in front. The L, U, and T were variations designed to fit restricted sites and special locations with respect to adjacent streets. Then the stores courageously turned away from the public street with two facing strips separated by parking between the storefronts. Later, this intervening parking space was contracted and transformed into an open, landscaped mall. The mall structure, with its shop frontages, became an island surrounded by parking space.

The Strip

The strip is basically a straight line of stores, tied together by a canopy over a pedestrian walk which runs along the storefronts. The strip is normally set back from the access street, and most of the parking is placed between the street and the building.

The neighborhood center is the best place for the strip arrangement. The most successful configuration places two major units—usually a market and the drugstore—at the ends of the strip. A strip is

3-22 SHOPPING CENTER BUILDING CONFIGURATIONS

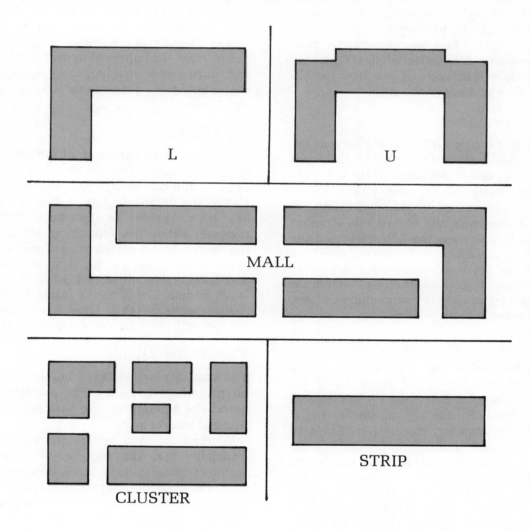

The strip—a line of stores tied together by a canopy over the sidewalk, which runs along the fronts of the stores. Economical for small centers, but must be kept within a reasonable length to avoid excessive walking distances and difficult merchandising.

The L—basically a strip, but with one end turned. Good for corner locations.

The U—basically a strip with both ends turned in the same direction.

The mall—essentially a pedestrian way between two facing strips. The mall may also take other shapes —an L, for example.

The cluster—a group of retail buildings separated by small pedestrian malls or courts.

generally the least expensive structure to build and is easily adapted to most site conditions. With strong sign control and good architectural treatment, the strip center can become an attractive and successful merchandising unit.

Care must be taken to avoid lengthening the strip beyond a comfortable walking distance. About 400 feet is normal, although there are successful strip centers of 750 feet and more. People are apparently willing to walk farther in a shopping center than they are downtown. Also, with adequate parking provided, people will drive back and forth within a center to various sections of the strip.

The L

The L is basically a strip with one end turned; the U is a strip with both ends turned in the same direction. In most cases, the intent of the L or U is to reduce the length of an otherwise overlong strip. The L can be turned in either direction according to the necessary site orientation. Another use of the L or U is to make the fullest use of a site which is nearly square; a strip development on such a site would waste site capacity and provide redundant parking. In general, the L is suitable for large neighborhood and smaller community centers, the U for larger community centers.

The Mall

Essentially a pedestrian way between two facing strips, the mall becomes a pedestrian street for back-and-forth shopping movement. It has become the standard pattern for the regional center and is being applied to community-size centers. The mall has come into its own, particularly for the regional center, because more and more regional centers are being designed for more than one department store.

The mall may be either open to the sky or roofed over, using glass or plastic skylights to allow natural lighting. The weather-protected area is usually heated and cooled according to the season. The enclosed mall, with its heating and air conditioning, has become the dominant pattern for regional centers, regardless of climate. Under current practices of mall construction, the enclosed mall is consistent with goals of energy conservation. The mall is designed with an efficient, centralized plant or rooftop units, low wattage lighting, and complete insulation.

Early shopping centers provided for pedestrian weather protection by constructing canopies or colonnaded roof projections along the storefronts.

For a neighborhood strip center, the front sidewalk was later glass-enclosed and air-conditioned to add the appeal of shopping comfort.

Straight malls are giving way to an offset design with "meandering" mall streets. But in most cases, department stores are not placed directly across a mall from one another.

Open mall centers are often remodeled and enclosed to improve customer appeal. Construction cost is offset by the increased sales volume, which results from the improved appeal and from the fact that, during poor weather, shopping in this type of center becomes a pleasurable activity rather than a simple necessity.

The Cluster

The cluster is an extension of the mall concept. In a regional center, the cluster takes on such variations on the customary letter shapes as the X, the Y, and the dumbbell. The cluster is a design that has been applied to the one-department-store regional center. The department store is placed in the center of the complex, surrounded by smaller stores, rather than placing it at one end of a mall and leaving the other end with no anchor or a weak anchor. The X and Y forms are the kinds of design solutions that have been developed for centers with three or four department stores.

The Specialty Center

The specialty center takes building forms having no prescribed patterns. The specialty center requires the building pattern best suited to the location and market area.

With any building pattern, there are basic design principles that the experienced developer and architect understand but the inexperienced overlook. For example, an enclosed mall, if it is too wide, is expensive to operate and discourages back-and-forth movement for impulse buying. If a mall is too narrow, it becomes crowded, hard to keep clean, and difficult to use for promotional activities. Forty feet is the most common width for malls. A mall can be widened into a court at one or two spots, both for design purposes and as a place for promotional activities.

Summary—Building Patterns

Common design errors, found in all building patterns, include unvarying widths or depths for all types of stores, difficulty in servicing smaller stores without interfering with pedestrian or auto traffic,

3-23 Specialty centers exhibit distinctive architectural styles and unusual building configurations. Marina Pacifica Shopping Village in Long Beach, California, is reminiscent of a New England village.

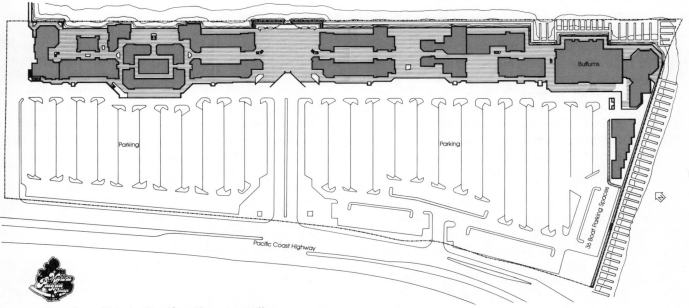

3-24 Site plan of Marina Pacifica Shopping Village.

3-25 A high-rise office building is part of Sharpstown Center, Houston.

and dead spaces that are difficult to lease because of their indirect pedestrian access. Multiple corners, setbacks, odd angles, and the like should be avoided in most small centers. In regional malls, however, this sort of special treatment may be used to avoid a tunnel effect in the mall and to create interest and visual excitement. In any case, the mall is the central feature of the center and therefore must possess individuality and character of design.

The stacking of levels in a regional mall center reduces walking distances and creates a more compact shopping area. The double-level or triple-level treatment is a solution called for by certain design limitations caused by site size and configuration.

In addition, a freestanding building has become an accepted feature of regional mall centers, both open and enclosed, for those tenant classifications

that provide customer convenience. Such tenants include supermarkets, drive-in banks, dry cleaners and laundries, barber and beauty shops, coin-operated laundries, specialized carryout fast-food services, shoe repair shops, and others. Restaurants and theaters may also be placed in freestanding buildings. Convenience buildings provide for the type of shops that need close-by parking, quick turnover, and fast customer service.

Building separation, when skillfully handled, creates a flexible tenant location pattern and allows the property to be used for one-trip shopping and greater customer convenience. The customary sea of parking is avoided by the distribution of convenience parking to each of the separate buildings. Tenants who prefer customer parking at their front door can thus be included in the regional center complex.

Facilities for Special Tenants

Freestanding Office Buildings

A freestanding office building for a single corporation or for multiple tenants brings more people to a center. The offices generate business for shops and restaurants. Because of this, the trend toward construction of office buildings on regional shopping center properties is a natural evolution. But, if provided, the building must have sufficient site area for the special parking and traffic it generates and must be capable of handling all-day parkers. However, the combined parking and traffic movement for office space and retail use will be less than the sum of the two individual requirements. Such shared parking must be carefully evaluated.

Hours for office tenant parking normally do not conflict with peak shopping hours. For this reason, the parking standard for shopping centers will accommodate office tenants until the net rentable area (NRA) of the offices reaches 20 percent of the center's GLA. When this point is reached, additional parking area should be constructed at the rate of four spaces per 1,000 square feet of office tenant space.[8] Parking space for the office building should be separated from the shoppers' parking and must be capable of handling the additional all-day parkers.

To determine whether a well-planned office building will help the center, the following factors should be evaluated:

- Apparent need for and desirability of offices in the area.
- Experience of other office buildings in the area.
- Possibility of using a section of the shopping center where high-density retail facilities or other facilities of greater benefit to the project would not be feasible.

Assuming there is a market for an office building within the shopping center complex, one of the first steps required is to check out the costs of construction and the economics of including the office component. It may be better to develop a completely separate office park nearby. Office park employees, like employees of an on-site office tenant, can use the shopping center for dining and noontime shopping.

Second Floor Offices

Although office tenants enjoy a location where they can shop and eat nearby during the lunch hour, offices placed above retail stores in shopping centers are generally not good rental properties. Office space on a second level of an enclosed mall center does not lease as rapidly as the retail space. If the shopping center management places enough emphasis on office leasing, most second-story office space will eventually fill up, but rental rates may well be lower than original expectations. Elevators are also required between the two floors, in addition to stairways, causing an added expense. Together with rental difficulties, complications of vertical circulation and service may justify the exclusion of this type of rental space from the shopping center building.

Medical Offices

As with other kinds of offices, doctors' and dentists' offices are probably best placed in freestanding clinic-type buildings either on the site or on an adjacent property. A one-story clinic building eliminates the elevator problem of the multistory professional building or the two-story shopping center building. Medical practitioners also require special and costly building features; because of this, having a separate medical building avoids the problem of having to charge a higher rent for the second floor of the center itself than would be charged for general office use.

If a medical building is included in the site, special parking must be provided. Unlike general office parking, medical building parking may interfere with parking for the shopping center; medical buildings should therefore have separate parking areas, with about six spaces per 1,000 square feet of NRA.

Banks

In states where branch banking is permitted, banks are common tenants in shopping centers. The bank is frequently placed in a freestanding building so that it can offer the convenience of drive-in service. Drive-in facilities require careful site placement of the structure to maintain good visual exposure while assuring easy traffic movement and adequate stacking areas for bank customers waiting to use the drive-up windows. This circulation pattern must be achieved without blocking

---

[8] See the section entitled "Parking Index" in *Dollars and Cents of Shopping Centers*. Also see *A Guide to Selecting Bank Locations* (New York: American Bankers Association, 1965).

3-26   Second-story offices at La Paz Plaza, Mission Viejo, California.

walk-in entrances or traffic circulation of the shopping center. The appropriate number of windows and stacking spaces depends on the volume of customers expected at the bank. The advent of computer-operated banking will result in convenient check-cashing units located within the mall.

Banks and savings and loan institutions often enter the center on ground leases and pay their own construction and outfitting costs. If placed in the center on other than a ground lease, these tenants pay a relatively high rental per square foot. A percentage lease based on deposit values is rare.

Bank leases are similar to other commercial leases in that the rental amount must be arrived at through negotiation. With freestanding buildings, however, net leases are quite common. On a ground lease with the institution constructing its own facility, the bank must become party to cross-easements and operating agreements.

Bowling Alleys

The popularity of bowling has waned. Like the furniture store, a bowling center is a large space user. Rental rates do not justify the inclusion of bowling, even in a regional center. A better investment for the bowling facility itself is a freestanding, single-tenant structure or an entertainment complex in an area outside the shopping center property.

Cinemas

The vogue in the cinema business is the multi-screen theater located in a freestanding building in a regional or community shopping center, with a seating capacity of 250, 350, or 400 in each auditorium and a common lobby, projection booth, and vending machines. Such theaters may also be part of the actual shopping center structure. Where the theater lobby opens directly onto the main pedestrian mall, the difference in operating hours between the theater and the stores may cause security problems. A benefit of the offset hours, however, is that the addition or inclusion of a movie theater does not require an increase in the number of parking spaces in the center.

The risk of overkill in theaters is reduced in shopping centers because successful centers are located within established market areas. The drawing power of the shopping center can provide a

3-27   Branch banks are most typically located in freestanding buildings. The major design problem is the avoidance of traffic circulation conflicts between bank users and shopping center customers. An important concern is sufficient room for drive-up window traffic.

good yardstick for the potential success of the cinema. In addition, the theater generates customer traffic through the shopping center before and sometimes after picture showings. Good bookings and active promotion are major factors in successful cinema operation. Revenue percentages from the theater's vending machines are included as part of the basis for determining the rental income paid to the center.

Gasoline Stations

With the pressures of the energy crisis and possible curtailment of gasoline consumption and sale, the long-term prospects of the gasoline station as a freestanding accessory tenant in the regional shopping center have become doubtful. The gasoline station is, however, one of the 20 most frequently found tenants in the neighborhood center. While it ranks 17th in the most recent survey, the gasoline station is probably found more often than this would suggest, since the survey does not take into account the corner service station site owned and developed independently of the shopping center.

The establishment of a new gasoline station is likely to be only marginally profitable for a shopping center development. Even so, until 1974, most community and regional shopping centers encouraged the service station to join the complex as a freestanding facility, either through an independent franchise operation or direct oil company land ownership or ground lease. One of the reasons for this encouragement was obviously that a gasoline and car service station provides an added convenience to shoppers and store employees. Department stores often value such a convenience for their customers; for this reason, they have ventured into gasoline service, either as a part of their TBA facilities or as a separate operation within the regional center.

There are two common types of lease agreements for service stations: fixed payment and variable payment. The fixed payment arrangement involves a flat monthly rental, whereas the variable payment is based on the monthly volume of gasoline sales. A typical rate under the variable payment arrangement is 1.25 cents per gallon for the land alone, with the tenant paying the cost of all improvements. The developer should keep in mind that gasoline sales at a shopping center station typically represent a higher proportion of gross service station revenues than they do at a station in an isolated commercial neighborhood, where services account for a larger share of total revenues.

Other lease arrangements are common: 1.5 cents per gallon or 5 percent of gross sales; 2 cents per gallon or $500 minimum per month, etc. (Six percent of gross sales is not as good as 2 cents per gallon.) Sometimes the tenant includes a declining rate provision in the variable payment rental; the per-gallon rate is reduced as sales exceed a specific level. For example, a station that pumps 60,000 gallons per month might pay 2.5 cents on each gallon up to 40,000 gallons and then 1.5 cents on the remaining gallonage. Like other leases, the variable gasoline station lease provides for a minimum rate which the tenant must pay even if his gallonage should drop. But with today's rapid changes in gasoline prices, the developer should insist on a lease which provides a percentage of total sales rather than a fixed gallonage rate. Most leases for service stations are actually contracts with an oil company, rather than with the individual station operator, because most gas station operators lease their stations from the oil company.

The location of the service station and the design relationship between the station and the shopping center have become important issues, especially in the neighborhood and community centers, where the service station has customarily sought a corner location with the remainder of the shopping center site wrapped around it. It is particularly important for the shopping center developer to maintain design control to keep the station design compatible with that of the main building mass. Cross-easements for joint access are also very important. Service station design and location have received a great deal of criticism; the developer may find that public approval for the shopping center will hinge on the proper design and location of the service station.

Other Establishments

Other possible nonretail uses are indoor tennis, ice skating, and other commercial-recreational enterprises. Such establishment within a center are possible if market conditions and planned arrangement of land uses justify multiuse installations. Both freestanding and integrated examples of these uses can be found.

Parking

The act of parking is the customer's first contact with the shopping center. The experience must be pleasant. The parking area must support the center's prime role—that of providing an attractive and convenient marketplace.

Parking is not a commercial use in itself, but it is an essential auxiliary to the commercial use in the center. Parking also ordinarily takes up more area than any other physical component of the center. And whether the parking is surface or structure, it must be carefully planned in any new project. Parking design requirements—parking area, driveway layout, access aisles, individual stall dimensions and arrangements, and the grading, paving, landscaping, and lighting of the parking surface—are major elements of the site planning process.

The chief concerns in providing the indispensable parking area are the number and best arrangement of the spaces. The problem is complicated when the off-street parking *area* requirements of a local zoning ordinance are not reasonably related to actual parking demand in the shopping center. When the parking area required by ordinance exceeds the demand, it becomes clear to center owners and tenants that actual number of spaces is a more suitable basis for measuring parking adequacy. Excessive zoning requirements also result in an expanse of unused pavement, causing both a poor appearance and a needless expense to the developer and the tenants.

Parking Standard

Parking demand at a shopping center, as compared with that of a freestanding store, is lightened by the fact that a customer visits several stores during a single shopping trip. Characteristics of multipurpose shopping, shared spaces, and rate of parking space turnover distinguish the parking requirements of shopping centers from those of freestanding commercial enterprises—a distinction not accounted for in zoning ordinances which establish fixed ratios of number of parking spaces to amount of building area for each commercial use.

Two terms are used to describe the relationship of parking provision to the shopping center structure:

Parking ratio is the site area assigned to parking use in relation to building area.

Parking index is the actual number of parking spaces per 1,000 square feet of GLA.

Parking ratio relates the *area* in parking to the area covered by building. Parking index counts the *number* of parking stalls.

For planning purposes and preliminary site evaluation, parking ratio serves as merely a useful tool for estimating the area needed for parking; it is *not* a suitable measurement for establishing parking standards. Parking ratio, when stated as 2 : 1 or 3 : 1, for example, is merely a convenience for making a preliminary estimate of the site's building and parking capacity; the number of spaces that will actually occupy this parking area depends on such variables as angle and size of car stalls, width of moving aisles and access drives, and the arrangement of other appurtenances of parking.

The area of retail selling space depends on tenant type, display of goods, method of selling, the number, size, and variety of items, and other variables. For this reason, selling space is an unsuitable unit for statistical comparisons of building area to parking provisions. But GLA is measurable. Furthermore, each tenant's GLA is stated in the lease document; GLA is thus a known and realistic factor for measuring the adequacy of parking provision in relation to retail use.

The generally accepted parking index for shopping centers is 5.5 spaces per 1,000 square feet of GLA. Based on 400 square feet per car, and taking both parking space and access driveways into account, the index is roughly equivalent to an area ratio of 2.2 square feet of parking area per square foot of building area. In other words, a 2.2 : 1 area ratio is a more appropriate formula for zoning ordinances than is a ratio of 3 : 1.

The study on which the standard is based shows that the standard parking index of 5.5 satisfies the demand for all shopping periods during a year, with the possible exception of 10 peak hours, or less than 0.5 percent of the total shopping hours in a year.[9] It is uneconomic to provide parking space for such limited peak demands. The standard includes parking spaces for employees and incorporates a reserve for traffic movement within the parking area. As a standard for the number of parking spaces needed in relation to tenant occupancy, the parking index is easy to apply. It does not require adjustments or explanations for area per car, parking patterns, car circulation, size and shape of the site, or other factors.

It should be mentioned, however, that the whole question of the standard parking index is currently being reexamined:

It is time to take a new look at the established parking standard for shopping centers, which has been 5.5 spaces per 1,000 square feet of gross leasable area (GLA) ever since TB 53, *Parking Requirements for Shopping Centers*, was published in 1965. This standard was appropriate for circumstances prevailing during the formative years of the shopping center industry, but conditions have changed materially over the past decade. Not only are there many more shopping centers today, but there is also a much greater variety of center types. Patterns of shopping activity have shifted, new land uses have been introduced into the center environment which do not conflict with peak parking demands of retail activity, and cars themselves are shrinking in size. Perhaps most significant of all, however, is the new awareness that land and energy resources are finite and that existing facilities must be more efficiently utilized than in the past. Viewed from this perspective, the traditional parking standard of 5.5 spaces per 1,000 square feet of GLA, which "accommodates the need for parking spaces at shopping centers for all but the ten highest hours of demand during the entire year," may provide an unrealistically high level of service.

This is the conclusion of Barton-Aschman Associates, Inc., which carried out a parking accumulation survey at 32 regional centers during the pre-Christmas shopping period in 1973, 1974, and 1975. During the 21-day data collection period, they found that ". . . less than eight percent of the daily parking accumulation counts exceeded or equaled the current standard of 5.5. Thirty-nine percent of the parking demand ratios determined fell between 4.0 and 5.0 and nearly 32 percent were less than 4.0." The average parking demand ratio for the 141 accumulation counts was 4.4, which should be adequate for most all but the 10 highest *days* of use. Keeping in mind that the survey was based on *days* of use rather than *hours* of use, the Barton-Aschman findings constitute major support for the view that the traditional standard might be excessive.

Based on information now available, it is not yet possible to definitively state what the appropriate new standard should be. But the direction of change is apparent, and perhaps a variable standard based upon such factors as center size and location might be appropriate. Even now, it can be stated that local governments should re-examine their zoning ordinances and parking requirements in the light of these findings and be prepared to respond with flexibility to proposed shopping center development projects.[10]

A center will generate an average of 40 trips per average day per 1,000 square feet of GLA. (A trip means one car in and one car out.) The range is 36

[9] *Parking Requirements for Shopping Centers*, ULI Technical Bulletin 53 (Washington, D.C.: ULI—the Urban Land Institute, 1965).

[10] *Land Use Digest*, Vol. 9, No. 9 (September 1976).

A New Parking System

By Roy P. Drachman

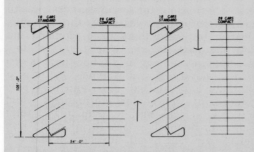

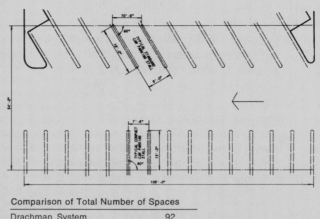

This plat shows the parking bay to be 54 feet, but the Drachman System will work in bays of only 50 feet in width with 60 degree angle spaces for standard cars. By using 45 degree angle spaces the width of the bay can be reduced to 48 feet.

Comparison of Total Number of Spaces

Drachman System	92
Normal System	72
Increase	20
Percentage Increase	29.16%

By simply restriping parking areas, owners and developers of shopping centers, office buildings, and other facilities can increase the number of car spaces by a minimum of 10 percent—in fact, it is possible that the number of cars can be increased by as much as 25 percent. With the high cost of land and the sizeable expenses involved in upkeep of parking areas, the more efficient use of parking facilities is of considerable interest to owners of commercial developments.

I have designed a new method for handling small cars in parking areas which has been successfully tested for six months at the Grossmont Regional Shopping Center in La Mesa, California. It is known as the Drachman System of Parking.

The rapidly growing trend for smaller automobiles points up the mistake being made by those owners and developers who have designed practically all the parking spaces in their parking facilities to accommodate only large cars.

There is no question that today the trend is towards small cars, compacts, or sub-compacts. Generally, the compact (Volkswagen as an example) has a "footprint" of 70 square feet. Many other small models have footprints of less than 70 square feet.

A survey made by George Devlin, president of National Planning Inc., a Detroit-based firm, showed that last spring 51 percent of all cars on California highways were compacts or sub-compacts —and that was before the current energy crisis struck with an even greater emphasis on smaller automobiles.

James Kelley, a Canadian developer and past president of the International Council of Shopping Centers, conducted a study on December 1, 1973 at the St. Lorentz Shopping Center in Ottawa, and found that during a four-hour period, 7,900 cars entered the parking areas at eight entrances. Forty-six hundred of these automobiles were compacts or smaller, totalling 58 percent. It is quite apparent that to have only large parking spaces, of which 40 or 50 percent are used by small cars, is a waste of land and money.

With this in mind, I developed my system of parking, which can be applied to any existing parking lot. If this system is used as the original design for a new center, the total area needed for parking can be reduced dramatically.

The main feature of this relatively simple system is the use of 90-degree angle spaces for small cars in the same bay where 45 or 60-degree spaces are provided for standard cars. The standard spaces are generally 8.5 feet or 9 feet by 18 feet, while the spaces for the compacts are 7.5 feet wide by 15 feet in length.

Since most parking bays are 50 to 55 feet wide, small cars can easily turn into the 90-degree spaces, but large cars cannot; not without backing at least once to maneuver the turn. Thus, few large cars get into small car spaces. This is particularly true on busy days when all spaces are well used.

While it is true there is nothing to keep drivers of small cars from using larger spaces, interviews with many compact-car drivers reveal they prefer to park next to other small cars because of the potential damage from large car doors.

Apparently there is a camaraderie among small-car owners that causes them to be careful about swinging their doors into adjacent autos. They fear large cars, particularly the station wagons with their wide doors and the usual number of careless children. This causes them to want to park among their own kind. We have found that 50-foot bays provide even more efficient use of the Drachman System because it becomes more difficult for the driver of a large car to make the 90-degree turn. Hal Logan, general manager and part owner of the Grossmont Center, marks all of the small spaces "compacts only."

One of the advantages of the Drachman System is that small-car drivers are not discriminated against by forcing them to park in some distant area. The spaces for compacts are distributed throughout the parking areas. In fact, because of the saving of land areas, all the spaces will be nearer the stores. This not only provides convenience for the shopper; it is beneficial to the developer as well.

3-28   The Drachman System of Parking (reprinted from *Urban Land,* September 1974).

to 56 trips. On a Saturday, the trips generated are 1.2 times the average daily rate. Daily turnover may be calculated for general purposes at 4 vehicles per space. The peak hour on access thoroughfares to a center occurs between 5 and 6 p.m., when the center generates only 2 trips per 1,000 square feet of GLA. Evening shopping peaks occur between 7 and 8 p.m. Peak traffic outflow occurs prior to closing, or between 8:30 and 9:30 p.m.[11]

The findings lead to the conclusions that off-street parking needs have been overestimated by shopping center developers, lenders, and tenants; and, in most zoning ordinances, the regulations for shopping center parking call for a substantially greater amount of parking spaces than is actually necessary.

As mentioned earlier in this chapter, office space can comprise as much as 20 percent of the center's GLA without a noticeable increase in peak parking demand; for greater GLA in office use, provision for parking may be calculated at one additional space for each 250 square feet of additional office area. A medical building generally requires six parking spaces per doctor, including one space for each doctor or technician.

Where there is a significant volume of walk-in trade, where a substantial proportion of the customers arrive by means of public transit, or where there are other mitigating circumstances such as strong competition, unusual size, limited trading area, or unusual arrays of those tenant classifications which have a consistently low parking requirement, *then* the parking index provision cited above should be reduced proportionately. The type of tenancy is a major determinant of parking space demand. A supermarket, for example, requires five times the parking space needed for a furniture store of equal size.

The size of American cars is changing. A 15½-foot compact length for nearly all domestic cars appears to be the direction in which car designs are headed. With the compact and subcompact as the dominant sizes, principles of parking space and layout should be restudied. When parking areas are specifically designed for a maximum car length of 15½ feet, rather than for the standard full-size American car, as many as 66 percent more cars can be parked in a given area. In 1973, 38 percent of all new cars sold in the United States (and 51 percent of all *registered* cars in California, a trend-setting state) were either compacts or subcompacts. Soon a 16-foot car will be in the luxury class. A California shopping center owner-developer reported that 42 percent of all cars on the parking areas of the shopping centers he controls were compacts. Similarly, a Canadian owner-developer found in 1973 that 58 percent of 7,900 cars entering his center's lot through any of eight entrances were compacts or subcompacts.

The increasing prevalence of smaller cars and the demand on car manufacturers for greater fuel economy mean that the wisdom of designing all parking spaces to accommodate full-size cars is questionable. By simply restriping, the capacity of parking areas of shopping centers, office buildings, and other facilities can be increased by 15 to 40 percent. With the high cost of land and the sizable expense involved in the upkeep of parking areas, owners of commercial developments should take considerable interest in the more efficient use of land and hence in a reduction in the size of parking facilities; if 40 to 50 percent of all parking spaces were redesigned for compact cars, storage capacity could be significantly increased without an attendant increase in lot area.

A relatively simple system of stall marking involves the use of 90-degree angles for small car spaces in the same bay where 45-degree or 60-degree spaces are provided for standard cars. The standard spaces are generally 8½ or 9 feet wide and 18 to 20 feet long, while the spaces for compacts are 7½ feet wide and 15½ feet long.[12]

Since most bays for angle parking are 50 to 55 feet wide, small cars can easily turn into the 90-degree spaces, but large cars cannot without backing at least once to maneuver the turn. Thus, few large cars go into small car spaces, especially on busy days, when most of the spaces are filled.

A self-policing system can also be established by marking spaces for compacts only. Sections of stalls for compacts can be distributed throughout the parking area, thus allowing all spaces equal convenience to the stores. Such an arrangement benefits the customer, the tenant, and the developer.

[11] From "Redevelopment Plan for the Bridgewater Regional Center," an unpublished report prepared in September 1973 for the Bridgewater (N.J.) Township Redevelopment Agency by Alan M. Voorhees & Associates and Economics Research Associates.

[12] The "Drachman System," an innovation of Roy P. Drachman, president of Roy Drachman Realty Company, Tucson, and trustee and past president of ULI. From Roy P. Drachman, "A New Parking System," *Urban Land*, Vol. 33, No. 8 (September 1974).

A number of factors affect parking demand and parking provision:

- Vehicle miles traveled to reach the center. If gasoline consumption is reduced, short travel distance (or convenience) becomes an important factor.
- Cost of fuel.
- Government regulations, such as those proposed under the Clean Air Act Amendments of 1970.
- Mass transit availability and cost.
- Walk-in trade.
- Size and type of center.
- Tenant composition.
- Total GLA.
- Character and income level of the trade area.
- Cost of land.

Layout

Ease of parking should be the guiding criterion for parking layout at any center. Parking at a shopping center must be simple, trouble-free, and safe. The shopper should be able to move through the parking area without prior knowledge of the layout.

A *parking bay* or *parking module* in a surface parking lot includes the driving aisle and the stalls on both sides. Aisles can also serve as pedestrian ways leading to the stores. Raised walks between the bays are unnecessary and expensive. In addition, such platforms interfere with sweeping and snow removal. Wheel stops also complicate mechanical cleaning operations. Only where parking spaces are adjacent to access driveways or where there are landscaped areas should wheel stops be introduced.

Access aisles should allow the shopper to walk directly toward, rather than parallel to, the building front. The maximum walking distance from a car to the stores should be 400 feet; try to limit the depth of parking from stores to 300 to 350 feet, except for employee parking areas.

Circulation for cars within the center should be continuous, preferably one-way and counterclockwise. A vehicle should also be able to maneuver within the site without entering a public highway. In a regional center, parking area circulation requires a belt roadway around the edge of the site and another around the building cluster. The inner belt allows for fire and emergency access and also for delivery and customer drop-off and pickup.

Main movement aisles are of two types—entrance and exit lanes, and belt lanes. Major aisles may allow for two-way movement. Minor aisles are one-way but need directional indicators, often a combination of arrows painted on the pavement and standing indicator signs.

Where there are several thousand car spaces, parking stalls should not be provided along the main aisles leading to the stores; this restriction eliminates congestion of access to the center. A surface parking facility of several thousand spaces should be divided into several sections for ready identification of parking location. Each of the divisions should contain a maximum of approximately 800 to 1,000 spaces.

For the convenience or neighborhood center, parking along the storefronts is a good arrangement. This design permits the convenience of quick visits to the stores and quick turnover of prime spaces. Here wheel stops, front bumper guards, or extended curb lines are required to prevent the intrusion of car fronts into the canopied walkway.

At one time, truck tunnels were commonly used at regional mall centers to separate shoppers and freight delivery. The economics of the truck tunnel, however, are now prohibitive. Instead, the enclosed mall center either schedules most deliveries for nonshopping hours or provides a screened or walled truck delivery court from which a group of stores can serviced.[13]

In general, shopping center traffic circulation is an area which requires the advice of a qualified parking or traffic consultant.

Patterns

There are two patterns for surface parking layouts: perpendicular and angular. Perpendicular or 90-degree parking combines economy of space with ease of circulation. It also offers the advantage of two-way movement through the aisle, as well as the safety of better sight lines, greater parking capacity, and shorter cruising distances. By contrast, angular parking spaces, with either 45-degree or 60-degree angles, are easier for the driver to swing into with one motion. Angle parking also requires the safer but perhaps less convenient one-way circulation, and it permits a lesser width of parking module.

---

[13] See *Guidelines for Planning and Designing Access Systems for Shopping Centers*, prepared by Technical Council Committee 5-DD, Institute of Traffic Engineers (Arlington, Va., 1976).

Source: Richard F. Roti & Associates, parking consultants.

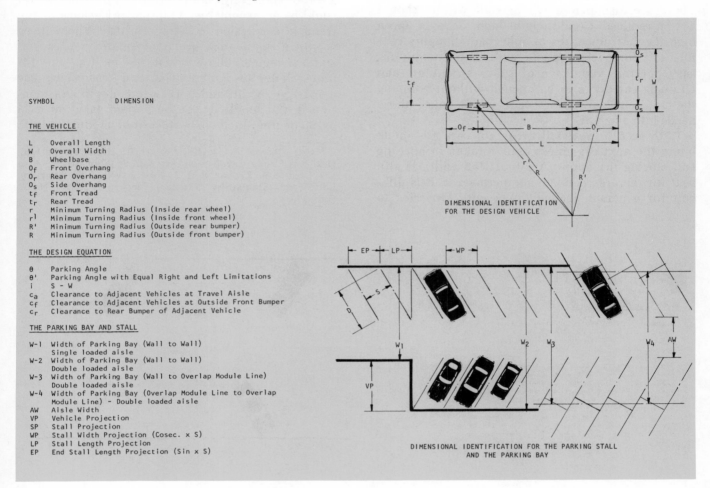

SYMBOL   DIMENSION

THE VEHICLE

L   Overall Length
W   Overall Width
B   Wheelbase
O_f Front Overhang
O_r Rear Overhang
O_s Side Overhang
t_f Front Tread
t_r Rear Tread
r   Minimum Turning Radius (Inside rear wheel)
r^1 Minimum Turning Radius (Inside front wheel)
R^1 Minimum Turning Radius (Outside rear bumper)
R   Minimum Turning Radius (Outside front bumper)

THE DESIGN EQUATION

θ Parking Angle
θ^1 Parking Angle with Equal Right and Left Limitations
i   S - W
c_a Clearance to Adjacent Vehicles at Travel Aisle
c_f Clearance to Adjacent Vehicles at Outside Front Bumper
c_r Clearance to Rear Bumper of Adjacent Vehicle

THE PARKING BAY AND STALL

W-1   Width of Parking Bay (Wall to Wall)
       Single loaded aisle
W-2   Width of Parking Bay (Wall to Wall)
       Double loaded aisle
W-3   Width of Parking Bay (Wall to Overlap Module Line)
       Double loaded aisle
W-4   Width of Parking Bay (Overlap Module Line to Overlap
       Module Line) - Double loaded aisle
AW   Aisle Width
VP   Vehicle Projection
SP   Stall Projection
WP   Stall Width Projection (Cosec. x S)
LP   Stall Length Projection
EP   End Stall Length Projection (Sin x S)

DIMENSIONAL IDENTIFICATION
FOR THE DESIGN VEHICLE

DIMENSIONAL IDENTIFICATION FOR THE PARKING STALL
AND THE PARKING BAY

The dilemma over perpendicular or diagonal parking is best solved by using the pattern that generally prevails in the community and that is best adapted to the particular site conditions. Each surface parking layout must be evaluated for circulation of pedestrians between the parked cars and the stores, for circulation of drivers moving in and out of the parking area or looking for a vacant space, and for use of space. Angle parking is used more widely across the nation than is perpendicular parking.

For perpendicular parking, the standard bay is 65 feet deep, comprising two stalls, each 20 feet deep, and a center aisle of 25 feet to allow for two-way circulation. The standard stall has a width of 9 feet.

Where 45-degree parking is used, the minimum bay width is 50 feet with a one-way aisle. With a two-way aisle, the bay increases to 60 feet in depth.

It is now entirely feasible to introduce two bay widths—one for small cars and the other for full-size cars. The compact car, with a footprint of less than 100 square feet, can easily be parked in a 75-degree or 90-degree stall, with a 48½-foot bay composed of two 15-foot stall depths and one 18½-foot aisle for one-way movement. Stall widths may be reduced from 9 feet to 7½ feet for small cars or to 8¾ feet for large cars without greatly diminishing the convenience to which customers have become accustomed over the years. Making this reduction will result in a surface space savings of about 16 percent in the small car section and about 7 percent in the large car section. To ensure this parking area economy, however, small car sections should still be designated to provide for self-policing by parkers.

Stalls

There are also places where stall widths should not be reduced. Conditions of high turnover and a high level of amenities at suburban shopping centers call for parking stalls with ample width for easy parking, avoidance of space straddling, and allowing car doors to be opened without bumping the adjacent car. The 9-foot width takes these needs into account.

With an 8½-foot stall, two-door cars are apt to bump the next car unless care is taken in opening and closing the doors. A 9-foot stall width is still best for the area close to a supermarket. It is difficult for a person loaded down with groceries to maneuver into a car parked with less room. While a 9-foot stall width is preferred, an 8¾-foot width could be an acceptable compromise because of the trend in car design to 6-foot widths. Where there is still a dominance of large American cars and station wagons, allow 9-foot stall widths and 18-foot stall depths. For compacts and foreign cars, use a 7½-foot width and a 15½-foot depth. As mentioned, the small car can be parked easily at a 75 or 90-degree angle in a 48½-foot module.[14] Still,

[14] See George A. Devlin, "New Directions in Parking Design," *Urban Land*, Vol. 34, No. 5 (May 1975). Also see George E. Kanaan and David K. Witheford, "Parking Lot Design Standards," *Traffic Quarterly*, Vol. 27, No. 3 (July 1793).

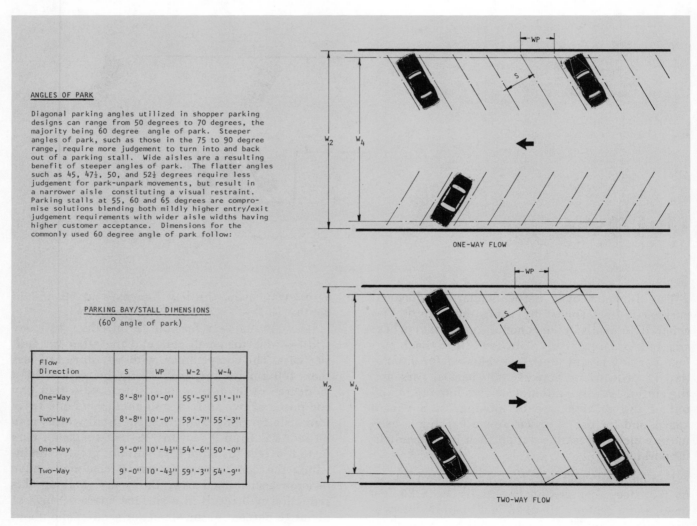

ANGLES OF PARK

Diagonal parking angles utilized in shopper parking designs can range from 50 degrees to 70 degrees, the majority being 60 degree angle of park. Steeper angles of park, such as those in the 75 to 90 degree range, require more judgement to turn into and back out of a parking stall. Wide aisles are a resulting benefit of steeper angles of park. The flatter angles such as 45, 47½, 50, and 52½ degrees require less judgement for park-unpark movements, but result in a narrower aisle constituting a visual restraint. Parking stalls at 55, 60 and 65 degrees are compromise solutions blending both mildly higher entry/exit judgement requirements with wider aisle widths having higher customer acceptance. Dimensions for the commonly used 60 degree angle of park follow:

PARKING BAY/STALL DIMENSIONS
(60° angle of park)

Flow Direction	S	WP	W-2	W-4
One-Way	8'-8"	10'-0"	55'-5"	51'-1"
Two-Way	8'-8"	10'-0"	59'-7"	55'-3"
One-Way	9'-0"	10'-4½"	54'-6"	50'-0"
Two-Way	9'-0"	10'-4½"	59'-3"	54'-9"

ONE-WAY FLOW

TWO-WAY FLOW

3-30 PARKING GEOMETRICS
Source: Richard F. Roti & Associates, parking consultants.

the convenience of having a parking space available is a greater consideration for any shopper than comfort in maneuvering in and out of the parked car.

Where the 9-foot stall width must be used, a 4-inch-stripe hairpin or looped line painted on the pavement surface is a good space indicator. The hairpin or looped line (16 inches between lines) is preferred over straight-line striping because it acts as a psychological aid in keeping cars within the allotted spaces and in keeping equal spaces between cars. In any case, all space markers should be painted; a button divider system is difficult to change if the parking pattern needs alteration. The length of parking stalls is of less operational interest than width, since compensation for a short stall can be made by aisle width, and since parkers tend not to pull all the way into the stall. Nevertheless, stall length must be determined in order to calculate space requirements.

Appearance and Construction

Parking areas must have a substantial sub-base and be well drained and must be paved. (Blacktop is the most common paving material.) Parking areas need such amenities as screening, landscaping, and lighting. They must be maintained to prevent potholes from developing and to keep litter from accumulating. Stalls must be clearly marked.

Where there is enough land or where land cost is not prohibitive, trees can be introduced in wells to avoid an otherwise barren appearance. However, trees must be protected from cars and from accumulations of salt and snow in colder climates. Landscaping intermediate spots in the parking area not only requires an initial expenditure but also adds extra maintenance costs to the shopping center management and thus increases the common area charges paid by the tenants. The aesthetic benefit derived, however, is of unmeasurable value.

3-31   This parking structure combines precast and poured-in-place concrete construction. Pedestrian skyways lead to the retail portion of the complex.

Surface parking is part of the open space at a shopping center. As such, through landscaping, it can become one of the amenity features of the commercial setting. Shopping center open space includes the parking area, malls, pedestrian ways, buffer areas, and all other parts of the site not covered by buildings, except for the access drives and uncovered service courts. The landscaping treatment of parking areas and of shopping center open space in general should aim for tastefulness and durability of design. Ground cover, shrubs, and bushes, massed at appropriate places on the site, and occasional trees in wells or clusters are suitable landscape provisions. Landscaping elements should be designed in such a way that they do not interfere with parking, parking area maintenance, or snow removal. Plantings should be hardy, easily maintained, and capable of thriving in the local climate.[15]

Depressing the parking level at any center by about 2 feet, in order to bring the tops of the cars below eye level from adjacent public streets, will increase the feeling of openness by allowing a line of view from the street to the store frontage. Berms constructed at the perimeter of the parking area can also improve the appearance of the center from adjacent streets and properties. These berms, either along public streets or between the various parking sections, can also be used as landscaping features.

Proper maintenance of the parking area is essential. Matters of policing, cleanup, night lighting, and orderly use cannot be ignored. Maintenance requires attention by the management organization and proportioned reimbursement by the tenants.

Employee Parking

Employees are all-day parkers and may be allotted stall widths of 8 feet. Employees cannot be allowed to occupy prime parking spaces that are needed for customers. If employees are not restricted in where they park, they may occupy customer spaces that should be turning over four or five times during a shopping day.

At best, employee parking is hard to control. Regulation is usually covered in a lease provision. The lease should provide that the landlord has the right to:

- Designate number and location of employee parking places.
- Receive, on request, the car license numbers of tenant employees.

- Cancel the lease if the tenant does not cooperate.
- Charge the tenant a specified amount per day for each employee car parked outside the designated area.

In practice, it may be difficult to achieve such ideal provisions.

In a strip convenience center, employee parking is best placed at the rear of the stores. A minimum width of 40 feet will be required for a combination rear service area and employee parking area. This will allow one row of cars and a driveway along the rear property line. A better arrangement is to provide a width of 60 feet, permitting the rear service area to function better as a truck delivery drive and parking area. The rear setback must be increased where space along the back property line is needed for planting as a buffer between the stores and adjacent residences. Or, if site area is at a premium, a screening wall can be placed on the property line.

In other types of centers, a special employee

---

[15] See J. Ross McKeever, *Shopping Center Zoning*, ULI Technical Bulletin 69 (Washington, D.C.: ULI—the Urban Land Institute, 1973). Also see *Maintenance and Repair of Asphalt Paved Parking Lots* (New York: International Council of Shopping Centers, 1975).

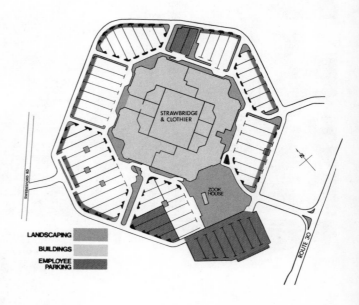

3-32 At Exton Square Mall in Exton, Pennsylvania, employee parking spaces have been placed outside the site's internal ring road.

parking area should be assigned and the requirements for employee parking enforced. In these centers, employee parking areas should be placed at the outer edge of the site, where they will not interfere with the more desirable parking spaces closer to the stores. In failing to designate special employee parking areas, a center may find its employees consistently occupying the spaces closest to the stores or filling the surrounding streets to the annoyance of neighbors. In some cities an ordinance permits the landlord, on signed complaint, to have the police ticket the car for a substantial fine or haul the car to a police impounding lot, thus causing the car owner to pay an even larger fine.

Value of a Parking Stall

It is often useful to place a value on each parking stall to indicate its relationship to the sales volume of the center once the center is in operation and once the parking demand has reached the capacity of the center's parking area. The value of a parking space can be determined by dividing the total annual sales volume of all tenants by the number of parking spaces. In a regional center with total sales of $75,000,000 and 5,000 parking spaces, for example, the value of a parking space is equal to $15,000 in annual sales.

If employees park their cars in the most convenient spaces, they are holding up stalls that should be generating retail sales. Employee parking at a neighborhood center, for example, can be analyzed this way: Assuming each parking space is known to generate $18,400 in annual sales and assuming 160 spaces are needed for employees, the sales loss —if employees occupy prime spaces and thereby drive away trade—could be almost $3,000,000. The employee parking problem can also be analyzed as follows: At an average rent percentage of 4 percent, an additional $120,000 in net rent could be produced from these spaces. At 6 percent return, this would produce $2,000,000. Each employee car space, capitalized at 6 percent, can be valued at $12,266.

To arrive at a parking stall and unit sales ratio, H. J. Logan, C.S.M., of Grossmont Center in San Diego, offers the following formula: Anticipate annual sales volume of the center. Assume customer sales of $5.50 to $7.50 per customer. Assume 1.5 customers per car. Adjust for number of turnovers per space. Use 300 business days per year. Result: the sales volume in relation to the number of parking spaces.

Commuter Parking

As more shopping centers receive the benefits of mass transit access, thus reducing parking demand, there is the likelihood of a problem of commuter parking occupying parking space designed to serve the shopping center patrons. This will be particularly true where the bus routes that serve the center also serve employment centers. The figures given above for the value of a parking space are clearly indicative of the economic issues. Private shopping center developers should not be expected to provide public parking lots for commuters. Like employee parking, this will be difficult to police and will require the cooperation of the community.

Where local laws will allow ticketing, the parking lots can be time-limited and tickets can be issued. Where this is not possible, private policing of the lots during the morning rush hour period may be the only solution. However, the shopping center developer also needs to be perceived as a good neighbor in the community, and a very tough control of commuter parking may result in negative feelings in the community toward the center in general and may in turn result in loss of business. Where excess land is available and where a parking conflict exists, it may be possible to lease a designated portion of the site to the transit authority for transit parking for at least the cost of maintenance and repair. Requests for tax abatement may also be possible. In the final analysis, parking in shopping centers is private parking for customers, and the developer must protect this use right to the extent that other uses would be detrimental to the center's operations.

Parking and Taxes

In some cities, the assessor values land used exclusively for parking purposes at the same rate as land used for business. In these cities, shopping center parking bears an inequitable tax load. Where commitments are made for the continued use of designated areas for parking, such as at shopping centers, the calculation for tax purposes should be adjusted to the restricted use of the parking area.

While it is true that parking areas contribute substantially to the success of a center, it is also true that this success is reflected in the higher taxable value of the land and structures occupied by the business use, as well as the value of the business itself. As the shopping center's parking area itself is not a *direct* revenue producer, its valuation for tax purposes should be based on its use as parking,

3-33 Structured parking at Northridge Fashion Center in Northridge, California.

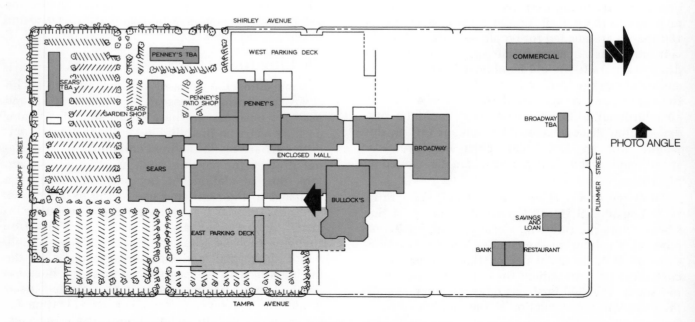

3-34 Site plan for Northridge Fashion Center. Arrow indicates photo angle of Figure 3-33.

not on its business use. Municipalities can follow this practice with good results. The valuation can also be based on acreage rather than on square feet. However, where real estate taxes on parking areas are included in common area maintenance charges paid by tenants, loading the taxes on the buildings to relieve the tax load on the parking area may actually impose an undue burden on the owner, rather than relieving him of an economic inequity. In addition, an income approach to value is used in some jurisdictions; land and building are not valued separately but rather as parts of a single package.

Parking Decks

To avoid excessive walking distances between the parked car and the store in regional centers and to solve parking space problems that may be created by a shopping center's development or by its expansion program (when a new department store is added after the original construction, for example) a self-operated parking structure can be built.

In many already constructed centers, adjacent land for parking area expansion either is not available or has become so costly that a structure or parking deck is a cheaper way of providing additional parking spaces. The structured spaces are closer to the stores, and depreciation can be taken on the parking structure, whereas it cannot be on land.

A parking deck has further advantages. When compact cars enter the facility, they can easily be channeled to compact spaces. Less space per car can be assigned because islands and other aesthetic appurtenances are eliminated. However, a parking garage also requires the provision of a ramp system, overhead clearances, column spacing, and ventilation for those parts of the structure which are below grade, although an entrance magazine—a temporary storage area for cars waiting to be parked—is not needed in a self-operated parking deck.

The multideck parking structure is particularly adaptable to sloping sites, where direct entrance to each level of the stores can be provided. For double-level or triple-level shopping centers, entrances can also lead from each level of the parking deck to the center.

Parking decks will appear in many areas because of the increased value of the land around a shopping center. Parking may also no longer be the highest and best use for expanses of ground near large retail centers. Other uses, such as hotels, office buildings, clinics, additional department stores, and commercial recreational facilities may be built on land now given over to surface parking; this means that present parking and any additional parking would be provided in structures.

The point at which a developer determines that he should build a deck for additional parking rather than buy more ground is the point at which the value of the land he would have to acquire exceeds the cost of construction of the parking deck. Present (1976) construction costs are somewhere around $8.00 per square foot, depending on the section of the country, building costs, and other factors. (In 1968, such costs averaged $5.50 per square foot.) Should land prices and construction costs rise to a point where the provision of free parking at a shopping center is no longer economical, developers may be forced either to charge customers a fee for parking or to turn parking areas over to the municipality for parking meter installation and public maintenance.

Security is a problem to consider in parking decks. Misfortunes to patrons range from vandalism and car theft to mugging and rape. Television monitoring equipment and adequate lighting can help prevent such incidents.

Summary—Parking

The factors which must be considered in providing parking for the shopping center vary in degree and extent according to type of center, location, tenancy, and trade area characteristics. In general, the parking arrangement depends on such amenity and convenience factors as the following:

- Site potential or parking spaces needed in relation to the GLA of the retail structure. The current standard index of 5.5 spaces per 1,000 square feet of GLA has proven satisfactory in most centers.
- Shape of the site and positioning of the buildings. These factors determine the necessary layout.
- Direction of traffic flow to the site, and volume in each direction, as well as any outside treatment needed for left turns or acceleration or deceleration lanes for entering and leaving the large center.
- Entrance and exit points; stackup lanes of adequate length to avoid congestion of periphery streets or on-site parking aisles. Exits should parallel entrances wherever possible, with exit lanes separated from entrance lanes by dividers or planters.

- Circulation within the site—outer perimeter and along the storefronts—for pedestrians, automobiles, buses, and emergency vehicles.
- Separation of customer and truck service traffic, when possible.
- Walking distance from the parking stall to the store (400 feet is the recommended maximum).
- A balanced parking area load according to individual tenant requirements.
- Adequate storm drainage allowance; a 3 percent grade assures good drainage into catch basins. Apply a high quality of surface and seal coat over a well-compacted subgrade.
- Width and angle of the parking stall; direction of movement through the aisles; ease of parking. Rely on painted lines and arrows and standing signs to control parking. Looped lines are preferred as stall indicators.
- Landscaping to break up the sea of asphalt paving and to generally improve the center's appearance.
- Economic factors, such as land cost, real estate taxes, operating costs, and escalator provisions in tenant leases to provide for maintenance of the parking area through common area charges to tenants.
- Lighting by use of moderate-height illumination standards, with the glow of perimeter lights cast away from any nearby residences to prevent annoyance.
- Use of bumpers or wheel stops only where unavoidable, in order to ease cleaning and snow removal operations.
- A straight driving lane of at least 100 feet at all important entrances of a large center. These straight driveways are needed to avoid turns by arriving parkers as well as the blocking of entrances, and can also serve as stacking lanes for cars leaving the center.

4.
Architectural and Engineering Design

The Architect's Task

The shopping center is an architectural challenge. The structure must house the business of retailing, the site must accommodate the parking of automobiles, and the building and site treatment must provide customer appeal and convenience while satisfying the tenants and compensating the owner. The whole concept calls for an architectural quality compatible with a specific environment—the type of center and its location, site topography, and building pattern. Achieving this quality also requires melding the principles of good planning, landscaping, architectural design, and engineering with skillful merchandising, public relations, and management. Compromises are made between what can be afforded and what may be left out, but the finished center must be an appealing and convenient place to shop; it must be a marketplace which meets the needs of its trade area. Only then can it be profitable for the community, the tenants, and the owner.

The architect's task, then, is special. The architect must conceive a design that achieves a general harmony of style while permitting a reasonable variation for tenant emphasis, all within the framework mentioned above. These requirements mean

that the architect-planner must blend his skills with those of other experts on the developer's team. This coordination of effort is necessary in designing a regional mall, but it is even more important for the smaller center, where an absence of applied skills has often resulted in a poor or mediocre appearance. In looking at the general run of strip centers, it is easy to see why the public considers many of them unsightly. A hodgepodge of materials, a lack of taste in signing, and an absence of architectural merit often combine to produce the visual pollution of the center.

Before a shopping center can be designed, the type of center, its key tenant types, and the general array of space for the tenants must be known. The developer's decisions and commitments affect the structural framework, particularly when an enclosed mall or special building cluster is intended. Just as the exterior design treatment is dictated by the size, shape, and location of the property, so the placement and grouping of tenants within the structure is based on the leasing or merchandising plan.

Decisions about mall configuration, structural framing, and mechanical equipment alternatives within the limits of cost should be made before ex-

4-1 The shopping center, a specialized environment for retail trade, presents a design challenge to the architect. These complexes are one of the most rapidly evolving forms of land use.

terior architecture is decided upon. The basic structure, especially for the straightforward enclosed and air-conditioned mall center, is similar to the framework of a well-constructed warehouse. Sophistication may come through an optional use of computer models that provide quick comparative analyses of various structural and systems alternatives.

Unless the center will have a basement, the foundation requires simple excavations for column footings and for grade beams to support bearing walls. A flat built-up roof over a long span joist roof design allows the wide spacing of load-bearing columns to provide as much flexibility as possible in individual store widths and depths. Building depths vary between 125 and 150 feet, although many shops may be no more than 40 to 60 feet deep, with the rear space designed to serve either as storage area or as overlap area for deeper adjacent units.

In addition to the structural and interior design controls imposed on the architect by the character and tenant makeup of the particular project, ex-

ternal controls are imposed by public response to conditions of the current era. For example, the growing concern with environmental and ecological matters means that building and site designs must harmonize with the community's character more than ever before. And in the long run, the "energy crisis" may have as much bearing on shopping center design as does site location. Energy-saving measures are being incorporated in the enclosed mall. A change can be made, for example, from rooftop air conditioners for each tenant to the use of chilled water circulated from a central plant, or to a hybrid system. Instead of untreated glass over central areas, translucent double Plexiglas sandwich panels and north clerestory lighting are being substituted. Buildings are being oriented for solar heating and cooling. Display windows on exterior walls are being eliminated or are being installed only where they face north or east. Other changes include greater insulation to reduce loss or gain of heat through skin materials (walls and roofs), automatic cycle lighting, and a decreased use of intensive heat-producing lighting systems with a corresponding increase in the use of paired-up sodium lamps instead of metal arc lamps of the same wattage. Graphics are being improved through the use of illuminated identification signs with black letters silhouetted on a light background, instead of brilliant self-lighted lettering. Energy-saving devices and innovative design techniques are limited only by the ingenuity and resourcefulness of architects, designers, and engineers.

Shopping center developers and designers must also deal with inflation as a force which is changing the "traditional" pattern of shopping center development. An attractive material or a construction technique requiring significant amounts of specialized labor may become too expensive. The architect's job will be to find new materials and new methods that will allow an equally attractive appearance at affordable costs.

It has always been important to achieve good building efficiency, but today's rising costs make this imperative. The design solution should maximize the leasable space and minimize those nonleasable spaces that are not required for customer use. With rising land costs, an inefficient parking layout is intolerable. With labor costs rising faster than income, an interior or exterior that has high maintenance requirements cannot be allowed.

However, maximum space at minimum cost is not the logical conclusion to these concerns. To be successful, a shopping center must be attractive

4-2 Split-faced masonry, brick, and metal panels were used to create the facade of Fairlane Town Center, Dearborn, Michigan. Entrances are distinguished by carefully articulated architectural massings.

and pleasant for the customer. The lack of quality in the finished appearance will surely project itself to the customer, thus reducing the earning capacity of the center.

Exterior Features
Building Materials

The exterior facing materials used in any center are one of the major determinants of the center's visual image. That image, which establishes the special identity of the particular center, must be one of harmony tempered by tasteful variation in selected details. A hodgepodge appearance must obviously be avoided, but the need for a unified exterior treatment should not be confused with the need, in some cases, to create distinctive images through the use of more than one major material. Criteria for the selection of materials include durability, ease of maintenance, waterproofing and insulation qualities, local availability, speed of assembly and erection, and, of course, appearance.

Masonry is an excellent external material. It offers the greatest flexibility in treatment and design variety by structured course work. Site casting of tilt-up wall sections allows for speedier construction, as does the use of other precast concrete wall panels, provided the production plant is within reasonable hauling distance of the site.

Metal panels are constantly being improved and are becoming more and more practicable for such uses as the shopping center. In some areas, wood which has been treated for weather exposure can readily be adapted for use in neighborhood and convenience centers.[1]

In an enclosed mall center, details of exterior architectural design are most important for emphasizing entrances to the center. A change of material or roof height, or a wall extension or indention, may be introduced to identify the entrances and to give them a distinctive appearance.

---

[1] See Louis G. Redstone, *New Dimensions in Shopping Centers and Stores* (New York: McGraw-Hill, 1973).

4-3 A canopied arcade shelters customers and contributes to the attractive appearance of Trailwood Shopping Center in Overland Park, Kansas. This neighborhood center is a project of the J. C. Nichols Company.

Canopies

For nonenclosed mall centers, the colonnaded walk or arcade is the traditional means of sheltering customers and weather-protecting the storefronts. In such conventional shopping centers, covered walkways are essential not only for inclement weather but also for enjoyable shopping in any kind of weather. The walkway may be glass-enclosed and air-conditioned where the temperature is uncomfortably high or low during most of the year; such a treatment is particularly suitable for a strip-type neighborhood or community center. Experience has shown that 12 to 15 feet is a good width for the enclosed walkway.

Canopies may be either cantilevered from the building wall or supported by freestanding columns or pillars. Width and height of the canopy will be determined by the proportions proper to the architectural style. With a canopy higher than 12 feet, the building wall below provides an ideal placement surface for signs. Such a design supports the architectural quality of the center and helps in the overall program of sign control.

When canopies are placed along building facades in nonenclosed malls, window shopping and window displays become important inducements to impulse buying and general price comparisons by shoppers. Furthermore, customers are free to view the merchandise displays without having to explain that they are "just looking." Canopies increase the attractiveness of wide window displays.

4-4 Landscaping can be used to develop a visual buffer. At the site shown here, the topography allowed the parking area to be depressed, thus screening cars from street view.

Windows also may be scaled to feature spot displays suited to certain kinds of shops. Mullion windows are suitable only when part of a period type of architectural style.

Landscaping

The image of the shopping center has been badly damaged by some past performances. In exposing a barren expanse of parking lot pavement to public

4-5   Landscape design should incorporate areas for bicycle parking, trash receptacles, and benches and other pieces of street furniture.

view, some centers have created the appearance of a sea of asphalt which has been universally considered unattractive. As mentioned in the last chapter, a surface parking lot is part of the shopping center's open space, and, when properly designed and landscaped, it can become one of the center's amenity features.

Landscaping within a parking area should generally be confined to trees and massed plantings in wells or in clearly defined planting areas. Landscaping elements should be placed where they will not interfere with the act of parking, parking area maintenance, or snow removal. In the provisions of site plan approval, under the zoning and building permit clearance documents, landscaping and landscaping specifications should be discussed as permissive rather than mandatory matters, although a total landscaping expenditure of 1 to 3 percent of total building costs is an acceptable requirement, depending on the size and character of the center. A performance standard approach will

allow creative design, whereas mandatory expenditures or specifications would place a cost burden on the developer but not necessarily result in well-conceived landscaping. Zoning requirements usually call for landscaping of parking lot boundaries and property line buffer strips. Zoning provisions which specify a percentage of total site area for landscape treatment, however, or which specify the placement, type, or diameter of trees are often overstepping the bounds of guarding the public welfare. Although the initial cost imposed by such requirements may seem insignificant, the developer must also consider the long-term maintenance costs of any landscaped areas.

Where a shopping center—usually of the neighborhood type—is to be located on a site close to a built-up residential area, more substantial buffers can be introduced to insulate the nearby residences. A planting strip, perhaps 20 feet wide, may be used for high, dense foliage, or, where planting is not practical, masonry walls or attractive fences may be provided.

4-6   Landscaping is also used as a key design element inside the shopping center. Here, full-grown trees line the mall.

Effective border treatment is an environmental amenity.[2] However, care must be taken that neither the location nor the height of landscaping features blocks sight lines necessary for the safety of drivers. As discussed in the previous chapter, hardy ground covers, shrubs, and bushes massed at appropriate places within the buffers are appropriate landscaping features, as are trees in wells.

Landscaping and its installation and maintenance are part of the expense of shopping center operation. Plantings and seasonal floral displays in appropriate places inside the center add greatly to customer appeal. In a mall layout, plantings, water displays, and sculptures can transform an interior pedestrian space into a community attraction and a gathering place for suitable community events.

Signing

The simplest way to define good signing is that it should be an integral part of the building design. The shopping center's graphics are the proper prov-

ince of the architect, who must achieve a design which prevents visual pollution. The services of a graphic designer are commonly used, but this should not relieve the architect of the task of creating a building design that provides well-designed locations for signage. These two professionals must work closely together from the early design preliminaries.

Sign regulation is an important part of shopping center management policy. In fact, the shopping center industry has led the way in sign control. Sign approval is one of the conditions included in the tenant's lease, and the developer's private control of the style and size of signs is often more severe than municipal regulations would be. Insisting on uniformity of scale, size, and placement is a worthwhile and important practice.

Offenders in shopping centers where signing lacks taste or restraint include not only local

[2] See Gary O. Robinette, *Plants, People, and Environmental Quality* (Washington, D.C.: National Park Service, U.S. Department of the Interior, 1972).

4-7 Tenants in early centers insisted on signs that could be read from the street. While the building design provided a standard location for signs, there was little design control of the signs themselves. Furthermore, a canopy often prevented customers on the sidewalk from seeing the signs, and in most cases no below-canopy signs were installed.

tenants but also the national and local chain merchants who use individual trademark signs. Department stores as well have logos and other special lettering forms, and these, too, must be coordinated with the overall design of exterior graphics.

Shopping center signing is typically subject to a municipality's sign control ordinance, which also governs conventional business and commercial districts. Unfortunately, such regulations—having been designed to control signs on individual business properties—are rarely suitable for application to a shopping center. Sign regulations are among the most controversial aspects of zoning law, and there are those who would argue that the legal basis for such regulation is debatable, since sign design control is an aesthetic consideration. Nevertheless, signing regulations which include design as well as size and locational criteria have been upheld in the courts and must be taken into account when establishing the center's program of graphic design.[3]

[3] See William R. Ewald, Jr., and Daniel R. Mandelker, *Street Graphics: A Concept and a System* (Washington, D.C.: American Society of Landscape Architects Foundation, 1971). *Street Graphics* is the most useful available guide to the appropriate provisions and administration of sign control ordinances.

4-8 Directional signs are also important.

4-9 Signs should be an integral part of building design.

Where a concept for signing has been developed as a special element of the architectural design, the developer may find the zoning authorities receptive to a carefully prepared signing program which deviates from the sign control ordinance, especially since the ordinance was very likely written to control the signing of single-purpose structures rather than shopping centers. The city can assist the developer by enforcing the approved program, thus relieving the developer of the need to negotiate with tenants who have very specific signing ideas which may be inconsistent with the developer's overall sign concept.

The businessman wants to be easily identified by the customer in the shopping center environment. He wants to be just as readily identified as his competitors. Finally, he wants that which identifies him and his goods and services to be uniquely his. But it has been found that where *all* signs in the center are required to conform to the same guidelines of size and style, each tenant is more amenable to the restrictions imposed on his signing. The conclusion to be drawn is that when graphic controls are uniformly applied, shopkeepers no longer feel that they must erect signs that are larger or more dazzling than those of their neighbors and competitors. In fact, proprietors in well-controlled shopping centers often find that their sales actually increase while their expenditure for signs is considerably reduced. These merchants discover not

4-10 Sign control inside the mall can be used to create a unifying design element.

4-11 A distinctive pylon identifies Winrock Center, Albuquerque. Pylons are an optional element in contemporary shopping centers, useful as an attractive architectural statement, but not a good means of advertising.

only that they are able to retain their individual identities within the framework of such controls, but also that they become identified with the shopping center as a whole—an entity that is larger and more memorable than any of the individual stores which comprise it.

In this respect, the shopping center has a great advantage over a single store on a downtown street or in a detached commercial strip location, because the developer of a well-managed center can insist on his own design and sign control. The shopping center normally does not need a pylon sign for visibility and identification. A well-designed center identification sign is acceptable, but the illuminated pylon sign commonly found in older centers often does not conform in taste to the shopping center concept.

Developers favor sign control by a declaration of permitted and prohibited signage as well as an approval clause in each tenant's lease. Such declarations forbid roof signs and large projecting signs and favor placement at a certain level on, above, or below a canopy, depending on the architectural treatment. The common feature for both public and private sign control regulations is the prohibition of moving or flashing parts.

Experience with sign control has shown that neat signing is appreciated immediately by the public and eventually by the merchants in the center, although the merchants often are initially reluctant to go along with the controls. As mentioned, the enforcement of uniformity is more difficult with trademark signs, but a compromise can usually be worked out which is compatible with the center's own specifications for color and lighting.

The problem is minimized when the architectural design of the center incorporates the details of size, style, location, and lighting of signs. Effectiveness of design depends on the designer's skill in achieving uniformity in character without necessarily requiring uniformity in typography. Specifications should be established by the center management, and permitted placement of signs should be spelled out and presented as a lease exhibit. If neon is permitted at all, uniformity of color of the neon signs is essential.

Developers may go so far—and many do—as to prohibit the use of paper or paste-on window signs. Many developers keep control of all signs, permanent or temporary, which are visible either through show windows or through store entrances.

4-12 Exterior signs can be used to lead the customer to restaurants and other special retail destinations.

Night Lighting

Exterior lighting is necessary for public protection and safety at any parking facility. Lighting in parking areas should provide about 1½ footcandles at the pavement surface. Greater levels of lighting —approximately 5 footcandles—should be provided in structured parking to assure personal safety. In the parking areas, poles should be placed in islands at the ends of parking bays. The level of intensity of outside lighting is a private management concern, not one for zoning specifications, although the developer could reasonably be required to ensure that the height of the standards and the direction of the lighting prevent a nuisance glare on adjacent properties.

To reduce electricity costs, no more exterior lighting should be provided than is necessary for security. The latest available nonglare and high-intensity lighting should be used to provide adequate illumination, to reduce spillover lighting, and to avoid excessive electricity costs. Lighting levels can be further reduced half an hour after closing time.

Truck Service Facility

The delivery court has become the principal truck service facility for the loading and unloading of goods. These functional areas must be screened and placed out of the customer's view.

4-14 Night lighting of signs is an important element of exterior design.

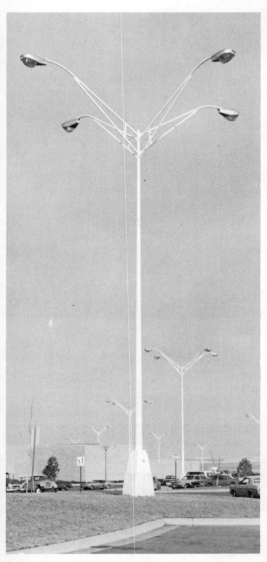

4-13 Tall light standards, while architecturally less pleasing than shorter standards, can help cut electricity costs. It is to be hoped that the conflict between aesthetic effect and energy use can be resolved by the development of more efficient light sources that can be mounted at lower heights.

4-15 Ideally, lighting fixtures for parking areas should harmonize with with the rest of the center in scale and architectural character.

4-16   Truck facilities can be screened by masonry wall extensions of the building line.

Small soft-line shops can be served by rear corridors leading from a service court. In a neighborhood or community nonmall center, occasional box deliveries from light express or parcel post vehicles can be made across the sidewalk without distracting the shoppers. Regional centers also successfully use over-the-sidewalk delivery by regulating delivery hours. The department store generally provides separate control of deliveries at its own service dock and by masonry screening at its truck service entry.

Early regional centers were designed with truck tunnels under the mall to serve all tenants. Though the tunnel offered the great advantage of complete separation of truck delivery traffic from pedestrian traffic, the tunnel was difficult and expensive to build, operate, and manage. The great costs involved now make the truck service tunnel unfeasible in shopping center development.

4-17   Loading and unloading facilities can also be depressed to remove them from view.

118

Interior Features

Tenant Spaces

When the tenant first looks at the space he has leased, it usually contains a certain frontage on the mall, unfinished party walls separating his space from that of his retail neighbors, an unfinished floor, and exposed joists for roof support. There is usually a rear door, and utilities have usually been stubbed to a point within the space.

Most developers use an allowance system for finishing the tenant space. The landlord lists a maximum dollar amount per square foot of GLA for specific tenant work such as storefronts, finished floors, walls, and ceilings, primary electrical conduits, secondary wiring, and so on; interior finishing and fixturing are not installed except as part of a specially negotiated turnkey job. The allowance may include floors and floor coverings, but the tenant pays for all light fixtures, counters, shelves, painting, and other custom fixtures and finishing. In essence, the owner furnishes the bare space. The work that the landlord is to do and the work that is the tenant's responsibility are plainly shown on working drawings and specifications and are spelled out in the lease. After the stipulated amount for an item has been reached, it is up to the tenant to pay for the rest. Through this system, the developer protects himself against excessive tenant demands that can upset construction cost estimates.

Recently some developers have attempted to assist tenants in certain phases of store planning, particularly the areas of storefronts, signs, and even the color coordination of sales areas. The idea behind this is the developer's recognition of the importance of reasonably harmonious store interiors in creating a pleasing and exciting retail image for the center as a whole. Developers have also begun to move from a "bare shell" to an "improved shell" in certain situations.

Tenant allowances depend primarily on the type of center and type of tenant. Allowances can range from nothing to a full turnkey job. Typical regional center allowances range from $3 to $6 per square foot. In smaller centers, the developer may have to provide a fully furnished tenant space. Highly desirable tenants will demand allowance concessions.

Building Flexibility

In any type of center, whatever structural column spacings are used, the design should allow for a measure of flexibility in store partitioning.

Except for intervening fire walls, the spacing of which is governed by the local fire protection code, partitions between tenant spaces should not be used as bearing walls. Tenant partitions should be built of materials and by methods that allow for easy removal. The design should provide for future store space reallocation and for readjustments in fixturing needed as tenants expand or shift their locations in the center. To allow for flexibility in operations, structural elements such as plumbing and heating stacks, air conditioning ducts, toilets, and stairways should be placed on end walls or on the walls least likely to be removed in enlarging a store or redividing the spaces, rather than on side partitions between tenants.

After construction begins, changes in the tenancy may require an altering of the tenant arrangement in order to improve the groupings of related shops, to accommodate tenant needs, or to free the "hot spot" locations for higher rental shops or more

4-18 An example of storefront design, drawn to assist future tenants.

119

4-19 The Rouse Company donated a sculpture of an Indian boy on a wild turkey to the borough of Paramus, New Jersey, location of Paramus Park Shopping Center. The sculpture is in one of Paramus Park's three court areas.

intensive use. By providing flexibility in design as well as non-load-bearing walls, tenant spaces can be enlarged or decreased. In this way, good locations can be created and a plan can be devised which will remain workable throughout the full leasing program.

In one-story neighborhood centers, heavy masonry piers should be avoided between storefronts. Such piers are expensive to install and difficult to remove, and they reduce window frontage. (Of course, such advice is impractical if the center is to have a traditional exterior architectural treatment.) Small steel columns with curtain walls of gypsum wallboard or exposed concrete block are used for interior partitions. For quick installation and to save labor costs and provide an incombustible and vermin-proof structure, the one-story building can use steel beam and column construction with steel truss or bar joist roof members carrying light precast concrete slab roof deck, and monolithic concrete floors covered with mastic-applied terra-cotta or vinyl tile.

Malls

The separation of foot traffic from motor traffic and the increased emphasis on amenities brought about the introduction of the open pedestrian mall in shopping centers.

The mall's attraction as a central open space was improved tremendously by its gardenlike treatment. Canopied walks, specimen trees, flowers, sculptures, and fountains created a general atmosphere of exhilaration in a commercial setting, a parklike amenity area where customers could rest on benches and generally relax and enjoy the surroundings. Later the appeal of this pedestian street was increased by enclosure and weather conditioning.

When a shopping center has a mall, there is no "best side of the street." The pattern encourages shoppers to move back and forth from one side of the mall to the other. For this reason, the mall is an asset in merchandising and a stimulus for impulse buying, as well as a pleasant and convenient place for the shopper.

Pedestrian flow along the mall is encouraged by careful placement of the tenants to maintain the shoppers' interest. In a mall center with more than one major tenant, the usual arrangement is the placing of a major tenant at each end of the mall. Where a department store is the single principal magnet, it is usually placed in the middle of one side of the mall, and the next strongest tenants are placed at the ends. Such a pattern can become a cluster in which the department store magnet is surrounded by small stores, with short pedestrian malls leading to the stores of secondary pulling power in order to strengthen customer circulation to the smaller intervening units.

In the present generation of centers the open mall is rarely used. Exceptions are found in places such as Hawaii where the climate is conducive to year-round outdoor living, and in specialty, convenience, or neighborhood centers. But the enclosed mall is now a nearly universal pattern except in small centers.

The fully weather-conditioned enclosed mall has assets not found in open mall centers, and many of these advantages can lead to increased sales volume. The design also permits open storefronts, which offer a savings in display window expense. The entire mall frontage of a store can, in effect, become open "window" area. When benches, plants, ornamental "spectaculars," and other mall furnishings are provided, the mall creates a setting for even greater merchandising vitality and center-wide promotion. Because of such advantages and because of the continuing popularity of enclosed malls, there is a trend of converting open malls to enclosed malls, as increased sales volumes are analyzed to justify the capital expense of conversion. An open mall can be roofed over by a "sky shield" or can be converted to a completely enclosed and weather-conditioned space for greater customer comfort and circulation and for increased merchandising attraction.

A straight-line mall is likely to produce a tunnel effect if its length is too great in relation to its width. To improve the visual effect, the pattern may assume such alphabetical shapes as the H, T, Y, Z, or L to provide shorter sight distances. At points where there is a change in the direction of customer flow between anchor tenants, a court or widened area can be introduced. Such an area offers the opportunity for dramatic architectural treatment and for premium space rentals. The space thus created is also a useful setting for special promotional events and displays—antique shows, for example, or Christmas or Easter displays. Fountains, sitting areas, seasonal floral displays, dramatic stairways, escalators, and sculptures can be featured attractions of the court area.

Whereas mall widths may range from 30 to 40 feet, the width may be increased to 60 feet or more for courts and other special areas, depending on the height and treatment of the ceiling. In multi-level malls, courts offer even greater opportunities for dramatic treatment. Here the ceilings can be as much as 50 feet higher than in the adjacent mall area. The mall in a small regional center (one of approximately 300,000 square feet GLA) may have a lower ceiling; 16 feet is a practical height for appearance and for keeping heating and air conditioning costs within reasonable limits. In larger regionals, a mall ceiling height of 20 feet has proven to work well. Variations in the ceiling height can be used to avoid long straight sight lines and to provide a more interesting and pleasing appearance than that of the single-height hallway. It is also important to consider acoustics; there must be no echo effect.

Since the mall customarily runs between major retail tenants—either the department stores, or a department store and a large variety store or food store—the architect's problem is to make this distance seem short while providing enough length for an array of tenants. If the storefronts are inviting and interesting in their variation, shoppers will not tire of walking as easily as they would if nothing distracted them from the chore of walking.

The developer's desire to provide enough retailing area for the stores that are properly part of the shopping complex—while keeping the mall length within a comfortable walking distance—bears directly on the depth of the stores. As a mathematical example: if the developer feels that the center requires 300,000 square feet of retail area, and if he divides this footage equally on both sides of the mall, establishing 700 feet as the desired length between the leading stores, then the average depth of stores on both sides of the mall might be 150 feet (taking into account the area of the anchor stores at the ends of the mall), since no basement or mezzanine areas are to be provided.

In enclosed mall centers, 15 percent of total GLA is the optimum amount to devote to common malls, courts, and corridors. An assignment of 25 percent of GLA is likely to be excessive.

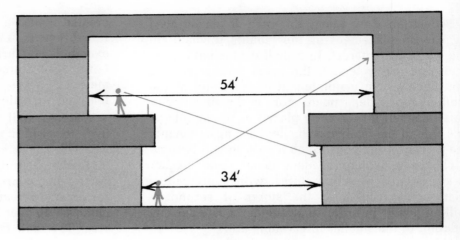

HAWTHORNE PLAZA
Hawthorne, California

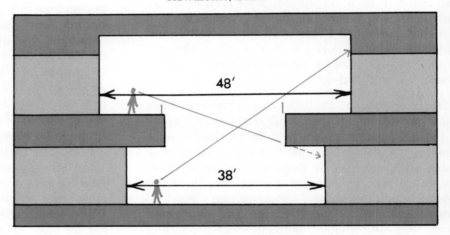

4-20 Cross sections of multi-level malls. The use of precast concrete framing at Hawthorne Plaza, rather than steel construction as used at Northridge Fashion Center, allows greater visibility between the upper and lower levels.

NORTHRIDGE FASHION CENTER
Northridge, California

Kiosks

The kiosk, a freestanding booth, is an innovation in retailing in enclosed malls. Kiosks encourage impulse buying and allow the flexibility of including very small tenant spaces—those of 100 square feet or so. Kiosks must be low enough that they do not not interfere with the view across the mall or with the view of tenant signs or lighting. If kiosks are too high, they will appear to be separate stores, will definitely separate traffic along the mall, and will deprive the nearby tenants of across-the-mall visibility of their merchandise.

The addition of carefully selected kiosks to a mall greatly aids in the creation of a gay, busy, marketplace atmosphere. Low counter-height kiosks are suitable for a variety of retail and service uses, such as candy, card, key, costume jewelry, and giftware sales, and travel agencies, ticket counters, newsstands, insurance agencies, and other outlets that can be readily secured during nonbusiness hours.

These small stands are placed in areas of heavy traffic and add a special flavor of activity and excitement to the center. Although in lease negotiations some of the major tenants may seek to restrict kiosks, a limited number of locations can be arranged to complement the mall operation and to provide substantial additional rental income at very little extra cost to the owner. In some cases, a mall tenant may wish to augment his sales by operating a kiosk in front of or near his store.

The developer must use care in introducing kiosks. He should not include food service outlets which require on-site cooking or which emit odors of any kind.

Multiple Levels

Vertical merchandising is being used more and more as the solution to restricted sites and to the problem of achieving store-to-store proximity for shopper convenience. The multilevel mall reduces site coverage and walking distances between stores and between the parking area and the stores. Multilevel treatment also allows the regional center to include a mix of uses in compact buildings on restricted-area, high-cost sites.

Multilevels are challenges to architects, since their proper design treatment requires a complex evaluation of site use, traffic movement, graphics, and amenities. This complexity is increased by the need to provide escalators, elevators, and stairways for vertical circulation. Still, the savings in required site area can help balance the greater capital costs of multilevel design.

Multilevel centers have distinct marketing advantages, provided the right distribution of tenants can be introduced for interplay between the shopping levels. It is important that the developer maintain careful control over tenant location when leasing a two-level center. Most mall tenants believe that their customer draw depends on a well-designed connection between the smaller tenants and the major stores. Hence the department store must have entrances from each level. Access to parking facilities from each level is also desirable. This can be readily accomplished on a site with a natural or artificial slope or in a center with structured parking.

Visibility of the various levels is a very important aspect of multilevel design. The use of open wells and dramatic two-story design elements, including shops floating between levels, are techniques that have been used to prevent isolation of one level from another. The placement and prominence of vertical transportation must also be carefully considered. End courts or central courts can feature the means of vertical transportation, creating a second gallery on the upper level and providing additional visual exposure for stores in the gallery area. Cross-bridges may be used to connect both sides of the upper level and to offer dramatic views of activity on both levels.

Two-story treatment is seldom advisable in neighborhood centers. Second stories do not necessarily increase earnings, and extra costs are involved for construction, plumbing, heating, lighting, and maintenance. It is uneconomic to provide elevators or escalators to reach the second floor.

Second floors, if included in small centers, are usually occupied by office rather than retail tenants. Office employees are all-day parkers, and office visitors are generally long-time, nonshopping parkers. Doctors and dentists are also poor tenants for the second floor of a neighborhood center because of the special plumbing, wiring, and maintenance they require. A better solution is the separate medical building.

4-21   At Foxhill Mall in Culver City, California, two levels of shops on one side of the pedestrian mall are faced by three levels on the other. The various levels are connected by escalators, bridges, ramps, and a "theme" tower.

Two-story treatment for a small center is likely to be successful only in an area of limited and high-cost commercial land, high population density, and a high level of disposable income. If second floor space is provided, suitable tenants are those that pull people to the center regularly and frequently, have visitors who will not park longer than an hour during shopping hours, and require no display space on the ground floor. Some service tenants, such as beauty shops, photographers, dance studios, and the like, are suitable for second floor locations. Stairs to second floors should be easy to climb, with intermediate landings; this is another reason for designing low ceiling heights on the first floor. Ideally, site topography will allow a design that provides at-grade access to the second level. An old real estate adage applies to most small shopping centers: You *rent* ground floor areas and "give away" basements and second floors.

Storefronts

Enclosed malls provide for the widest possible display of merchandise for those stores which front on the pedestrian malls. Storefronts may be completely or partially open; merchandise can be placed before the public without the barrier of glass. With no doors to open, customers enter the tenants' sales area under the most favorable circumstances. The full store width becomes the entrance to a combined front display and sales area. Shoplifting can become a problem, however, if store space layouts are not designed for control by store personnel at front sales locations.

Devices for closing the storefronts in enclosed malls range from sliding glass doors to open grilles which drop from overhead. The variety of attractive display possibilities for storefronts is almost limitless. It is often less expensive to merchandise storefronts in an enclosed mall, because tenants are able to do away with window backs and other expensive display materials.

Store Size

Do not make stores too big. There is a saying in the shopping center industry: Any store size is all right if it is not too big. As discussed in Chapter 2, the leasing program will include plans for store sizes. A merchant on a long-term lease may want the biggest store possible, if only to accommodate possible expansion. The developer-owner should have structural flexibility and, if possible, a flexible leasing agreement which allows a tenant to be

moved if the need for a larger (or smaller) space is demonstrated.

Small stores add character to the center. In planning small store spaces, care must be taken that suitable depths are provided; this usually entails overlapping a large store as an L behind the small store.

The following considerations are important in planning store sizes:

- Try to hold each tenant to the minimum space needed, as it is better for the tenant to be a little tight on space than to be rattling around in too much room with insufficient sales to justify his rent, especially with today's higher building and operating costs which are reflected in higher rents. Most tenants will recognize the prudence of gauging their space to the projected volume of sales.
- Try to limit frontages for major tenants to permit exposure of as many different merchants as possible to the mall or pedestrian way.
- Variety in retail tenant mix is more important than the size of any particular store space. There is evidence that centers with a variety of retail tenants are considerably more successful than those with only a few large stores.[4]

Store Width

A standard store width cannot be given for any particular type of tenant. Chain store companies have studied the matter for years and have employed the best talent in the store planning field to ascertain the proper width for their stores. Merchants generally have their own ideas about store size, based on their experience and study, and will usually advise the developer of their needs. Unfortunately, the merchants' ideas often do not coincide with the developer's need to restrict mall store widths in order to keep the mall to reasonable length and to allow frontage on the mall to as many tenants as possible.

In nearly all present-day centers, the architectural design calls for structures with wide spans between the structural columns. Stores are fitted into these structural steel frames without too much regard for column location. With clever layout, columns are disguised as part of the fixtures and often can be used as part of the store's decorative features.

---

[4] For median store sizes (in GLA) by tenant classification, see *Dollars and Cents of Shopping Centers* (Washington, D.C.: ULI—the Urban Land Institute, triennial).

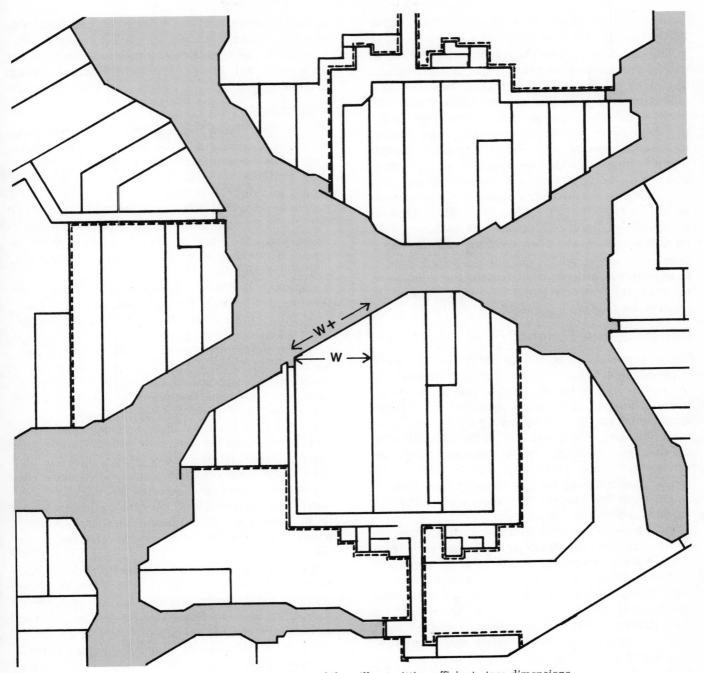

4-22 Angled frontages increase storefront exposure while still permitting efficient store dimensions.

The developer should keep in mind that he has only so much frontage "for sale." Usually the amount of available frontage in a center is limited while the store depths are not. The developer should prevent a merchant from using too much of this valuable commodity for a wide but shallow store when the merchant can do as much volume in the same square footage with a greater store depth.

Store Depth

The ability to provide stores of varying depths is an asset in any center. A range of depths from 40 to 150 feet is often both required and feasible. The use of curtain walls where possible at the rear of stores permits future deepening at minimum cost. Where it is necessary to construct buildings with a uniform depth, small stores may be "carved out" of deeper space, leaving rear overlap areas for the neighboring larger stores.

The developer must avoid creating excessive depths from which neither he nor the tenant can obtain an adequate return. Where shopper traffic moves on two frontages, where delivery is at the back of the store and ground-level storage facilities have to be provided, or where there are no basements, greater store depth is needed. Lesser depth is possible where storage and service facilities are in the basement and where only one side of the store has pedestrian traffic. Greater store depths in regional centers are generally a product of specifically planned uses, such as large high-quality stores, multiscreen theaters, and the like.

In small stores which may be deepened later, it is wise to place the electric panels and equipment on the side walls to avoid the need to relocate them if the rear wall is moved.

Store Ceiling Height

The appropriate clear ceiling height for the store depends somewhat on the exterior architectural treatment and certainly on the total area of the store. There is a trend toward lower ceilings, encouraged partly by the savings in energy consumption for lighting and air conditioning afforded by the lower ceiling, and by the accompanying savings in construction and maintenance costs. Lower finished ceilings cut heating and maintenance costs but require architectural "breaks" to produce a pleasing appearance.

The distance from the floor slab to the underside of the bar joists holding the roof may vary from 9 to 13 feet, depending on the architectural style of the building, the depth of the stores, and the type of tenants. It is usual for the air space between the finished ceiling and the roof to contain air conditioning ducts, electric wires, recessed light boxes and panels, telephone wires, plumbing lines, and other utility hardware; such equipment requires from 2 to 3 feet of space between the finished ceiling and the roof. Developers have found that the installation of T-bars and lay-in acoustical finished ceilings provides easy future access to the utility lines.

Although many stores have 11-foot finished ceilings, some small stores may have ceilings as low as 9 feet. Certain specialized, larger-space-using tenants, such as variety stores and supermarkets, require finished ceilings as high as 13 feet. In storage areas out of view of the customers, no finished ceiling is needed, but many fire codes require lay-in panels or other materials with a 2-hour fire-resistant rating. The use of mezzanines for either selling or storage will obviously require different ceiling heights.

Basements

At one time, large regional centers needed basements to accommodate the truck service tunnels. Basements were fairly easy to provide, because they could be scooped out at the same time the tunnel was dug. Now, however, with truck service courts and service delivery areas built on a level with the main building, basements have been eliminated and are generally considered too costly in terms of income-producing space for present-day center construction.

Although the new generation of shopping centers do not require them, basements have been used in some areas for storage and heating equipment and for store expansion space. The original cost of providing basement space is relatively low, especially in colder sections of the country where foundation footings 4 or 5 feet below grade are necessary. However, the basement is still an added capital cost and a low income producer.

Cost-saving features in basement construction include the use of concrete block foundations where subsurface conditions permit, with the first floor support provided by transverse beams. This construction method eliminates the need for basement stair headers and permits basement stairs to be relocated and widened without undue expense when revising store spaces and tenant arrangement.

Stairways leading to a basement should be constructed of concrete or steel. Where the basement is to be used for merchandising, a 5-foot stair width should be provided. Some stores, such as furniture and variety chains, specifically request basement areas for merchandising and may require vertical transportation.

Interior Walls

Party walls between retail stores in enclosed mall centers can be constructed of any of a variety of materials, depending on the local building and fire codes. Some codes require fire walls which extend to the underside of the roof. Sometimes the material is concrete block; sometimes metal stud partitions with gypsum wallboard are used. The latter provides maximum flexibility for future changes in store sizes.

Partitioning between the sales and the storage areas of a store can usually consist of stud and gypsum wallboard construction. The wall finish may be anything from paint to wallpaper to painted decoration to a vinyl cover finish for special uses. Most fire codes require extension of this partitioning to the underside of the roof.

Plumbing

Since plumbing lines must run under the floor slab, they are best installed while subfloor construction is exposed. Stores that do not have special plumbing requirements usually confine plumbing fixtures to small toilet areas and washbasins, but restaurants, beauty and barber shops, and other stores with more complex requirements find plumbing a major item of improvement cost.

Plumbing requirements for a shopping center are essentially the same as those for freestanding stores. Water heating equipment, if required, is generally provided by the tenant. Restaurants and major stores will provide restrooms for customers. Where so permitted, groups of small tenants can be served by shared restrooms provided by the developer and maintained by the group through common area charges.

The lease should specify the responsibility for providing vents and drains for tenants, such as supermarkets, restaurants, and dry cleaners, who require large plumbing installations. Where there is no basement, under-floor installations should be deferred until the tenant spaces are leased, because the formulation of the tenants' requirements will lag behind the developer's construction schedule.

Sprinklers must be installed in enclosed malls and in other mall buildings. The system required depends on local fire insurance rates and building codes and on available water supplies. In most cases, sprinkler systems pay for themselves in lower insurance costs over a period of 5 to 7 years.

Lighting

Electric wiring for lighting and other purposes is usually installed before the finished ceiling and wall cover are put in place in the sales area. The wiring which leads from a panel box in the rear of the store is generally the responsibility of the tenant.

Ceilings in the enclosed mall space are frequently skylighted. As mentioned earlier, side wall clerestory treatment is better for energy conservation. Such treatment permits natural daylight to filter in,

4-23 Natural lighting has been used here to illuminate an escalator.

thus benefiting both the mall atmosphere and the specimen planting customarily found in enclosed malls.

Lighting of enclosed mall areas is usually designed so as not to detract from the light intensity of the store windows but yet to provide a pleasing, natural effect. Combinations of fluorescent and incandescent lighting plus indirect lighting may be used. Incandescent lighting requires a greater number of fixtures, more wiring, and greater wattage than fluorescent lighting to produce the same number of footcandles. In addition, incandescent lighting generates greater heat.

Too much attention is usually given to lighting store interiors rather than to lighting the merchandise. To reduce consumption of electricity, light colors could be used to eliminate the need for high wattage floodlighting. Store interiors can be designed to reduce the number of outlets and the length of wiring runs to effectively reduce installation and operating costs. By using high lumen output lights, fewer fixtures are needed.

Flooring

Special floor covering is usually put over the concrete slab in the tenant sales area, although it is often omitted in the storage area. Floor coverings range from various tile materials to carpeting. Wood flooring is not recommended for stores unless the whole decorative scheme calls for it. Stores will often have different floor coverings in different parts of the sales area, depending on the character of the merchandise and the manner of merchandise presentation.

Floor surfaces of enclosed malls consist of anything from polished concrete, to a vinyl floor covering with variations in textures, to terrazzo. The developer should be careful in choosing the surface material; it must not be so rough that it interferes with cleaning, yet the floor must not be slippery. Terrazzo and quality tile floors are serviceable and economical. The use of a small pattern design will allow for easier replacement if cracks appear from heavy use.

The floor of enclosed malls can be made more attractive and less cold in appearance if a carefully designed variety of materials is used, rather than unvarying, dead-white terrazzo. The entryway of most stores can be made more dramatic and appealing if the floor materials are noticeably different from those used in the main mall. Different floor materials and floor designs help break up the monotony of lengthy malls or walkways.

4-24   Attractive, durable, easily maintained flooring is an important design consideration.

Heating and Air Conditioning

There are two basic methods of heating and cooling the shopping center: individual units for each store, or a central plant for the entire center. Individual units are tenant responsibilities. The central plant is the responsibility of the shopping center management and offers the greatest centerwide convenience. Hybrid systems, which employ large, multitenant rooftop units, are also available. The pros and cons of individual units and central plants are essentially a cost and income study.[5]

With energy savings a critical need in the HVAC system, the mechanical engineer must evaluate all possible systems and the availability of various fuels. Intelligent judgement, based on thorough analysis, is necessary not only for new projects but also for improvements in operating centers. Solutions are complicated by the differences in needs and requirements of the various tenant classifications.[6]

By using an extra building insulation envelope, including a heat-reflective roof coating, air conditioning loads are reduced. In enclosed malls, the services of air conditioning engineers should be used to check each tenant's system to assure proper balance so that stores do not "bleed off" conditioned air from the mall area.

In many areas, substantial additional income is available to the owner through the submetering of energy from the local utility company; in other words, the owner buys at the wholeshale rate and sells at the retail. The legality of submetering must be investigated, because state and local utility laws vary greatly, as do the practices and policies of electric companies. For this reason, both legal counsel and the advice of a heating engineer should be sought.

[5] See Victor Gruen and Larry Smith, *Shopping Towns USA* (New York: Reinhold, 1960), pp. 183–85, 205.

[6] See the section entitled "Sale of Utilities to Tenants" in *Dollars and Cents of Shopping Centers* (footnote 4 above). Also see pp. 100–106, "Mechanical Systems," in Redstone, *New Dimensions* (footnote 1 above); and Gilbert F. Hellmer, "Energy Saving Alternatives for New and Existing Buildings," *Buildings*, Vol. 68, No. 11 (November 1974).

5.
Operation and Management

The Lease as an Operational Tool

The lease document is the foundation for the successful operation of the shopping center. The lease and its provisions establish the level of income that the developer-landlord anticipates from his enterprise. The shopping center lease varies extensively from a standard commercial lease.

A lease is a contract by which a landlord gives a tenant the use and possession of the demised premises for a specified period of time in exchange for payments of specified amounts. *Leasing* refers to such conveyance. The conveying party is the lessor, and the party to whom the terminable use right is conveyed is the lessee. In real estate, the terminable use right conveyed to the lessee is a leasehold. Rents are estimates of the value for use possibilities of the leased premise. Although they are not discussed here, many possible and probable causes might be identified which separately or in combination can increase or decrease the value of future use possibilities for a particular premise.

Since the lease is a legal instrument, it must be drafted by a lawyer informed in the field. No universal leasing document can be described which will apply to all shopping centers, all tenant types, and all jurisdictions.[1] But the area of tenant leasing must be carefully studied at the very outset of the development venture, as mentioned earlier in this book; regardless of the type or location of the center, the matter of leasing must be part of the preliminary investigation and planning process. It is in the lease that the various tangible and intangible elements of shopper attraction are shaped, drawn together, and controlled. The lease document's treatment of details, and its handling of the many facets of the shopping center, will in large measure determine the center's final atmosphere, customer appeal, and degree of financial success.

This section is not intended to be a leasing manual. Rather, it discusses the practices currently employed in shopping center leasing to balance landlord risk with tenant performance, including the use of percentage devices established in the provisions of participating lease agreements.

---

[1] See the sample lease in Appendix C. This lease is presented only as an example and is not intended as a definitive or universally applicable document.

131

Percentage Leases

A shopping center developer-owner is confronted with two basic economic needs which must be met in his leasing. First, he must be assured of an adequate income stream to meet his fixed expenses. Second, he must receive a reasonable return on his equity; he must receive a return which reflects the value of his property. If properly structured, the combination of minimum guaranteed rent plus percentage rent, or rent as a percentage of sales, can answer both needs.

Besides providing a basic return on the investment, minimum rents should cover the fixed expenses of shopping center operation—principal and interest on the mortgage, real estate taxes, insurance, maintenance, housekeeping, and other expenses. The percentage rent, when added to the minimum guaranteed rent, should provide for the potential of an increasing return on investment. The adequacy of the minimum rent structure is assured by special lease provisions, such as escalator clauses and the establishment of a formula for shared common area charges and real estate taxes, which protect the landlord against inflation.

In the retail field, the percentage lease has become the most widely used kind of rental contract for both tenant and landlord. In its simplest form, the percentage lease is an instrument wherein the tenant agrees to pay a rental equal to a stipulated percentage of the gross dollar volume of the tenant's sales. In shopping centers, the most common type of percentage lease is one in which the tenant agrees to pay a specified minimum rent even if the negotiated percentage of gross sales is less than the agreed minimum. This combination of minimum rent and percentage rent takes the needs of both landlord and tenant into account; the guaranteed minimum protects the shopping center owner if the tenant's sales are not high enough to produce the necessary rental income. But the owner receives less when times are rough, and more as the tenant's business prospers, since total rent charges fluctuate with the volume of business.

Percentage lease rates and the amount of the minimum rental are based on the ability of the merchant to pay, the kind of business, the volume of business per square foot of leased space, the markup on merchandise, the business value of the tenant space and of the shopping center location, the amount of competition, and other factors.[2]

There are several types of percentage leases. As noted above, the one which is most commonly used provides for a minimum guaranteed rental from which the owner will derive enough income to cover amortization and operating costs, plus a basic return on his investment. This protects the owner during the early years of a development and during periods of recession. During periods of normal business activity, both parties participate in the high level of trade.

As discussed in Chapter 2, the breakpoint in gross sales volume—under which the minimum rent applies, and over which the percentage rent applies—can be determined mathematically once the minimum rental and the rate of percentage rent are established. To illustrate: if the owner knows his minimum rental should be $6,000, and if the agreed-upon percentage rate is 6 percent, gross sales of $100,000 would be the breakpoint. But if gross sales fell below this figure, say to $50,000, the owner would still be paid $6,000; with a straight percentage lease, he would receive only $3,000 in this instance. When sales exceed the $100,000 level, the rate of percentage applies to the overage. For this reason, overage rents are the goal to which the landlord strives for both the tenant's operations and his own. The overage offers the cushion in shopping centers, the "balance after operating expenses."

Because of its balancing of tenant and landlord interests, the percentage lease with a minimum guarantee is used for almost all types of tenants in shopping centers. As with every rule, however, there are exceptions; these exceptions are likely to be financial institutions and nonretail tenants such as banks, building and loans, and small loan companies; service shops; and offices for such tenants as insurance agencies, doctors, and dentists. Where only fixed guarantees are involved, it is wise for the developer to consider short-term leases. With fixed rentals, the owner is at a disadvantage. He is not properly provided with incentive income as he proceeds to develop and promote his center. With short-term leases, he is better able to protect himself for adjustment of rental income in line with rising value of the center location, higher operating costs, and other changing circumstances.

The Lease Document

An attorney will draft the lease, but the developer should establish the business terms upon which the

[2] Median and ranges of percentage rents by tenant classification and by type of shopping center are detailed in *Dollars and Cents of Shopping Centers* (Washington, D.C.: ULI–the Urban Land Institute, triennial).

document is based. A well-constructed and well-drawn lease is also a management tool, as it sets down the rules and regulations of conduct for both tenant and landlord.

Any sample lease form for a shopping center should be used very carefully. The developer must avoid any legal form based on another jurisdiction. Many factors prevent a rigid leasing formula from being applicable to all parts of the United States. Lease provisions must also conform to the circumstances and requirements of the particular shopping center type. Above all, it is unwise to enter into any important transaction, such as a long-term lease for a commercial property, without the counsel of an attorney who resides in the city where the center is located and who is familiar with statutes, ordinances, and court decisions applicable to the development and operation of a shopping center in that particular jurisdiction.

Besides establishing obligations, responsibilities, and leasehold arrangements, the lease incorporates the means of preserving the shopping center's character and appearance as a merchandising complex over a long period of time. When drafted properly, lease provisions establish beneficial relationships between the developer and the tenant.

For a well-planned operation, lease clauses should cover all facets of agreement, including:

- Description and permitted use of the premises, including an identification of the premises as a portion of the shopping center, which in turn is given a property description.
- Description of the gross leased area.
- Rental terms, including minimum guaranteed rent and rate of percentage rent.
- Basis for payments for such joint or common area expenses as mall and parking maintenance and lighting.
- Basis for HVAC and utility payments.
- Real property tax escalator clauses.
- Membership in the merchants association and participation in promotional and other activities of the association, including details of association dues.
- Insurance premiums for public liability, property damage, and fire insurance and extended coverage for fixtures and merchandise.
- Definition of gross sales.
- Auditing of tenants' accounts.
- Reporting of monthly sales figures.
- System of paying rent.
- Security deposit.

- Term of lease.
- Occupancy conditions.
- Maintenance of the premises by both the landlord and tenant, including such tenant responsibilities as trash removal, strict rodent control (for tenants offering food or food service), window displays, advertising signs, and painting of interiors.
- Conditions required of landlord for tenant occupancy.
- Clauses to allow changes in site plan.
- Parking index.
- "Standard" commercial clauses such as continued occupancy, default under the lease, surrender of possession, change in tenant corporation, and miscellaneous items, including notices and waiver of claims.
- A plan of the site and building layout indicating the demised premises, as an appended exhibit to the document.

Shopping center leases also include other operating provisions, such as utility service agreements, use provisions, reuse clauses, and provisions governing hours of operation. In fact, the entire operating and promotional policy of the center can be outlined in the lease. However, such policy is not necessarily incorporated in the lease, except for a spelling out of the basis and scale of assessment for participation in the merchants association.

Any shopping center lease should prepare for the possibility of the future addition of stores and the expansion of the parking area, either through the purchase or conversion of additional land or through the building of parking structures. As mentioned in the discussion of parking in the last chapter, the construction of a parking deck allows amortization and depreciation to be applied to the cost of the structure, whereas these cannot be applied to the cost of land. In areas of high land cost, these financial advantages may justify the double-decking of parking to accommodate an increase in parking demand, but this will not be the case where the cost of the structured parking must be borne solely by the new expansion area rather than by the center as a whole.

The following is a more detailed discussion of various lease clauses. Throughout, it attempts to be helpful rather than definitive; this material should be considered only as notation to aid the developer in shopping center planning and negotiation. It is intended only as discussion, and not as a full treatment of items found in the clauses of a lease. Omitted are the interpretations, the adjustments, and the innovations—the ingredients of distinction—that must be considered and applied to the specific site and the local conditions. In addition, the order of discussion of these items is not intended to suggest the proper order of clauses in the lease document.

Definition of Terms

In general, a section of the lease which defines terms used in the document makes it easier for both tenant and landlord to understand exactly what is provided in the lease. As with other lease clauses, the drafting of definition clauses will require legal assistance to ensure that the definitions are full, accurate, consistent, and applicable throughout the lease.

Modification-Financing Clauses

A modification-financing clause is a valuable tool for the developer. The following is an example of such a clause:

> The owner shall not be obligated to proceed with the construction of the lease premises unless and until financing acceptable to the owner is obtained. Should such financing not be obtainable within six months after completion of final plans and specifications, the owner may so notify the tenant in writing, and this lease shall thereupon cease and terminate and each of the parties hereto shall be released and discharged from any and all liability and responsibility hereunder. If the owner can obtain financing only upon the basis of modification of the terms and provisions of this lease, the owner shall have the right to cancel this lease if the tenant refuses to approve in writing any such modification within thirty days after the owner's request therefor, which request may not be made after delivery of possession. If such right to cancel is exercised, this lease shall thereafter be null and void, any money or security deposited hereunder shall be returned to the tenant, and neither party shall have any liability to the other by reason of such cancellation.

Rent Provisions and Sales Records

Monthly collection of percentage rentals, with year-end adjustments, is a good procedure. In instances where the tenant will not accede to clauses which establish such a payment system, the procedure might be adjusted so that the tenant pays a monthly percentage rental equal to the average percentage rental paid during the previous year, with a year-end adjustment.

The term *gross sales* should be carefully defined since this is the benchmark for determining percentage rentals. The reporting procedures should be carefully drawn. In order to ensure the accuracy of the reports, the landlord should be provided with annual statements of each tenant's gross sales and should have the right to cancel the lease in the event of a substantial discrepancy. The landlord would also do well to include a provision enabling him to cancel the lease if a specified sales volume is not reached by the tenant within a specified period of time. This provision is important when dealing with an independent mechant of unproven ability.

All percentage leases should give the owner the right to check the tenant's books at any time. Accounting and payment should be arranged on a monthly basis if possible, and the tenant's monthly statement should show daily sales. Where a tenant has other stores at lower percentage rates or at fixed rentals, the possibility of the tenant's running sales through those stores must be considered. An outside accountant should be used for tenant auditing, especially during the first 2 years of operation, and periodically thereafter. In the case of a small shop where bookkeeping and accounting methods make it difficult to check on the tenant's sales volume, a high basic rent per square foot and a short lease term are the preferred arrangement.

Guaranteed rent is usually paid monthly, in advance, and this should be established in the lease provisions. Monthly reports should be required on volume of business done, even though settlements of percentage rent may be made on other bases.

The lease should provide that rental percentages apply to all sales on and from the premises, in order to include mail orders not otherwise accounted for. No deductions are normally allowed for uncollectable accounts, but items commonly deductible from gross sales are cash refunds to customers, sales taxes, excise taxes, and allowances for goods returned to suppliers.

When a lease provides that excess percentage rent is to be adjusted annually and credited against the minimum guaranteed rental for the following year, a risk arises of accumulating a rent-free period. To avoid this situation, it is best that excess percentage rent be refunded.

Term of Lease

The lease's duration is stated in months or years, with separate clauses for commencement of the term and for establishing the tenant's sales reports on a monthly and annual (fiscal year) basis.

Leases should not be made for too long a period;

some developers go so far as to say that tenants should be educated to the idea of no long-term leases, or even that small tenants should not be given leases of more than 5 years. With local tenants, at least, the developer is better off with short-term leases. Soft-line tenants need longer leases, and a good credit rating also calls for a longer lease.

Department stores should be required to lease for at least 20 years. Other major tenant leases should be for the next longest term—10 to 15 years. For the smaller chain and local tenants, leases should normally run 7 to 10 years. Mortgagees are unlikely to give credit to longer lease terms for most local tenants. Shorter lease terms give the landlord the right to renegotiate with the majority of smaller tenants for a higher minimum rent or to weed out poor performance tenants.

Caution should be used in granting renewal options to any tenant. Options generally favor the tenant. The tenant typically obtains a rental ceiling and a choice in his extension of the lease—both of which may be detrimental to the landlord's interests. Options based on sales performance are preferable, so that "merit" in terms of dollar income to the landlord has a function in lease renewal.

Options theoretically help the tenant to avoid making an initial long-term obligation. But when leasing to untried tenants, the landlord should have the right to terminate if the tenant is unproductive in percentage rent payment. If a tenant who has proven in his other stores that he produces high volumes should request a long-term lease, such as one of 10 or 20 years, a renewal option in the basic lease may be practical but still should usually be avoided, although each case must be treated individually.

Use Clauses

Use clauses are of critical importance to the developer in maintaining a proper tenant mix and should be drafted carefully with the assistance of legal counsel.

Excessive protection against competition should not be given to a tenant. Customers like competitive shops, and more than one dress shop, men's store, and the like are desirable for the completeness and competitiveness of a center. In fact, the basis of a first-class regional center is a good number and variety of apparel shops which offer a range in quality and price. The more men's and women's stores with a complete range of price and merchandise, the better off the shopping center is

going to be from the standpoints of both sales volume and customer traffic.

Competition is the stimulant in retailing. In general, "exclusives" should not be included in the lease. Sometimes tenants request the right to be the sole outlet for a type of merchandise, but such requests must be refused. The proper level of competition and the solution to tenants' anxieties about excessive competition depend on negotiation and on the size of the center. It is evident from experience that where two candy stores, for example, are included in a regional center, each is likely to do a greater volume of business than if there were only one such store in the center.

Exclusives in price and merchandise lines should not be granted by clauses in a lease. Furthermore, restrictions on such anticompetition clauses were reinforced by two Federal Trade Commission consent orders announced in 1974.[3] The consent orders became landmark decisions governing terms that department stores once were able to impose as protection for their key tenant status. Certain terms of the FTC ruling against two department stores in the *Tysons Corner* consent order apply to all major tenants and shopping centers:

(1) The stores may not fix prices;
(2) Advertising by the center or by other tenants cannot be controlled by the two stores;
(3) Discount selling in the center cannot be prohibited; and
(4) The amount of space leased to other tenants cannot be limited by the two stores.[4]

The other FTC consent ruling applicable to a department store as a tenant held that the store could not arrange with the other tenants in the center to prevent the inclusion of any tenants in the center. The consent order also granted a number of rights to the leading tenant—the department store in a regional center—including the right to negotiate lease clauses that protect the store's location and the right to establish reasonable categories of retailers from which the developer or landlord may select tenants to be located in the area proximate to the store, provided that such categories do not specify price ranges or lines of merchandise or identify particular retailers. The order significantly reduces—

[3] *Gimbel Brothers, Inc.,* FTC Dkt. 8885, Consent Order announced November 29, 1973, 39 Fed. Reg. 7164 (1974), Final Order, January 30, 1974; and *Tysons Corner Regional Shopping Center,* FTC Dkt. 8886, Consent Order announced March 5, 1974.

[4] "FTC and Shopping Centers: Dos and Don'ts for Major Tenants," *Real Estate Law Report,* Vol. 3, No. 11 (April 1974), p. 2.

the control that a major retail tenant may exercise over other retailers in a shopping center. This is important not only to the major tenant but to the smaller tenants, as well, who now have a wider field when negotiating their own leases. The developer is no longer in a position to say to the smaller tenants that his hands are tied because the major tenants insist upon certain controls.[5]

The business use clause should cover the matter of vending machines and mail orders by providing that the tenant must report gross sales, not net, and that the vending machines must be limited either to lines similar to the principal merchandise or to employee use.

For the developer's protection, a *radius clause* is often included in the lease. Through this clause, the tenant agrees to refrain from owning or operating another store within a specified distance of the center. The distance depends on the type of business involved. Variations involve permitting other tenant stores within a given distance of the center but requiring a portion of the sales volume of such other stores to be ascribed to the tenant's sales at the center.[6]

Tax Stop Clauses

The most important innovation in shopping center leases has been the tax stops or escalator clauses which account for future tax increases and establish either full-share or cost-of-living indices to compensate for increased costs of operation and maintenance of the common area facilities. An escalator or tax stop clause—one that requires the tenant to pay real estate taxes from the first dollar or from other specified dollar levels or at least his pro rata share of any increase in real estate taxes after the first full year's assessment—must be included in the lease. To allow the tenant to deduct this sum from his percentage rent, if any, has become generally unacceptable; outright payment (nonrecapture) has been substituted.

With the continued soaring of real estate taxes, the tax stop is especially important from the viewpoint of the mortgagee (lender), who is interested in the continued availability of funds to service the loan. As reported in *Dollars and Cents of Shopping Centers: 1975,* the largest single category of expense in almost every shopping center is real estate taxes. In the current survey, real estate taxes amounted to 32 percent of total operating expenses in regional centers, 40 percent in community centers, and 45 percent in neighborhood centers. But while real estate taxes have increased, percentage

rents have not risen fast enough to give the landlord the measure of protection he needs.

Another form of tax stop includes payment of all taxes on the parking lot as part of the common area charges in which the tenants participate.

Change Provisions

A clause is necessary to protect the developer against a change in the type of tenancy which results from a change in a tenant's ownership control. Even where the lease includes a use clause, a change in a tenant's corporate control can affect the tenant's operation. For this reason, a lease clause which provides for due notice to the landlord of such a change or for cancellation of the lease is a necessary safeguard.

The tenant's right to assign his lease or to sublet without the landlord's consent must also be either expressly limited or prohibited in the lease. An assignee of a lease is liable for percentage rent; a subtenant may not be. For this reason, a percentage rental clause should cover sales by subtenants, concessionaires, accessory tenants, and other outlets which operate within or from the center.

As part of the site plan exhibit which accompanies the lease document, the developer should reserve the right to change the plan for expansion or other purposes without objection from the tenants or cancellation of the tenant's lease. The developer should reserve the right to change the site plan without tenant approval of the change, unless such a change may result in a shifting of the tenant's location.

The tenant wants assurance that the parking index will be guaranteed. The developer may, however, want to reserve the right to use for other purposes as much as 10 percent of the parking area designated on the site plan or of any parking over and above a specified index. He also must reserve the right to modify the parking layout, and the lease should include a clause which allows him to double-deck the parking area. Any area to be developed later should be marked on the site plan as "Reserved" or "Future Building" or should be otherwise provided for with suitable language in the lease.

Under the terms of the *Gimbel Brothers* FTC consent order discussed earlier, a leading tenant

---

[5] Ibid., p. 1.

[6] Since radius clauses are currently under legal scrutiny, legal counsel should be obtained in developing the language of any such lease clause.

was granted the right to approve the location, size, and height of all buildings as well as parking area location, roadways, utilities, and common areas. The leading tenant may also have the right to approve the proposed layout for future expansion and may require that any expansion not provided for in the initial layout must not interfere with efficient traffic flow or change the parking ratio. According to the consent order, changes—

> shall be accomplished only after any and all covenants, obligations, and standards (construction, architecture, operation, maintenance, repair, alteration, restoration, parking ratio, and easements) of the shopping center shall be made applicable to the expansion area, and shall be made prior in right to any and all liens, encumbrances, and all other covenants, obligations, and standards applicable to the expansion area.[7]

A condemnation clause is another lease provision which must be included to account for changing circumstances. Such clauses are lengthy and technical but are necessary to protect against the conditions which arise when land or premises are condemned by an eminent domain process. Generally, the clause applies to the lease of a larger tenant which includes a parking index guarantee. Care should be taken to ensure that the tenant does not have the unlimited right to cancel in the event of loss of a portion of the land or improvements because of condemnation.

Ratios should be established to determine at what point the tenant may cancel; such a point might be a taking or damage to the store area of 10 to 20 percent, or a reduction in parking area below a ratio of 2 square feet of parking area to each square foot of GLA. The landlord should retain the right to redesign parking or provide substitute parking if a portion of the parking area is taken by condemnation.

Common Areas

Common area refers to everything outside the gross leasable area. It includes parking and its appurtenances, service roads, loading areas, service courts, delivery passages, pedestrian walks, malls (open or enclosed), canopied sidewalks, public restrooms, landscaped areas, and all access roads not in public ownership. The common area clause requires that the tenant pay his share of the cost of operation and maintenance of these areas, and it establishes the basis on which these charges are assessed.

There are several ways of distributing the charge among tenants. The most common are:

- A fixed charge for a stated period.
- A variable charge based on a percentage of sales.
- A pro rata charge based on the proportion of the tenant's GLA to the total center GLA, either including or excluding department stores.[8]

The fixed charge method has obvious problems for the landlord. It places a ceiling on expenditures, which tenants like, but which, with rising costs, may prevent satisfactory maintenance. A ceiling on these costs could also affect the developer's financing because the lender will recognize that the developer may not have sufficient funds available for the service of the debt if part of the income from rents must be diverted to pay for common area charges. Developers should avoid allowing the tenant to establish any such ceiling on the common area charges. The lease usually specifies the type of cost items allocable to maintenance of the common area, and the tenants' contribution must cover all of these items.

The variable charge is also unwise because it is subject to fluctuations over which the landlord has no control.

The pro rata system is the preferred method of assessment and is also the most sensible. Under this system, each tenant pays his proportional share and no payment ceiling is established. No share of the costs is chargeable to the landlord.

If at all possible, real estate tax assessments should be included in common area charges. It is recommended that a specific amount per square foot be paid monthly by the tenant, with adjustments made at the end of the year. During each subsequent year, monthly payments would be $\frac{1}{12}$ of the payments during the preceding year, with additional adjustments made at the end of each year.

The tenants' payment for enclosed mall heating and air conditioning should also be prorated. Where electricity is submetered, the mall should be metered separately.

The following are typical cost items included in the common area charges:

---

[7] "FTC and Shopping Centers" (footnote 4 above), p. 2.

[8] Median and ranges of common area charges per square foot GLA by tenant classification and by type of shopping center are detailed in *Dollars and Cents of Shopping Centers* (footnote 2 above).

- Lighting, including electricity or gas and replacement of bulbs, tubes, or wicks.
- Utility costs for air conditioning and heating the mall areas in an enclosed mall center.
- Planting, including water, plant replacement, insecticides, and fertilizer and other material.
- Sweeping and cleaning of all common areas.
- Snow removal. In cold climates, this is best contracted for on a basis of time and quantity.
- Trash removal, including hauling from the premises, unless specified elsewhere in the lease as a tenant responsibility.
- Parking space striping, curb painting, and painting of signs, including directional signs and area identification signs.
- Rental or purchase of equipment needed for maintenance operations, and personal property taxes and insurance on such equipment.
- Real estate taxes on the common area.
- Security.
- Insurance premiums for liability, property damage, and fire insurance.
- Wages of maintenance crews for all maintenance items, plus workmen's compensation insurance and other employee benefits.
- Uniforms of maintenance crews, including uniforms of truck or cart drivers in large regional centers.
- Reasonable charges for administration of the operations and collections required for common area maintenance. This management charge usually accounts for 10 to 15 percent of the total common area charge.

In addition to the common area charges, the common area clause provides for the developer's control of parking and other common areas and for the enforcement of compliance with rules, such as the restriction of employee and tenant parking to specified areas, with specific conditions, such as default of lease, spelled out for noncompliance.

The lease will obviously distinguish between landlord and tenant responsibilities in the common areas and the respective responsibilities in the individual tenant spaces. As discussed in the last chapter, more and more developers are operating on a leasing policy whereby the tenant is leased a shell (four walls, roof, and floor) and given an allowance for finishing the space; as a rule, tenant fixtures, floor coverings, and lighting are not installed by the landlord. In some instances, however, one or all of these may have to be furnished and financed by the lessor in order to

secure an important tenant. If the landlord must furnish the merchant with fixture money (except in the case just mentioned of the vitally important tenant for whom exceptions are made), this money should be repaid either as an additional 1 or 2 percent of the tenant's gross sales or as a separate fixture account until the amount has been recovered. The merchant does not receive this money as a gift but only as a loan. In any event, the lease clauses will describe the construction responsibilities of both landlord and tenant, as well as the conditions of the tenant's acceptance of the premises. A description of the allowance system is included as part of the division of responsibility between landlord and tenant.

Merchants Association

The merchants association can be the strongest single element in the successful operation of the tenant complex as a unit in order to improve the shopping center's image in the community. The lease clause should provide for the formation of the association and should call for mandatory membership for all tenants. This lease clause is essential; it establishes a vehicle for the joint promotional efforts of all tenants. The clause should set up the basis for contribution to the association—usually a specific amount per square foot of GLA with some fair device for escalating the contribution to account for inflation. (For a discussion of the actual operation and management of the merchants association, see page 145.)

Rather than having a specified amount that each tenant contributes to the merchants association—even though tenants like the "fixed" idea, and most developers use that arrangement—one might consider a clause that requires each merchant to pay a percentage of his gross sales to the merchants association fund. The disadvantage of this type of clause is that it does not permit a fixed promotional budget. To overcome this problem, some leases require a tenant to advertise at some stated percentage of sales, not through but in addition to the merchants association assessment.

The landlord customarily makes a contribution, either in dollars or in services, equal to 20 or 25 percent of the amount raised through tenant assessment. In this way, the merchants association fund becomes a joint tenant-landlord operation.

It is also customary to have a preopening and opening charge stated in the lease, requiring the tenant to pay a specified amount per square foot of GLA into the opening promotional fund for a new center and obligating the owner to contribute an amount equal to 25 pecent of the tenants' contribution. This money is spent over a period of 3 or 4 months before and during the early operating phase of the center.[9]

Some major developers are experimenting with a *promotional fund* as an alternative to the merchants association. A contribution is still required of each tenant, but the recipient is not a merchants association but the fund, which is controlled solely by the developer. Under this arrangement, some sort of advisory board is set up, composed of merchant representatives, and the developer then consults with this board on the use of the promotional fund.

Sign Control

Exterior signs and other graphics are regulated by the lease contract. A definite restriction on signs and their use should be established. As discussed in Chapter 4, the restriction should specify sign approval by the landlord and should set forth criteria in such areas as projection, placement, size, and color.

No rooftop signs should be permitted. Chain stores do not like to give up trademark signs, but they will go along with placement, size, and color controls. In strip centers, window advertising should be regulated so that placards and paper posters do not detract from the appearance of the shopping center as a whole. Sidewalk displays of merchandise should also be prohibited. In regional centers, the lease customarily includes an exhibit of permitted types of signing.

Other Clauses

In addition to the clauses mentioned above, which apply especially to the shopping center and which establish the basis for center operation and for tenant-landlord relationships, the shopping center lease will include the usual clauses found in commercial real estate leases. These clauses deal with contingencies, co-tenancies, indemnity insurance, utility services, remedies and defaults, surrender of premises, liens, guarantees, and so on. Since such clauses are quite technical, nearly all of them require legal phrasing based on the state and local jurisdictions in which the center will be located.

Provisions for setting store hours should be included in the lease. To allow the center to operate as a unit, it is customary to link store hours of small tenants to the hours of the major tenant or tenants, with whom there will be a specific hours agreement. Lighting of window displays and interior lighting during night operations and after closing hours also need to be covered by a lease clause.

Naturally, there will be objections to parts of the lease by some tenants, and there will be compromises. The extent and outcome of this give-and-take will depend on the bargaining positions and negotiating skills of the two parties.

In a well-planned center, the landlord should be able to incorporate many protective factors in his leasing program. The important lease provisions for the developer and his center are those which cover minimum and percentage rents, maintenance control of the parking area and other common areas, merchants association participation, and firm operating expense and tax protection.

Details of Management

As we have just seen, many of the details of shopping center operation and management are set forth in the lease. Through the lease provisions, the shopping center management establishes control of the completeness and mix of the tenant array; establishes control of and assessments for common area operation and maintenance; and provides for the enforcement of sign control, hours of operation, employee parking, tenant housekeeping, and maintenance of interior premises. Furthermore, through the organization and operation of the merchants association, as detailed in the lease, the center management helps foster and strengthen an image for the center which is attractive to shoppers in the trade area.

The lease provides for smooth center operation and management by clearly dividing responsibility between the landlord and the tenant; it describes that which the tenant is obliged to maintain and that which the landlord is required to perform. Structural maintenance and capital improvement of the buildings, for example, are the owner's responsibility, as is the repair of outside walls, roofs, sidewalks, and canopies. The owner, with tenant contributions, also maintains and repairs parking lots and landscaped areas, whereas the tenants are responsible for the repair and maintenance of the tenant spaces.

[9] Sample lease provisions pertaining to merchants associations, including clauses which establish the tenant's and landlord's contributions to the association fund, may be found in William W. Callahan, *Shopping Center Promotions: A Handbook for Promotion Directors* (New York: International Council of Shopping Centers, 1972).

In addition to dividing the responsibility of work between tenant and landlord, the lease establishes who will bear the financial burden of the various areas of center upkeep and operation. In most centers, this distribution of financial support is made simpler by the separation of each tenant's rental payment from his contribution to common area operation. The lease then describes which expenses are to be borne by the owner and which are to be considered common area expenses. Lighting of the parking area, for example, is considered a maintenance cost and is therefore charged to the tenants through a provision in the lease. It is also usually best for tenants to pay for their own utilities, either through separate metering, or—to eliminate the cost of metering—through an engineering estimate system. The distribution of air conditioning charges depends on whether the system involves a central plant or individual package units. In either case, capital costs and operating charges are divided between landlord and tenant through lease provisions. And in this matter as in all other areas of center operation and maintenance, the chosen arrangement must be made legally enforceable through inclusion in the lease.

The lease can also be seen as the second of three steps which help assure the center's proper operation and management and its ultimate success as a business venture. The first of these steps is the consideration of such development criteria as a strong location with respect to access from the trade area, proper site planning, proper selection of merchants, and appropriateness of store sizes and building layout for the individual tenants' merchandising abilities and for the needs of the trade area. The second step includes the leasing program and the many operational arrangements that are set forth in the tenant lease. The third step is the ongoing operation and management of the center. Only so much groundwork can be laid; after that point, it is up to the center management, in its day-to-day decisions and policies, to guide the center toward success for both the owner and the merchants.

The requirements for successful center operation are strong and enthusiastic merchants, a general manager who is given a free hand and who possesses promotional skills and a knowledge of merchandising, and a developer-owner who is keenly interested in promoting the center. For successful promotion, the market must be known and the various facets of marketing—buying, inventorying, displaying, pricing, selling to please customers, promoting, and advertising—must be appreciated by the developer and employed by the merchants. The shopping center is no longer simply a real estate operation but a complex for merchandising; it is a business.

No one has yet found a way to measure the energy, the know-how, or the capability of management. The intangible qualities of managerial efficiency and effectiveness are probably as important as locational advantage or historical experience in contributing profit or loss to a shopping center's operation. Before going ahead with a discussion of the details of shopping center management, however, it should be noted that just as only so much planning can be done before actual management must take over, so the shopping center manager and his staff can only contribute so much to the success of the center. The mechanics of management and the decisions made by the manager cannot assure a thriving marketplace. Likewise, the developer can only provide the setting for success, because it is largely the merchants who determine the customer draw and who cause the center to succeed or fail. For this reason, the most important responsibility of the shopping center management is to stimulate the merchants to create a marketplace which is more than usual or commonplace. The merchants must be encouraged to tailor their array of goods and services and their ranges of colors, sizes, prices, and styles of merchandise to the current and changing demand of the buying public. Only in the presence of such responsiveness to the market can the center become *the* place to shop.

Management Arrangements

Since a shopping center must be treated as an ongoing merchandising operation rather than as a straightforward real estate venture, there must be a comprehensive and responsive arrangement of center management. The owner, whether or not he is also the manager, must provide leadership and drive. One of the owner's most important efforts will be to shepherd the merchants association and to plan stimulating and meaningful association meetings. Once a month, for example, the meeting should feature a well-planned discussion of interest and benefit to all association members. To ensure the appropriateness of association meetings and activities, it is a good idea for the secretary of the association to be a professional experienced in public relations and retail merchandising. The shopping center manager himself could have either retail experience or real estate management experience, although in general it is easier to train an experienced merchandiser to deal with real estate operations than it is to instill a working knowledge of merchandising in a person whose background is real estate management.[10]

Depending on the size of the center and the arrangements for operation worked out earlier in the lease negotiations, the shopping center owner-developer provides for maintenance and management in one of the following ways:

- The owner-developer acts as or employs his own manager to supervise the maintenance and management force, including the supervision of promotion and advertising, whether this work is handled by outside contract or by the center's management staff. The owner also retains the promotion director as a key member of the management staff. In some arrangements, the owner pays the promotion director's salary as part of his contribution to the merchants association.
- The owner-developer turns over the center's operations to a management firm, if he does not have such capacity in his own organization. This is a common practice in neighborhood centers.

Where center operation is handled by a management firm, fees are involved and are usually determined by negotiation. The fee necessarily depends on the extent of services rendered; a higher fee would be charged if advertising, promotion, and coordination of the merchants association were included in the contract.

A leasing and management contract should be considered as two separate agreements. If only leases are secured and no other management functions are peformed, the prevailing rates in the area for real estate management may be used as a guide. In shopping center leasing, commissions paid to the broker who secures a tenant lease do not vary much from those paid for securing commercial leases downtown, even though the clauses in a shopping center lease vary from those in other commercial leases. For management alone, fees are generally based on a percentage of the gross rentals collected.[11]

Special Management Concerns

In addition to maintenance and other areas of shopping center operation, there are a number of management concerns which may be troublesome and which require the landlord's special attention. These include, among others, the matters of sign control, enforcement of parking regulations, evening and Sunday operation, and the whole area of real estate taxes.[12]

Sign Control

The need for strict sign control has already been mentioned several times. The size, location, and design of all signs and other graphics are matters over which the owner and manager must maintain rigid control. If management directives are to succeed in preventing poor or incompatible signing, sign control must be put into the lease in a vigorous and enforceable form. Lease clauses should limit the amount of space that the tenants' signs may occupy, require that no signs be placed on the roof, and provide that any lettering to be placed on any glass must be approved by the landlord.[13]

The shopping center management should not offer concessions in matters of sign control. In today's merchandising, many tenants, such as chain drugstores, favor the placement of paper signs on display windows to promote certain merchandise or to announce sales. But the practice is probably not effective, and it is likely to give the center as a whole a shabby appearance. The careful management of any center involves rigid control over exterior paper signs.

Where a new signing program is part of the renovation of an existing center, the owner would do well to "give a little and take a little" by offering to pay half the cost of new signs. Whatever policy is adopted, all tenants must be offered the same arrangement.

---

[10] For a complete reference source for shopping center management, see Horace Carpenter, Jr., *Shopping Center Management: Principles and Practices* (New York: International Council of Shopping Centers, 1974).

[11] The International Council of Shopping Centers offers its members the "Shopping Center Management Agreement" form, containing recommended language for operating contracts. The form can be a valuable aid to developers, management brokers, and attorneys in concluding shopping center management contracts. Also available to ICSC members is "Auditing Tenants' Gross Sales," Shopping Center Report 11, by Roger S. Smith (New York: International Council of Shopping Centers, 1966).

[12] ICSC members are referred to the "Shopping Center Maintenance Schedule Checklist," available from ICSC.

[13] See the sample sign agreement under Appendix C (Exhibit C, Part III).

Parking Enforcement

There will be a considerable number of employee cars at any center. In fact, the standard index for parking—5.5 spaces per 1,000 square feet GLA—includes an allotment of at least 10 percent of the total parking area to accommodate employee parking. In many centers, employee parking will require an even greater percentage of the parking area.

Regulations which designate certain portions of the parking area for employee parking are included in the lease; the lease further provides that flagrant violations can lead to cancellation of the lease. This is necessary since the center's parking areas are private property and thus the parking regulations cannot be enforced by the local police. At any rate, the center management must continually check to see whether these regulations are observed and must work with individual tenants and through the merchants association to enforce such regulations; otherwise, employees will occupy prime parking spaces best used for customer parking.

Parking violations by the public are another matter. Since persons who misuse parking spaces may also be customers of the center, diplomacy and finesse must be used in dealing with violations. The greatest problem arises when commuters find the shopping center a convenient place to leave their cars all day. These parkers either work nearby or park their cars at the center before taking another form of transportation to their place of employment. Such a situation calls for a municipal ordinance, such as that already in effect in Kansas City, Missouri, which permits police enforcement of parking regulations on private lots.

With practices of real estate assessment continuing to cause problems for shopping center owners and other business owners, there may come a time when center owner-developers will be forced, in effect, to turn their parking areas over to the municipality for maintenance and enforcement. The municipalities in turn would be forced to support these operations by installing parking meters on the lot or by otherwise charging for customer parking.

Evening and Sunday Operation

Evening shopping is a major new force in retailing. The practice has shifted the peak hours of trade and the traditional shopping schedules to such a point that centers which stay open only three or four nights a week are considered conservative in their operation. Evening sales now typically account for 30 to 40 percent of a center's trade, as shown in Figure 5-1.

Late afternoon and evening shopping causes less interference with evening rush hour traffic. It also means that merchants will open later in the morning on weekdays. This affects the center's operations, particularly the early demand on the parking area. The challenge then faced by management is to achieve greater trade volumes in off-peak hours through effective advertising and promotion.

After-dark operation also requires better lighting of walks and parking areas and greater attention to store illumination for both interior and exterior design. Incandescent and fluorescent lights should be mixed to get a balance between warm and cold light. The lights and glamour of centers at night are important, but they must be achieved at a level of intensity which will avoid excessive energy consumption. Holding down the costs of lighting and heating or air conditioning the center while expanding the hours of evening operation calls for skillful planning and design by the center management and the tenants.

5-1	ESTIMATED DAILY DISTRIBUTION OF SALES (YEAR-ROUND)						
TIME OF DAY	Monday	Tuesday	Wednesday	Thursday	Friday	Saturday	Sunday*
MORNING (before 12)	19%	22%	21%	19%	25%	27%	29%
AFTERNOON (12–6)	41	40	41	41	34	51	40
EVENING (after 6)	40	40	39	40	41	23	31

*Where center has Sunday hours.   Because of rounding, not all daily totals appear equal to 100 percent.
Source: International Council of Shopping Centers.

Sunday openings are another trend. Shopping center operators report that weekend shopping accounts for an even greater proportion of the sales volume than it traditionally did in central business districts. Business activity starts building on Thursday and reaches its peak in the afternoon on Saturday, the heaviest shopping day. In some areas, however, Sunday openings produce the highest sales volumes *per hour* of the week.

Store hours can be handled by agreement through the merchants association rather than as a specification in the lease. However, the lease should prohibit the independent action of a tenant who chooses not to remain open during regular daytime, evening, or Sunday hours. Many centers are open six nights per week and a limited number of hours on Sunday. The hours of small tenants should be tied to the hours established by the major tenants.

Real Estate Taxes

Real estate taxes and assessments are another special problem for the shopping center owner, because real estate taxes represent the landlord's greatest exposure to operational expense. As reported in *Dollars and Cents of Shopping Centers*, real estate taxes in 1975 accounted for 32 percent of total operating expenses in regional centers, 40 percent in community centers, and 45 percent in neighborhood centers.

For protection from increasing real estate taxes, tax participation by the tenants through a lease clause is essential. Since tenants pay for tax increases through rent increases, the tenants become concerned about and interested in the local assessment practices and may help in finding tax relief.

Future taxes are often estimated too low. To be on the safe side, taxes should be figured at the local rate and to nearly full value as represented by whatever method the local assessor uses as his basis for assessment. Assessments get changed frequently but the trend is ever upward, as shown in Figure 5-2.

There is a difference in value between land used for building and land used for parking, and this difference should be reflected in the tax assessment of the shopping center property. The land used for parking should be valued as parking area, not as commercial property similar to that occupied by the commercial structure. The contribution made by the shopping center parking area to the public benefit supports the thesis that more reason-

5-2 INCREASE IN REAL ESTATE TAXES PER SQUARE FOOT GLA

TYPE OF CENTER	1960	1975
NEIGHBORHOOD	$0.20	$0.32
COMMUNITY	.20	.30
REGIONAL	.24	.36
SUPER-REGIONAL	—	.63

Source: *Dollars and Cents of Shopping Centers.*

able valuations are needed for shopping centers. Standard assessment factors used for downtown properties—front foot values, corner influences, standards of depths, and so on—should not be applied to the shopping center, where roughly 25 percent of the land is used for building and 75 percent for free parking.

Accounting

Many references have already been made to ULI's triennial publication, *Dollars and Cents of Shopping Centers. Dollars and Cents* analyzes the balance left in shopping center operations after operating expenses are subtracted from gross receipts. It presents current data on the various components of shopping center income and expense as well as other data on centers in the United States and Canada. Its purpose, then, is to provide a source of reference for finding and evaluating levels of performance in shopping center operations. From the balance after operating expenses presented in the book must be subtracted the noncomparable items of depreciation, debt service, and income taxes in order to arrive at an actual return on investment.

The categories of measurement used in *Dollars and Cents* and the accounting methods which the presentation of data reflects are based on another ULI publication, the *Standard Manual of Accounting for Shopping Center Operations.*[14] Whereas *Dollars and Cents* is intended as neither a directive nor a manual but rather as a reference work on current levels of shopping center performance, the *Standard Manual* was developed by a special ULI committee because of the need for uniformity in shopping center accounting methods to allow consistency of presentation and meaningful compari-

---

[14] *Standard Manual of Accounting for Shopping Center Operations* (Washington, D.C.: ULI–the Urban Land Institute, 1971).

sons of operating results. Specialized accounting methods for the industry were not required for asset and liability accounting, which is much the same for shopping centers as for other businesses. Rather, it was in the area of income and expense accounting that specialization and standardization were needed. Income accounting in shopping centers is largely a reflection of the revenue received through provisions in the tenant lease, including rental income from tenants, income from common area services, income from the sale of utilities to tenants, where submetering is involved, and income from miscellaneous sources. Expense accounting in shopping centers, on the other hand, must be tailored to provide center owners, developers, and managers with useful data for budget projections and for comparisons within the industy. The *Standard Manual* was designed to meet these accounting needs and to facilitate this sharing of information in order to improve the practices and performance of shopping center management and operation. Much of the information which follows is based on the *Standard Manual*.

Income Accounting

The total income or total operating receipts are derived from all money received from rent, common area charges, and other income. Total rent is the income from tenants for the leased space, including the minimum guaranteed yearly rent (or the straight percentage rent where there is no minimum guarantee) and the overage rent received as a percentage of sales above the established breakpoint. Because of the many different rental arrangements commonly used, only the figures for total rent are realistic for rental comparisons (including those found in *Dollars and Cents of Shopping Centers*) across the industry. But in income accounting in the individual shopping center, the records should be designed to show readily the data in each of the following categories as established in each tenant's lease:

- GLA in square feet.
- Sales—annual volume and per square foot of GLA.
- Rate of percentage rent.
- Percentage rent where no minimum guarantee is established.
- Minimum guaranteed yearly rent.
- Overage rent earned for the year.
- Charges to tenants for common area services,

including charges for heating and air conditioning an enclosed mall.
- Charges under escalator clauses, accounted separately for each type of charge.
- Utility charges for the year, where applicable.
- Miscellaneous income, including revenue from such facilities as public telephones, pay toilets, and vending machines.
- Total rent and total charges.

Expense Accounting

The standard system of expense accounting is based on two objectives. The first and most important is the need to classify and present accounting data according to the accounting and information needs of the shopping center management. The second objective is to provide accounting methods which facilitate the industrywide gathering and analysis of operating expense data. To accommodate these two objectives, shopping center expenses are divided into categories in two ways: a system of *functional* categories, and a system of *natural* categories. The functional categories can be applied to all centers; they provide the framework for comparison across the industry. The natural division of expenses, on the other hand, ties the functional expenses with the primary objects of expenditure. The following is a breakdown of expenses according to these two systems:

Functional Expense Categories
- Building maintenance.
- Parking lot, mall, and other public areas.
- Central utility systems.
- Office area services.
- Advertising and promotion.
- Finance expenses.
- Depreciation and amortization of deferred costs.
- Real estate taxes.
- Insurance.
- General and administrative.

Natural Expense Categories
- Payroll and supplementary benefits.
- Management fees.
- Contractual services.
- Professional services.
- Leasing fees and commissions.
- Materials and supplies.
- Equipment expenses.
- Utilities.
- Travel and entertainment.

- Communication.
- Taxes and licenses.
- Contributions to merchants association.
- Insurance.
- Losses from bad debts.
- Interest.
- Depreciation.
- Amortization of deferred costs.
- Ground rent.

Taken together, the two categories provide a logical basis for analytical comparisons of individual shopping center results with industry data as well as day-to-day information for management purposes. The standard system is designed to serve as the expense classification for a complete system of accounting, with two exceptions—financing costs and depreciation of the structures (real and appurtenances). Depreciation practices—or the spreading of a capital expense over a period of years—vary significantly. Of course, depreciation is also a deduction in arriving at taxable income, and the portion of capital costs to be borne by the operations of a given accounting period is a significant factor in the determination of net income for that period. For these reasons, variations in depreciation practices can produce greatly different results. In shopping centers, as in many other real estate undertakings, the taxpayer (the shopping center owner) may have the objective of matching depreciation expense as nearly as possible to the excess of rental and other income over deductible expenses other than depreciation. As a means of achieving this objective, the taxpayer must make several choices from a broad range of alternatives. He must choose from among available depreciation methods. He must either depreciate each asset as an individual item or must select a basis for grouping depreciable assets. For each item or asset grouping, a useful life must be chosen. Finally, the taxpayer must elect whether he will follow "guideline" or traditional depreciation procedures.[15]

Since there is substantial difference in the size and complexity of regional, community, and neighborhood centers, it is logical that the needs of management for accounting information will also vary. If a large shopping center wants to use the standard system of expense accounting as a tool for financial planning and budgetary control, it should also establish for internal use a subdivision of functional categories or an expansion of natural divisions consistent with assignments of responsibility and supervisory personnel.

Merchants Association

An association of merchants is vitally important for the promotion of a shopping center of any size. The association acts as a clearinghouse for suggestions, ideas, and programming of merchandising events, and it serves as a quasi-court for handling complaints and differences of opinion. Experience has shown that association membership must be mandated in the lease and that assessments for the association's activities should be collected at the same time as the rent.

As the opening of the center draws near, the owner-developer devotes his attention to management and promotion. Even before construction is completed, he organizes his tenants for preopening and opening activities and for the daily operations that will follow. As owner, he must produce a satisfying image for the center and must foster teamwork among the merchants. He must resolve any conflicting interests in the group. He must bring about cooperation among individuals representing large tenants, small tenants, national chain stores, parent companies, and local independents. He must be assured of a business environment that invites customers to come to the center rather than just to one store. An atmosphere of tenant and landlord cooperation for mutual benefit is the key to reaching the full sales volume potential of the center. The degree of success depends largely on the effectiveness of the merchants association.[16]

Membership

As stated earlier, a lease clause is the recommended vehicle for the establishment of the merchants association. The lease is the landlord's strongest tool after the center's location itself; the possibility of lease cancellation is a very potent operational aid.

Mandatory membership in the association may be resisted as a lease requirement, although tenants are likely to find such a requirement more acceptable if the landlord is also required to contribute to the association budget. Fortunately, most chain stores no longer resist mandatory membership clauses. If the lead tenant does not join the association, it is hard to get other tenants to go along

[15] For a discussion of selecting a depreciation method, see the *Standard Manual*, pp. 10–14.

[16] See Robert S. Nyburg, *Shopping Center Merchants Associations* (New York: International Council of Shopping Centers, 1959). Also see Callahan, *Shopping Center Promotions*, cited in footnote 9.

with the clause, and the solution becomes one of setting up separate provisions for the association with each tenant. But once the leading tenant agrees to belong to the merchants association and contribute to the advertising program, other tenants—local and chain stores—are more readily persuaded. Tenants who once would not sign a lease with a mandatory membership clause now agree to the formation of a merchants association which includes an owner's representative. They will belong to and support the association because of the wide participation.

Operation

Operation of the association should be left largely to the merchants, who will work through committees to carry out association activities under a professional program director.

The owner can rely on either of two operational policies. He can act as merely the agent for the association, relying on the members' interest and organization for operation of the center, in which case an executive secretary or professional promotions director will be hired and paid for by the association; or he can actively run the association, relying on the officer-members and committees to cooperate in the advertising and promotional programs.

The owner must recognize his responsibility for promoting the center. The association members should expect to be presented with a comprehensive promotions program for their approval and a promotions director to execute the program. When the owner pays the salary of the promotions director, the owner keeps control of the promotions, even in small centers. Associations have trouble when the landlord leaves the merchants to their own devices; in general, tenants are slow to appreciate what an association can do for them.

An association may be organized as a profit corporation with charter and bylaws. A nonprofit corporation has tax advantages, but it is also limited in its activity. The profit organization operates more broadly and can escape year-end taxation by investing all its tenant assessments in promotional events and other activities.

Bylaws set forth all pertinent information and rules, including election of officers, duties of officers, quorum, order of business for monthly meetings, date of annual meeting, appointment of committees, and, usually, the establishment of a board of directors consisting of a president, vice

president, secretary, and treasurer. The usual standing committees are finance, advertising, special events, and publicity. The authority to assess dues and fees for advertising, promotion, seasonal decoration, and other activities is spelled out in the formal lease document. In joining the association as required in the lease, the tenant also agrees to abide by the association's charter and bylaws.

A part-time or full-time paid secretary is a necessity for successful operation. The many items of correspondence, newsletter preparation, notices, billings, and other responsibilities cannot be assumed by any one member, whose main effort must always be to make his own store pay. In small centers, it is not always possible for the association to maintain a staff; staff work must then be handled as part of the owner's contribution.

Where a full-time or part-time promotion manager is not employed by the association, a representative of a local public relations firm can be contracted with for promotional work. A large agency which is not locally based can be used, but the representative who handles the center's work should be local. In general, the more local the management responsibility, the better the operation.

The merchants association can be charged with a wide range of activities—joint advertising of the center, including the use of the center's name on advertising mastheads, letterheads, bill heads, and statements; special centerwide promotion; seasonal events and decorations; enforcement of parking lot regulations, particularly those regarding employee parking; business referrals and credit systems; store hours and night openings; merchant directory; and centerwide news bulletins or special newspapers for trade area distribution. The importance of getting the merchants involved cannot be overstressed; unless they are involved, merchants will merely accept what is offered. In some cases, the association can be charged with parking lot maintenance and lighting, trash collection, and snow removal, but it is probably better to avoid conflicts by letting the center management perform the maintenance services and charge back the pro rata share to each merchant as part of the common area charges.

Dues

The basis of assessment for contributions to the cost of the association's activities varies widely. The most equitable method is for all tenants to contribute to the advertising fund, usually on the basis of each tenant's GLA. Less usual methods include a straight percentage of gross sales; a combination of a sales volume percentage and the basic formula of square feet occupied; contribution according to front footage occupied; a percentage of the tenant's annual rent in relation to the total annual rent of the center; individually negotiated assessments unrelated to the merchant's size or volume; and combinations of these methods, although formulas which combine several of these methods may be difficult to administer. Tenants, such as banks, whose leases do not include percentage clauses should pay into the promotion fund on the basis of square feet occupied. A lease can also specify the amount to be contributed for pre-opening and grand opening promotion and for the first year of operation. Management either matches the amount raised through the merchants' contributions or—the more usual practice—pays 25 percent of the annual budget.

If the tenant does not pay his dues, he is violating the lease and the landlord must take action. Lease termination is preferable to a suit, which neither the tenant nor the landlord wants.

Owner Participation

The owner-developer must not only organize the merchants association but must also participate in and guide its activities. He must contribute to the operating fund, as mentioned earlier. An active association requires an active and energetic effort by the owner to stimulate interest, originate and launch promotions, prepare budgets, and coordinate all activities of the association.

To stimulate the merchants, the tenants can be sent a monthly association bulletin which includes sales volume increases and decreases from the previous month and from the previous year. This information can be presented by tenant clasification—shoes, ladies' wear, and so forth. The preparation of this bulletin will also require that the tenants report their sales volumes monthly so that the management can report sales volumes and sales trends without revealing the volumes achieved by individual tenants. The monthly bulletin, as part of the educational program for the merchants, will also contain other news and information about future programs of interest to the merchants.

After the center has been in operation for several years, certainly after 5 years, the trade area should be reexamined. Addresses of credit accounts held by merchants should be checked to see whether the market is being reached. The income level and other characteristics of the trade area can change without the merchants' being fully aware of it. Because of this, merchandise patterns should be examined to see whether prices, styles, sizes, and other qualities are appropriate for the current market.

A center can also be upgraded by relighting, refurbishing, remodeling, adding an enclosed mall, or making other physical improvements. In most centers, sales volumes level off as the center gets older. Significant gains rarely take place, and sales may even decline. But when an older center is expanded or enclosed or otherwise improved, new life is pumped in and sales may increase.

Developers and tenants are convinced that an effective merchants association is of great mutual benefit. The association's advertising and promotional programs increase customer traffic and boost the sales. As the merchants realize greater profits, they become more competitive and tend to better serve their customers. As sales volumes go up, the owner-developer receives greater overage rents. Since the owner has every reason to be interested in the volume of business done by each tenant and by the aggregate of all stores, he should be careful to furnish the leadership, talent, and organizational skills necessary for the effective centerwide promotion of merchandise, public events, and community services.

Promotion

A successful center is a promoted center. Promotion is important to owners of both large and small centers; in both cases, the owner depends on effective promotion and the consequent high level of sales for a satisfactory level of percentage rents.

Promotions and special events are not only traffic builders but also image makers. Generally speaking, money spent for promotions can be higher in the first few years of operation or until the center is fully accepted throughout the trade area. The schedule of promotional expenditures must be based on a thoroughly programmed budget approved by the association. To develop such a program, there must be a clear assignment of responsibilities and top-level cooperation among the center's retailers.[17]

The *type* of promotion undertaken by the center

---

[17] As a guide to association bylaws, budgets, promotional events, and other activities, see Callahan, *Shopping Center Promotions* (footnote 9 above).

is a major factor in the center's growth. The promotion is aimed at attracting customers, not just curious crowds. "Pack the stores, not the parking lots" is a maxim that applies to promotional events. Carnival-type promotions are of limited benefit and should be restricted to the offering of attractive merchandise and sound values.

Developers emphasize that center promotions should be planned around a major tenant's own promotion. Timing and merchandise offerings should not be duplicated. Most developers have found it a good idea to focus on five or six major promotions during the year and then to supplement these with appropriate minor events. Promotional events and activities should be set up and fully budgeted a year in advance, and association members should be furnished a full description of the program and budget. A record should be kept of each promotional event so that the owner or promotions director can review completed promotions to see why they were or were not successful.

Cooperative advertising, primarily newspaper and radio advertising, is the kind of promotion most often used. It is important to advertise the center because, in the public's mind, the individual shops within the center must be associated with the image of the center itself. Spot announcements on daytime radio and television are a good way of reaching the public. Full-page newspaper advertising is also worthwhile. The shopping center company contracts with the paper for the advertisement in its own name and then sells space to the individual merchants at a lower rate than they would pay for separate ads. In this way, the adver-

tising is identified with the center's logo and the image that it conveys. Filling up a full-page ad may not be easy for the center management, but the resulting increase in sales volumes can be worth the effort.[18] Upcoming promotional and advertising activities should be announced through the monthly bulletin so that the merchants can cooperate in these events.

Christmas, Easter, Halloween, and other holidays are special occasions for promotions and seasonal decorations in the center. Other worthwhile promotional schemes include giveaways, children's attractions, and special sales during birthdays or anniversaries. A "Suburban Living Fair" or "Urban Living Fair" can replace the old midsummer clearance event. Special promotional events always benefit from the use of live models to illustrate such things as patio cooking, urban living, and the use of children's play equipment. For all promotional activities, the developer-owner should keep in mind that replacement and refurbishing of display materials are needed.

Whatever the promotion activity, the wider the participation by the tenants, the greater the impact and success of the promotion. Joint participation enables small tenants to bid for business through methods ordinarily limited to large merchandisers. In addition, the participation of all tenants helps maintain the center's positive image in the mind of the buying public.

---

[18] For a compendium of promotions ideas for stores and shopping centers, see Joseph R. Rowen, ed., *NRMA Sales Promotion Encyclopedia Vol. 3* (New York: National Retail Merchants Association, 1973).

6.
Case Studies

This chapter is a series of nine shopping center case studies. Its intent is to present representative examples of the three major types of shopping centers and to communicate the direction of contemporary development.

Developer membership in ULI, and a willingness to share experiences with a wider audience, were prerequisites of inclusion. Further, each development had to be of superior quality, with features worthy of emulation. However, the profiles are not presented as necessarily the best examples of their respective types. Such a decision would be difficult to make, and many other projects would have served equally well.

Contemporary development experience was also important; each project has either been completed or structurally modified since 1970. Another consideration was geographical distribution. All major regions of North America are represented.

The projects appear in order of size, from The Mercado, with 43,000 square feet of GLA, to Fair-

lane Town Center, with 1.4 million square feet. The narrative is based on lengthy on-site interviews with the developers and other project professionals. Statistics reflect project conditions as of September 1976. Economic data, in particular, have been treated uniformly to permit comparisons; these data have also been generalized to protect developer confidences. Readers interested in profiles of shopping center economic performance are referred to *Dollars and Cents of Shopping Centers,* mentioned earlier in this book.

Some conclusions suggested by individual projects may appear inconsistent with the perspective of the entire industry. This is to be expected, for shopping center development is not so much a science as an art. Special concepts successful in one situation often have only limited application elsewhere. Rules of thumb have a way of becoming quickly outmoded. Compare, for example, the trend-setting centers of 10 years ago with those of today, some of which are presented in the following pages.

THE MERCADO

6-1 A series of one- and two-story freestanding buildings provide a dramatic setting for specialty shops.

The Specialty Center

The seventies has witnessed a surge of interest in specialty shopping developments, a trend deriving from a variety of factors associated with increasing affluence, casual lifestyles, and a growing interest in self-expression and personal satisfaction through handicrafts, art, and entrepreneurship. At its present stage of evolution, the specialty shopping center offers imported goods, gifts, handcrafted items (often created on the premises), and luxury merchandise of all kinds. It also normally contains a mix of specialty restaurants and food shops to attract return customers.

The original specialty shopping areas typically consisted of random clusters of street-front shops in high-income areas within cities or in destination resorts such as Palm Beach, Florida, and Carmel, California. These were followed by more carefully planned groupings of specialty shops with off-street parking, such as the Town and Country Villages in Palo Alto and San Jose, California. The next step in the evolution of specialty centers was Bal Harbour Shops in Bal Harbour, Florida. This noteworthy center, concentrating the broadest array of luxury shops in South Florida, used traditional shopping center design of the mid-sixties. The success of this center and of similar projects gave rise to a number of developments oriented toward the merchandising of imported and specialty goods, but usually directed toward a broader, middle-income market.

Specialty centers do not lend themselves to precise physical definition. They may range from neighborhood to regional in scale, and exhibit a wide variety of physical configurations and architectural styles. Few have an anchor tenant, thus distinguishing them from community and regional centers. The common feature of specialty centers is the use of a unique architectural style which is both intimate in scale and strongly pedestrian in character, in the fashion of Ghirardelli Square in San Francisco. Many recent centers have sought to create a special experience for the shopper and a sense of discovery and adventure through the use of irregular circulation patterns and dramatic spatial relationships within the shopping environment. These elements are intended to make shopping an entertaining experience as well as a necessity of day-to-day life.

Most specialty center tenants are local and independent, although a few national chains specialize in imported merchandise. This local character of the tenant mix is both the primary strength and the fundamental weakness of the specialty center. For the center to be successful, the artisans, shopkeepers, and restaurateurs must create a unique identity for the center and give it a much wider market area than the commercial square footage would otherwise generate. Artists and craftsmen, however, often lack managerial skills and business experience, a circumstance which can lead to tenant instability and high turnover.

The Mercado and Rancho Bernardo

The Mercado is a specialty shopping center which illustrates many of the potentials and problems associated with this type of commercial development. With 43,000 square feet of GLA and a site of 7.7 acres, The Mercado consists of a carefully designed grouping of arts and crafts shops, boutique fashion stores, and unusual restaurants. Among the 40 tenants are eight restaurants and food stores, eight clothing stores, and seven art, craft, and gift shops, as well as a variety of other specialized retail outlets, offices, and service uses.

The Mercado has been built in an attractive Early California style and consists of a series of interconnected, two-level, freestanding structures, clustered around two interior courtyards. The shops have been placed in an irregular fashion with varied entrance spacing, narrow corridors, spacious open areas, and dramatic changes in elevation to communicate the center's theme, An Adventure in Shopping. As an adjunct to the retailing operations, the courtyards are used for stage performances, musical entertainments, art fairs, shopping displays, and other activities.

The Mercado is located in Rancho Bernardo, a 5,900-acre master-planned community approximately 25 miles north of downtown San Diego but still within the city limits. The development was initiated in the early sixties; with more than 15,000 residents, it is now approximately 35 percent complete. Rancho Bernardo is being developed by AVCO Community Developers, Inc., a New England-based conglomerate and Fortune 500 company which acquired the project from its original owners in 1969. The specialty center concept was implemented shortly after AVCO assumed control. Construction took 1 year, and the center opened in late 1970.

Within the framework of AVCO's development program, The Mercado was conceived of as one means of establishing an image for Rancho Bernardo and attracting potential residents to the new community. Profitability was not the primary concern at the outset. On the Rancho Bernardo community plan, The Mercado site was designated SC (Specialized Commercial). Elsewhere in the development, convenience and general merchandise sales are accommodated by a series of four neighborhood centers and one town center, all except one of which are either complete or under construction. The center is adjacent to the interchange between Interstate Highway 15 and Rancho Bernardo Road,

the primary at-grade arterial serving the development. The 114-acre Bernardo Town Center, which consists of a community-scale shopping center and a series of freestanding commercial, retail, office, and institutional buildings, is located diagonally across the interchange from The Mercado. This positioning suggests both the importance The Mercado has in the overall development program and the synergistic relationship between it and the town center.

The site itself is essentially flat, having been graded from the slope of a hillside. Access is provided from the collector streets bordering the site on the east and south. The Mercado buildings are clustered against the hillside, with parking in front of the buildings, and a service street closed to through-traffic separating the two structural groupings.

6-2   A fountain is the visual focus of the first courtyard.

6-3   Multilevel retail space with balconies overlooking the courtyard.

Physical Design

With its red tile roofs, white stucco walls, tile and cobblestone floors, and dark wooden balconies, The Mercado has a strongly indigenous Early California appearance. This design theme is highly appropriate, not only because of the center's location, but also because of its specialty orientation. Building materials appropriate for a subtropical location provide a well-conceived background image for the craft stores, art galleries, boutique shops, and restaurants which constitute the tenant mix. These building materials are also sufficiently unusual that they reinforce in a major way The Mercado's role as a destination center drawing from the entire San Diego metropolitan area. The Early California design theme has been extended to the landscaping plan, which uses a variety of tropical vegetation. Twenty-two percent of the site is devoted to landscaping, an amount sufficiently high to impart a naturalistic feel to the entire development. Supergraphic signage adds a contemporary touch.

The Mercado is a neighborhood center in terms of scale, although, as noted in Chapter 1, neither the amount of GLA nor the size of the site actually determines the shopping center type. Buildings and courtyards occupy 17.3 percent of the property, and the remainder consists of parking, circulation, and landscaping. The center was built in two phases in 1969 and 1970. Following completion of the first courtyard, a movie theater was dropped from the development plan and it became possible to add a second courtyard. This courtyard, located farther from the main parking area, took longer to lease than the first, an experience suggesting that alternative expansion plans should be planned at the outset.

The Mercado's highly individualized layout includes a series of narrow passageways leading from the parking areas into the interior courtyards, as well as the highlighting of the pedestrian areas by careful placement of outdoor restaurants, sculptures, a gazebo, and similar amenities. Individual buildings are integrated by means of archways,

6-4 The Early California–style architecture includes red tile roofs and white stucco walls. Supergraphics add a contemporary touch.

walls, balconies, and roofline extensions, as well as by the use of common materials.

This innovative approach to center design posed several problems, principally relating to pedestrian circulation. The quaint placement of shop entrances creates an interesting merchandising environment but required adjustment at several points so that stores could be better seen by potential customers. In addition, the numerous stairways serving the second-level shops should have been supplemented with elevators to increase shopper traffic on the upper level.

There is on-site parking for 301 vehicles, giving The Mercado a somewhat higher parking index than typical for neighborhood-scale centers. Service areas and service access facilities are at the rear of the buildings.

Development Strategy

The strategy of using a specialty center as a marketing tool was based on a combination of market and economic research and architectural planning. Center tenants were subsidized at the outset, and in 1972 they paid an average rent of $5.19 per square foot and common area charges of $0.65 per square foot. During the early years of operation, the developer also assumed the cost of advertising except for a fee amounting to 2 percent of gross sales. At least two other physical elements of the community, the golf course and 150-room Inn at Rancho Bernardo were also utilized in similar fashion as part of this marketing strategy.

Subsequently, the pace of growth at Rancho Bernardo slowed considerably and it became apparent that a major shift in AVCO's development strategy was required. After evaluating a variety of approaches, the company decided to limit the scope of its real estate activities to land development alone, a decision based on the perception that management and development are entirely different businesses and are not necessarily compatible with one another. Between 1973 and 1975, all operational facilities at Rancho Bernardo were sold, including shopping centers, office buildings, apartments, and industrial space. The Mercado was purchased by The Mercado Associates, a partnership of three local investors, for $1,520,000. The new owners immediately placed the center on a profit-making footing by raising common area charges to cover actual overhead costs and increasing rents by an average of 20 percent.

Tenant Mix

The largest tenant category (in terms of GLA) is clothing and shoes, with eight stores occupying 23.9 percent of the center. Almost as large is the "other retail" category, with 14 outlets accounting for 23.2 percent of the center. The Mercado also has four restaurants, four food stores, one dry goods store, three furniture stores (home furnishings), three office users, and three service facilities. Four tenant spaces, comprising 3.1 percent of the center, were vacant as of September 1976.

Tenant classifications found in *Dollars and Cents of Shopping Centers* only indirectly communicate the unique mix of tenants found at The Mercado. The "other retail" category, for example, includes nine art galleries and art and gift shops, a toy store, a jeweler, a clock store, and a bath accessories shop. The four food stores include a delicatessen, a health-food store, a confectioner, and a gourmet food operation. Similar diversities are found in other tenant categories. There are four artisans operating at The Mercado: a woodcarver, a metalworker, a painter, and a needlecrafter. One area originally intended as a "farmers' market" was subdivided after initial construction because of health code problems, anticipated difficulties in management, and the realization that greater income would be generated from other types of shops.

As with many other specialty shopping centers, there has been substantial tenant turnover at The Mercado. In 1976, fewer than half the tenants of 4 years before were still present. Some tenant operations had retained their original names under new ownership, and others had closed, changed their names, expanded, or relocated within the center. Both AVCO and the new owners have had to provide some tenants with managerial assistance and advice. Nevertheless, the present combination of older and newer tenants is significantly stronger than the original tenant mix. The stores around the second courtyard were the last to lease, a reflection of the difference in accessibility. Still, some of the most successful operators at The Mercado have second-story locations, and good marketing appears to be more important than location as a determinant of retail success.

Management and Operation

The management staff, including the center manager, assistant manager, and two full-time maintenance personnel, was transferred to The Mercado Associates along with the property. There is no merchants association, and the management handles advertising and promotion. A common area charge to cover the cost of maintaining the courtyards, walkways, parking areas, and landscaping is assessed against each tenant on a square footage basis. Such charges, which amounted to $96,000 or $2.21 per square foot of GLA in 1975, are defined to include real estate taxes, insurance, utilities, trash collection, and maintenance costs applicable to the common areas. A typical lease provides for a rent of approximately $6 per square foot, plus a percentage rent of 6 to 8 percent of gross receipts.

Even though it has sold its operational facilities and transferred its management control, AVCO Developers, Inc., has maintained overview control for the exterior of The Mercado through a declaration of building restrictions and architectural control running with the land and designed to protect AVCO's interests during a communitywide development period expected to exceed two decades. These legally enforceable controls and restrictions apply to signage, exterior alterations, colors, and lighting improvement design. Plans and specifica-

6-5 Entrance to one of The Mercado's outdoor restaurants. Note the tile floor and the use of trees in the dining area.

tions for proposed improvements must be submitted to the three-member Rancho Bernardo Architectural Review Committee for approval. Permitted uses and those requiring prior written approval of the architectural committee are also specified. As part of the documents, certain uses are identified as being consistent with The Mercado's specialty shopping center designation:

> . . . specialty food market, not to exceed 5,000 square feet gross floor area; antique shops, book stores; music stores, leather goods and luggage shops; photographic studios, equipment and supplies; restaurants and bars; travel agencies; florists; gift shops; garden nursery and florists; artwork, pottery and hobby shops; apparel shops, not to exceed 2,000 square feet gross floor area; barber and beauty shops; curtain and drapery shops; confectioneries; jewelry stores; studios for teaching art, dancing and music; and candle shops.

It is this mix of uses which perhaps best defines the specialty center as a retail development type.

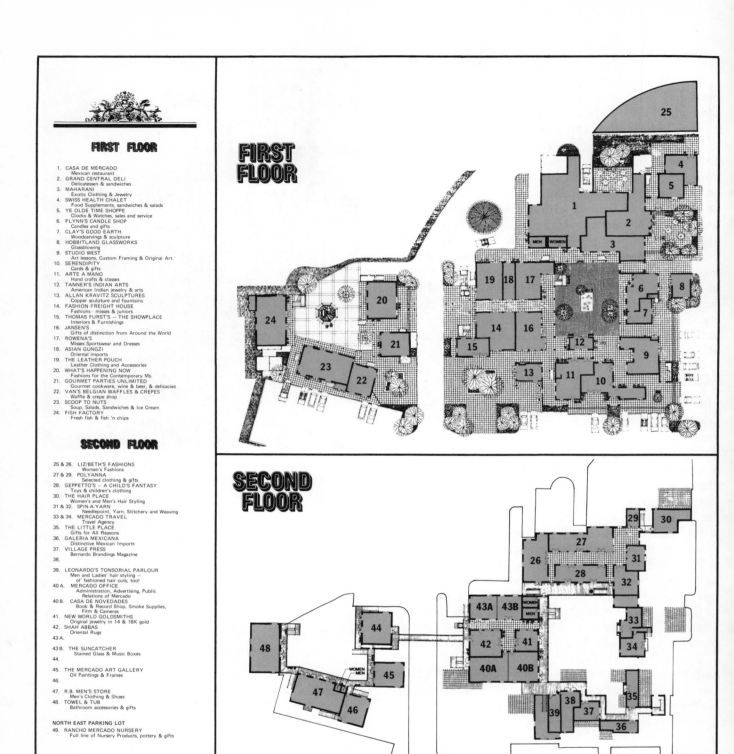

FIRST FLOOR

1. CASA DE MERCADO
   Mexican restaurant
2. GRAND CENTRAL DELI
   Delicatessen & sandwiches
3. MAHARANI
   Exotic Clothing & Jewelry
4. SWISS HEALTH CHALET
   Food Supplements, sandwiches & salads
5. YE OLDE TIME SHOPPE
   Clocks & Watches, sales and service
6. FLYNN'S CANDLE SHOP
   Candles and gifts
7. CLAY'S GOOD EARTH
   Woodcarvings & sculpture
8. HOBBITLAND GLASSWORKS
   Glassblowing
9. STUDIO WEST
   Art lessons, Custom Framing & Original Art
10. SERENDIPITY
    Cards & gifts
11. ARTE A MANO
    Hand crafts & classes
12. TANNER'S INDIAN ARTS
    American Indian jewelry & arts
13. ALLAN KRAVITZ SCULPTURES
    Copper sculpture and fountains
14. FASHION FREIGHT HOUSE
    Fashions - misses & juniors
15. THOMAS FURST'S — THE SHOWPLACE
    Interiors & Furnishings
16. JANSEN'S
    Gifts of distinction from Around the World
17. ROWENA'S
    Misses Sportswear and Dresses
18. ASIAN GUNGZI
    Oriental imports
19. THE LEATHER POUCH
    Leather Clothing and Accessories
20. WHAT'S HAPPENING NOW
    Fashions for the Contemporary Ms.
21. GOURMET PARTIES UNLIMITED
    Gourmet cookware, wine & beer, & delicacies
22. VAN'S BELGIAN WAFFLES & CREPES
    Waffle & crepe shop
23. SCOOP TO NUTS
    Soup, Salads, Sandwiches & Ice Cream
24. FISH FACTORY
    Fresh fish & fish 'n chips

SECOND FLOOR

25 & 26. LIZ/BETH'S FASHIONS
          Women's Fashions
27 & 29. POLYANNA
          Selected clothing & gifts
28. GEPPETTO'S — A CHILD'S FANTASY
    Toys & children's clothing
30. THE HAIR PLACE
    Women's and Men's Hair Styling
31 & 32. SPIN-A-YARN
          Needlepoint, Yarn, Stitchery and Weaving
33 & 34. MERCADO TRAVEL
          Travel Agency
35. THE LITTLE PLACE
    Gifts for All Reasons
36. GALERIA MEXICANA
    Distinctive Mexican Imports
37. VILLAGE PRESS
    Bernardo Brandings Magazine
38.
39. LEONARDO'S TONSORIAL PARLOUR
    Men and Ladies' hair styling —
    ol' fashioned hair cuts, too!
40 A. MERCADO OFFICE
       Administration, Advertising, Public
       Relations of Mercado
40 B. CASA DE NOVEDADES
       Book & Record Shop, Smoke Supplies,
       Film & Cameras
41. NEW WORLD GOLDSMITHS
    Original jewelry in 14 & 18K gold
42. SHAH ABBAS
    Oriental Rugs
43 A.
43 B. THE SUNCATCHER
       Stained Glass & Music Boxes
44.
45. THE MERCADO ART GALLERY
    Oil Paintings & Frames
46.
47. R.B. MEN'S STORE
    Men's Clothing & Shoes
48. TOWEL & TUB
    Bathroom accessories & gifts

NORTH EAST PARKING LOT
49. RANCHO MERCADO NURSERY
    Full line of Nursery Products, pottery & gifts

6-6   Site plan—The Mercado.

PROJECT DATA—THE MERCADO

DEVELOPER/MANAGEMENT (1970–75)

AVCO Community Developers, Inc.
16770 West Bernardo Drive
San Diego, California 92127

LAND USE INFORMATION

Site area   7.7 acres
Land allocation

	Site area	Percent of site
Buildings	29,936 sq. ft.	8.9
Courtyards	28,276 sq. ft.	8.4
Parking, circulation, and open	203,148 sq. ft.	60.7
Landscaping	73,616 sq. ft.	22.0
Total	334,976 sq. ft.	100.0

GLA   43,364 sq. ft.

Parking
Spaces   301
Ratio   3.5 : 1
Index   7.0

ECONOMIC INFORMATION

Total sales (1975)	$2.9 million
Sales per sq. ft. GLA	$66.65
Merchants association dues	none (2 percent of gross sales promotion charge)
Common area charges	$2.21 per sq. ft.
Rentals	
Median amount	$6.60 per sq. ft. GLA
Percentage rents	6 to 8 percent
Capital costs (1970)	
Land and land improvements	$879,000
Buildings and equipment	$1,180,000
Overhead and development	NA

TENANT INFORMATION

Number of tenants   44
Percent leased   93.9

Tenant Classification	Number of stores	GLA	Percent of total GLA	Average percentage in neighborhood centers (from *Dollars and Cents of Shopping Centers: 1975*)
Food	4	4,758 sq. ft.	11.0	26.5
Food service	4	8,976 sq. ft.	20.7	5.1
General merchandise	——	——	——	16.3
Clothing and shoes	8	10,358 sq. ft.	23.9	5.5
Dry goods	1	1,080 sq. ft.	2.5	3.8
Furniture (home furnishings)	3	2,137 sq. ft.	4.9	4.8
Other retail	14	10,055 sq. ft.	23.2	16.9
Financial	——	——	——	3.0
Offices	3	1,275 sq. ft.	2.9	4.7
Services	3	2,084 sq. ft.	4.8	5.6
Other	——	——	——	4.7
Vacant	4	2,631 sq. ft.	6.1	3.1
Total	44	43,354 sq. ft.	100.0	100.0

Tenants by ownership type

Type	Number	Percent	Average percentage in neighborhood centers (from *Dollars and Cents*)
National chain	——	——	20.4
Independent	40	100.0	58.3
Local chain	——	——	21.3

TALL OAKS VILLAGE CENTER

6-8   A residential section of Tall Oaks Village.

The Neighborhood Shopping Center

Tall Oaks Village Center is the third of five neighborhood-scale shopping centers planned for Reston, a new community approximately 18 miles west of Washington, D.C., in suburban Fairfax County, Virginia. The center occupies a 7.5-acre site and contains 68,000 square feet of GLA. Within the framework of Reston's commercial center planning, village centers have been designed to serve the everyday convenience shopping needs of persons residing within a radius of ½ to 1 mile. In addition, these village centers are intended as the focal points for a variety of neighborhood activities and interests; this function is expressed at Tall Oaks by means of a clock tower built of sculptured timbers, located in the center's open plaza. In size, anticipated function, and tenantry, the facility closely approximates the neighborhood center prototype.

This development is also of interest because it reflects an evolution in Gulf-Reston, Inc.'s thinking about the position of the commercial function within the urban environment. Experience gained in the construction and operation of Reston's first two neighborhood shopping centers, Lake Anne Village Center and Hunters Woods Village Center, has been applied to Tall Oaks.[1] Likewise, the two centers yet to be built will benefit from the Tall Oaks experience. Planning and design for Tall Oaks Village Center were completed in late 1972, and construction began in mid-1973. The grand opening was held during the Thanksgiving holidays in 1974.

Tall Oaks Village Center has been designed in a modified U configuration. The primary tenant and anchor, a grocery store of 39,000 square feet, occupies the northern half of the center. Adjoining the grocery store is an open plaza bounded by smaller structures, with space for an additional 19 tenants. Parking spaces for 407 automobiles are provided in attractively landscaped bays adjacent to the grocery store, with vehicular access provided by a collector street serving the residential portion of the neighborhood. A freestanding convenience grocery store has been positioned next to the collector street, across the parking area from the anchor tenant.

The Commercial Function at Reston

Of Reston's 7,400 acres, 300 acres or 4 percent of the entire development has been designated for a full range of commercial uses. Initial plans called for seven village centers, an International Inn and Conference Center, and a Town Center serving regional commercial and office needs. After Gulf Oil took over the development of Reston, the number of village centers was reduced from seven to five in order to expand the population based served by each of the centers. The Town Center and International Center concepts have been retained without substantial modification.

The International Inn and Conference Center, located adjacent to an exit ramp from the Dulles Airport Access Highway, opened in late 1973. Consisting of a 302-room hotel, a 165,000 square foot office tower, and 25,000 square feet of retail space in a shopping arcade, this facility has been positioned to respond to the growing demand for meeting and conference room space in northern Virginia. The primary rationale for including such a facility within Reston was the development's strategic location astride the primary access road to the airport.

The Town Center, which will perform a combination of regional office and retail functions for Reston and adjacent areas of Fairfax County, is still in the planning stage. However, several components of the county's government center, which will be physically integrated with the office and retail uses, have been funded, and a county emergency medical facility is now under construction. A total of 180 acres has been designated for the Town Center, but the actual physical dimensions will depend on the resolution of several outside factors. Among the most important of these is traffic access; major improvements in at-grade arterial streets will be required before the Town Center site becomes feasible for its proposed function. A second consideration is the potential expansion of commercial development in the Tysons Corner area, a rapidly growing urban subcenter located approximately 8 miles east of Reston, between Reston and Washington, D.C. Because of

---

[1] See "Hunters Woods Village Center," *Project Reference File*, Vol. 3, No. 15 (July–September 1973).

6-9　The open plaza at Tall Oaks introduces natural elements into the shopping environment.

these considerations, the regional commercial function at Reston could range from 500,000 to 1,500,000 square feet of GLA. Construction of the Town Center should be underway by the early eighties.

The largest modification in the commercial plan for Reston has been the designation of a 23-acre site adjacent to the Town Center for automobile-oriented retail uses. Conceived of as a cluster of freestanding buildings with common parking areas, this complex is visualized as the site of such uses as discount stores, automobile dealerships, and furniture stores.

Site and Service Area

Tall Oaks Village Center is located at the intersection of a major at-grade arterial, Wiehle Avenue, and a local collector street, North Shore Drive, which serves the adjacent residential area. The shopping center site is heavily wooded and slopes from north to south, and these natural characteristics were retained by means of a natural buffer area between Wiehle Avenue and Tall Oaks

and by providing access to the center from the local collector street.

The central portion of Reston, where Tall Oaks Village Center is located, is substantially built out. In immediate proximity to the center are three attached residential clusters with a total of 469 units. These, together with a planned 200-unit high-rise tower for the elderly and an elementary school site, comprise the Tall Oaks neighborhood. Actual service area, however, is far larger, including nearby single-family residential areas and overlapping the trade area of Lake Anne Village, situated approximately ¾ mile away. In practice, Reston residents have tended to patronize stores on the basis of the tenant rather than the location, and the original concept of fully integrated villages of 15,000 to 20,000 persons has not evolved in quite the manner anticipated.

Across North Shore Drive, but accessible via a pedestrian underpass, are a kindergarten and a Reston Home Owners' Association swimming pool. These uses, along with the planned residential tower, reinforce the community center function of Tall Oaks, besides contributing significantly to pedestrian traffic.

Planning and Engineering Features

In the original planning documents, the Tall Oaks site was described as the location of Reston's "hilltop village." As built, however, this aspect has been minimized in favor of highlighting the site's heavily wooded character. Primary design constraints included maximization of building coverage and GLA obtainable on the site, facilitation of both pedestrian and vehicular access, and preservation of the natural features of the site to the extent feasible. To a significant degree, however, aesthetic rather than marketing considerations dictated the final design.

Tall Oaks has an inward focus, away from the adjacent streets. The center has been divided into two main activity areas: the grocery store adjacent to the parking lot, and the open plaza, highlighted by the clock tower and defined by freestanding buildings which house the smaller tenants. Total building coverage amounts to 69,894 square feet, a figure somewhat higher than typical for neighborhood centers. Service access is provided around the periphery of the complex.

Two undisturbed natural areas, separated from one another by a wooden pedestrian bridge, have been integrated into the open plaza. This device has permitted the introduction of a mature wooded environment into the center of this urban public space, and, in concert with the natural buffers and parking lot landscaping, establishes the tone for Tall Oaks.

The center is tied to Reston's pedestrian pathway system from two directions. From the south, an asphalt walkway passes beneath North Shore Drive and proceeds up a broad flight of stairs to the plaza. From the north, a walkway located in a wide landscaped median runs the length of the parking lot to the grocery store arcade and the plaza. Where the path crosses the roadway between the grocery and the landscaped median, the paving has been raised and given a contrasting texture and color to give elderly shoppers curb-free access to the center and to warn drivers to give pedestrians the right-of-way.

Overall circulation has not worked as well as expected. Concentrating all parking at the northern end of the site has made it more difficult for shoppers to patronize stores on the open plaza, a problem which has been aggravated by the area's limited visibility from the parking lot. Actual use of the pedestrian system has also been lower than expected. This appears to be due to the fact that the village center is on the eastern edge of Reston, limiting the residential area in the immediate neighborhood. Once the high-rise housing for the elderly is built, pedestrian use of the paths and the open plaza should increase substantially.

6-10 A walkway is located in a landscaped median in the parking area. Where the walkway crosses a driving lane, paving has been raised and given a contrasting color and texture.

Architectural Character

Tall Oaks was designed to be an attractive and positive element within the landscape and highly compatible with adjacent residential areas. A human scale was achieved by sloping the roofs of the covered arcade which runs the length of the grocery store and along the freestanding buildings fronting on the open plaza. Individual tenant spaces have been subordinated to the total design concept, which provides the dominant visual statement.

Kenitex, a stucco-like, buff-colored material, gives the buildings an attractive texture and appearance. The design was worked out jointly by the architect and Gulf-Reston, Inc., in an evolving process, with input from the company's operating division.

Land Use Controls

Development approvals for the center were obtained in stages, the first of which was the inclusion of the entire Reston development in the Fairfax County comprehensive plan. This was a prerequisite for rezoning Reston to RPC (Residential Planned Community) status. Later, the developer was required to furnish the county with a development plan showing major uses, the circulation system, open space networks, and the primary elements proposed for the new community, including village centers. As a final step before actual construction, an engineered site plan was submitted to the county planning commission for approval. The RPC zone specifies uses permitted within village centers and refers to other sections of the county zoning ordinance relative to off-street parking; the developer is given flexibility in building placement and setbacks. Developer-established controls applied to neighborhood center development include commercial property protective covenants and restrictions contained in the bylaws of the Reston Home Owners' Association.

Management and Operation

All commercial facilities in Reston are built and managed by the developer as profit centers. This strategy permits Gulf-Reston, Inc., to participate in the growth of values as the community matures and also allows the company to generate continuing cash flow, thus giving the developer a means of raising additional capital through the sale of income properties.

All tenants except service organizations and office tenants are required to join the Tall Oaks Merchants' Association, which has been incorporated under the laws of Virginia. Because of their functions, a dentist and the Christian Science Reading Room were not required to join. Organization and responsibilities of the merchants association are spelled out in the bylaws, which have established a seven-member board of trustees to manage the center. One trustee is elected by the lessor, the rest by the membership. Functions of the association are "to generally promote the welfare and business goals of its members; to provide a forum for the exchange of ideas relative to business politics; to lend guidance in all aspects of

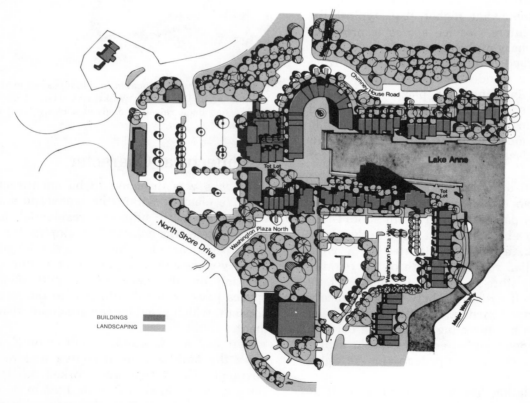

BUILDINGS
LANDSCAPING

6-11   Site plan—Lake Anne Village Center.

good consumer relationships; to promote Tall Oaks Center . . . and to serve as a vehicle for joint promotional events. . . ." Dues are calculated on the basis of $0.15 per square foot per year, with the lessor contributing an amount equal to 25 percent of the money paid by tenant members. In addition, an informal group composed of the presidents of all the village center merchants associations meets periodically as a steering committee to coordinate common interests related to planning and zoning issues, to communicate with the developer, and to work on other matters of mutual concern.

Common area charges, which cover the total cost and expenses incurred in operating and maintaining the common facilities, were accrued at the rate of $0.36 per square foot of GLA in 1975. This covered landscaping and gardening, insurance, repairs, line painting, lighting, depreciation of maintenance equipment, repair of utility lines, policing, and removal of snow, trash, rubbish, garbage, and other refuse.

Neighborhood Center Development at Reston

There are three neighborhood shopping centers at Reston: Lake Anne Village Center (1965), Hunters Wood Village Center (1970), and Tall Oaks Village Center (1974). In combination, they represent almost two decades of operational experience and provide a basis for judgements about the role of neighborhood shopping centers in the urban framework. From his experience, the developer offers several comments from this perspective:

• In line with commonly accepted development practice, neighborhood shopping centers should fulfill a convenience retail function. The more specialized stores now located in Reston's village centers can be expected to gravitate to the Town Center once it is built. A secondary function is that of the local community center, an objective accomplished at Reston by placing churches, recreational facilities, and certain other facilities within the center environment.

• Neighborhood centers are commonly in the range of 50,000 to 60,000 square feet of GLA. Hunters Wood, with 106,000 square feet of GLA, was found to be too large, and Tall Oaks was scaled down accordingly. There is no plan to develop community-scale shopping facilities within Reston, although Hunters Wood approaches this category in many respects.

6-12   The Tall Oaks logo.

6-13   Townhouses have direct pedestrian access to Tall Oaks Center.

6-14   The key tenant, a grocery store.

- Carefully defined service areas, with a typical radius of ½ to 1 mile, are fine from the theoretical standpoint. In practice, however, they do not work well. Reston's 27,000 residents are almost as automobile-oriented as other suburbanites, and they base their shopping trips on other factors besides distance, such as store preferences, store management, and the objective of the planned trip. Tall Oaks, for example, has the largest grocery store in Reston and is patronized by those seeking the widest selections of merchandise, even when it means driving past a closer center.

- A grocery store is the best anchor tenant and can be supplemented by a variety store or other large space user in addition to service uses and other small tenants. Office uses represent an appropriate neighborhood center function, as do smaller freestanding uses such as gas stations, convenience grocery stores, and fast-food outlets. Residential uses should not be located directly over the retail area, as was done at Lake Anne Village Center. Apartments above the stores opening onto Lake Anne's waterside plaza have had very high turnover. On the other hand, placement of residential uses in convenient proximity to shopping facilities, as is visualized with the high-rise tower at Tall Oaks, is an important way of contributing to a center's economic and social vitality.

- The biggest challenge facing the designer of a neighborhood center is to optimize both pedestrian and vehicular circulation. While the conventional strip center places all the parking in front of the stores to the detriment of pedestrian circulation, Tall Oaks has gone to the opposite extreme in sacrificing accessibility to the plaza area by placing all parking at the northern end of the site. This problem could have been mitigated by a more central placement of the complex on the site.

Tenant Characteristics

The largest tenant, with 56.7 percent of center GLA, is a Giant grocery. This tenant is sufficiently dominant to distort the composition of the center

6-15 Neighborhood sandwich shop has an outdoor eating area.

as compared with the *Dollars and Cents of Shopping Centers'* neighborhood shopping center tenant composition averages. In practice, however, the mix of uses, which includes 5,363 square feet of office space, two restaurants, two financial institutions, and other retail and service uses, is compatible with the convenience orientation objective of neighborhood shopping centers. Of 23 tenant spaces provided in the design, 15 have been leased, at rates ranging from $4.10 to $13.50 per square foot. Individual stores have between 996 and 38,763 square feet of GLA.

Tall Oaks has been less than totally successful in operation. Almost 10 percent of the center is vacant, and sales per square foot of GLA have been lower than anticipated. This problem appears to derive from three primary causes: insufficient number of experienced, aggressive merchants; deficiencies in the basic design, which does not adequately emphasize pedestrian circulation, and the center's opening at the beginning of an economic recession. The primary anchor is located next to the parking lot, not where it can draw shoppers past the smaller tenants, and a plan for a secondary anchor for the plaza end never materialized. Nor is the plaza area particularly visible or accessible. Recent improvements to draw the attention of shoppers to this area have included draping flags at the plaza entrance and opening up windows on the building frontage along the parking lot.

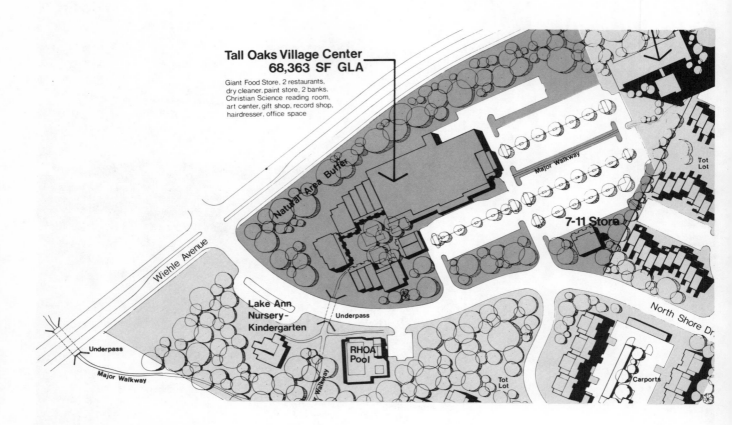

**Tall Oaks Village Center
68,363 SF GLA**

Giant Food Store, 2 restaurants,
dry cleaner, paint store, 2 banks,
Christian Science reading room,
art center, gift shop, record shop,
hairdresser, office space

6-16   Site plan—Tall Oaks Village Center.

PROJECT DATA—TALL OAKS

DEVELOPER/MANAGEMENT

Gulf-Reston, Inc.
11440 Isaac Newton Square North
Reston, Virginia 22090

ARCHITECTURE

Collins & Kronstadt–Leahy Hogan Collins
1111 Spring Avenue
Silver Spring, Maryland 20910

LAND USE INFORMATION

Site area   7.5 acres

Land allocation

	Site area	Percent of site
Buildings	65,600 sq. ft.	20.2
Parking and circulation	135,270 sq. ft.	41.6
Landscaping and buffer area	124,523 sq. ft.	38.2
Total	235,393 sq. ft.	100.0

GLA   68,363 sq. ft.

GBA   69,894 sq. ft.

Parking
  Spaces[1] 407
  Ratio   2.01 : 1
  Index   5.9

ECONOMIC INFORMATION

Total sales (1975)	$3.7 million
Sales per sq. ft. GLA[2]	$60 (approximate)
Merchants association dues[3]	$0.15 per sq. ft.
Common area charges	$0.36 per sq. ft.
Rentals	
Amount	$4.10 to $13.50
Length	3 to 20 years
Percentage rents	variable[4]
Capital costs (1973–74)	
Land and land improvements	$ 800,000
Buildings and equipment	1,800,000
Overhead and development	200,000
Total	$2,800,000

[1] Includes 40 spaces designated for use by residents of the planned high-rise building for the elderly.

[2] Occupied space.

[3] Developer contributes an amount equal to 25 percent of the tenant contribution.

[4] An average based on percentage of sales volume.

TENANT INFORMATION

Number of tenants   15
Percent leased   90.5

Tenant Classification	Number of stores	GLA	Percent of total GLA	Average percentage in neighborhood centers (from *Dollars and Cents of Shopping Centers: 1975*)
Food	2	41,386 sq. ft.	60.5	26.5
Food service	2	4,817 sq. ft.	7.0	5.1
General merchandise	——	——	——	16.3
Clothing and shoes	——	——	——	5.5
Dry goods	——	——	——	3.8
Furniture (home furnishings)	——	——	——	4.8
Other retail	3	3,506 sq. ft.	5.1	16.9
Financial	2	2,604 sq. ft.	3.8	3.0
Offices	3	5,363 sq. ft.	7.9	4.7
Services	3	4,246 sq. ft.	6.2	5.6
Other	——	——	——	4.7
Vacant	——	6,441 sq. ft.	9.5	3.1
Total	15	68,363 sq. ft.	100.0	100.0

Tenants by ownership type

Type	Number	Percent	Average percentage in neighborhood centers (from *Dollars and Cents*)
National chain	4	26.7	20.4
Independent	2	13.3	58.3
Local chain	9	60.0	21.3

SOUTHGATE PLAZA

6-18 Franklin's variety store is a key tenant at this community shopping center. A major remodeling has given the complex a unified facade.

The Community Shopping Center

Southgate Plaza is of particular interest for two reasons: first, it closely approximates, in size and tenant mix, the ULI prototype for community shopping centers; second, it illustrates one of the major trends now apparent in shopping center development, namely, the renovation and expansion of older centers. The initial section of Southgate Plaza was built in 1954, and three subsequent expansions over the next 20 years have brought the center to its current size of 154,000 square feet of GLA. This process has also involved the evolution of the center from its original configuration as a neighborhood strip center to a full-scale community shopping center with a junior department store and a variety store as anchor tenants.

Southgate Plaza is located in Lake Charles, Louisiana, approximately halfway between Houston and New Orleans and 34 miles inland of the Gulf of Mexico. As the oil and gas capital of southern Louisiana, the city and Calcasieu Parish, which together comprise the Lake Charles SMSA, experienced explosive growth between 1950 and 1970. In 1970, the community had a population of 145,415. Expansion has slowed in the past 5 years, however, and the current population is estimated to be 150,500. Family incomes in the community tend to be significantly above the Louisiana average, and a broad segment of the population is in the middle-income range, reflecting the unionized character of the local work force.

The initial site acquisition of 17.2 acres was made in 1954 by Weingarten Realty, Inc., the real estate affiliate of a Houston-based grocery chain. Weingarten was expanding, and it recognized the retail potential in Lake Charles. At that time, commercial activity was concentrated in the downtown area, and Southgate Plaza was the first major shopping center outside the CBD. Since that time, the center has been developed on an incremental basis, with new sections being added in response to growth in the market.

Weingarten Realty, Inc., has been involved with Southgate Plaza and other neighborhood- and community-scale centers in the Texas and Louisiana area for more than 20 years. Based on the experience gained in building and operating more than 20 shopping centers, the firm has determined that centers of 100,000 to 250,000 square feet are particularly viable in communities with populations of 50,000 to 100,000, where it is possible for smaller centers to fulfill a combination of community- and regional-scale retail functions. In larger metropolitan areas, the community-scale center is most appropriate in specialized marketing situations and in locations where it does not compete directly with a regional center.

Renovation and Remodeling

A current major activity of the company is expansion and refurbishment of existing centers, either already owned or acquired for the specific purpose of upgrading. A typical improvement program for an existing center involves restructuring the tenant mix, physical expansion (often combining demolition with new construction), reorganization of pedestrian and vehicular circulation, and a variety of exterior modifications, such as new facade treatments, coordinated signage programs, repainting, and landscaping.

Weingarten has found that there can be as much as a 20 percent saving in upgrading or redeveloping an existing facility rather than building a new one. Economies in such projects are associated with reuse of structures and parking areas and reduced expenditures for site work. Before an existing center is revitalized, however, two conditions must be present. First, population and economic trends within the market area must justify the investment. Second, site area must be sufficient to support a modern facility.

One neighborhood-scale center (Greinwich Terrace) recently acquired for this purpose is located in Lake Charles a short distance from Southgate Plaza. The company's most interesting renovation project to date, however, has involved the acquisition and upgrading of River Oaks Shopping Center in Houston. As discussed in Chapter 1, this venerable center, one of the first in the United States, was begun in 1937 by Hugh Potter, one of the founders of ULI. Despite a strategic location at the entrance to Houston's most exclusive neighborhood, mismanagement had reduced River Oaks to little more than a low-grade commercial strip. The redevelopment program, which is being carried out over a 4-year period, is designed to restore the features which distinguish shopping centers as a planned commercial land use. Incompatible structures and signs are being removed, and a unified design scheme is being applied to the entire complex. River Oaks has been modernized and expanded and has been given a new logo and a contemporary aesthetic treatment. The original buildings have been repainted, and awnings have been added to the crescent-shaped structures at the western end of the center. Major structural improvements include new plumbing, wiring, and roofing. The tenant plan devised to restore River Oaks' position as a high-income specialty center combines high-fashion and general merchandise tenants; as their leases come due, existing stores are evaluated in terms of their contribution to an optimum tenant mix. Through careful business management, the renovation program has been self-amortizing. Cash flow has been significantly increased since the project was acquired in 1973, and the new tenants have been willing to pay higher rents in exchange for modernized space in a well-located center.

As part of its major program of upgrading retail facilities in established Houston neighborhoods, a second shopping center, Heights Plaza, was completely renovated during 1976. In this instance, a 63,000 square foot neighborhood center, portions of which dated back to 1930, was entirely rebuilt on a staged basis, with the center remaining open throughout the redevelopment process. Weingarten

Realty, Inc., initiated the process by assembling adjacent residential lots to expand the Heights Plaza site area. Next, a new, larger supermarket was constructed on the former parking area, and the original supermarket structure was demolished, providing space for a new drugstore and six smaller tenants, which were shifted out of an older portion of the original center. Parking now occupies the former location of the grocery store. As completed, the project involved a 14.5 percent expansion of the site area and a 62.9 percent expansion of leasable space, with almost the entire center now consisting of modern construction. The development program also provided for three freestanding fast-food outlets on the arterial street frontage across from the center.

The Evolution of Southgate Plaza

While the pattern of growth and expansion at Southgate Plaza differs in important respects from the renovation and remodeling experiences of River Oaks and Heights Plaza, this retail complex nevertheless exhibits many aspects of shopping center development which are becoming increasingly common.

The center is situated approximately 1 mile south of downtown Lake Charles on Ryan Street, a major north-south arterial. The original 17.2-acre parcel was selected for two reasons: first, it was undeveloped and had 870 feet of frontage on a major arterial; second, it was in an established residential

6-19 Looking east on West Gray Avenue toward downtown Houston. Deterioration of River Oaks Shopping Center is apparent in this pre-renovation view.

6-20 River Oaks Shopping Center is adjacent to Houston's River Oaks neighborhood, the most prestigious in the city.

area in the rapidly growing southern half of the city. Subsequent acquisition of contiguous parcels has brought the site to its present size of 20.7 acres. Physical changes in the area over the past two decades, including the construction of Interstate Highway 210—the Lake Charles bypass, three blocks to the south—and development of Prien Lake Mall, a twin-anchor, enclosed shopping center, just four blocks away, have tended to verify the accuracy of the original locational decision. The parcel itself has access from five streets: Ernest, Eighteenth, Ryan, Eddy, and Alamo. The interior portion of the property remains undeveloped in 1977, although it lies in the direction of Prien Lake Mall, a circumstance which has enhanced Southgate Plaza's development potential.

The evolution of the shopping center has taken place within a generalized framework established by the developer. The project was conceived from the outset as a strip center, with building design and placement and acquisition of additional property being guided by this consideration. In size and tenant mix, Southgate Plaza is a community center, although it did not expand to this magnitude for more than 15 years after opening. Further expansions are planned and will increase the center considerably beyond its present size of 154,000 square feet and 26 tenants. The sequence to date has proceeded as follows:

- 1954—the original component of the center opened, a 26,800 square foot Weingarten's supermarket.
- 1958—the first section of retail stores was added by building 63,000 square feet of leasable space to the south of the supermarket. This expansion brought the size of the complex

171

6-21　Planters have been used as sidewalk landscaping elements.

to 90,000 square feet and 21 stores, with the supermarket as the anchor tenant. At this stage, Southgate Plaza had become a neighborhood shopping center.

- 1969—an additional 3.5 acres were purchased in order to permit expansion of the center northward along Ryan Street to Eighteenth Street. This acquisition gave the developer almost a quarter mile of frontage on the at-grade arterial. The next phase of development was the erection of a 10,700 square foot Walgreen drugstore on the newly acquired property, formerly occupied by a mix of residential and commercial buildings. Southgate Plaza had now grown into a community-scale shopping center with a total of 22 stores and more than 107,000 square feet of retail space. Anchor tenants included the supermarket and TG&Y, a variety store.
- Between 1969 and 1974, competition appeared in the form of Prien Lake Mall, an 800,000 square foot enclosed regional shopping center.

Responding to this circumstance, the developer carried out a major expansion of the Southgate Plaza and initiated an extensive renovation of the complex. An additional 46,000 square feet of retail space was created by extending the center north to Eighteenth Street. Tenant mix was significantly broadened by adding a junior department store as an anchor at the north end of the center. The renovation coincided with the expansion program and established a uniform facade for the front of the center. In addition, the parking lot was resurfaced and restriped, planter boxes and landscaping were added, and a coordinated signage program was implemented.

Physical Design

Southgate Plaza is a conventional strip center, consisting of an irregular row of stores integrated by means of a unified roof line and "French style" mansard canopy running the length of the center above a pedestrian walkway. The center has 1,350

6-22　At a community center scale, a specialty clothing store such as Riff's can perform the role of anchor tenant.

feet of frontage, as compared with the 400 feet viewed as optimal for strip centers. This circumstance, however, does not seem to have had a negative economic impact on the center. Surface parking for 678 vehicles is located between the street and the storefronts, with additional unstriped space for parking provided behind the center. The complex consists of three freestanding buildings, interconnected by means of the mansard roof, with irregular setbacks ranging from 200 to 320 feet from the right-of-way. The 1958 and 1969 expansions were given deeper setbacks in order to accommodate additional vehicles in front of the stores and to permit better traffic circulation within the parking area. Nevertheless, the present parking arrangement is deficient in several respects. Parking is still allowed along more than two-thirds of the pedestrian walk, hampering customer movement in and out of the shopping center. In addition, vehicular circulation is parallel to rather than at right angles to the storefronts. A new parking layout to rectify these problems is under study, and additional spaces will be provided at the rear of the center. A combination of 45-degree parking and one-way traffic lanes has been used.

Development plans call for expansion of the center into the undeveloped interior portion of the property over the next few years. This area is visualized as the location of a series of freestanding office buildings, service-oriented businesses, and entertainment uses. Each structure will have its own adjacent parking area and will front on private drives which will be extended into the site from Ernest and Eighteenth Streets. The first step in this expansion program will be a 14,000 square foot, four-screen cinema building. An attractive open mall between the central and south buildings will permit pedestrian movement between the new section of the center and the older part fronting on Ryan Street.

As presently configured, Southgate Plaza consists of 153,900 square feet of GLA in 26 individual stores, ranging in size from 507 to 30,045 square feet. The tenant mix corresponds to the community shopping center average, with 30.6 percent of tenant space occupied by three general merchandise outlets, the two largest being a variety store and a junior department store. The parking ratio, a measure of the relationship between built area and parking area, is 3.3 to 1. Parking accounts for 74.5

173

percent of total developed site area, and the parking index is 4.4.

Marketing and Development Strategy

For many years, Southgate Plaza was the largest retail complex in Lake Charles outside the downtown area. Because of the relatively small population of the city (77,998 in 1970), Southgate was able to assume some of the stature of a regional center and to draw upon the entire metropolitan area for its trade. In characteristic community center fashion, Southgate Plaza offered an array of convenience and general merchandise goods in considerable depth. With the completion of Prien

Lake Mall in 1972, however, this locally dominant position disappeared. The impact of the new regional center on Southgate Plaza was both immediate and substantial: four tenants, including jewelry, fabric, shoe, and cosmetic stores, shifted to the regional center, and several others closed. Within a year, vacancy increased from 3 to 13 percent. It was apparent that Southgate Plaza would have to be repositioned in the marketplace in order to sustain its economic viability. The redevelopment program was based on the developer's judgement that Southgate Plaza would have to be modernized, refurbished, and expanded in order to remain competitive. As implemented, the concept sought to retain the former customer base by main-

6-23 Side yard treatment.

taining a parity with the regional center and the downtown in terms of tenant mix, merchandise, and attractiveness. The redevelopment program embodied two major phases: physical improvements to the center, and an upgrading of the tenant mix.

Total square footage of the center was increased by 43 percent with the addition of seven new retail stores. The key to this expansion was the significant broadening of the tenant mix; the largest additions were a 5,779 square foot restaurant, and a 30,045 square foot junior department store called The Fair. At the same time the developer began a program to upgrade tenants in the older portion of the center. The most significant accomplishment in this direction was the attraction of a top ladies' clothing store, Riff's, from the downtown area to Southgate Plaza. At the expense of both tenant and landlord, Riff's remodeled both the interior and exterior of its 10,740 square foot store and expanded it in the process.

The upgrading process also involved restructuring the financial profile of the center. Rents for small tenants were raised from a median level of $2.25 per square foot before renovation to the range of $4.20 to $6.00 for leases coming up for renewal after the improvements were completed. The rate of percentage rents for small tenants was also raised.

The program of physical improvements was necessary to give the center a contemporary and unified appearance. Because of its age and the periodic expansions which had taken place, Southgate Plaza had a disjointed facade, and it had visual deficiencies characteristic of early centers, including inadequate sign control, aesthetically poor use of exterior building materials, and a poorly designed and constructed parking area. These drawbacks, however, were remedied by establishing a uniform roof line for the center with the "French style" mansard roof of brown anodized steel panels and by repainting exterior masonry a uniform mustard color, adding planters and landscaping, rebuilding the parking area, and rearranging the traffic circulation pattern.

This strategy appears to have been successful. By September 1976, the vacancy rate had been reduced to 4.3 percent of GLA, and the center is now substantially larger than it was when the vacancy rate was much higher. Cash flow has significantly improved, and, in physical terms, the center now presents a highly contemporary face to the community.

Management and Operation

Southgate Plaza is managed by the owner-developer, who handles maintenance responsibilities and acts as the agent for the merchants association. A Houston-based executive of the company has the overall management and leasing responsibility for Southgate Plaza and three other Weingarten centers in southern Louisiana. A full-time, on-site employee is responsible for landscape maintenance and cleanup. Other maintenance tasks are handled on a contractual basis. Security is provided by the Lake Charles Police Department.

The merchants association was established by the developer. Its sole responsibility is to publicize the name and location of Southgate Plaza through centerwide promotional activities, special events, and advertising. The association has not been formally incorporated, and there are no bylaws. Through individual lease provisions, center tenants are either encouraged or required to join the association. Yearly dues of $5 per front foot are required of the tenant members with the developer presently contributing 25 percent of the total association budget.

The experience at Southgate Plaza has confirmed the statement that the lease, which establishes the working relationship between tenant and landlord, is the most important management tool available to the shopping center operator. Lease provisions specify not only the financial obligation but also the operational requirements concerning trash removal, signage, interior decoration, hours of operation, and permitted uses. Weingarten Realty, Inc., has relied heavily on the lease to implement its center modification strategy, and several tenants were not renewed as part of the reorganization program at Southgate Plaza. With respect to signage, tenants previously were permitted any type of sign not more than 4 feet high and not longer than 4 feet less than the length of the storefront. Renegotiated leases have established a unified format and color scheme for tenant signage, and all signs must be approved by the management. The new standard requires that all signs be white and internally lighted and that they use cut-out lettering.

Leases for small tenants range from 1 to 5 years, and up to 20 years for anchor tenants. Percentage leases require most tenants to pay 5 to 10 percent of gross receipts plus a guaranteed minimum. The new leases also contain a provision for a common area maintenance fee of up to $0.24 per square foot to cover the cost of exterior maintenance.

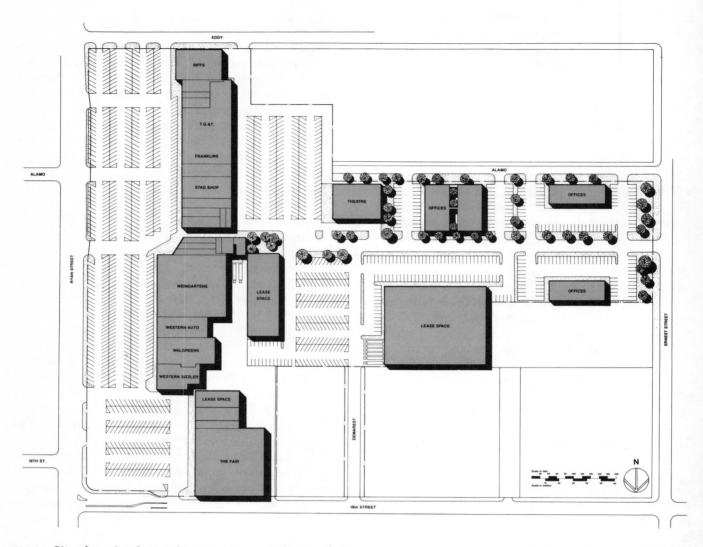

6-24 Site plan—Southgate Plaza. Parking next to the southerly and most recent extension of the shopping center is oriented toward the shopping center, rather than at right angles to it.

6-25   PROJECT DATA—SOUTHGATE PLAZA

DEVELOPER/MANAGEMENT

Weingarten Realty, Inc.
600 Lockwood
P.O. Box 1698
Houston, Texas 77001
Completion of renovation   1974

LAND USE INFORMATION

Site area   20.7 acres
Land allocation

	Site area	Percent of site
Buildings	3.7 acres	17.8
Parking and circulation	12.2 acres	58.9
Landscaping[1]	0.02 acres	0.1
Subtotal	16.1 acres	76.8
Undeveloped	4.8 acres	23.2
Total	20.7 acres	100.0

GLA   153,889 sq. ft.

GBA   159,889 sq. ft.

Parking
   Spaces   678
   Ratio   3.3 : 1
   Index   4.4

ECONOMIC INFORMATION

Total sales (1975)	$13.0 million
Sales per sq. ft. GLA	$84.48
Merchants association dues[2]	$5 per front foot
Common area charges	up to $0.24 per sq. ft. GLA
Rentals	
Amount	$4.20 to $6.00 per sq. ft. GLA[3]
Length	1 to 5 years for small tenants, up to 20 years for anchor tenants
Percentage rents	5 to 10 percent for new leases; formerly 2.5 to 5.5 percent
Capital costs (1974 renovation)	$195,000[4]

[1] Landscaping occupies 1,000 square feet.
[2] Developer contributes 25 percent of the association budget.
[3] Tenant furnishes heating, air conditioning, lighting, floor coverings, and interior partitions.
[4] Includes rebuilding facade, resurfacing of parking lot, landscaping, and sign improvement.

TENANT INFORMATION

Number of tenants   26
Percent leased   95.7

Tenant Classification	Number of stores	GLA	Percent of total GLA	Average percentage in community centers (from *Dollars and Cents of Shopping Centers: 1975*)
Food	1	26,826 sq. ft.	17.4	15.7
Food service	2	7,579 sq. ft.	4.9	3.7
General merchandise	3	47,090 sq. ft.	30.6	35.8
Clothing and shoes	5	27,928 sq. ft.	18.2	7.8
Dry goods	—	—	—	3.0
Furniture (home furnishings)	1	3,500 sq. ft.	2.3	3.7
Other retail	7	25,066 sq. ft.	16.3	14.5
Financial	2	1,825 sq. ft.	1.2	2.5
Offices	—	—	—	2.2
Services	5	7,459 sq. ft.	4.8	3.6
Other	—	—	—	4.3
Vacant	—	6,616 sq. ft.	4.3	3.3
Total	26	153,889 sq. ft.	100.0	100.0

Tenants by ownership type

Type	Number	Percent	Average percentage in community centers (from *Dollars and Cents*)
National chain	12	50.0	27.0
Independent	7	29.2	49.0
Local chain	5	20.8	24.0

TROLLEY SQUARE

6-26   Trolley Square has a turn-of-the-century design theme.

The Theme Center

Trolley Square is an innovative entertainment and specialty shopping center located in the former car barns and maintenance shops of the Salt Lake City streetcar system. The 13-acre complex consists of four freestanding masonry buildings which incorporate an intricate network of internal pedestrian shopping streets, courtyards, and common open areas connected by landscaped walkways. Trolley Square features a turn-of-the-century theme that employs antiques and architectural artifacts for both functional and decorative purposes. These elements give Trolley Square an ambience that distinguishes it from competing suburban shopping centers.

The project was designed to make shopping a recreational and leisure-time experience. It emphasizes the human scale, with boutiques and a varied and stimulating physical environment that places Trolley Square in the forefront of innovative commercial design. In 5 years, Trolley Square has become one of Salt Lake City's major attractions. The developer believes the carefully devised nostalgic atmosphere helps explain the success of the project.

Trolley Square is situated in an aging, low-density residential section of Salt Lake City, some nine blocks southeast of downtown. The development has 114 tenants in 250,000 square feet of GLA. Tenants include 15 restaurants, six movie theaters, 16 apparel shops, a farmers' market, arts and crafts shops, gift shops, and boutiques.

Renovation got underway in 1970, following 12 months of project planning and design. The first components of the complex opened in June 1972. Development is occurring on a phased basis and expansion is continuing as additional sections of the vacant industrial buildings are converted to commercial use. Of the total GLA, 87.3 percent had been committed by mid-1976.

The streetcar complex was built in 1908 by the Utah Light and Railway Company, which had been acquired 4 years previously by E. H. Harriman, the railroad magnate, who was determined to make the system a model of its kind in the United States. At a cost of more than $3 million, Harriman erected the complex of mission-style buildings to house and serve a fleet of 144 streetcars operating over more than 100 miles of track. There were four main structures: a car house to store the streetcars and for general maintenance; a machine shop for mechanical overhauls; a sand house to store grit for winter operations; and a carpentry and paint shop for car body work and construction.

The site of the streetcar complex was a square city block, 660 feet on a side, covering 9.8 acres. Total building coverage was 270,000 square feet, or 62.9 percent of the block. In addition, there was a 97-foot-high water tank with a 50,000-gallon capacity.

Brick bearing wall and steel truss construction was used in the buildings, whose roofs were built of 8-inch to 10-inch slabs of concrete and contained 208 skylights, each 16 feet long and 8 feet wide. The modified mission-style architecture featured a curved cornice topped by contrasting concrete wainscoting. The most distinctive feature of the design was a series of reinforced concrete arches at the ends of the car house.

The car house, covering 126,000 square feet, was the largest building. It consisted of a series of four bays (a fifth was added later) that together were 420 feet long, 58 feet wide, and 34 feet high at the peak, separated from one another by interior masonry and concrete walls. Each bay contained four streetcar tracks with grease pits in the concrete floor, and the entrance to each bay had rolling steel doors.

Following abandonment of the streetcar system in 1945, the buildings housed the city bus line until 1969, at which time the use of the buildings was phased out.

Development Strategy

Trolley Square is being developed by a group of seven Salt Lake City investors headed by Wallace A. Wright, Jr., a local realtor. The site was acquired in two parts, the first from National City Lines in 1969, and the second from the Utah Light and Power Company in 1973. Subsequent purchases in adjacent blocks have brought the total land holding to 13 acres, with acquisition continuing.

Various factors, including market assumption and the location, structural type, and condition of the buildings were of crucial importance in the decision to go ahead with the project. The complex was strategically located in an old section of Salt Lake City, approximately midway between downtown and the University of Utah campus. Around the car barns were a variety of low-density residential and commercial structures that were beginning to be displaced by buildings with high-intensity uses. The block itself was bordered on the east by Seventh Street East (State Route 71), a major highway providing primary access to the growing residential area to the south and east. These factors, together with low land prices in the area, suggested an opportunity for a major upgrading of that part of Salt Lake City.

As is the case with many adaptive use projects, the developers were attracted to the complex because it offered an extensive area under roof at relatively modest cost. Furthermore, additional space could be created by adding floors under the high ceilings. The streetcar buildings were solidly built, and an evaluation revealed that no major structural improvements would be required.

One problem identified, however, was leakage around the skylights.

Perhaps the most noteworthy aspect of the decision to proceed with Trolley Square was the developer's determination that a project of this type could succeed in a community the size of Salt Lake City, whose metropolitan area had a population of 557,735 in 1970. While this assumption has proven correct, it represented a major gamble at the time, since developments of the type planned for Trolley Square had previously been attempted only in large and sophisticated metropolitan areas.

Public Involvement and Approvals

Trolley Square is located in the C-1 Commercial District, which permits a commercial adaptive reuse project without a zoning variance. Unexpected problems, however, arose over the off-street parking provision of the city zoning ordinance,

6-27   The mission-style architecture of the original structures was particularly suitable for conversion to a specialty center.

6-28 Converting obsolete structural elements to new uses is an important principle in adaptive reuse.

which requires one space per 300 square feet in a commercial building, one space per 10 seats in a theater, and one space per 200 square feet of restaurant floor space. This provision does not take into account the spread in peak demand of a combined shopping and entertainment center with extensive evening activities. Nevertheless, provision of adequate parking has been a continuing problem at Trolley Square, which previously had fewer than three spaces per 1,000 square feet of GLA. The developer responded to the problem by constructing a 210-space underground parking structure on the western end of the center site in 1976. Additional structured parking is planned for present surface lots on adjacent blocks.

Project Planning

From the outset, Trolley Square was planned as a pedestrian-oriented shopping and entertainment complex, modeled after such successful West Coast developments as Ghirardelli Square. In order to create a self-contained shopping center of this type, a minimum of 150,000 to 200,000 square feet of space was needed. If less space had been available, it would have been necessary to rely on adjacent commercial establishments to attain the market scale required. The turn-of-the-century design theme was integral to the concept, and the developer decided to place a far heavier emphasis on entertainment facilities than is typical in shopping center developments. Only limited provision was made for office space.

The expansive and unimpeded interior spaces gave the designers great flexibility. Internal layouts of the bays were generalized and then refined in response to the commercial success of the initial components and marketing demand. Flexibility has been a key part of the development strategy. Some areas originally designated for one type of tenant have been changed to suit alternative tenants.

Because there was 250,000 square feet of GLA to be rented, development was divided into phases. First to open were the theaters and several restaurants, since it was thought that they could stand on their own, whereas, for other commercial tenants to be successful, there would have to be more activities to generate the necessary pedestrian traffic.

Redevelopment Process

Several important considerations guiding the redevelopment process included capitalizing on the spacious interior of the car house by creating additional rental space; using discarded building materials, structural elements, and furnishings to give the completed project a unique ambience and reduce the cost of construction; minimizing structural changes in the buildings; and emphasizing the visual and structural integrity of the complex through careful design modifications. This approach, which afforded the twin benefits of minimizing cost outlays while creating a unique and nostalgic shopping environment, has given Trolley Square a truly distinctive identity and an intangible quality that is unobtainable in new construction. While new space for the activities contained in Trolley Square could be provided at a competitive cost, the character of the finished structure would be entirely different.

After decades of hard use, the buildings were cover with grime and the site itself was a barren, gravel-covered square of earth surrounded by a chain link fence. Removal of a thick coat of yellow paint revealed the original rose-colored brick and contrasting concrete wainscoting. Roof leaks around the skylights were sealed with polyurethane insulation, and a new main entrance was created by widening and redesigning the doorway on the south side of the trolley barn. The few original windows in the complex were replaced, and additional windows and entrances were created by cutting through the brick walls and replacing garage doors with glass walls and rescaled doorways. The sense of visual unity throughout Trolley Square was enhanced by the use of uniform exterior materials, including ornate steel framing, painted black, for the new windows and doors.

As part of its conversion into a branch office of the First Security Bank, one wall of the sand house was replaced by a Plexiglas dome containing a new stairway leading to the second floor. In the machine shop, which was converted into the theater building, the old garage doors were replaced by murals of old-time movie stars, and a curved glass enclosure was extended from one side of the building to make space for a restaurant. The water tower was painted gold and converted into an observation tower by adding a circular wrought-iron staircase and decorative elements. The major effort, however, involved the car house. Bay windows were built along the narrow space separating it from the theater building. Arcades were added on both ends of the structure by replacing the rolling steel doors with recessed glass set within steel frames.

That portion of the site not occupied by buildings was completely redesigned for pedestrian and vehicular use, and the four main buildings were given a landscaped setting with connecting brick-paved pedestrian pathways.

Important savings were achieved by using recycled building materials, the value of which, when imaginatively used, is frequently unrecognized. Among these was a steel marquee which once had spanned a downtown street to advertise a movie theater. This marquee was moved to Trolley Square, where it now forms an arched entry to the parking area. Forty vintage street lamps were either attached to the buildings or placed along the four sides of the block. Six trolley cars were moved to the site; one now serves as a gas station, another as a savings and loan office, and the other four as shops. A cupola from a demolished mansion has been converted into a gazebo.

The major renovation cost was incurred in converting the vacant building interiors for commercial use, which required formulating and implementing an overall concept for internal circulation on a staged basis. In the trolley barn, the pedestrian system takes the form of a modified H, with a main central corridor diagonally crossing the five bays. The corridor has a central opening at the second bay, which provides a primary internal focus. The bays themselves contain pedestrian shopping streets 7 to 12 feet wide, with shops fronting the streets on both sides. The corridor system is connected to the pedestrian streets by openings in the masonry walls which separate the individual bays.

Interior space in the trolley barn was expanded by approximately 50 percent by adding second and third levels overlooking the main floor. These lend an exciting visual dimension to the project and provide a combination of shops, balconies, stair-

6-29   TROLLEY SQUARE BUILDINGS

Building	GBA	GLA	Area Rented	Area Vacant	Percent Rented	Number of Tenants	Former Use
North Building	NA	38,713 sq. ft.	21,624 sq. ft.	17,089 sq. ft.	55.9	3	Carpentry/ paint shop
First Security Bank	NA	4,151 sq. ft.	4,151 sq. ft.	—	100.0	1	Sand house
Theater Building	NA	39,926 sq. ft.	39,926 sq. ft.	—	100.0	7	Machine shop
Trolley Barn	NA	162,387 sq. ft.	147,901 sq. ft.	14,486 sq. ft.	91.1	101	Car barn
Other (S&L, Gas Station)	NA	4,500 sq. ft.	4,500 sq. ft.	—	100.0	2	NA
Total	314,619 sq. ft.	249,667 sq. ft.	218,102 sq. ft.	31,565 sq. ft.	87.4	114	

6-30 Imaginative interior design. Note skylights and exposed structural members.

6-31   Relationship of Trolley Square to downtown Salt Lake City.

ways, and elevation changes which highlight the shopping bazaar design concept. The second and third floors are built of prestressed concrete core decks resting on steel beams.

Heating, electrical, and lavatory systems were added. The central heating plant, a four-pipe system with fan coil units for heating and gas absorption chillers, was located in the trolley barn. This system makes rooftop units unnecessary and is more efficient than having individual units in each building. The central plant is connected with the separate buildings by means of an underground pipe system located in the former grease pits. The system operates on natural gas but can, if necessary, be converted to coal, oil, or electricity by changing or converting the boilers.

Vintage architectural elements were used to create the special appearance of the interior and were obtained at a cost no greater than that of furnishing conventional shopping center interiors. These elements include streetcars, antique elevators, discarded street furniture, wood beams, and similar

items. Facades from demolished mansions have been used as storefronts in the interior streetscapes. Many shops incorporate stained glass windows, gables, doors, chandeliers, wood paneling, and other relics in their design. One of the most striking elements is a stained glass dome from a demolished California cathedral. All store interiors, though paid for by tenants, must be approved by the developer.

Walls were cleaned and the steel roof trusses were painted black. Wrought-iron railings, window screens, and other details of modern construction reminiscent of turn-of-the-century design are used to visually integrate the overall interior.

Since Salt Lake City lies in an area prone to earthquakes, it was necessary to meet the seismic building code standards. This was accomplished by designing new floors so that seismic bracing could be added to the buildings. Steel seismic bracing was also added to some of the new openings to support the old brick bearing walls, which were not originally reinforced.

Tenant Mix

Entertainment activities, including theaters and restaurants, have been heavily emphasized and account for more than one-third of the GLA. (One unusual tenant, occupying 6,900 square feet, is an arcade amusement center.) This orientation heightens the festive atmosphere suggested by the design scheme and extends patronage of the complex into the evening hours.

Although there are a few national franchise outlets, most of the tenants are local merchants who bring to Trolley Square an understanding of local interests and tastes, an invaluable marketing asset.

A full range of retail outlets are located in the complex, as well as a number of stores selected to create additional vitality and interest. Among these are a farmers' market, a flower shop, and several craftwork shops, including a leatherworker, a silversmith, and a diamond cutter. The other major tenant component is clothing and shoes, which occupies 10.8 percent of the GLA. A 15-story hotel tower with 242 rooms is planned for the space above the fifth bay.

One objective of the tenant mix was to stimulate daily or weekly return traffic, thereby establishing Trolley Square as a major shopping location. The developer believed that Trolley Square could succeed only if it became an integral element of the community, meeting the continuing shopping needs of area residents rather than catering to tourists who would visit once or twice a year. The 15 restaurants, which account for more than a fifth of total center space, have helped accomplish this objective, which, to a considerable degree, has been achieved.

Managment and Operation

Trolley Square is operated like a conventional shopping center, with the developer leasing space and assuming responsibility for overall project management and control. Tenants must belong to the merchants association, which promotes the interests of all occupants of Trolley Square by conducting promotions, special events, and publicity programs. Voting rights and dues are based on a sliding scale that varies from $0.12 to $0.50 per square foot, according to the size of the space occupied. The association's operating budget for 1976 amounted to $50,000, of which 25 percent was contributed by the developer. Annual operating and maintenance costs for common areas and facilities are shared by the tenants on a proportional basis.

Minimum retail leases generally range between $6 and $8 per square foot. Office space is leased at $5 per square foot. The leases specify rules and regulations established by the developer and also include a percentage clause, which gives the developer an average of 6 percent of gross sales of certain tenants above an established breakpoint as determined by the guaranteed minimum rent. The leases also contain a performance clause, which permits the developer to cancel the lease if predetermined sales levels are not reached within a specified period of time. The renewal option, if given, adjusts the rent according to shifts in the consumer price index.

The project is managed by Trolley Square Associates, which employs a manager, an operations manager, and a secretarial, security, and janitorial staff of approximately 15 full-time and 15 part-time personnel. Much of the construction work was carried out by the building arm of the firm, Trolley Square Construction Company.

6-32 Trolley Square's four-screen theater contributes to return traffic and evening activity.

185

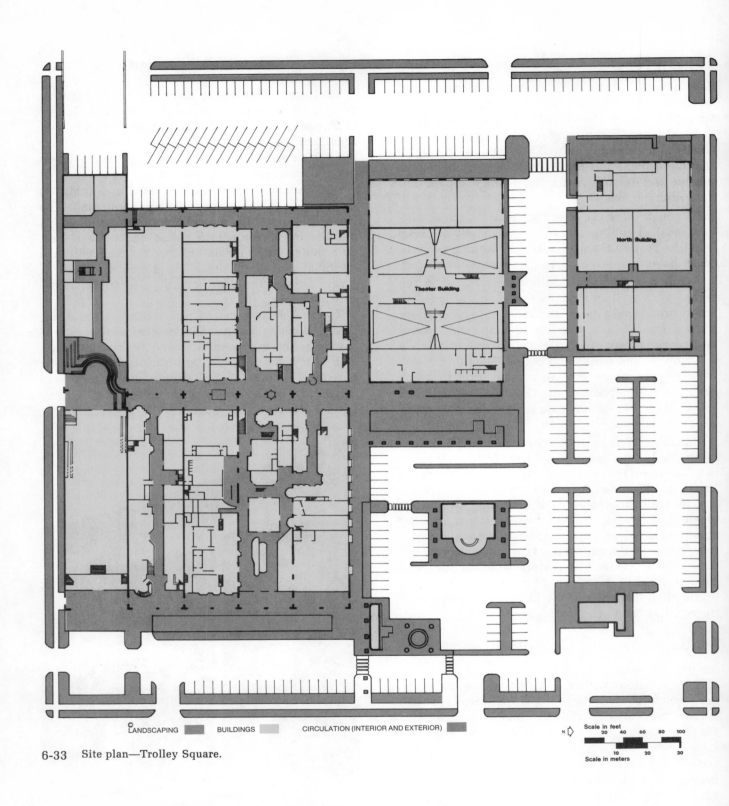

LANDSCAPING ▦ BUILDINGS ▢ CIRCULATION (INTERIOR AND EXTERIOR) ▦

N ⬦ Scale in feet
20 40 60 80 100
Scale in meters
10   20   30

6-33   Site plan—Trolley Square.

186

PROJECT DATA—TROLLEY SQUARE

DEVELOPER/MANAGEMENT

Trolley Square Associates
199 Trolley Square
Salt Lake City, Utah 84102

ARCHITECTURE

Architect/Planners Alliance
139 Trolley Square
Salt Lake City, Utah 84102

Year of completion   1977

ECONOMIC INFORMATION

Total sales (1975)	$11.2 million
Sales per sq. ft. GLA[2]	$91
Merchants association dues	$0.12 to $0.50 per sq. ft.
Rentals	
Amount	$6 to $8 per sq. ft. GLA[3]
Length	2 to 15 years (average 5 years)
Percentage rents	4 to 20 percent (average 6 percent)

LAND USE INFORMATION

Site area	13.0 acres	
Central block	9.8 acres	
Land allocation		

	Site area	Percent of site
Buildings	6.2 acres	47.7
Parking and circulation	5.6 acres	43.1
Landscaping	1.2 acres	9.2
Total	13.0 acres	100.0

GLA	249,667 sq. ft.
GBA	314,619 sq. ft.
Parking:	
Spaces	1,010[1]
Ratio	0.9 : 1
Index	4.0

[1] Includes 210 structured spaces and 800 surface spaces; does not include 200 spaces on the street.

[2] Based on an average of 141,664 sq. ft. of leased GLA, excluding theaters; if theaters are included, sales per sq. ft. are lowered to $77.

[3] For new tenants.

TENANT INFORMATION

Number of tenants   114
Percent leased   87.3

Tenant Classification	Number of stores	GLA	Percent of total GLA	Average percentage in community centers (from *Dollars and Cents of Shopping Centers: 1975*)
Food	9	10,028 sq. ft.	4.1	15.7
Food service	15	53,115 sq. ft.	21.3	3.7
General merchandise	——	——	——	35.8
Clothing and shoes	16	27,001 sq. ft.	10.8	7.8
Dry goods	7	5,668 sq. ft.	2.3	3.0
Furniture (home furnishings)	4	4,247 sq. ft.	1.7	3.7
Other retail	41	49,003 sq. ft.	19.6	14.5
Financial	3	7,388 sq. ft.	3.0	2.5
Offices	7	12,131 sq. ft.	4.9	2.2
Services	8	9,781 sq. ft.	3.9	3.6
Other	3	32,840 sq. ft.	13.2	4.3
Special	1	6,900 sq. ft.	2.5	——
Vacant	——	31,565 sq. ft.	12.7	3.3
Total	114	249,667 sq. ft.	100.0	100.0

Tenants by ownership type

Type	Number	Percent	Average percentage in community centers (from *Dollars and Cents*)
National chain	8	7.0	27.0
Independent	21	18.4	24.0
Local chain	85	74.6	49.0

CEDARBRAE MALL

6-35   A regional-scale mall functioning as a community-oriented shopping center. Two grocery stores have served as secondary anchor tenants since Cedarbrae Mall opened.

The Evolution of Cedarbrae Mall

Cedarbrae Mall demonstrates a successful strategy for maintaining the economic viability of a shopping center during a period of population growth and increasing competition in the center's trade area. Given the possibility that renovation and expansion of existing centers may become the largest single area of shopping center development activity within a few years, the Cedarbrae Mall experience assumes a particular interest. This Canadian center, located in metropolitan Toronto, has adapted to rapid population growth in the area and the construction of a 1.1 million square foot regional center 2 miles away. A continuing program of expansion and modernization was initiated shortly after the center was completed in 1960, and has involved expansion of the center from 187,000 to 354,000 square feet of GLA, the addition of a department store as the anchor tenant, the creation of an enclosed pedestrian mall, and adjustments in tenant mix. Of even greater importance has been the developer's success in giving the center a new identity by restructuring it from a regionally oriented center serving an extensive trade area to a community-oriented center accommodating primarily local service and shopping needs.

There have been two major sequences of expansion and renovation, the first occurring in 1962 when a freestanding Simpsons department store, with 100,000 square feet of GLA, was incorporated into the original strip center. In 1970, planning began for a second expansion, which eventually added 24 shops and 27,000 square feet of GLA to the center. During this phase, many of the older stores were remodeled and the entire center was enclosed at a cost of $2 million. These improvements were completed in late 1972.

In physical terms, the center has grown from community to regional in scale, as Canadian centers are somewhat smaller, on the average, than their U.S. counterparts. In marketing terms, however, Cedarbrae Mall has once again become a community-scale center.

Cedarbrae Mall contains 64 mall tenants, the Simpsons department store, and 13 office tenants occupying second-level space accessible from the mall. Large space users which do not require highly visible locations, including a furniture showroom and a bowling alley, are located in the basement. The enclosed pedestrian mall is 1,020 feet long, contains 38,000 square feet of common area, and is anchored at both ends by supermarkets. Simpsons occupies a central position along the mall and has been set back slightly to form a pedestrian court. The periphery of the 28.3-acre site accommodates surface parking for 2,200 vehicles. Service functions are accommodated at the rear of the complex, between the building line and Green Cedar Circuit, a local collector street which forms the boundary between Cedarbrae Mall and Cedarbrae Collegiate Institute, a technical school with 2,200 students.

The Site

Cedarbrae Mall is located in Toronto's eastern suburbs at the intersection of two major at-grade arterials, Lawrence Avenue East and Markham Road. The immediate environs consist of freestanding retail buildings, a community-scale strip shopping center, several high-rise apartments, and extensive areas of single-family detached homes. This mix of uses is greatly different from that existing at the time the center was built, when much of the borough of Scarborough was undeveloped. Rapid urbanization since that time has been accompanied by a substantial increase in trade area population. For the first few years after Cedarbrae Mall was completed, most development in the area took the form of single-family subdivisions. More recently, however, there has been a shift to high-rise apartments and condominiums. This trend toward increased residential densities has been the most important factor in enabling Cedarbrae Mall to maintain its pattern of steady sales growth in the face of expanded retail competition. Walk-in traffic and public transportation account for almost 30 percent of center patronage, a marked increase from the early sixties, when population densities were much lower, bus routes on adjacent streets carried many fewer passengers, and most shoppers arrived by car.

The original retail development pattern in Scarborough consisted largely of small to medium-size strip centers. Between 1962, when Simpsons opened its first suburban store in Cedarbrae Mall, and 1973, the center was the only major shopping complex in the borough, and it accommodated most of the retail shopping needs of Toronto's eastern suburbs. In 1968, however, Trizec Corporation acquired a 56-acre parcel with freeway frontage 2.5 miles from Cedarbrae Mall and proceeded to develop Scarborough Town Centre, a 1.1 million square foot super-regional shopping center with 132 mall stores and three anchor tenants—Simpsons, Miracle Mart, and Eaton's. The center's land use plan also positioned the borough's municipal offices within a ring road encircling the property. When Scarborough Town Centre opened in early 1973, it immediately became the largest retail complex in the eastern section of metropolitan Toronto and also assumed many community functions previously either dispersed or located at Cedarbrae Mall.

Development Strategy

Cedarbrae Mall was built by the Fairview Corporation, Ltd., a predecessor corporation of the present owner and manager, Cadillac Fairview Corporation, Ltd. As one of the largest integrated land development firms in Canada, Cadillac Fairview is also active in the fields of new community, residential, and urban development, in addition to its shopping center holdings. The firm's Shopping Centres Group has a portfolio of 34 completed centers with 11.8 million square feet of GLA in 17 Canadian cities. Its retail strategy is to build and operate centers for long-term asset growth and income generation, thereby contributing to the company's total cash flow. Cadillac Fairview believes that modernization and expansion of existing centers is an important area of shopping center development activity. During 1974 and 1975, the company completed two major expansions of older centers, The Centre Mall in Hamilton, Ontario, with 700,000 square feet of GLA, and Fairview Park Mall in Kitchener, Ontario, with 725,000 square feet of GLA. Recent projects such as Les Promenades–Saint Bruno, outside Montreal, reflect both an awareness of the growing role shopping centers play as locations for community activity and social interaction and the conviction that centers must be planned in such a way as to fulfill the expectations of the communities in which they are located. In fact, the strategy of expanding and enclosing Cedarbrae Mall was based on the firm's multiple commitments to main-

tenance of center productivity and expansion of shopping centers' social and community functions.

In view of the challenge posed by Scarborough Town Centre, it was apparent that a major upgrading of Cedarbrae Mall's shopping environment would be necessary to maintain the center's long-term economic viability. The decision to be made by Cadillac Fairview was not whether a remodeling program should be undertaken but rather the precise nature of the improvements to be carried out.

The development program adopted had two primary elements, one physical and the other operational. After considering various construction alternatives, one of which would have involved erection of deck parking and additional retail space, a design solution was adopted which specified limited expansion of retail space and enclosure of the pedestrian area. These improvements afforded the benefits of extending center patronage into the evening hours, broadening the range of merchandise and services available in the center, and creating a climate-controlled shopping environment which would attract shoppers and increase pedestrian traffic during the cold Canadian winters. A further benefit was that this improvement could be carried out at a relatively low cost.

The organizational modifications involved conversion of Cedarbrae Mall from a regional center serving an area with a radius of 7 to 8 miles to a community-oriented center with a more localized focus and a primary trade area with a radius of 1½ to 2 miles. The 26 new mall tenants were selected on the basis of their contribution to the goal of expanding merchandise selection within the center while providing for basic community needs and generating regular pedestrian traffic. A market analysis was undertaken to point out the mix of merchandise and services required to meet consumer needs in the redefined trade area. The developer also adopted a variety of techniques to reinforce the local position of the center, including organizing promotional activities in conjunction with charitable groups, having students from Cedarbrae Collegiate Institute paint large murals next to the Simpsons store, and broadening the number of community activities and programs held at the center. A fire prevention program held by the local fire department, for example, has become an annual event. This strategy acknowledged that it would not be possible to replicate either the merchandise selection or the scope of activities available at Scarborough Town Centre, but presumed that physically upgrading the center and giving it a new role would enable Cedarbrae Mall to retain a profitable and useful position within the community.

Evidence since the completion of the center in November 1972 suggests that this strategy has been quite successful. Retail sales, which had increased at an average annual rate of 8 percent before enclosure, have been increasing at over 12 percent annually since the mall was enclosed. Even during the months of heavy construction, sales decreased only slightly, and sales for 1972–73 were 20.7 percent higher than those in the preceding 12 months. During fiscal 1975, retail sales averaged $143 per square foot of GLA. It seems that the $2 million investment in Cedarbrae Mall, the minimum amount felt to be required to sustain the center over the long term, will have the effect of maintaining the center as a viable retail complex for the foreseeable future. Sales growth in the coming years will depend on population growth near the center, increases in disposable income, inflationary trends, and changes in buying patterns.

Expansion and Enclosure

The addition of Simpsons department store in 1962, an improvement not anticipated when the complex was designed, reinforced the center's original role of serving the shopping needs of most of Scarborough. Plans to further expand the center beyond 283,000 square feet of GLA and enclose the pedestrian area were formulated after the development program for Scarborough Town Centre was announced. Actual construction took 8 months, beginning in April 1972, but before work on the project could begin, zoning had to be modified to permit a higher building coverage.

A portion of the parking lot was used for two retail structures facing the original building line

6-36 Expansion and enclosure involved building new retail structures facing the original building line. Shown here is the exterior appearance of this new construction.

on each side of Simpsons. The 30-foot space between the storefronts was converted into an enclosed pedestrian mall by extending the original exterior canopy to the new building line and supporting it with a series of structural columns and attachments to existing masonry walls. A suspended acoustic tile ceiling was installed, and the original concrete sidewalks were replaced with polished terrazzo highlighted by banding at the columns. A sprinkler system was installed for the entire center in order to conform to the local building code. Entrances were redesigned and window walls were introduced to bring light into the pedestrian corridor.

The new center space was aesthetically improved by introducing artistic elements into the center's interior. The central court in front of the Simpsons store features two pieces of sculpture in small reflecting pools and large murals on each side of the entrance. Hanging pots were used at the window areas and potted trees were placed along the pedestrian mall. Visual interest has been enhanced by a space-frame sculpture hung from the ceiling. The original tenants were encouraged to modernize their store facades, and new tenants' facades were given a contemporary appearance with unified signage.

The exterior appearance of Cedarbrae Mall has been significantly improved; the original canopy and its discordant mix of signs have given way to a uniform facade of buff-colored brick selected to match the appearance of Simpsons and the supermarkets. Additional landscaping was introduced and the parking area was restriped. Despite the fact that the expansion was built on the center parking lot, only 110 parking spaces were lost.

One essential redevelopment criterion was that the center remain in operation during the 8-month construction period. Steps taken to minimize disruption of the shopping center operation included erecting hoarding along the mall to separate the shoppers from workmen; carrying out particularly disruptive construction activities, such as polishing the terrazzo floors, after business hours; and keeping shoppers apprised of progress by periodic news bulletins and other promotional techniques.

Cost of the enclosure was divided between the tenants, who contributed $1 per square foot, and the developer, who assumed the remainder of the expense. One provision of the enclosure agreement allowed tenants to charge their initial increase in percentage rents against their share of the improvement cost.

Based on his experience, the developer offers several comments about the difficulties associated with expansion and enclosure of shopping centers:

- It is difficult to obtain accurate cost figures before construction is started.
- It is necessary to keep a center open during the construction phase in order to minimize the disruption of customer shopping habits.
- The need to periodically upgrade the premises to meet changes in building code requirements must be anticipated.
- Cooperation and support from both local government and the tenants are essential.
- Long-term lease arrangements can be expected to impose limitations on what can be accomplished.

Cadillac Fairview also emphasizes that the scope of the improvement program was dictated in large measure by the nature of the original construction and the need for the center to be upgraded to contemporary standards. The firm no longer builds open centers and, had it been possible, would have carried out more extensive changes in tenant composition than were actually made. In size, however, the developer feels that the center is appropriate to conditions in Canada and points out that many of the company's 34 centers fall within this size range.

Tenant Mix

Cedarbrae Mall's primary orientation is apparent in the tenant mix, which more closely resembles that of a conventional community center than that of other centers the same size. Cedarbrae Mall contains many uses not commonly found in centers with more than 350,000 square feet of GLA. Financial, office, and service uses—including banks, insurance agencies, finance companies, doctors, lawyers, dentists, opticians, barbers, beauty shops, travel agents, a tailor, and a cleaner—occupy 7.1 percent of the total GLA, a much higher percentage than the regional center average listed in *Dollars and Cents of Shopping Centers: 1975*. Supermarkets are another major component of the center, representing 17.0 percent of the GLA, whereas the average for regional center supermarkets is 5.5 percent. Furniture stores, variety stores, and a bowling alley are also major space users at Cedarbrae Mall. Underrepresented in terms of square footage are such destination shopping uses as food service, general merchandise, clothing and shoes,

Portfolio of The Shopping Centres Group

	Year Opened	Company's Interest (%)	Size of Site (acres)	Total Leasable Area (000 sq. ft.)	Area of Non-Owned Buildings (000 sq. ft.)	Number of Stores & Services	Parking Spaces
Barrie, Ontario							
Georgian Mall	1973	100	22	201	93	42	1,100
Calgary, Alberta							
North Hill Shopping Centre	1958	100	32	510	208	95	2,400
Edmonton, Alberta							
Bonnie Doon Shopping Centre	1959	100	31	415	–	90	2,500
Giffard, Quebec							
Les Galeries Ste. Anne	1973	70	18	228	–	25	1,150
Hamilton, Ontario							
The Centre Mall	1955	100	66	678	335	74	3,800
Eastgate Square	1973	70	41	525	–	107	3,000
Gage Square	1974	70	7	67	–	4	500
Kitchener, Ontario							
Fairview Park Mall	1966	100	52.8	727	337	92	3,678
Levis, Quebec							
Les Galeries Chagnon	1974	70	42	536	126	63	2,400
Mississauga, Ontario							
Millway Shopping Centre	1976	100	4.5	45	–	11	226
Rockwood Mall	1974	42	24	291	–	37	1,400
Montreal, Quebec							
Domaine Shopping Centre	1959	100	13	235	25	60	900
Maisonneuve Shopping Centre	1959	100	9	139	–	30	550
Greenfield Park Shopping Centre	1961	50	26	375	17	45	2,100
Fairview Pointe Claire	1965	50	74	628	–	79	3,900
Les Galeries D'Anjou	1968	50	74	937	–	145	5,300
Le Carrefour Laval	1974	51	74	870	123	128	4,500
Ottawa, Ontario							
Montreal Square	1973	70	5	58	–	12	300
Vista Centre	1973	100	6.5	70	–	20	430
Regina, Saskatchewan							
Southland Mall	1975	50	28	255	–	35	1,400
Richmond Hill, Ontario							
Hillcrest Mall	1974	100	46	566	–	85	3,000
St. Catharines, Ontario							
Fairview Mall	1961	100	24	261	67	30	1,600
Saint John, N.B.							
Fairview Plaza	1960	100	15	192	99	18	500
Thunder Bay, Ontario							
Thunder Bay Mall	1972	70	16	140	–	22	900
Toronto, Ontario							
York Mills Shopping Centre	1953	100	6	51	–	17	250
Don Mills Shopping Centre	1955	100	33	411	52	86	2,400
Parkway Plaza	1958	100	19	280	–	65	1,200
Cedarbrae Plaza	1960	100	30	403	114	77	2,300
Parkwoods Village Shopping Centre	1960	100	6	78	39	20	250
The Towne Mall	1967	100	1	71	–	14	150
Peanut Plaza	1970	50	5	90	–	18	600
Fairview Mall	1970	50	47	570	–	113	3,300
University City	1974	100	4	44	–	13	200
Winnipeg, Manitoba							
Polo Park Shopping Centre	1959	100	60	848	263	83	4,600
			961.8	11,795	1,898		

6-37

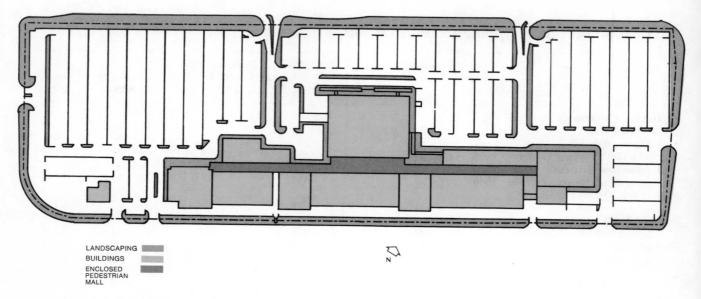

LANDSCAPING
BUILDINGS
ENCLOSED
PEDESTRIAN
MALL

N

6-38   Site plan—Cedarbrae Mall.

and dry goods, the mainstays of most regional centers. The Simpsons store, for example, is smaller than most newer department stores in regional-scale centers.

Despite many individual tenant changes, the tenant mix of Cedarbrae Mall remains substantially the same as it was when the center first opened. Many occupants are more characteristic of early centers than of those being built today. Grocery stores, for example, which anchor both ends of Cedarbrae Mall, are usually omitted in contemporary centers. One advantage is that since many of these uses are appropriate to community orientation and since many of these stores are locally owned, they are closely attuned to community merchandise preferences.

Management and Operation

As owner and operator of the center, Cadillac Fairview maintains an on-site staff of a manager, a bookkeeper, a secretary, a security chief, three security personnel, a maintenance superintendent, and a four-person maintenance staff.

Tenant membership in the merchants association is mandated through provisions of the lease. Tenants are given one vote for the first 750 square feet of GLA and another vote for each additional 500 square feet, with a maximum of 30 votes per tenant. Dues are $0.30 per square foot, with the developer contributing an amount equal to 25 percent of the tenant contribution. Although not a member, Simpsons contributes an annual fixed amount and is actively involved in association affairs, although it has no vote. The association has a board of directors made up of a member of each merchandise category, but the owner manages the association affairs and retains the right of veto.

Basic rents are $9 to $10 per square foot. Percentage rents range generally from 6 to 8 percent and are based on the tenant space. Simpsons, the exception, operates on a ground lease. Approximately 60 percent of the stores, those with sales above a breakpoint specified in their lease, pay percentage rents. Common area charges for center maintenance and insurance averaged $0.85 per square foot in 1975.

PROJECT DATA—CEDARBRAE MALL

DEVELOPER/MANAGEMENT

Cadillac Fairview Corporation, Ltd.
1200 Sheppard Avenue, East
Toronto, Ontario, Canada M5W 1W2

LAND USE INFORMATION

Site area   28.3 acres
Land allocation

	Site area	Percent of site
Buildings	7.9 acres	27.9
Parking and circulation	18.1 acres	64.0
Landscaping	2.3 acres	8.1
Total	28.3 acres	100.0

GLA   354,320 sq. ft.
GBA   392,320 sq. ft.

Common area   38,000 sq. ft.
Parking
  Spaces   2,200
  Ratio   2.3 : 1
  Index   6.2

ECONOMIC INFORMATION

Total sales (1975)	$29 million
Sales per sq. ft. GLA	$143[1]
Merchants association dues	$0.30 per sq. ft.
Rentals	
Amount	$9 to $10
Length	generally 10 years
Percentage rents	generally 6 to 8 percent
Capital costs	
Total	$2 million[2]
Per sq. ft.	$30.50

[1] Excluding majors.

[2] $26.60 per sq. ft. for new retail; $35.25 per sq. ft. for new mall.

TENANT INFORMATION

Number of tenants
  Mall tenants   64
  Office tenants   13
  Department stores   1
  Total   77
Percent Leased   100.0

Tenant Classification	Number of stores	GLA	Percent of total GLA	Percent of developer GLA	Average percentage in regional centers (from Dollars and Cents of Shopping Centers: 1975)
Food	4	60,080 sq. ft.	17.0	23.7	5.5
Food service	6	7,382 sq. ft.	2.1	2.9	2.9
General merchandise	3	136,800 sq. ft.	38.6	14.3	53.4
Clothing and shoes	19	37,567 sq. ft.	10.6	14.8	16.9
Dry goods	1	2,063 sq. ft.	0.6	0.8	1.4
Furniture (home furnishings)	2	16,046 sq. ft.	4.5	6.3	1.4
Other retail	20	43,646 sq. ft.	12.3	17.2	10.1
Financial	7	9,949 sq. ft.	2.8	3.9	1.6
Offices	7	5,533 sq. ft.	1.6	2.2	0.4
Services	7	9,604 sq. ft.	2.7	3.8	1.2
Other (bowling)	1	25,650 sq. ft.	7.2	10.1	3.0
Vacant	—	—	—	—	2.2
Total	77	354,320 sq. ft.	100.0	100.0	100.0

Tenants by ownership type

Type	Number	Percent	Average percentage in regional centers (from Dollars and Cents)
National chain	34	44.2	41.1
Independent	10	13.0	25.2
Local chain	33	42.8	33.7

THE CITADEL

6-40 Outdoor restaurant.

The Urban Subcenter

The Citadel presents a striking design solution to the problem of providing for orderly development within the context of an automobile-oriented, suburban shopping center environment. The primary component is a twin-anchor, multilevel shopping center which occupies the central portion of a 160-acre site. A ring road separates the shopping center from the peripheral portions of the property, which are being developed with a variety of uses compatible with The Citadel's primary retail function. These supporting elements include attached residential, hotel-motel, and office uses. While the integration of project components is less sophisticated than that of the mixed use development, the project represents a significant advance over the typical situation wherein peripheral development is unrelated to the shopping center. The project's combination of components should have the effect of reinforcing The Citadel's position as the primary urban subcenter in Colorado Springs when completed in the early eighties. At that time, there should be approximately 3,500 persons living and working within The Citadel. A system of plazas, pedestrian linkages, and accessways through the structures physically integrates the entire development. Heavy emphasis on aesthetics has taken the form of sculpture, landscaping, reflecting pools, and other amenities. Most striking of all has been the use of a pre-Columbian design motif, which has been applied to building interiors and exteriors, the pedestrian areas, signage, and the land use plan itself.

The project was formulated in 1966 following acquisition of the property by the J. C. Penney Company, which planned to develop a regional shopping center on the site. Since 160 acres was more than necessary for a regional shopping center alone—ULI suggests 80 acres as the maximum area required for a project of this type—the remainder of the site was preplanned for a range of compatible uses. This approach had the advantage of allowing the developer to participate in the increases in property value and development potential associated with the development of a regional shopping center, and also permitted proper buffering of the development from adjacent residential areas.

Three years was required to obtain necessary government approvals and to complete the marketing, traffic, engineering, and design studies. Construction of The Citadel began in late 1970, and the center opened for business in early 1972. Development has since proceeded on the peripheral parcels, with 54 percent of the available acreage having been either developed or committed to eventual use. Elements completed through September 1976 include 142 townhouse and garden apartments, two freestanding office buildings, a 52,000 square foot neighborhood shopping center, and a TBA store operated by J. C. Penney, Inc.

The Site

The Citadel, well placed to benefit from the community's rapid growth, occupies a quarter section at the intersection of two major at-grade arterial streets in the eastern section of Colorado Springs. The environs consist of a combination of tract subdivisions, apartment projects, and strip commercial developments. The Citadel is the only regional shopping center in the city. Outside of downtown Colorado Springs, the only other major commercial activity in the city is limited to half a dozen neighborhood and community-scale shopping centers, the largest having 260,000 square feet of GLA. Most of these centers are also located in the rapidly growing eastern portion of the city, within a 3-mile radius of The Citadel.

The site is 2,500 feet on a side and slopes from east to west, a circumstance which dictated a two-level design scheme for the shopping mall. Entrances on the west are located at the lower level, entrances on the east at the upper level.

Design

The regional shopping center, with its 69-acre site, is at the center of the property. The 91 acres around the peripheries of the site have been designated for residential use, including a combination of 900 townhouses, garden apartments, and high-rise apartments, as well as a 300-room motor hotel, office and retail buildings, and a convenience shop-

6-41 A bank is one of several freestanding commercial buildings at The Citadel.

ping center. Development densities range from suburban to urban. Access to the ring road, which defines the shopping center site, is provided by access roads which penetrate the site from the adjacent arterials. These streets, built by the developer and dedicated to the city, have been set back a minimum of 400 feet from the arterial intersections to minimize traffic congestion.

The Citadel's design scheme, which has given the development a unique image and character, takes its inspiration from the temples, stelae, and bas-reliefs of the pre-Columbian Indian culture of Central America. This concept is apparent in the rectangular geometry of the site plan and building configurations, the use of geometrical patterns on horizontal and vertical surfaces, and informal and irregular tropical landscaping in the mall courts. No attempt has been made, however, to directly copy or adapt any pre-Columbian structure; instead, the intent has been to recreate the essence of the pre-Columbian style.

A provision in the operating agreement authorizes the architect to review and approve all building exterior designs, materials, and signage for conformance to The Citadel's design concept. The palette of materials available for use is limited to rust-colored face brick, exposed concrete aggregate, and ribbed concrete wall surfaces. Applica-

tion of these design guidelines has given The Citadel a feeling of continuity and identity that is unique and dramatic. While this design, in and of itself, cannot be said to contribute to the center's success, the design—in concert with a good location and other factors—strongly reinforces The Citadel's positive image in the minds of shoppers.

Essential to the concept is the physical integration of the various project components. This has been accomplished by using broad pedestrian plazas which stretch from the shopping center to the ring road. The east and west greenways are called the Plaza of the Waters and the Plaza of the Sun. Each contains appropriate sculpture, pools, fountains, walkways, an amphitheater, and other amenities. The plazas are also the location of freestanding commercial buildings which enhance the activity cycle in these areas. The Plaza of the Sun is the planned location of a third department store. When this store is built, the plaza will be shifted directly west, across the ring road, to provide an important public space within the residential area. The full impact of the pedestrian linkages will only be realized after the entire development has been completed. Current residential and office populations remain small, and most persons patronizing the shopping center rely on automobiles for access.

6-42 This twin-anchor suburban center is situated in the most rapidly growing section of Colorado Springs.

Surface parking spaces for 4,442 vehicles are provided around the four sides of the center, with additional spaces provided for the uses in the peripheral areas. The parking index, 6.0 spaces per 1,000 square feet of GLA, exceeds the ULI standard and appears to be significantly higher than necessary. This criteria, however, was established in the zoning ordinance and could not be modified at the time the project was approved. Parking for the residential areas is provided at the rate of 1.5 spaces per unit.

Storm drainage, a matter of particular concern because of the high portion of the shopping center site given over to buildings and parking, has been accommodated by means of a 48-inch line circling the center site and draining to the southwest.

Development Strategy

The Citadel project represented a conscious effort on the part of the developer to create an imaginative and innovative development at a very favorable suburban location. The name, The Citadel, reflects the fact that the local economy is heavily weighted toward the military, as the area includes Fort Carson and the Air Force Academy.

The J. C. Penney Company's original intent was to supplement its smaller downtown outlet, but the downtown store was closed once the 172,000 square foot Citadel department store had opened. Following municipal approval of the project, General Growth Properties of Des Moines, Iowa, was selected to develop the 27.6-acre central portion of the property as a shopping mall. Associated Dry Goods purchased 13.8 acres at the north end of the site for a 110,000 square foot outlet of its Denver Store. The J. C. Penney Company has retained ownership of the southern portion of shopping center acreage and the peripheral areas, but has elected to sell this land rather than to develop and manage it. This strategy, based on a corporate decision identifying merchandising as the company's primary area of expertise, was initiated in 1972 and is continuing. Peripheral site purchases to date include General Growth Property's acquisition of 5.7 acres for a neighborhood shopping center and 346 rental apartment units, and the acquisition of 7.7 acres by two financial institutions, The Citadel Bank and Western S&L, which have erected office buildings on their properties.

The Shopping Mall

The multilevel shopping mall, anchored at the ends by Penney's and the Denver Store, consists of two irregular pedestrian streets, each 504 feet long, superimposed over one another. The West Mall is situated at right angles to the main corridor and ends at the Plaza of the Sun, giving the overall mall a T configuration. The 92 stores face each other across a 32-foot corridor, which opens at intervals into a series of interior courts. The courts at the department store entrances are highlighted by glass sculpture. The central court, at the intersection of the two malls, is a 12,000 square foot atrium capped by a skylight. In addition to the stairs and escalator connecting the two levels, the central court contains a massive water sculpture, a Mayan stele, tropical plantings, and seating areas. Openness in storefront design is emphasized to heighten eye appeal and marketability. Most stores are 50 percent or more open to the corridor, with roll-down grilles, sliding glass panels, and folding partitions used to secure the stores when closed.

The pre-Columbian design motif has been introduced into the interior by the use of precast concrete panels, quarry slate and tile for floors and wall surfaces, tropical plantings, and the application of Central American decorative elements to store facades. Tenants have also been encouraged to incorporate the motif into their store designs and signs, and many have done so.

The Citadel was designed with the main entrances facing east. To date, however, traffic flow has been heavier from the west, toward the more urbanized portion of the market area. There are

6-43 The design motif has been applied to building exteriors as well as to building interiors, pedestrian areas, signage, and the land use plan itself.

at-grade screened truck docks, including one for each of the department stores, on all four sides of the structure to serve the center's tenants. Built of rust-colored brick as extensions of the mall facade, these service areas have been skillfully planned to blend in with the overall design.

Marketing

The primary trade area for The Citadel consists of the two-county Colorado Springs SMSA, which had an estimated population of 292,000 in 1975. This figure represented a 22.0 percent increase over that of 1970. The secondary trade area is much wider and includes most of southern Colorado and portions of adjacent states. Until the fall 1976 opening of the 511,000 square foot, $30 million Pueblo Mall 40 miles south, The Citadel was the only regional center in a vast, multistate area, but Pueblo Mall has now eliminated approximately 25 percent of The Citadel's secondary market area. Denver, little more than an hour's drive to the north, also draws off a considerable amount of trade that would otherwise be available to retail outlets in Colorado Springs. The size of the market area served by The Citadel has presented a challenge to the center operator. In a reverse of the typical pattern in the nation, The Citadel relies on television, radio, and newspapers (in that order) to reach its far-flung audience.

The construction of a second multi-anchor regional shopping center in Colorado Springs is planned for the early eighties. Before this becomes an economically viable possibility, however, several factors will need to change. First, the rate of population growth in the area, which has slowed since 1973 because of a moratorium on gas connections, will have to pick up substantially. Second, the Colorado Springs region will have to improve on its position of having the lowest per-capita

sales of any metropolitan area in the state. A more likely prospect, at least for the near future, would be the addition of a third anchor department store at The Citadel.

The Citadel's mall was leased over a period of 40 months and is now fully occupied. The overall economic success of the shopping center appears to derive from the following factors: a dynamic and rapidly growing metropolitan area; a CBD which has traditionally offered only limited retail competition; community size sufficient to sustain a single regional shopping center but too small to accommodate two major centers; extensive secondary trade area; and a design concept which has produced a unique and pleasant environment for shopping. Development of the peripheral parcels, however, has been slower than originally anticipated, a circumstance attributable at least in part to the depressed state of the real estate industry between 1974 and 1976.

6-44   Plaza of the Waters, one of several pedestrian areas stretching from the shopping center to the ring road.

Management and Operation

Operation and management are carried out under the operating agreement signed by land purchasers in The Citadel and administered by the master developer, the J. C. Penney Company. General Growth Properties built, leased, and now manages the mall and has established a merchants association to carry out a coordinated advertising program for the center. Membership is mandatory, with dues originally established at $0.10 per square foot but now increased to $0.25 per square foot. The two department stores are voluntary members and pay a fixed amount based upon closed-end agreements. The developer contributes an amount equal to one-third of the tenants' contribution. Common area charges for landscaping, interior maintenance, security, and other operational costs totalled $1.15 per square foot in 1975 but are flexible on the basis of actual cost. The department store tenants also pay a fixed common area charge as determined by prior agreement.

The center operates from 10:00 a.m. to 9:00 p.m. during the week, with shorter hours on Saturday and Sunday. The restaurants and movie theater, which close later in the evening, are located on the West Mall, which can be closed off from the rest of the center by a wrought-iron folding gate. This has proven to be a convenient means of extending the operational cycle of the center while minimizing security problems for most of the center after the business day.

Tenant Mix

The 92 individual stores in the mall account for 50.1 percent of the shopping center's GLA. The tenant mix closely approximates the averages listed in *Dollars and Cents of Shopping Centers: 1975* for regional centers. Slightly under half of all GLA is given over to the two main department stores. Heavy emphasis has been placed on soft goods—which are represented by 36 outlets and 132,000 square feet of GLA. The 32 stores in the "other retail" category include a broad array of merchants whose goods range from books and stationery to wine and cheese. Of the 94 tenants, 57.9 percent are national chain stores, 29.4 percent local chain stores, and 12.7 percent independent retailers.

Land Use Controls

The property was zoned for agriculture at the time it was acquired, and rezoning was necessary in order to accommodate the proposed development concept. This was accomplished by applying different zoning categories to the various parts of the property. These include PBC-3 (Planned Business) for the regional shopping center, PBC-2 (Planned Business at a lower density) for the convenience center, PUD (Planned Unit Development) for the residential areas, and R5 (Conditional Residential, a category permitting office uses at a specified density) for the remainder.

6-45   Two of three projected anchor stores are now in place.

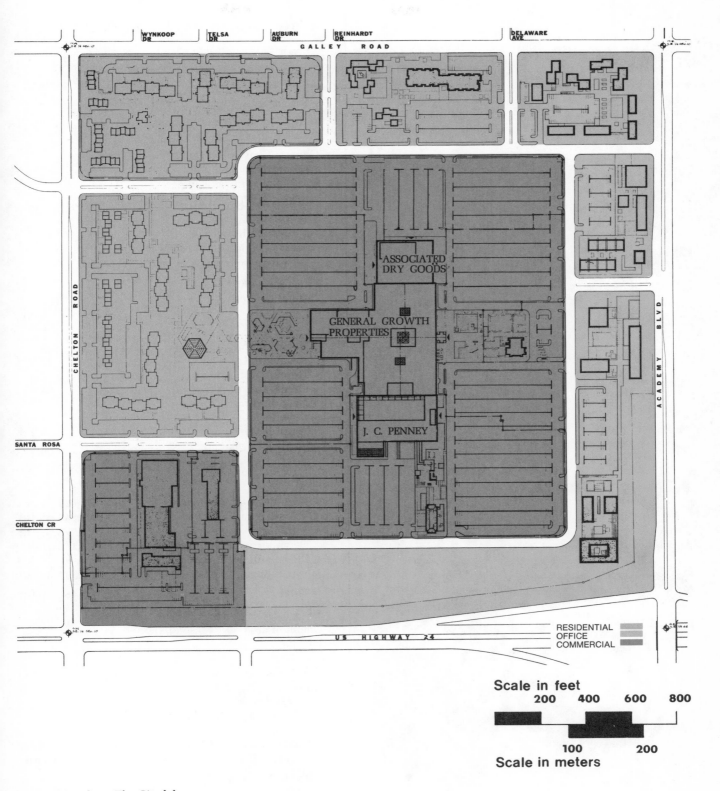

Labels within image:

WYNKOOP DR • TELSA DR • AUBURN DR • REINHARDT DR • DELAWARE AVE

GALLEY ROAD

CHELTON ROAD

ACADEMY BLVD

ASSOCIATED DRY GOODS

GENERAL GROWTH PROPERTIES

J. C. PENNEY

SANTA ROSA

CHELTON CR

US HIGHWAY 24

RESIDENTIAL
OFFICE
COMMERCIAL

Scale in feet
200 400 600 800

100 200
Scale in meters

6-46 Site plan—The Citadel.

6-47 Pre-Columbian design motif.

6-48   PROJECT DATA—THE CITADEL

DEVELOPERS

J. C. Penney Company, Inc.
1301 Avenue of the Americas
New York, New York 10019

General Growth Properties
1055 Sixth Avenue
Des Moines, Iowa 50306

ARCHITECTURE/PLANNING

The Ramos Group
101 West 11th
Kansas City, Missouri 64105

LAND USE INFORMATION

Site area   160.0 acres
Land allocation

	Site area	Percent of site
Regional shopping center	68.8 acres	43.0
Residential	40.0 acres	25.0
Hotel-motel	4.2 acres	2.6
Office and commercial	38.9 acres	24.3
Neighborhood shopping center	5.7 acres	3.6
Auto center	2.4 acres	1.5
Total	160.0 acres	100.0

Area sold or developed   95.9 acres

GLA

Regional shopping center	566,022 sq. ft.
Mall tenants	(282,244 sq. ft.)
Department stores	(283,778 sq. ft.)
Neighborhood shopping center	52,146 sq. ft.
Freestanding commercial buildings (TBA store)	30,297 sq. ft.
Total	648,465 sq. ft.

GBA	723,416 sq. ft.
Common area	74,951 sq. ft.

Parking
Spaces   4,442
Ratio   4.0 : 1
Index   6.0

Land Ownership

J. C. Penney (department store, peripheral parcels)	118.6 acres
General Growth Properties (the mall)	27.6 acres
Associated Dry Goods (Denver Store)	13.8 acres
Total	160.0 acres

ECONOMIC INFORMATION

Total sales (1975)	NA
Sales per sq. ft. GLA	NA
Merchants association dues[1]	$0.25 per sq. ft.

Common area charges	$1.00 per sq. ft.
Rentals	
Amount	$4.50 to $18.00 per sq. ft. GLA[2]
Length	5 to 20 years
Percentage rents	4 to 10 percent

[1] Developer contributes an amount equal to one-third of the tenant contribution.

[2] Higher rents are charged to kiosk tenants.

TENANT INFORMATION

Number of tenants	
Mall tenants	100
Department stores	2
Total	102
Percent leased	100.0

Regional Center

Tenant Classification	Number of stores	GLA	Percent of total GLA	Percent of developer GLA	Average percentage in regional centers (from *Dollars and Cents of Shopping Centers: 1975*)
Food	4	8,017 sq. ft.	1.4	2.8	5.6
Food service	7	19,974 sq. ft.	3.5	7.0	2.9
General merchandise	3	297,107 sq. ft.	52.5	5.3	53.4
Clothing and shoes	36	131,771 sq. ft.	23.3	46.4	16.9
Dry goods	1	4,230 sq. ft.	0.8	1.5	1.4
Furniture (home furnishings)	5	13,675 sq. ft.	2.4	4.8	1.4
Other retail	32	73,793 sq. ft.	13.0	26.0	10.1
Financial	2	1,107 sq. ft.	0.2	0.4	1.6
Offices	—	—	—	—	0.4
Services	2	960 sq. ft.	0.2	0.3	1.2
Other	1	13,580 sq. ft.	2.4	4.8	3.0
Special	1	1,808 sq. ft.	0.3	0.7	2.2
Subtotal	94	566,022 sq. ft.	100.0	100.0	100.0

Neighborhood center

Tenant Classification	Number of stores	GLA	Percent of total GLA
Food	1	33,419 sq. ft.	64.1
Food service	1	1,386 sq. ft.	2.6
Clothing and shoes	1	6,600 sq. ft.	12.7
Other retail	1	3,341 sq. ft.	6.4
Financial	1	1,400 sq. ft.	2.7
Vacant	—	6,000 sq. ft.	11.5
Subtotal	5	52,146 sq. ft.	100.0
Freestanding commercial building	3	30,297 sq. ft.	—
Total	102	648,465 sq. ft.	100.0

Tenants by ownership type

Type	Number	Percent	Average percentage in neighborhood centers (from *Dollars and Cents*)
National chain	59	57.9	41.1
Independent	13	12.7	33.7
Local chain	30	29.4	25.3

PARAMUS PARK

6-49   A view of Paramus Park from the ring road.

An Economic Success Story

Few shopping centers have had more immediate and dramatic success than Paramus Park. During its first 12 months of operation, this enclosed mall regional center generated sales in excess of $174 per square foot of developer GLA and was the top performer among the Rouse Company's 24 shopping centers. A further sales increase of 15 percent took place in fiscal 1976, and Paramus Park is now calculated to have generated sales of $214 per square foot during the revised fiscal year ending December 31, 1976. These sales figures place Paramus Park in the highest rank of centers in the nation, and they exceed by a wide margin the upper decile of regional centers reported in *Dollars and Cents of Shopping Centers: 1975*. These sales were achieved by combining a skillful merchandising strategy with an attractive physical plant and a carefully devised tenant mix in a strong but outwardly saturated market location.

The center is not unusual in physical terms; Paramus Park has a modified S configuration with 276,000 square feet of GLA in its enclosed mall, anchored at the ends by department stores. Rather, it has been subtle adjustments in the conventional shopping center formula, combined with the unique development opportunities of the affluent suburban location, that have given Paramus Park its competitive edge.

Development Strategy

Paramus Park is located in the populous northern New Jersey suburbs of New York City. Household incomes in the immediate environs are significantly higher than state and national averages. The population of the trade area, which includes all or portions of Bergen, Passaic, and Essex Counties in New Jersey and Rockland County, New York, stands at 1.5 million. Bergen County, in particular, has been an attractive location for retail development, and the Rouse Company wished to locate a center there to complement its Willowbrook and Woodbridge Center developments, which serve the central and southern portions of the northern New Jersey metropolitan area.

The development strategy presumed that a new center would have to modify existing shopping patterns, as the market area was already well served with retail facilities. There are five regional shopping centers and two freestanding department stores within a 20-minute drive of Paramus Park. These, together with subsequent expansions and enclosures of older open mall centers undertaken after the Paramus Park project was initiated, have brought total shopping center GLA in northern New Jersey to 5.8 million square feet. Included are the following major developments: Bergen Mall, a 20-year-old enclosed mall with two department stores; Garden State Plaza, a 1.3 million square foot regional center with three department stores; The Fashion Center, a two-anchor fashion center; Nanuet Mall, an enclosed mall center with two department stores; Riverside Square, a former freestanding department store which has been expanded into an enclosed mall with an additional department store as a new anchor tenant; and Willowbrook, a 1.4 million square foot regional center with three anchor tenants. These centers provide a wide range of shopper goods for the middle to upper income groups and have physical plants ranging from the outdated to the fully modern and highly competitive.

A further consideration for the developer was that only limited population growth was projected for the multicounty trade area and that a new center would consequently have to be oriented toward the existing market. Between 1970 and 1975, the population of Bergen County remained stable. Older industrialized towns in the eastern and southern sections are now losing population, while suburban and rural townships in central and northwestern Bergen County are growing. Personal incomes are increasing rapidly, however, and the expectation of increasing disposable incomes provided an important rationale for starting the project.

Sales experience to date at Paramus Park has shown that a market did exist and that a new regional shopping center can be developed in an apparently well-served area of stable population by basing the development decision on anticipated growth in disposable income and by creating a more appealing shopping environment. The pros-

MAJOR RETAIL DEVELOPMENTS, NORTHERN NEW JERSEY AND ROCKLAND COUNTY, NEW YORK

Center	Location	Major Tenants	GLA (Sq. Ft.)	Year Opened
Bergen Mall	Paramus, N.J.	Stern's Ohrbach	1,200,000	1957
Garden State Plaza	Paramus, N.J.	Bamberger's Gimbel's J. C. Penney	1,340,000	1957
The Fashion Center	Paramus, N.J.	Lord & Taylor B. Altman	450,000	1967
Nanuet Mall	Nanuet, N.Y.	Sears Roebuck Bamberger's	800,000	1969
Paramus Park	Paramus, N.J.	Abraham and Straus Sears Roebuck	758,000	1974
Riverside Square	Hackensack, N.J.	Bloomingdale's Saks Fifth Avenue	585,000	1976*
Willowbrook	Wayne, N.J.	Bamberger's Sears Roebuck Ohrbach	1,400,000	1969

*Expansion of freestanding Bloomingdale's department store.

pects for future sales growth at Paramus Park appear to be good; a market survey for the period from 1977 to 1981 has projected that retail sales in the trade area will increase at a compound rate of 7.4 percent in current dollars.

Before starting the project, the developer sought out prospective tenants and prepared preliminary and specific market analyses. For its current projects, the Rouse Company has added an additional step, an expectation survey of prospective shoppers, undertaken in order to assure the validity of initial judgements about prospects for a new center and to determine the appropriate nature of the complex to be built.

At Paramus Park, the challenge was to broaden the market through merchandising and design. To accomplish this, the developer tailored the project to the marketplace by creating a unique and distinctive shopping center, one conveying a feeling of both quality and excitement to the affluent residents of northern New Jersey. The strategy assumed that a contemporary approach and above-average product design and amenities would generate a positive response on the part of the shopping public. The center is being merchandised between existing middle-income and high-income-

oriented centers, thereby appealing to as broad a segment of the market as possible.

Paramus Park was given a unique tenant mix heavily weighted toward soft goods, gifts, and jewelry, and it includes a gourmet food area, the Pic-Nic. The physical design is distinguished from older centers in the area by a sophisticated use of building and plant materials, both interior and exterior.

The development process was initiated in 1969, when Federated Department Stores, Inc., bought land for an outlet of its Brooklyn-based Abraham and Straus division. The Rouse Company negotiated with Federated and then entered into a joint venture with Connecticut General Life Insurance Company to develop a shopping center on the site. In early 1970, a commitment was obtained from Sears, Roebuck and Company to locate in the new center. It took approximately three years to ready the 59.8-acre site for construction, because of unstable soil conditions which required fill, settling, and compaction. Construction got underway in 1972, and the complex was completed in 24 months. Paramus Park opened in March 1974, and the center was 92 percent leased and 84 percent occupied by the end of the first month's operation.

The Site

Since the developer entered Bergen County after the area had been substantially urbanized, it was necessary to locate the new center on a bypassed parcel in a manner which violated virtually all the principles of shopping center location, except the fundamental one of positioning a center in the middle of its trade area. The 59.8-acre area is landlocked, and although Paramus Park has frontage and good visibility along the Garden State Parkway, there is only limited access from that direction. Primary access to the center is from New Jersey Route 17, a heavily traveled arterial west of the property, separated from the center by existing development, including highway-oriented commercial, industrial, and warehouse uses. Two access roads and a partial interchange between the center's access ways and Route 17 had to be built by the developer to make the site usable for retail commercial purposes. Paramus Park is screened from view along Route 17, and this lack of visibility, together with the poor environment provided by the neighboring commercial strip, reinforced the need to develop the center as a distinctive and self-contained shopping environment.

Soil conditions presented an additional problem, since the property had formerly been a celery farm and was overlain by a layer of peat averaging 22 feet in depth. Before construction could begin, it was necessary to surcharge the site and allow settling and compaction to take place. Pilings were then used to create a suitable foundation for part of the mall structure.

Despite these site deficiencies, the property was deemed acceptable in view of the desirability of locating within the borough of Paramus, which, because of the ready access provided by the intersection of three major arterials—State Routes 4 and 17 and the Garden State Parkway—has be-

6-51   Innovative design was an important part of the development strategy.

come the suburban retailing center of northern New Jersey, with four major shopping center developments within its boundaries. The central business districts of Passaic, Paterson, and the older industrial communities in the area do not effectively compete with the suburban malls, which now account for a majority of retail activity in Bergen County.

The primary trade area, which is seen as the area within a 10-minute drive of Paramus Park, has a population of 259,000. The secondary trade area, between 10 and 20 minutes of the center, has a population of 643,000. The tertiary trade area, 20 minutes to half an hour from the center, has an additional 580,000 residents. This area, with the borough of Paramus as its center, is approximately 20 miles from east to west and 30 miles from north to south.

Physical Design and Innovations

From the Garden State Parkway, the traveler's attention is first drawn to an internally lighted steel pylon identifying Paramus Park and bearing the center's logo. Beyond this pylon can be seen the horizontal mass of the center itself, anchored at one end by a two-level Sears store and at the other by a three-level Abraham and Straus store, with a combined store area of 483,000 square feet. Between these two stores are 114 mall shops, with 276,000 square feet of GLA.

Between the center and the internal ring road on the edge of the property are surface parking spaces for 4,227 vehicles and the 15,000 square foot freestanding Sears auto accessories store. The silhouette of the center is made distinctive by a series of sloping, tinted-glass skylights resting on an expanded steel frame and placed at angles to the hexagonal masonry block walls of the mall structure.

Two of the center's three primary components, the mall structure and the Abraham and Straus department store, were designed by the architectural firm of RTKL Associates, Inc. Compatible but distinctive exterior materials used for these portions of the center include buff-colored hexagonal concrete block for the mall and 8-inch-square brick masonry highlighted by ribbing at the top and at the entrances to the Abraham and Straus store.

A park theme, incorporated in the name, provided the basis for design decisions regarding material selection, architectural treatment of public areas, and the overall tone of the mall itself. The

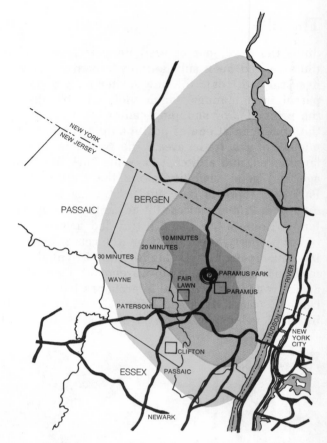

6-52   Trade area as defined by driving times of 10, 20, and 30 minutes. Paramus Park draws shoppers from up to 20 miles away.

emphasis on landscaping is apparent in the extensive planted areas used to define traffic circulation patterns and highlight the angular pattern of the exterior walls. The five loading docks for the mall and department store tenants have been carefully screened as extensions of the exterior facade, and the ring road has been set off from the parking areas by a grass strip, which has been extended along the primary access roads to the center structures. Adjacent to the building itself is an internal service road for both shopper and service vehicles.

Two of the four pedestrian entrances are mini-parks articulated with contrasting patterns of concrete aggregate, extensive plantings, bicycle racks, and seating areas. The other two entrances are covered for shopper convenience. Parking stalls are at right angles to the mall structure, and all spaces inside the ring road are within 400 feet of the shopping center building. Patronage has been so heavy that two additional lots have been rented to accommodate the overflow, despite a parking index of 5.5.

6-53　Mature ficus trees, placed in cast-iron grates, line the pedestrian mall. Skylights admit natural lighting.

Paramus Park incorporates a number of internal shopping center design innovations intended to maximize shopper convenience and satisfaction and to boost sales. The designers have created an intimate and exciting environment for shopping by emphasizing the human scale and by creating visual interest through design. Tropical plantings, rust-colored tile floors, a varied and colorful design scheme, sculpture, skylights, and a waterfall occupying the central court serve as the backdrop for shopping, leisure, and programmed activities. Patterns of light and shadow from the skylights play along the pedestrian way, which was built only 35 feet wide to allow shoppers to view both sides of the street at once. This street effect is heightened by a landscape plan featuring mature ficus trees planted in a linear fashion in cast-iron grates along the enclosed mall. The mall is 1,200 feet long and has a distinctive S shape, which serves both to maximize the use of the irregular site and to compartmentalize space into a series of carefully defined vistas. Each segment ends in a mall court

or department store entrance. One mall court features a weathering steel sculpture of an Indian boy on a turkey, the symbol of the borough of Paramus, donated to the community by the developer. Another court contains extensive plantings and seating areas. The primary aesthetic feature of the center, however, is the multilevel waterfall and tropical planter area in the central court, which provides a backdrop for the Pic-Nic, the food service area.

Tenant Mix

The success of Paramus Park can be explained in part by its carefully devised tenant mix, which differs not only from the pattern established by other Rouse Company shopping centers but also from the averages shown in *Dollars and Cents of Shopping Centers: 1975.* Retail activities which generate destination traffic, particularly in the soft goods and food lines, have been heavily emphasized. More than 57 percent of the mall tenants'

GLA is devoted to clothing and shoe stores. This figure is over twice as high as ULI's regional shopping center composition average and almost 40 percent greater than that of other Rouse centers. The high concentration of competing retailers combines the strong initial attraction of this kind of merchandise with the opportunity for comparison shopping.

The two department stores, Sears and Abraham and Straus, which account for slightly more than half of the center's GLA, have also emphasized the soft goods lines.

Merchandise which can be readily obtained elsewhere, or which is not ideally suited to a shopping center, or which generates low sales per square foot of GLA, is either absent or available only in limited selections at Paramus Park. Movie theaters, variety stores, and furniture stores have been avoided entirely.

Food and food service uses are important at Paramus Park because of the innovative way they have been packaged and merchandised, not be-

cause of the square footage they occupy (10.1 percent of center space, roughly equivalent to food tenant coverage in most regional centers). A common practice is the scattering of food outlets throughout a center. At the Pic-Nic, however, 21 fast-food outlets, restaurants, gourmet food stores, and ice cream and candy stores are concentrated in an area especially designed for the purpose. This food service area is the most innovative feature of the center. Given the relatively limited square footage allocated to food and food service, however, the high sales achieved at Paramus Park cannot be attributed to the Pic-Nic alone.

Another innovation has been a reduction of individual store spaces in order to boost sales per square foot. The developer believes that concentrating a greater number of tenants in a given area increases a center's variety, interest, and competitiveness. The 114 mall tenants occupy an average of 2,417 square feet of GLA. By comparison, the tenants at Northridge Fashion Center, a four-anchor regional center in Los Angeles' San Fer-

6-54　A tropical waterfall in the central court is flanked by escalators and an elevator.

6-55　At the Pic-Nic, a common dining area overlooks the central court.

nando Valley, have a more typical average of 3,398 square feet of GLA.[2]

Tenant mix is weighted toward locally owned and operated stores, which comprise 40.3 percent of all Paramus Park tenants, a considerably greater proportion than the national average of 33.7 percent for regional centers. Local tenants, it is felt, are more sensitive to merchandise preferences and can respond more easily to market shifts.

The Pic-Nic

A special feature of Paramus Park—and one which is being adopted in more and more centers throughout North America—is the Pic-Nic, the concentrated food service area overlooking the central court on the mezzanine level. The Pic-Nic, with its 21 restaurants, ice cream and candy stores, gourmet food shops and fast-food outlets, is an exten-

sion of the center's park theme. It occupies 24,300 square feet of GLA and has been successful since the day it opened. It has also been the most important draw along the mall; two-thirds of the shoppers report that they have something to eat at the Pic-Nic, and merchant sales average $250 per square foot per year. The fact that this figure has not increased significantly since the center opened suggests that the area has been operating at capacity since the beginning.

A separate location on the mezzanine has given the Pic-Nic its own identity while complementing the activity along the rest of the mall. The food service area is accessible by stairways, escalators, and an elevator, which are integral elements of the central court and are actually built into the waterfall structure. This spatial relationship helps

[2] See "Northridge Fashion Center," *Project Reference File*, Vol. 2, No. 4 (January–March 1972).

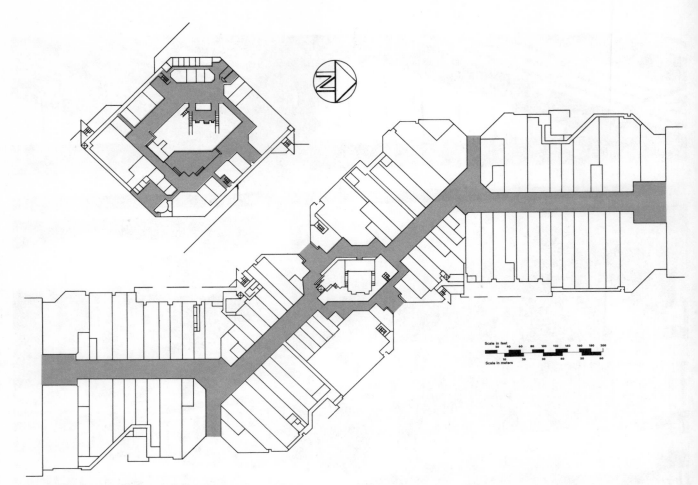

6-56   Interior layout of Paramus Park.

to draw shoppers up to the mezzanine level. Retail outlets along the four-sided arcade open onto a looped pedestrian corridor and a common seating and dining area beneath an expansive skylight. This sidewalk café area, with its colorful umbrellas, the waterfall, and tropical vegetation, provides a dramatic setting for informal dining. Approximately 650 persons can be accommodated, sitting and standing, at one time. The center's administrative offices, community room, and restrooms, also located on the mezzanine level, further emphasize the upper level as a center of activity.

The Pic-Nic benefited from the Rouse Company's initial experience with a fast-food area at Sherway Gardens, a regional shopping center in metropolitan Toronto, Canada.[3] Gourmet Fair opened in 1971 and consists of 18 food and food-related tenants in 10,600 square feet of GLA, situated along Sherway Garden's central mall corridor. In designing the Pic-Nic, the company made a much more substantial commitment to the concept of a concentrated food service area; the Pic-Nic is more than twice the size of Gourmet Fair and was given a prominent location where it would complement but not conflict with the rest of the center. The area has a light and airy picnic-in-the-park motif, in contrast to the conservative decor at Gourmet Fair. The operation and management of the food service area have also been separated from that of the other retail tenants. Nonfood tenants were kept out of the Pic-Nic area, and service, storage, and loading facilities were designed and sized to meet the special needs of food and food service outlets.

Food preparation, crowds, and large amounts of trash have required special management attention. The Pic-Nic has its own maintenance staff to handle trash disposal and clean the tables in the eating areas. Lease provisions were designed to maintain quality control by specifying that the landlord can "modify standards of merchandise and merchan-

[3] See "Gourmet Fair at Sherway Gardens," *Project Reference File*, Vol. 2, No. 14 (July–September 1972).

dising. . . . that tenants must remove from sale and from Pic-Nic any food or other merchandise which in the judgement of the Landlord does not meet the aforesaid standard" and that all complaints against tenants must be adjusted promptly and satisfactorily.

Tenant mix was determined in advance, and each lease specifies the kind of food to be offered. Even so, continuing vigilance has been necessary to ensure adherence to these provisions.

Management and Operation

Paramus Park, Inc., a wholly owned subsidiary of the Rouse Company and Connecticut General Life Insurance Company, is a joint venture project of the two companies. The development is managed by the Rouse Company, which also has reciprocal agreements with Sears and with Abraham and Straus, whereby the company maintains the department stores' properties within the center. On-site staff include a vice president–general manager, a promotions director, a bookkeeper, a secretary, a security staff, and maintenance personnel. Total employment in the center, including the staffs of the department stores and the mall tenants, is approximately 2,000.

Common area revenues are used to maintain, operate, and insure the enclosed mall and the landscaping and parking areas, with the department stores contributing to these costs. Tenants must become members of the Paramus Park Merchants Association, which advertises and promotes the center, and must pay $0.30 per square foot into the association fund. The developer contributes an additional 25 percent.

Paramus Park is part of a companywide computer network which interconnects all Rouse Company shopping centers and provides an invaluable array of data on center and tenant performance. Monthly sales data for each tenant—including square footage of GLA, store type, rent, and percentage rent provisions—are programmed into a computer console in the management office and are then transmitted to a central computer at the Columbia, Maryland, headquarters of the company, where they are automatically aggregated by tenant, store type, and store size. Printouts provide comparison figures for all centers in the system, thus enabling the shopping center manager to monitor the performance of each of his tenants and to identify problems and opportunities much more rapidly than he could without the computer sys-

tem. Annual sales pace, for example, is updated each month to allow a comparison between current performance and performance of the previous year.

Shopper Survey

A survey carried out in mid-1975 by the company's department of market research provides an interesting profile of Paramus Park's shoppers and shopping patterns. The results show that the shoppers are quite affluent, with incomes exceeding both the metropolitan area and county averages. The median family income of survey respondents was $22,500, with 35.2 percent earning more than $25,000. The typical shopper is a female in her early thirties, living within 15 minutes of the mall. However, a significant proportion of the shoppers (14.4 percent) live outside New Jersey, primarily in neighboring Rockland County, New York.

6-57 PARAMUS PARK SHOPPERS SURVEY

AGE DISTRIBUTION

AGE GROUP	PERCENT
18–24	23.0
25–34	33.8
35–54	34.4
55+	8.4
Refused	0.4
Median 32	

FAMILY INCOME

INCOME LEVEL	PERCENT
Under $10,000	5.0
$10,000–$14,999	11.6
$15,000–$19,999	20.2
$20,000–$24,999	21.6
$25,000–$49,999	26.8
$50,000+	8.4
Refused	6.4
Median $22,500	

TRAVEL TIME TO PARAMUS PARK

MINUTES	PERCENT
0–10	26.8
11–20	47.4
21–30	15.4
31–60	9.0
Over 1 hour	1.4
Median 15 minutes	

Source: The Rouse Company

The typical shopper visits the center once every 3 weeks and stops at four or five stores during a shopping trip. Clothing was by far the most popular purchase item: 49.4 percent of those surveyed said they had either bought or intended to buy clothing at Paramus Park. An additional 18.8 percent said they intended to buy household-related items. Median expenditure for all respondents was $16.90.

Comparing Paramus Park with other shopping centers in northern New Jersey, shoppers indicated that they were drawn to the center because of its attractive design and tenant mix. In response to a question about which shopping centers a shopper would choose to search for particular items, Paramus Park scored especially well in gifts and jewelry, for which it is more than twice as popular as its closest competitor.

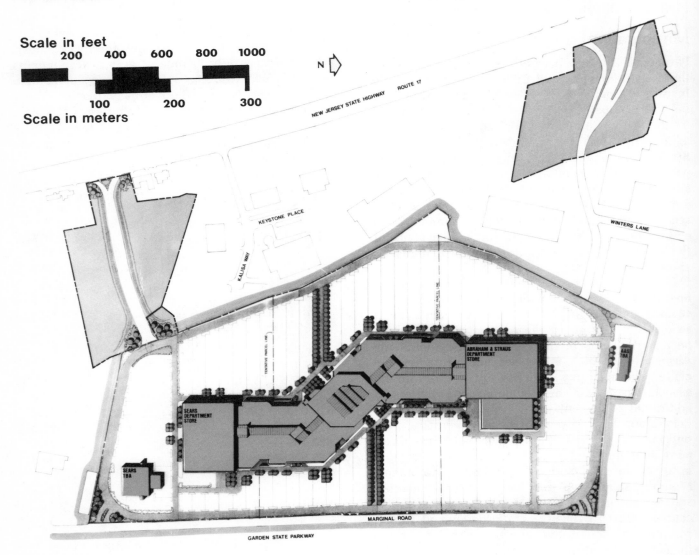

6-58   Site plan—Paramus Park.

PROJECT DATA—PARAMUS PARK

DEVELOPER
The Rouse Company
Columbia, Maryland 21044

ARCHITECTURE/PLANNING
RTKL Associates, Inc.
The Village of Cross Keys
Baltimore, Maryland 21210

LAND USE INFORMATION
Site area   59.8 acres (main site)

Land allocation

	Site area	Percent of site
Buildings	15.0 acres	25.1
Parking and circulation	37.8 acres	63.2
Landscaping	7.0 acres	11.7
Total	59.8 acres	100.0

GLA[1]   758,222 sq. ft.

GBA[2]

Mall building	386,630 sq. ft.
Abraham and Straus	300,000 sq. ft.
Sears Roebuck and Company	182,688 sq. ft.
Total	869,318 sq. ft.

TENANT INFORMATION
Number of tenants

Mall tenants	114
Department stores	2
Total	116
Percent leased[4]	100.0

Parking
Spaces[3]   4,227
Ratio   2.5 : 1
Index   5.5

Land ownership

Paramus Park Associates	24.3 acres
Abraham and Straus	21.5 acres
Sears Roebuck and Company	14.0 acres
Total	59.8 acres

ECONOMIC INFORMATION

Total sales[5]	$58.0 million
Sales per sq. ft. GLA	$214

Rentals

Amount	$6 to $29 per sq. ft.
Length	1 to 15 years
Percentage rents	4 to 10 percent

[1] Total floor area designed for tenant occupancy and exclusive use, including freestanding ancillary structures.

[2] Total floor area of the center, including freestanding ancillary structures.

[3] Striped surface spaces within the ring road. The developer plans to add 550 spaces and is renting two additional lots.

[4] As of September 1976.

[5] Projected mall sales for calendar year 1976.

Tenant Classification	Number of stores	GLA	Percent of total GLA	Percent of developer GLA	Average percentage in regional centers (from *Dollars and Cents of Shopping Centers: 1975*)
Food	8	8,399 sq. ft.	1.1	3.0	5.6
Food service	14	19,633 sq. ft.	2.6	7.1	2.9
General merchandise	2	485,000 sq. ft.	63.8	——	53.4
Clothing and shoes	56	157,060 sq. ft.	20.6	57.0	16.9
Dry goods	——	——	——	——	1.4
Furniture (home furnishings)	4	10,724 sq. ft.	1.4	3.9	1.4
Other retail	29	75,229 sq. ft.	9.9	27.3	10.1
Financial	1	2,401 sq. ft.	0.3	0.9	1.6
Offices	——	——	——	——	0.4
Services	2	2,087 sq. ft.	0.3	0.8	1.2
Other	——	——	——	——	3.0
Vacant	——	——	——	——	2.2
Total	116	760,534 sq. ft.	100.0	100.0	100.0

Tenants by ownership type

Type	Number	Percent	Average percentage in regional centers (from *Dollars and Cents*)
National chain	41	36.0	41.1
Independent	27	23.7	25.3
Local chain	46	40.3	33.7

HAWTHORNE PLAZA

6-60   Hawthorne Plaza under construction in the fall of 1976.

Locational Trends in Shopping Center Development

Changing market conditions and evolving development opportunities are bringing about major adjustments in shopping center design and location. It is becoming more and more difficult to apply many of the basic parameters within which the industry has operated since its inception more than 25 years ago. Population growth in the suburbs has slowed. Use of the automobile and its relationship to energy resources is a matter of growing concern. There is renewed interest in the revitalization of urban areas, as seen in the commitment by many local governments to renovate their downtowns. Both citizens and all levels of government are playing a far more active role in the development process. With land and construction costs rising rapidly and with more than 17,000 shopping centers now in place, the saturation point for conventional commercial developments in many suburban areas cannot be far off. These trends make it clear that the shopping center of the future will differ in a number of important respects from the center of the past decade. Consequently, the formula approach to shopping center development, common during the sixties and early seventies, is now being adjusted. A number of centers that have already opened suggest the direction of future development, and many other such centers are in the planning and construction stages.

One of the most important of these innovative centers, in terms of location, physical configuration, and projected market, is Hawthorne Plaza, an 840,000 square foot multilevel regional shopping center being developed by a partnership of Ernest W. Hahn, Inc., Carter Hawley Hale Properties, Inc., and Urban Projects, Inc. The project occupies a 34-acre redevelopment site in the central section of Hawthorne, California, an incorporated community of 54,142 (1970 Census) in the Los Angeles basin, several miles southeast of the Los Angeles International Airport. The site, previously occupied by a variety of obsolete commercial and residential uses, was acquired, cleared, and redeveloped under the California Community Redevelopment Law. This statute permits the forming of public-private partnerships for carrying out redevelopment projects and offers considerably greater flexibility than the old federally funded urban renewal program.

Hawthorne Plaza, destined to become the retail focus of a community where commercial activity had been limited to strip commercial development along major arterials, was adapted to a relatively limited site area by combining an efficient multilevel merchandising design with structured parking. For the first time in decades, Hawthorne has a true center for its social and economic life, and further redevelopment in the area, capitalizing on the opportunities presented by Hawthorne Plaza, is probable.

In the early sixties, the Hawthorne city government recognized the need to revitalize its deteriorating commercial base, but a decade was required to establish the necessary local agencies, determine an appropriate course of action, and obtain developer and financial commitments. Land acquisition and clearance began in 1973 and construction in July 1975, and the center held its grand opening early in 1977.

From the preliminary evidence provided by Hawthorne Plaza and other innovative commercial developments built over the past several years, it is possible to make some judgements about how shopping centers are adapting to changing conditions. Most new centers can be expected to incorporate some of the following characteristics:

- They will be tightly configured and will make extensive use of multilevel designs and structured parking.
- Downtown locations, or sites which have been redeveloped for commercial use, will become more common as the suburbs become saturated and developers seek to tap existing, unserved markets.
- Projects will be more carefully integrated with their surroundings, both in response to settings which are more urban and as a consequence of increased public involvement in the development process.
- As markets become more specialized, shopping centers can be expected to exhibit a growing variety of sizes, designs, and market orientations.
- In comparison to open-site suburban locations, future centers in downtown locations will re-

6-61　Commercial frontage on Hawthorne Boulevard before redevelopment.

quire far more complex financing and governmental approvals processes. Public-private cooperation in order to accomplish mutual goals will become common.

The California Community Redevelopment Law

The California Community Redevelopment Law is designed to enable communities to acquire, clear, and redevelop blighted areas through a partnership of public and private interests. Of particular significance is the fact that this law establishes a mechanism for offering redevelopment land to developers at prices competitive with suburban locations. This aspect of the redevelopment process is particularly important in central business districts, where the assemblage of sufficient land is usually impracticable for a private investor, both from financial and operational standpoints. Moreover, the law allows municipalities to identify with some precision both the size and type of permitted new uses for a redevelopment area, before the site is acquired and cleared. Because of the flexible public-private relationship, properties remain in use and on the tax rolls until required for develop-

ment of a specific project. Since political controls are local, much of the red tape associated with federally funded renewal projects is eliminated. In many instances a site can be cleared and redeveloped in less than 3 years. At Hawthorne Plaza, for example, only 3 years will have passed between the time the first structures were demolished and the opening of the completed new commercial complex. The entire redevelopment area was committed to specific uses before the first parcel of land was acquired, and construction actually began before all the site had been cleared. According to developer Ernest W. Hahn, it was the flexibility, precision, and financial incentive offered by the Community Redevelopment Law which made Hawthorne Plaza possible.

The actual redevelopment process, as spelled out in the California legislation, is relatively straightforward. All cities and counties in the state are authorized to establish a redevelopment agency. Once an agency has been established, a survey of blight in the community is undertaken and one or more project areas are identified for redevelopment. A redevelopment plan for the project area is then formulated by the agency and the planning commission, and is adopted through ordinance by the governing body. Next, the agency implements the redevelopment plan by acquiring the land through negotiation or condemnation, clearing the site, relocating displaced residents and businesses, and disposing of the land for private redevelopment in conformance with the plan.

The Community Redevelopment Law authorizes an agency, on its own initiative, to obtain financing from any legal source. It may sell lease revenue and tax allocation bonds secured by revenues to be generated by the redevelopment process. This tax increment financing provision constitutes a greatly flexible approach to redevelopment financing, since the jurisdiction neither incurs a financial liability nor is required to obtain formal approval by the voters through a referendum, although, in some instances, lease revenue bond financing may be subject to a referendum vote. Tax increment financing works this way: the jurisdiction establishes the assessed (base) value of the property within the project boundaries at the time the project is begun. As the property is made more valuable through redevelopment, the difference (the increase, or *increment*) between the new developed value and the base valuation is allocated to the redevelopment agency to retire its indebtedness (the tax allocation or lease revenue bonds). Meanwhile, the local taxing bodies can continue to receive the same amount they were getting before redevelopment. Once the bonds are paid off, the taxing agencies of the community receive the full financial benefit of the improvements.[4]

Selection of the developer is a crucial step in this process. The community must satisfy itself that the developer can and will carry out the project as

[4] For a further discussion of the use of tax increment financing in shopping centers, see "Central City Mall" and "San Bernardino Civic-Cultural Center Complex," *Project Reference File,* Vol. 3, Nos. 9, 10 (April–June 1973).

6-62   Aerial view of the redevelopment site prior to demolition reveals low-density development and an inefficient pattern of land use.

agreed. This is accomplished by a Disposition and Development Agreement (DDA) between the agency and the developer. The DDA is executed before any acquisition, relocation, demolition, or land disposition takes place, and it specifies the obligations and responsibilities of each party, as well as the nature of the completed project. For Hawthorne Plaza, Ernest W. Hahn, Inc., was selected as the developer because it was a locally based firm with strong ties with the community and because it had established a record of successful shopping center development throughout the West.

The Redevelopment Process

Before deciding to initiate a regional shopping center project, the community spent several years discussing various redevelopment strategies for its deteriorating strip commercial areas. The Community Redevelopment Agency of the City of Hawthorne was formed in 1968 and, one year later, the location and general dimensions of the Hawthorne Plaza Project were approved by the city council.

The site of the proposed shopping center was bisected by railroad tracks, placing a severe constraint on building layout and design. Working for the city's economic consultant, the architectural and planning firm of Charles Kober Associates prepared a number of alternative site plans. Although these layouts eventually progressed from a two-department-store center south of the railroad tracks to the present design, the limitations of site shape and size always demanded multilevel building design, structured parking, and sophisticated pedestrian-automobile connections.

Even while the preliminary site planning was progressing, the developer was selected and tentative commitments were obtained from department stores. In 1973, a DDA was reached between the limited partnership and the redevelopment agency. Under the terms of the agreement, the agency committed itself to convey 26.5 acres of the redevelopment site to the developer, to construct a three-deck parking structure on the balance of the property, and to provide parking on the basement level of the center. The developers committed themselves to purchase the property for $5.5 million and to build a regional shopping center of not less than 800,000 square feet on the site. The city council created the Parking Authority of the City of Hawthorne in late 1973 to carry out necessary financing for the parking facilities, administer leases between the agency, the city, and the developer,

and to hold title to the 7.1 acres retained in public ownership.

Financing for the project was raised through the sale of $25,230,000 in lease revenue and tax allocation bonds. The lease revenue bonds generated $21,230,000 for site acquisition and clearance and for relocation and construction of the parking facilities. The bonds are secured by rentals received by the parking authority under a lease with the city, which, in turn, is subleasing the parking structure to the developer for $300,000 per year. The developer has assumed full responsibility for parking structure operation, maintenance, and repair. To make the bonds marketable, the developer agreed to build the parking facilities for a fixed price of $10.2 million. Proceeds from the sale of $4 million in tax allocation bonds have been used for site acquisition, consulting fees, and city public works improvements necessitated by construction of Hawthorne Plaza.

The developer provided the agency with a $5 million advance of funds to cover land assembly, clearance, and relocation costs before sale of the bonds. Since these funds—together with the $500,000 developer deposit—equalled the purchase price of the property, the agency was, in effect, selling the land before it had been acquired. Acquisition and clearance of the 167 separate parcels within the 8-square-block area took 2 years and was accomplished by mid-1975. The original zoning, C-2 general commercial and B-3 multifamily residential, was modified to conform to the project design. Site preparation began before all the older structures had been removed, and construction was completed in less than 2 years. As managing partner, Ernest W. Hahn, Inc., is responsible for coordinating center design, leasing, management, and operation. The firm is also the contractor for Hawthorne Plaza.

A primary motivation for the redevelopment project was the need to increase the community's tax base. Hawthorne Plaza should be of substantial financial benefit to the city. In 1969–70, the fixed assessed value of the redevelopment area was $1,405,887, and the property generated only $175,000 in property taxes. After the center opens, assessed value is projected to rise to $15,000,000, and, in the first full year of operation, 1977–1978, property taxes should increase more than tenfold, to $1,900,000. The increment will be used to pay off the lease revenue and tax allocation bonds, allowing the community to start realizing the full benefit

6-63

HAWTHORNE PLAZA REDEVELOPMENT DATA

	1969–70	1977–78
Assessed valuation	$1,400,000	$15,000,000
Market value	$5,200,000	$60,000,000
Property tax paid	$ 175,000	$ 1,900,000
Retail sales tax generated	$ 10,000	$ 615,000
Financing		
Lease revenue bonds		
Series A 1974	$ 4,700,000	
Series B 1974	16,530,000	
Subtotal	$21,230,000	
Tax allocation bonds		
Series A 1976	4,000,000	
Total	$25,230,000	

6-64   HAWTHORNE PLAZA LEASE PLAN

PROPOSED TENANT*	PERCENT OF GLA
Shoes	11.0
Women's ready-to-wear	16.8
Men's ready-to-wear	7.5
Jewelry	3.3
Gifts	4.8
Food	11.8
Household	6.4
Junior department store	15.6
Seasonal, miscellaneous, non-retail	22.8
Total	100.0

*Non-ULI categories.

of an expanded tax base. If it chooses, Hawthorne may use any excess increment to redeem the bonds more rapidly or to initiate additional redevelopment projects, subject to certain limitations within the bond prospectus. The increase in sales tax revenues, however, will be of immediate benefit to the community. The state of California returns a maximum of 1 percent of the combined 6 percent state and local sales tax to the jurisdiction in which the taxable transaction took place. In 1974, taxable retail sales for the city of Hawthorne amounted to $109 million, a sum which generated $1,090,000 for the municipality. If, as expected, Hawthorne Plaza's retail sales are in the range of $85 per square foot, the city's retail sales will increase by 65 percent, a net gain of $174,000 to the city treasury, minus the estimated $10,000 in sales tax generated yearly within the project area before redevelopment.

Development Strategy and Marketing

Hawthorne Plaza has been built to serve an established trade area previously unserved by a regional shopping center. Approximately 569,000 people live within 5 miles of the center. Included in the primary trade area are all or part of the suburban Los Angeles municipalities of Hawthorne, Lawndale, Carson, El Segundo, Inglewood, Lomita, and Gardena, among others, as well as unincorporated county areas and the Los Angeles International Airport. In this area, municipal boundaries merge imperceptibly and residential development is a mix of single-family homes and garden apartments, most built during the forties and fifties. Population densities are relatively high, and Hawthorne Plaza is expected to generate some walk-in trade. Public transportation, however, was a marginal consideration and should not account for more than 2 to 3 percent of the customers. The development program has not been predicated on any expectation of major population growth within the market area, which is almost entirely urbanized.

The closest regional shopping centers to Hawthorne Plaza are the 930,500 square foot Del Amo Shopping Center and the 1,110,000 square foot Del Amo Fashion Square across the street from each other in the city of Torrance, about 5 miles south of Hawthorne. In October 1975, Ernest W. Hahn, Inc., opened the 927,000 square foot Foxhill Mall in Culver City, 6 miles northwest of Hawthorne Plaza. There are also several freestanding department stores and smaller convenience shopping centers in the trade area.

Marketing studies carried out as part of the development process show that the median income per household in the trade area is slightly above the Los Angeles SMSA average. Disposable incomes, however, tend to be higher than this figure would suggest, since many residents are homeowners who acquired their properties many years ago and have relatively low mortgage payments. Most households fall within the middle-income range; relatively few are in either the high-income or low-income categories. This pattern reflects the industrialized character of Hawthorne and adjacent communities and the high proportion of blue-collar residents. The largest employers in Hawthorne are the Northrop Corporation and Mattel, Inc. Minorities are expected to account for 30 to 40 percent of shopper patronage.

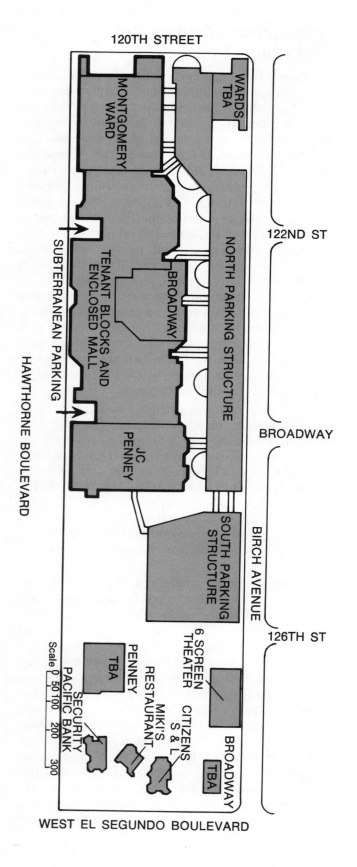

120TH STREET

MONTGOMERY WARD

WARDS TBA

SUBTERRANEAN PARKING

HAWTHORNE BOULEVARD

TENANT BLOCKS AND ENCLOSED MALL

BROADWAY

NORTH PARKING STRUCTURE

122ND ST

BROADWAY

JC PENNEY

SOUTH PARKING STRUCTURE

BIRCH AVENUE

126TH ST

Scale 0 50 100 200 300

TBA

PENNEY

MIKI'S RESTAURANT

SECURITY PACIFIC BANK

6 SCREEN THEATER

CITIZENS S & L

BROADWAY

TBA

WEST EL SEGUNDO BOULEVARD

Hawthorne Plaza is being positioned to serve this predominantly middle-income market through tenant mix, merchandise offerings, and store decor. The three anchor tenants include The Broadway, Montgomery Ward, and J. C. Penney, which will account for 54 percent of GLA. The 134 mall tenants will occupy a total of 317,000 square feet of GLA. The developer expects that it will take 2 to 3 years for Hawthorne Plaza to become fully established within its market area. As mentioned earlier, sales for the first full year of operation are projected to exceed $85 per square foot.

Shopping center development is proceeding rapidly throughout the Los Angeles Standard Consolidated Statistical Area (SCSA), which consists of Los Angeles, Orange, San Bernardino, Riverside, and Ventura counties and has an estimated population of 10.2 million. Between 1970 and 1976, 12 centers, each with more than 700,000 square feet of GLA, opened in the region. During the same period, a number of other centers were modernized and expanded. These new facilities are bringing about a major restructuring of metropolitan Los Angeles' retail function, although the future pattern is not yet fully apparent. Many older, established retail areas are declining in comparison with new regional centers, most of which have freeway locations and have been carefully positioned to draw from a relatively wide trade area. The city of Hawthorne, for example, is expected to become a major retailing center for the first time in its history, not only by retaining residents who formerly shopped elsewhere, but also by attracting new shoppers from other parts of the South Bay area. Community retail sales should nearly double during Hawthorne Plaza's first full year of operation. Another consequence of Hawthorne Plaza's development will be that the old retail center of Inglewood, previously the dominant commercial and office center of this part of the metropolitan area, will face increasing retail competition. Inglewood is bracketed on both sides by new regional centers—Foxhill Mall to the north and Hawthorne Plaza to the south—and these centers will directly affect much of the Inglewood trade area. The city has responded to this challenge by undertaking a major office-governmental redevelopment project in the downtown area.

6-65 High site coverage, characteristic of new shopping centers in urban areas, is shown in Hawthorne Plaza's site plan.

6-66   Artist's street elevation depicts imaginative use of vegetation in this multilevel center.

The Site

Hawthorne Plaza is situated at the intersection of the city's primary at-grade arterials, Hawthorne and El Segundo Boulevards. These streets have enough capacity to ensure ready access to the center, even though Hawthorne Plaza does not have a freeway location. The proposed Century Freeway would pass along 120th Street, just north of the center, but even though much of the right-of-way has been acquired, it now appears unlikely that the freeway will ever be built. El Segundo Boulevard intersects the San Diego Freeway a mile west of the center site and should be a primary route of regional access to and from Hawthorne Plaza.

The site is rectangular, and it has approximately 2,500 feet of frontage on Hawthorne Boulevard and 580 feet of frontage on El Segundo Boulevard. To the north and east, the center is separated from the adjacent residential neighborhood by Birch Avenue, a local street. The 34-acre redevelopment area encompasses an eight-square-block tract which had been platted in 1905, by the Hawthorne Improvement Company, into a highly individualized layout with geometric curving blocks, boulevards, and landscaped parks. Over the years, this land plan could not be adapted to evolving development patterns, and the unplanned mixture of commercial and residential uses in the area degenerated into some of the most blighted properties in the city. This circumstance, together with a strategic location in the center of the community, provided the basis for selecting this particular area for redevelopment. Another unusual aspect of Hawthorne Plaza's location is that the site is bisected by a spur line of the Southern Pacific Railroad. Extended negotiations were required between the railroad and the developer to incorporate the rail line into the final design.

Physical Design

Shopping centers designed for downtown locations differ in important respects from those built on spacious suburban sites. Some understanding of the constraints imposed by Hawthorne Plaza's limited site area may be gained by comparing the center with the suburban Laguna Hills Mall, both shopping centers designed by Charles Kober Associates for Ernest W. Hahn, Inc. At Hawthorne Plaza, 840,000 square feet of GLA had to be accommodated on 34 acres. Laguna Hills, completed in 1973, has only 2 percent more leasable space but is located on a site twice as big. This additional space permitted a design involving a single-level enclosed mall, anchored by three department stores and surrounded by surface parking. Hawthorne Plaza, on the other hand, uses a multilevel design, has been adapted to an urban setting, and occupies a redevelopment parcel.

Hawthorne Plaza's retail structure, with 1.1 million square feet of gross building area, fronts on Hawthorne Bouevard and is connected by 17 pedestrian bridges to two three-level parking garages at the rear of the site. In a strongly articulated arrangement of these primary components, the pedestrian bridges provide direct access to the enclosed mall and to the three department stores. Retail and parking have a clear visual relationship to one another, which is essential when structured parking is used. Montgomery Ward and J. C. Penney anchor the north and south ends of the mall, respectively, and The Broadway occupies a central location in the structure, with the mall angling around it. The retail complex and the north parking structure have been placed to the north of the railroad tracks, while the south parking structure is located on the other side of the railroad tracks and is connected with the rest of the center by

vehicular-pedestrian bridges. At-grade access is provided to the lower and middle levels of the parking structures, and exterior semicircular ramps permit internal circulation and access to the upper parking deck. A lower-level central circulation street, with entrances off 120th Street and Hawthorne Boulevard, provides access to both the service docks and the below-grade parking, which extends beneath the retail structure and the north parking structure. The remainder of the property is occupied by six freestanding commercial buildings, including a bank, a six-screen theater, a savings and loan, a restaurant, and two auto accessory stores, all served by surface parking. The DDA originally specified an office building with 95,000 square feet of leasable space at the south end of the site. Marketing studies, however, revealed a limited demand for office space in Hawthorne, and the DDA was amended to allow for the lower density uses. Overall building coverage, including parking structures, amounts to 57.2 percent of the site area.

In contrast to many regional centers, Hawthorne Plaza has a unified exterior design which employs common exterior materials, including light tan split-faced fluted masonry and rough textured stucco. The project has been given a sculptured appearance through the use of irregular massings and articulated setbacks, angles, and indentations. Walls and setbacks are extensively landscaped with trees, planter areas, and vines, all placed at various heights. The intention is to break up the mass of the building front and to soften its impact for people driving by on Hawthorne Boulevard. There are two screened loading docks and two vehicular entrances to the lower level and a single pedestrian entrance along the Hawthorne Boulevard frontage. Since Hawthorne does not have a downtown, in the conventional sense, the center has a largely inward orientation while respecting the streetscape.

Hawthorne Plaza, conceived as a social center and a vital, animated environment unique in the community, has a cheerful and informal interior design theme. The enclosed mall is an irregular, two-level pedestrian street approximately 925 feet long and from 34 feet wide on the lower level to 54 feet wide on the upper level. The two levels are connected by escalators and elevators that also serve the lower level parking area. The interior design features a series of open courts, skylights, seating areas, and extensive landscaping. Setbacks ensure good visibility between the upper and lower levels. The unusual internal configuration—with the mid-mall department store placed within the retail structure and the mall angled around it—was dictated by site limitations. Nevertheless, by creating the effect of a winding shopping street, the design introduces an element of drama and excitement not usually found in regional shopping centers.

The traditional parking index of 5.5 spaces per 1,000 square feet of GLA was reduced to 5.0 at Hawthorne Plaza. This adjustment reflects site limitations, the higher level of pedestrian traffic, and the developer's belief that the traditional standard is too high. The company's recent centers have an average parking index of 4.5, and several have indexes as low as 4.0. At Hawthorne Plaza, 85 percent of the 4,226 spaces are located either within the subterranean parking area or within the interconnected multilevel parking decks.

Charles Kober Associates has designed two shopping centers in downtown locations since the Hawthorne Plaza design was finalized, and the continuing evolution of this urban form is apparent in these more recent centers. Hawthorne Plaza, with its vertical design, established the basic configuration of urban centers. It exhibits consistency of color and exterior building materials, but the major tenants dictated the exterior configuration of their stores and used different construction mod-

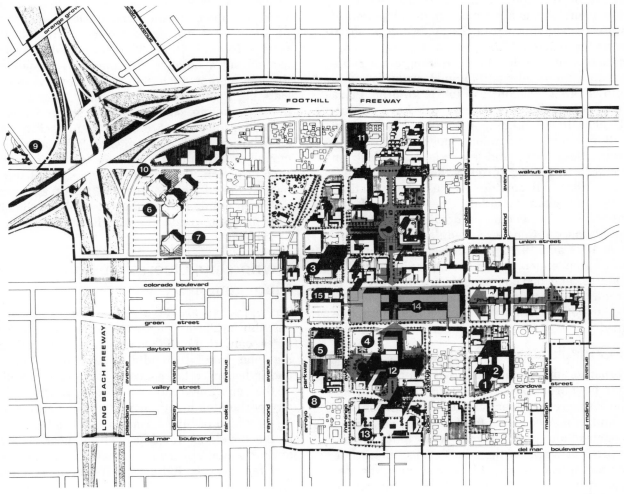

1 HILTON HOTEL
2 GROSVENOR PLAZA OFFICE TOWER
3 P.T.&T. HEADQUARTERS
4 PASADENA CENTER
5 BANKAMERICARD CENTER
6 PARSONS HEADQUARTERS
7 PARSONS EXPANSION
8 BROWN & CALDWELL

9 ORANGE GROVE VILLAGE
10 COMMERCIAL OFFICE PLAZA
11 PARK CENTER OFFICES
12 PASADENA CENTER HOTEL
13 PLAZA CORDOVA
14 RETAIL CENTER
15 FINANCIAL OFFICE COMPLEX

DOWNTOWN REDEVELOPMENT PROJECT

PASADENA CENTER
PEDESTRIAN CONNECTION

6-67   Retail is skillfully integrated into Pasadena's downtown redevelopment plan. Strong pedestrian relationships are to be established between the planned regional shopping center and the rest of the CBD.

ules. The firm's second urban center, Glendale Galleria, recently completed on a 28-acre suburban CBD site in Glendale, California, carried the process one step further. The four department store tenants agreed to a uniform exterior design, and all used the same brown brick and subordinated their individual facilities to the whole. The Glendale center incorporates other refinements of the Hawthorne design scheme while retaining most of its fundamental characteristics. The Pasadena Retail Center, a redevelopment project planned for the heart of this long-established southern California community, is a prospective development of even greater significance in the evolution of shopping center design. This project reflects a concerted effort by the developer to integrate a shopping center into a substantially pedestrian-oriented downtown area. In contrast to Hawthorne Plaza and Glendale Galleria, Pasadena will have an outward focus in addition to its internal pedestrian mall. Some shops and offices open directly onto Colorado Boulevard, and an existing pedestrian mall will be extended through the center at right angles to the mall corridor. By using compatible building and plant materials, the feeling of the downtown is to become a dominant statement within Pasadena Center. Scheduled for development in 1977 and 1978, this project is expected to contain three anchor tenants, approximately 130 mall stores, and 600,000 square feet of GLA. It is apparent that this design experience will be reflected in other urban projects throughout the country.

The Construction Sequence

The construction sequence on redevelopment sites tends to be more complex, primarily because of the limited land area. Proper scheduling is particularly important, since each contractor must coordinate his construction requirements with those of all other firms at work on the site. Because the prime contractor at Hawthorne Plaza was also the developer, it was possible to maintain a high degree of control during the construction sequence. In this instance, "fast-track" construction was used, involving proceeding with construction before all plans were completed. Foundation construction, for example, began as soon as the foundation plans were completed, even though the balance of the mechanical, structural, and architectural design was unfinished.

The first floor of the retail mall structure is built of precast concrete, and the roof and supporting columns are built of structural steel, while the parking structures employ a poured-in-place, post-tensioned, clearspan design. In contrast to many regional shopping centers, Hawthorne Plaza has common walls and is, in effect, one large building. Each department store, however, required its own structural module as dictated by individual merchandising layouts. Construction activity moved from south to north on the site, and excavation began before all the existing structures had been cleared. Most utility lines required to serve the property were already in place, although primary water lines had to be upgraded. Development costs of the center are projected to total $58.30 per square foot of GLA. The municipality has also carried out a number of projects to accommodate the new center, including street improvements on Hawthorne Boulevard and Birch Avenue, utility undergrounding, construction of storm drains, and relocation of a city fire department facility. Along Hawthorne Boulevard, median parking was removed to permit five moving lanes of traffic in each direction. The Birch Avenue right-of-way has been widened from 50 feet to 54 feet, and parking has been eliminated on the west side of the street. This program, funded by tax allocation bonds, cost $3,175,000.

Ownership, Operation, and Management

Three parties are involved in the ownership of Hawthorne Plaza. The developer holds title to 23.4 acres, comprising the enclosed mall, at-grade parking, and the freestanding commercial buildings, and is leasing retail space to mall tenants and two of the department stores on a long-term basis. The city parking authority owns the two parking structures, which occupy 7.1 acres and are being leased to the developer for $300,000 per year. The third anchor tenant holds title to its own land (3.1 acres) and facilities, including the freestanding auto accessory stores.

Management and operations are the responsibility of Ernest W. Hahn, Inc. The managing partner expects to operate Hawthorne Plaza with a staff of 40 persons, including a manager, an assistant manager, a promotions director, 20 maintenance men, four landscape gardeners and eight to 12 security personnel. Total employment for the center is expected to be about 1.8 persons per 500 square feet of GLA, or about 3,000. Viewed from this perspective, the center will become the third largest

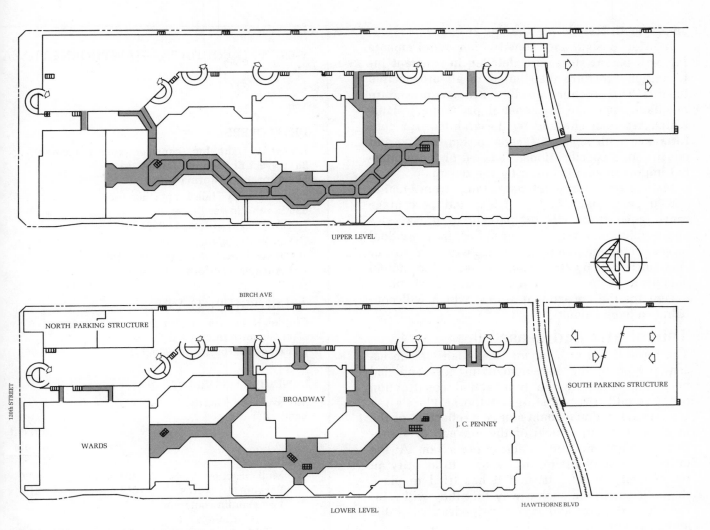

UPPER LEVEL

BIRCH AVE

NORTH PARKING STRUCTURE

120th STREET

BROADWAY

SOUTH PARKING STRUCTURE

WARDS

J. C. PENNEY

LOWER LEVEL

HAWTHORNE BLVD

6-68   Building plan—Hawthorne Plaza.

employer in Hawthorne the day it opens.

Interior design and construction requirements for mall tenant stores are detailed in a tenant information brochure distributed to all prospective tenants. The brochure specifies a review procedure of submitting to the developer all preliminary plans, which are then checked by the architect for conformance with signage, facade design, utility, and construction specifications. The cost of these internal improvements is borne by the tenants.

Median rents for mall tenants range from $4.50 to $28.00 per square foot of GLA, and percentage rents range from 3 to 10 percent of gross sales above minimum rents, as specified in individual leases. Common area maintenance will be a further cost incurred by the tenants, with the actual charges to be determined yearly on a pro rata basis, except for the department stores, which will contribute a fixed amount.

Tenant Mix and Lease Plan

The formulation of a tenant lease plan was an essential step in the development process and had been completed by the time actual construction began in mid-1975. Most of Hawthorne Plaza's 141 tenants are national chain stores, a reflection of the local market and typical of the makeup of super-regional shopping centers across the nation. At the outset, Ernest W. Hahn, Inc., sought to identify an optimal mix of tenants, and it has tried to place the mall tenants in such a way that they will reinforce one another and maximize pedestrian traffic and sales volume.

As a practical matter, stronger tenants tend to get the better locations, but an effort has been made to distribute them more widely to achieve centerwide balance. Particular attention has been paid to tenants in the main courts; weaker tenants, from the standpoints of sales volume and visual attraction, have commonly been placed on the side courts.

The Community Redevelopment Law requires that an effort be made to relocate former occupants of the redevelopment site into the new commercial facilities, but only two local stores are relocating in Hawthorne Plaza. Most other businesses operating in the redevelopment area were either economically marginal or inappropriate for a shopping center location.

A merchants association, managed by the developer, has been formed and will be primarily responsible for advertising and promotion, with dues determined by the size of each store.

DEVELOPERS

Ernest W. Hahn, Inc. (construction/management)
2311 West El Segundo Boulevard
Hawthorne, California 90250
Carter Hawley Hale Properties, Inc.
550 South Flower Street
Los Angeles, California 90071
Urban Projects, Inc.
10850 Wilshire Boulevard, Suite 1050
Los Angeles, California 90024

ARCHITECTURE/PLANNING

Charles Kober Associates
2706 Wilshire Boulevard
Los Angeles, California 90057

LAND USE INFORMATION

Site area   34.0 acres
Land allocation

	Site area	Percent of site
Buildings		
Mall structure	10.4 acres	30.5
Parking structures	7.1 acres	21.0
Freestanding commercial buildings and TBAs	2.0 acres	5.7
Surface parking and circulation	11.8 acres	34.6
Landscaping	2.3 acres	7.0
Railroad right-of-way	0.5 acre	1.2
Total	34.1 acres	100.0

GLA[1]

Mall tenants	316,555 sq. ft.
Department stores	486,600 sq. ft.
Freestanding buildings	36,846 sq. ft.
Total	840,001 sq. ft.

GBA[2]

Department stores (with TBA)	515,674 sq. ft.
Developer mall building	508,288 sq. ft.
Developer freestanding buildings	37,080 sq. ft.
Total	1,061,042 sq. ft.

230

Parking
Spaces

Structured	3,589
Surface	637
Total	4,226
Ratio	1.9 : 1
Index	5.0

Land ownership

Developers	1,019,528 sq. ft.	23.4 acres
The Broadway	134,621 sq. ft.	3.1 acres
Parking Authority	308,898 sq. ft.	7.1 acres
Railroad right-of-way	18,034 sq. ft.	0.4 acres
Total	1,481,081 sq. ft.	34.0 acres

ECONOMIC INFORMATION

Total sales[5]	$71,400,000
Sales per sq. ft. GLA[5]	$85
Merchants association dues	assessment formula
Common area charges	not presently estimated
Rentals	$4.50 to $28.00 per sq. ft. GLA

[1] Total floor area designed for tenant occupancy and exclusive use, including freestanding ancillary structures.
[2] Total floor area of the center, including freestanding ancillary structures.
[3] As of July 1976.
[4] As of September 1976.
[5] Projected first full year of operation.

TENANT INFORMATION

Number of tenants

Mall tenants	138
Department stores	3
Total	141
Percent leased[3]	84.1

Tenant Classification	Number of stores	GLA	Percent of total GLA	Average percentage in super-regional centers (from *Dollars and Cents of Shopping Centers: 1975*)
Food	8	10,885 sq. ft.	1.3	4.7
Food service	14	27,973 sq. ft.	3.3	4.6
General merchandise	4	448,453 sq. ft.	53.6	38.0
Clothing and shoes	36	93,995 sq. ft.	11.2	26.0
Dry goods	1	4,570 sq. ft.	0.5	1.9
Furniture (home furnishings)	3	7,271 sq. ft.	0.9	1.8
Other retail	18	75,494 sq. ft.	9.0	12.7
Financial	3	14,653 sq. ft.	1.7	1.9
Offices	——	——	——	0.5
Services	3	3,782 sq. ft.	0.4	1.4
Other	1	18,539 sq. ft.	2.2	3.9
Vacant	50	134,382 sq. ft.[4]	15.9	2.6
Total	141	840,000 sq. ft.	100.0	100.0

Tenants by ownership type

Type	Number	Percent	Average percentage in super-regional centers (from *Dollars and Cents*)
National chain	65	71.4	43.6
Independent	18	19.8	29.8
Local chain	8	8.8	26.6

FAIRLANE TOWN CENTER

6-70   Fairlane Town Center, a prototype suburban subcenter.

The Suburbanization of Detroit's Retail Function

Shopping center development activity in metropolitan Detroit has occurred in three distinct phases. Beginning with the first center construction in the late fifties, each phase has represented a noteworthy elaboration of center form and design, and each has embodied an increasingly sophisticated response by retailers and developers, not only to the rapid expansion and dispersal of population in the Motor City, but also to the dramatic growth in personal income and the geographic shifts of middle-income and upper-income residential areas. Perhaps nowhere else in the country has the evolution from single-anchor, retailer-developed centers to regional-scale retail complexes been so clearly manifested, and perhaps nowhere else has a metropolitan area's retail function faced more volatile and changing circumstances.

In 1940, the Detroit metropolitan population stood at 2.5 million persons, 64 percent of whom lived in the city itself. Retail activity was concentrated in the central business district, where the symbol of fashionable shopping was J. L. Hudson's six-story downtown department store. Non-CBD retailing was concentrated along the major thoroughfares radiating outward from the urban core. The remainder of Wayne County and adjacent Macomb and Oakland counties stood on the threshold of dramatic growth but remained substantially rural in character.

By 1976, for reasons well known in many cities throughout the country, Detroit's traditional pattern of retail activity had been transformed. Population shifts, extensive freeway construction, and the decline of the core city have led to almost total suburbanization of the city's retail function. Not since 1958 have retail sales in the city exceeded those of the suburbs. By 1976, suburban areas accounted for more than two-thirds of the metropolitan population and an even greater share of retail trade. Outlying concentrations of office and commercial activity have grown up, rivaled the downtown, and then surpassed it. One shopping complex alone, Northland, in suburban Southfield, accounts for more retail trade than the Detroit CBD, yet the pace of change is so rapid that Northland now faces competition from newer, larger, and more sophisticated suburban retail complexes, such as Somerset Mall and Oakland Mall.

Between 1954 and 1976, 22 community-scale and regional-scale shopping centers, with a total of 16.4 million square feet of floor space, were built in the metropolitan area—all in the rapidly growing suburbs. During this period, not one community or regional center was built inside the city limits of Detroit, whose population and retail trade have been steadily declining. Today, little more than J. L. Hudson's remains to suggest the scale of what was once Detroit's retail heart. However, a belated effort to reverse this decline is now underway, in the form of Renaissance Center, a massive mixed use development on the downtown waterfront, incorporating four office towers, a 70-story hotel, and 340,000 square feet of retail space.

Shopping center development activity began in the fifties, when the J. L. Hudson Company decided to develop a series of suburban stores to retain customers who had moved out of the city. A decentralization plan, prepared by Victor Gruen & Associates, proposed the construction of four shopping centers in a ring around the city, each at least 10 to 12 miles from downtown and equidistant from one another.[5] Each of the new centers would be anchored by a Hudson's department store and would contain between 600,000 and 1,000,000 square feet of GBA. Although two of them were not completed until the sixties, the four centers—Northland, Eastland, Southland, and Westland—were built substantially as originally visualized, in both size and location. Each center consisted of a single department store anchor and peripheral shops in a setting of landscaped open courts, with parking provided around the edge of the site. At the time they were built, these centers were models of innovative design and were emulated throughout North America.

Since that time, the four centers have been modernized and expanded to remain competitive with more contemporary suburban retail competition. At Northland, the addition of a second department store has brought the GBA to 1.7 million square feet, and extensive development, in the form of

[5] Victor Gruen and Larry Smith, *Shopping Towns USA* (New York: Reinhold, 1960), p. 37.

POPULATION 1940–1975—DETROIT URBAN AREA

AREA	1940	1950	1960	1970	1975
(CITY OF DETROIT)	(1,623,452)	(1,849,568)	(1,670,144)	(1,511,336)	(1,386,817)
WAYNE COUNTY*	2,175,542	2,435,235	2,666,297	2,666,751	2,536,700
MACOMB COUNTY	107,638	184,961	405,804	625,309	669,000
OAKLAND COUNTY	254,068	396,001	690,259	907,871	967,500
TOTAL	2,537,248	3,016,197	3,762,360	4,199,931	4,173,200
CITY OF DETROIT AS A PERCENT OF TOTAL URBAN AREA POPULATION	64.0	61.3	44.4	36.0	33.2

*Includes the city of Detroit.
Source: U.S. Census of Population.

office buildings, hotels, and adjacent commercial development, has made Northland the nucleus of a new suburban downtown. Eastland, Southland, and Westland are now enclosed, and second department stores have been added.

Between 1964 and 1968, a number of shopping centers were built in the Detroit suburbs. The three largest were Oakland Mall in Troy, Livonia Mall in Livonia, and Macomb Mall in Roseville. This second phase of shopping center development activity was characterized by the implementation of innovations made possible by the design and marketing experience of the four centers in the earlier phase. Each of these newer projects featured an enclosed mall design, over 750,000 square feet of GBA, and two anchor department stores. As such, they reflected the evolution toward more carefully merchandised centers, where mall tenants have spaces of roughly equivalent attractiveness and can benefit from pedestrian traffic between the anchor tenants, which are placed at the ends of the enclosed mall. These centers also broadened the consumer base by having two department stores and a wider selection of merchandise. The second generation centers form a second ring of retail development, approximately 6 miles farther from the CBD in the direction of Detroit's major areas of population growth.

The most recent phase consists of three even larger regional centers, two of which opened in 1976 and one of which is scheduled to open in 1977. The three centers, Fairlane Town Center, Lakeside, and Twelve Oaks, are visualized as becoming the primary suburban focal points in their respective areas of the metropolitan region. Each will have a trade area substantially larger than those of the regional centers of the sixties. Despite such superficial differences as the fact that one has a two-level mall and another has a three-level mall, these centers closely resemble each other in both physical design and tenant mix. Each has more than a million square feet of GBA and a projected total of five or six department stores (thus qualifying them as super-regionals), over 150 tenants (many common to both of the centers which have already opened), and multilevel enclosed mall designs. Center sites of more than 200 acres have been assembled to accommodate retail expansion as the market matures and to permit the orderly development of office buildings, hotels, and other uses compatible with a primarily commercial orientation. Careful planning of peripheral areas is the most significant departure from the second generation centers, and it constitutes an important step in the evolution of shopping centers toward fully integrated urban subcenters.

Fairlane Town Center

The Taubman Company, developer of Fairlane and Lakeside, believes that the most recent retail developments became possible because of deficiencies in the second generation centers; they were undersized, often poorly located, and they tended to fragment the metropolitan trade area. In the opinion of the developer, these deficiencies created an opportunity for a third generation of centers to capitalize on the ultimate development potential created by a regional-scale shopping center. Fairlane, Lakeside, and Twelve Oaks represent the framework for a series of true urban subcenters.

CENTER	YEAR OPENED	BUILDING AREA (SQ. FT.)	ANCHOR TENANTS WHEN OPENED	LOCATION	CHANGES
FIRST GENERATION					
Northland	1954	1,725,000	1	Southfield	Enclosure Second department store
Southland	1970	547,000	1	Taylor	Enclosure Second department store
Eastland	1957	1,330,000	2	Harper Woods	Enclosure
Westland	1965	642,000	1	Wayne	Enclosure Second department store
SECOND GENERATION					
Livonia Mall	1964	770,000	2	Livonia	None
Oakland Mall	1968	1,100,000	2	Troy	None
Macomb Mall Center	1964	750,000	2	Roseville	None
THIRD GENERATION					
Fairlane Town Center	1976	1,496,000	3	Dearborn	Additional department store under construction
Lakeside	1976	1,558,000	4	Sterling Heights	Additional department store under construction
Twelve Oaks	1977	1,020,000	2	Novi	Under construction in 1977

Source: *Shopping Center Directory*, 17th edition (National Research Bureau, Inc.).

The most ambitious of Detroit's three new regional shopping complexes is Fairlane Town Center, a joint venture of The Taubman Company and Ford Motor Land Development Corporation (FMLDC). It is to be the central element of Fairlane, a 2,360-acre new community being developed on the former estate of Henry Ford. The project is located in Dearborn, a suburban community 8 miles west of downtown Detroit and 9 miles south of the Northland shopping center in Southfield. Dearborn is also the headquarters of the Ford Motor Company. Upon completion in 1980, the 282.6-acre shopping development will consist of a 1.5 million square foot super-regional center, with six department stores, 200 shops and services, and surface parking for 8,140 vehicles. The shopping center is separated by a ring road from 150 acres of low-rise and mid-rise office buildings, hotels, medical facilities, and other uses selected for compatibility with the extended activity cycle being given the Town Center. Total employment in the Town Center, expected to reach 8,000 persons, will provide an important base of support for the retail component. Integration of the diverse uses comprising the Town Center is being furthered by an automated "people-mover," the Automatically Controlled Transportation (ACT) system, featuring driverless, rubber-tired vehicles controlled by computer and operated on elevated guideways.

Detailed development planning for Fairlane began in 1968, when William L. Pereira and Associates and Economics Research Associates were commissioned to master-plan the Ford property. Their

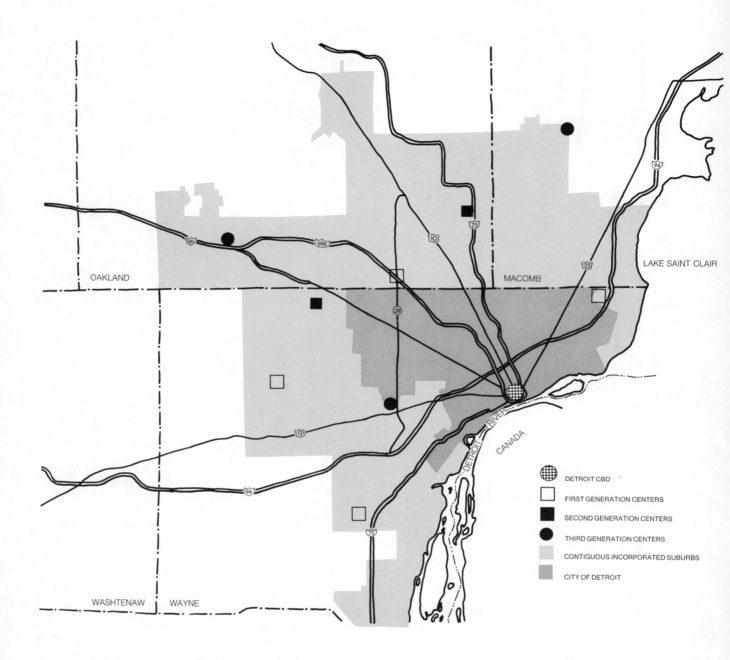

OAKLAND

MACOMB

LAKE SAINT CLAIR

DETROIT RIVER

CANADA

⊕ DETROIT CBD

□ FIRST GENERATION CENTERS

■ SECOND GENERATION CENTERS

● THIRD GENERATION CENTERS

CONTIGUOUS INCORPORATED SUBURBS

CITY OF DETROIT

WASHTENAW   WAYNE

6-73   Distribution of retail activity in metropolitan Detroit.

plan proposed maximizing the value of the strategically located property—said to be one of the largest tracts of underdeveloped metropolitan land under one ownership in the country—by developing a combination of residential, office, industrial, research, and retailing functions in a setting of open space, wooded greenbelts, and water areas. The conceptual phases of the process took approximately 2 years, and construction of Fairlane's initial elements—a twin tower office complex—

began in February 1971. The entire project is expected to take at least 15 years to complete.

The Town Center was placed in a rectangular parcel bounded by three at-grade arterials, Evergreen Road, Hubbard Drive, and Michigan Avenue, and a major north-south expressway, the Southfield Freeway, which separates the center from Ford World Headquarters, just to the east. Within a 1-mile radius is an extensive concentration of other Ford facilities, including the company's re-

6-74   Northland as it appeared in 1954. This retail complex, now the nucleus of a major urban subcenter, was recently enclosed and expanded. The American Institute of Architects has named Northland to its list of the nation's most significant architectural works.

search and design unit and the offices of Ford Motor Credit and the Lincoln-Mercury Division. Just to the south are Greenfield Village and the Ford Museum.

Besides the shopping center, two primary components of the Town Center are already complete: the 800-room Hyatt Regency Dearborn Hotel, owned by FMLDC and operated by the Hyatt Corporation under a long-term management contract, and a 19-acre health care facility occupying a complex of low-rise buildings in the northwest quadrant of the property.

The joint venture to develop a regional-scale retail complex in Fairlane Town Center was drawn up in 1970 by The Taubman Company and FMLDC. The agreement delineated the extent of personal participation on the part of principals of both firms, and designated The Taubman Com-

pany as project developer, general contractor, leasing agent, and manager. FMLDC, which holds an equity share, donated 121.6 acres inside the ring road as the location of the shopping center, but retained the peripheral parcels.

The development process, from conception to completion, took about 6 years, including 3 years of actual construction. Fairlane Town Center opened in March 1976, 50 percent leased and 30 percent occupied.

The center consists of 1.4 million square feet of GLA, including a 595,000 square foot, three-level enclosed mall and three department stores, J. L. Hudson Company, Sears Roebuck and Company, and J. C. Penney. These anchor tenants account for slightly more than half of the total leasable space. A fourth anchor, Lord and Taylor, will be under construction by early 1977. The development

6-75   A multilevel mall.

plan calls for two additional anchor tenants, which will increase the GLA at Fairlane Town Center to more than 1.5 million square feet. These additional components should be complete and occupied by 1980.

Super-Regional Shopping Centers

Aware that much of the economic potential of regional shopping center locations was being lost to competitive strip developments and freestanding department stores—and aware that many center locations could have supported a larger, more fully integrated retail complex than had actually been built—developers began to expand their centers in the late sixties. This expansion helped reduce the spillover effect, which in other centers had taken the form of competing strip commercial developments and had meant that competitors

were accruing much of the economic increment created by the shopping center.

The planning and design strategy which evolved to resolve this problem consisted of developing multimodal centers with as many as six department stores and enough land to provide for expansion. Retail complexes began to grow rapidly in size, and centers with more than a million square feet of GLA and from 3 to 6 anchor tenants became common. The International Council of Shopping Centers estimates that there are now more than 200 of these very large centers in existence, and ULI took note of this trend in *Dollars and Cents of Shopping Centers: 1975* by adding the super-regional classification to the list of shopping center categories used to discuss center size and operational performance. As discussed in the first chapter of this book, the super-regional shopping

NAME	GBA AT FULL DEVELOPMENT (SQ. FT.)	MAJOR DEPARTMENT STORES	LAND AREA (ACRES)	SHOPS AND SERVICES AT FULL DEVELOPMENT	OWNER/ DEVELOPER
Fairlane Town Center	1,496,446	J. C. Penney J. L. Hudson Sears Roebuck Lord & Taylor (under construction) Two others to be selected	282.6	200	The Taubman Company Ford Motor Land Development Corporation
Lakeside	1,582,531	Crowley, Milner & Co. J. C. Penney J. L. Hudson (under construction) Sears Roebuck Lord & Taylor	276.0	185	The Taubman Company
Twelve Oaks Mall	1,045,298	J. L. Hudson Lord & Taylor J. C. Penney Sears Roebuck	84.5*	165	Dayton Hudson Properties

*Excluding residual property.

center offers a variety and depth of shopping goods and services comparable to that formerly found only in the central business district of large metropolitan areas. This range of offerings includes a wide selection of general merchandise, apparel, and home furnishings, as well as a variety of services and recreational facilities. By definition, the super-regional has a total GLA of 750,000 square feet or more and includes three or more full-line department stores, each with at least 100,000 square feet of GLA. In practice, most super-regional centers also have at least 100 mall stores.

The Taubman Company, however, prefers to define a center in terms of its impact on a given trade area, rather than in terms of its physical size and number of department store anchors alone. A center scaled to capture more than 40 percent of the major tenant retail sales in a particular area becomes the dominant commercial force in that area, regardless of the center's size, which may range from 450,000 to more than 2,000,000 square feet. Nevertheless, in building centers scaled to the requirements of various metropolitan areas, the developer of Fairlane has built no fewer than 14 centers which meet all the defining criteria of super-regional shopping cen-

ters. This experience also suggests that most large metropolitan areas, except those which are already overstored, can support at least one center in this size range.

Success at the super-regional scale must be based on a center's ability to attract a disproportionate share of the market—a share propotionately greater than the increment in GLA—because of the greater variety and selection of merchandise it offers. In a refinement of the regional center strategy where the department stores constitute the primary draw, the mall itself becomes an attraction equivalent to the anchor tenants. This marketing strategy presumes less frequent shopping trips, and also presumes that the center will dominate major-ticket shopping in its trade area.

For this to occur in Detroit, Fairlane, Lakeside, and Twelve Oaks Mall will have to draw heavily from the existing market of the older centers. Their respective trade areas blanket the metropolitan area, and the established centers will need to reorient themselves in the face of the impact of the new centers; the renovations recently completed at Northland, Southland, Eastland, and Westland provide evidence that such adjustments are already being made.

6-77   With 2.2 million square feet of GLA and four department stores, Woodfield Mall in Schaumburg, Illinois, is the largest shopping center in the world.

Woodfield

The best known of the developer's super-regional shopping centers because of its metropolitan area impact has been Woodfield, located in the Chicago suburb of Schaumburg. This center opened in 1971, and upon completion of a second phase 2 years later, it became the largest shopping center in the world, with 2.2 million square feet of GBA and four anchor tenants. Market capture for the center is approximately 45 percent in a trade area encompassing most of Chicago's western suburbs and including such competing retail complexes as Golf Mill and Randhurst. Woodfield exemplifies the evolution of the suburban shopping center into a carefully articulated urban subcenter, and is now the focus of the largest concentration of suburban office space in metropolitan Chicago. Several development concepts which were introduced at Woodfield have been further refined at Taubman's Detroit area centers. The first such concept is a physical plan which combines orderly development on peripheral parcels of the retail complex with a strong automobile orientation. All three centers have a ring road for internal circulation, and all three have large sites; Woodfield's site, the smallest, covers 191 acres. Development is proceeding rapidly on the land outside Woodfield's ring road. This area now includes office buildings, a movie theater, an ice arena, and freestanding restaurants. A similar development pattern is planned for the Michigan centers. Fairlane, however, carries this integration concept one step further with the addition of the multimodal transit plan, which integrates the Town Center area by means of the ACT people-mover system.

The second characteristic is a developer strategy based on a market capture in excess of 40 percent. A variation of this strategy was required for Detroit, where the suburban shopping centers are more firmly established. Consequently, greater emphasis has been placed on generating business from areas served by already established centers.

240

The third characteristic relates to interiors, which have been modified in the two most recent centers by reducing the size of central courts, adding more department stores, and substituting a more elaborate X configuration for Woodfield's straightforward cross design.

Center Design and Construction

Fairlane Town Center has a unified exterior facade of buff-colored brick panels and carefully articulated structural massings. The anchor stores have been given distinctive detailing and are identified by large, internally lighted signs. Even distribution of pedestrian traffic between the upper and lower levels of the center, a major design problem in multilevel centers, was accomplished by creating upper and lower parking areas, each with direct access to the respective level of the enclosed mall. The site, which was essentially flat and had been used for farming, had to be extensively graded to create the necessary 18-foot change in grade. The ACT people-mover station was situated on the middle level of the center. Rooftop areas containing air conditioning units and other mechanical equipment were screened from the view of the mid-rise and high-rise buildings in the vicinity.

The center occupies 121.6 acres within the ring road and includes the center structure and a free-standing J. C. Penney auto accessories store. The remainder of Fairlane Town Center consists of 161 acres designated for development compatible with the area's urban function, and 7 acres of local streets, which are owned and maintained by FMLDC.

The parking area, with surface spaces for 8,100 cars, is organized into four quadrants, two on the upper level and two on the lower level, separated from each other by landscaping and pedestrian ways. All parking has been positioned at a 45-degree angle, with internal vehicular circulation oriented toward the retail structure. As the center expands, spaces will be eliminated to make way for department store building pads but will be replaced by an equivalent number of new spaces on outlying undeveloped ground currently unused but designated for parking in the development plan. The parking index at Fairlane is 6.3 spaces per 1,000 square feet of GLA, equivalent to that in most recent Taubman centers.

Landscaping has been generously distributed throughout Fairlane and accounts for 10 percent of the site area. Natural plantings have been used on the sloping ground between the upper and lower parking areas, where large trees, shrubs, ground cover, and grass impart a naturalistic effect which is visible throughout Fairlane. Within the parking area, access roads have been given a more formal treatment, with mature trees placed in rows to aid the motorist's visual comprehension of the center. Next to the center structure itself is a pedestrian environment of sidewalks and planter and seating areas which has been separated from the truck docks by changes in grade, masonry extensions of the center walls, and other design techniques.

The Mall Interior

The distinctive interior feature of most very large shopping centers is a series of expansive open courts, and Fairlane, with 138,000 square feet of common area, is no exception. The internal pedestrian network consists of upper and lower modified X systems superimposed over one another and a more limited middle level centering on the ACT station. Because of the design constraints

6-78 Elevators move shoppers between floors at Fairlane Town Center.

6-79 This aerial view shows the automated transit system connecting Fairlane Town Center with the Dearborn Hyatt Regency Hotel.

imposed by the people-mover, incorporated into the center as part of the agreement between The Taubman Company and FMLDC, there are twin interior courts rather than a single grand court at the intersection of the mall axes. The south central court was designed as an activity center, with a stage and seating areas, and the north central court was designed as the location of a large terraced fountain, which provides an attractive community focal point. Additional courts, each highlighted by a contemporary sculpture of grand scale and designed on the basis of 30, 60, and 90-degree angles on a horizontal plan, were created at the apexes of the grand court locations. This design foreshortens visual distances within the

mall interior, maximizes the exposure of mall stores, diminishes walking distances requred to visit all stores, and creates changing vistas of excitement and interest for shoppers. Aesthetically, the interior is a contemporary urban environment rendered distinctive by terrazzo floors, white ceilings articulated with geometrically shaped skylights, and white walls which contrast dramatically with the colorful storefronts.

Access among the three retail levels is provided by stairs, ramps, escalators, and twin elevators flanking the ACT station. These, together with seven carefully placed entrances and exits, permit ready movement between levels and minimize the amount of "dead" space. Everything possible was

6-80　Fairlane's automated transit system consists of an elevated guideway resting on concrete columns. The system enters the center between the Sears and Hudson's department stores.

done to make the store locations attractive to potential tenants. One way was to angle the mall facades to create a high frontage-to-depth ratio, thereby heightening the visual impact of individual stores. The resulting pedestrian streetscape consists of irregular storefronts, each unique but coordinated within a design and operational framework established by the developer. Some tenants have preferred an open and casual facade, while others have chosen an enclosed, formal appearance, depending on the tenant's merchandising philosophy and anticipated pedestrian traffic. This mix of store facades appears to be characteristic of most recent centers, and there is no apparent marketing advantage in either approach, other considerations being equal.

The mall areas are lighted by an unusual system which uses the skylights as the primary light source during the daytime and lighting fixtures in the evening hours. Illumination requirements for the mall area are weighted in such a way that a large percentage of the light is emitted from stores and storefronts. It is thought that this system has re-

duced lighting system demands at Fairlane Town Center to one of the lowest levels ever achieved in a regional center. Natural light reduces energy requirements in the daytime and makes the displays of merchandise more attractive.

Automated Transit System

The automated transit system is the most innovative feature of Fairlane, as it represents perhaps the first time that a regional center has been designed for other than automobile and pedestrian access. The initial half-mile segment of the looped system, which connects Fairlane with the Dearborn Hyatt Regency Hotel, started operating in early 1976. The facility consists of an elevated guideway resting on concrete columns and running between a station within the shopping mall and one adjoining the hotel lobby. The automated system, with its two bidirectional vehicles, is programmed to operate under peak load conditions of 1,800 persons per hour. Each electrically powered, computer-controlled vehicle is designed

243

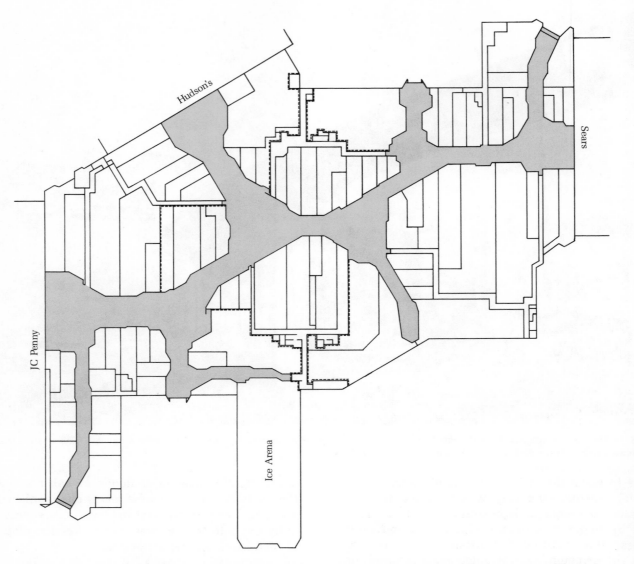

6-81 Layout of the lower level mall interior. The ACT provides direct access to the middle level of the center.

to accommodate 24 passengers and cruise at 25 miles per hour. A 500-foot bypass lane near the midpoint of the system allows vehicles traveling in opposite directions to pass each other. The ACT was developed by Ford Motor Company as a prototype urban transit system. Original plans to extend the system to Ford International Headquarters were eliminated because of the expense and because of difficulties associated with a freeway crossing. Nevertheless, even in its modified form, the looped system has the potential of becoming an important means of access to the shopping center for the Town Center's working population, once the line is completed and the peripheral parcels are fully developed. Meanwhile, the sys-

tem functions as a tourist attraction and runs at capacity most of the day.

Ownership, Operation, and Management

Principals of both The Taubman Company and FMLDC are participating financially in the development. FMLDC contributed the 121.6-acre parcel inside the ring road but has retained ownership of the peripheral parcels, which are being developed separately from the shopping center for both sale and lease. Both the entry roads and the ring road, 8.5 acres in all, are privately owned and maintained by FMLDC. The three department stores have purchased their respective building pad areas, a total of 12 acres, and have signed operating agreements with the developer, who has overall management responsibility for the shopping center.

As managing partner, The Taubman Company has been responsible for center design, construction, and operation. The Taubman Company has determined that using its own staff permits greater control and efficiency than contracting out for services. There are approximately 70 full-time, on-site staff members, including the manager, assistant manager, promotion director, maintenance superintendent, ice arena manager, and office, security, and maintenance personnel.

Mall tenants at Fairlane Town Center get unimproved space, which they must finish at their own expense according to developer specifications. Considerable leeway in signage, storefront design, and interior configurations is allowed. Each tenant installs his own rooftop HVAC unit and services his space through a series of ducts and shafts provided by the developer. HVAC units are maintained individually, but the electrical system was designed so that each tenant is serviced and metered separately from a primary power source.

Certain prospective tenants, sought after by the developer to locate in the center, may receive a tenant allowance to help with utility extensions, finish off internal spaces, and carry out other improvements. One way the developer was able to obtain high rents for most of the mall space was to begin leasing only 6 months before the department stores opened, thereby establishing better rents than if arrangements with some tenants had been completed while the shopping center deal was still being put together.

Tenants participate in the maintenance of the mall, parking areas, and building exterior, with common area charges expected to be in the range of $1.40 to $1.80 per square foot of GLA for the center's first full year of operation. The developer will absorb the cost of vacant space until the center is 75 percent occupied, at which time this cost will be borne by the tenants. The department stores are making a smaller contribution to common area maintenance, partly because their heavy promotion reduces the need for mall tenants to advertise on their own.

There is an initial annual charge of $0.25 per square foot for merchants association dues, with the developer adding 25 percent of the tenants' contribution. The association's bylaws provide for a board of nine members, five of whom represent the mall tenants and four of whom represent the department stores and the developer. The association's responsibility is "to promote Fairlane Town Center . . . through the sponsorship of commercial, cultural, educational, community and other programs; and, in furtherance of such purpose, to engage in and conduct promotional programs and publicity, special events, decorations, cooperative advertising in the general interest and for the benefit of the Center."

Market Area and Tenant Mix

Fairlane's primary trade area, from which 80 percent of all department-store-type sales are drawn, includes portions of the city of Detroit and its western, southern, and near-northern suburbs, with a population of 1 million persons. Also in this area, which is roughly 10 miles from north to south and 20 miles from east to west, are two regional-scale retail developments: Westland Shopping Center, with J. L. Hudson, J. C. Penney, and approximately 40 tenant stores; and Southland, with J. L. Hudson, J. C. Penney, and approximately 40 tenant stores. The remaining 20 percent of Fairlane's patronage comes from elsewhere in the metropolitan area, Ann Arbor, other parts of Michigan, and Windsor, Ontario.

The mall area's tenant mix has been structured to provide the most complete presentation of soft goods available within the trade area. Over three-quarters of the developer's 595,000 square feet of GLA has been leased, with almost 100 shops now open. Among others, the tenants include 52 clothing and shoe stores, nine restaurants, three specialty food stores, two bookstores, three record and electronics stores, three jewelry stores, and three gift, card, stationery, and flower shops. Two of the tenants, the six-screen cinema and the ice skating arena, were incorporated into the center to generate pedestrian traffic and to extend the activity cycle of Fairlane into the evening hours. These facilities occupy 47,000 square feet of GLA and will generate lower revenues per square foot than most other tenants. They are located in a self-contained extension on the western side of the retail complex, with separate access. The three department stores account for more than half of Fairlane's leasable space, a figure which will increase to more than two-thirds when the three additional anchor stores are built. Total sales at Fairlane are projected at $160 million for the first full year of operation, or about $130 per square foot for the entire center, department stores included.

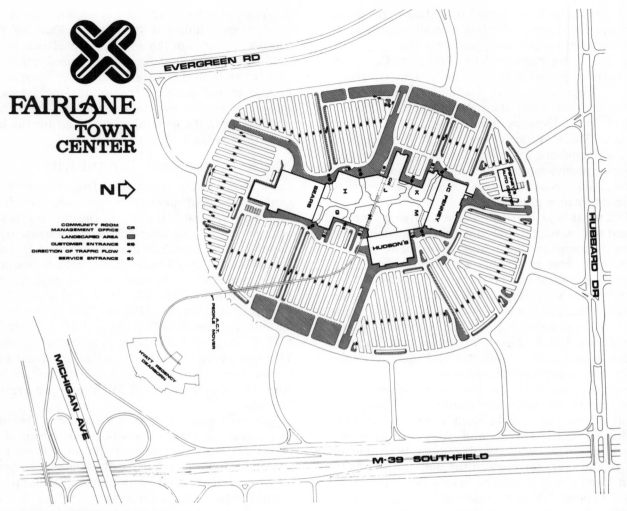

COMMUNITY ROOM
MANAGEMENT OFFICE CR
LANDSCAPED AREA
CUSTOMER ENTRANCE ⟹
DIRECTION OF TRAFFIC FLOW →
SERVICE ENTRANCE ⟹

EVERGREEN RD

HUBBARD DR

MICHIGAN AVE

A.C.T.
PEOPLE MOVER

HYATT REGENCY
DEARBORN

M-39 SOUTHFIELD

6-82 Site plan—Fairlane Town Center.

6-83 PROJECT DATA—FAIRLANE TOWN CENTER

DEVELOPERS

The Taubman Company, Inc. (construction/
management)
26250 Northwestern Highway
Southfield, Michigan 48076

Ford Motor Land Development Corporation
One Parkland Boulevard
Dearborn, Michigan 48126

ARCHITECTURE/PLANNING

Brown-Heldt Associates, Inc., planners
730 Montgomery Street
San Francisco, California 94111

Wah Yee Associates, architects
25711 Northwestern Highway, Suite 416
Southfield, Michigan 48036

LAND USE INFORMATION

Site area
  Total development 282.6 acres
  Shopping center 121.6 acres[1]
Land allocation

	Site area	Percent of site
Buildings	34.3 acres	28.2
Parking and circulation	75.0 acres	61.7
Landscaping	12.3 acres	10.1
Total	121.6 acres	100.0

Parking
  Spaces[4] 8,097
  Ratio 2.2 : 1
  Index 6.3

GLA[2]

Mall tenants	595,373 sq. ft.
J. C. Penney	214,210 sq. ft.
J. L. Hudson	239,900 sq. ft.
Sears Roebuck	224,877 sq. ft.
Subtotal	1,273,559 sq. ft.
Lord & Taylor (opening 1978)	120,000 sq. ft.
Total	1,393,559 sq. ft.
Common area[3]	138,322 sq. ft.

GBA

Mall	797,078 sq. ft.
J. C. Penney	224,497 sq. ft.
J. L. Hudson	249,694 sq. ft.
Sears Roebuck	224,877 sq. ft.
Total	1,496,146 sq. ft.

Land ownership

J. C. Penney[5]	4.1 acres
J. L. Hudson[5]	3.1 acres
Sears Roebuck[5]	4.9 acres
Fairlane Town Center	101.1 acres
Ford Motor Land Development Company[6]	8.5 acres
Total	121.6 acres

ECONOMIC INFORMATION

Total sales[10]	$160 million
Merchants association dues[11]	$0.25 per sq. ft.
Common area charges	Calculated per square foot for mall tenants. Projected to total $1.40 to $1.80 for 1976.
Rentals	
Amount	$13.0 per sq. ft., average
Percentage rents	4 to 12 percent

[1] Includes entry roads.
[2] Total floor area designed for tenant occupancy and exclusive use.
[3] Public mall space; does not include service areas.
[4] Striped spaces within the ring road.
[5] Building pads.
[6] Entry roads and ring road.
[7] Mall shops, as of September 1976.
[8] Six-screen cinema and ice skating rink.
[9] Not rented as of September 1976.
[10] Projected first full year of operation.
[11] Developer contributes an amount equal to 25 percent of the tenant contribution.

TENANT INFORMATION

Number of tenants	
Mall tenants	101
Department stores	3
Total	104
Percent leased[7]	79.1

Tenant Classification	Number of stores	GLA	Percent of total GLA	Percent of developer GLA	Average percentage in super-regional centers (from Dollars and Cents of Shopping Centers: 1975)
Food	3	8,991 sq. ft.	0.7	1.5	4.7
Food service	9	43,427 sq. ft.	3.4	7.3	4.6
General merchandise	3	678,186 sq. ft.	53.3	———	38.0
Clothing and shoes	52	266,943 sq. ft.	21.0	44.8	26.0
Dry goods	1	2,862 sq. ft.	0.2	0.5	1.9
Furniture (home furnishings)	7	24,407 sq. ft.	1.9	4.1	1.8
Other retail	23	68,589 sq. ft.	5.4	11.5	12.7
Financial	1	1,769 sq. ft.	0.1	0.3	1.9
Offices	———	———	———	———	0.5
Services	3	7,325 sq. ft.	0.6	1.2	1.4
Other[8]	2	46,911 sq. ft.	3.7	7.9	3.9
Vacant[9]	———	124,149 sq. ft.	9.7	20.9	2.6
Total	104	1,273,559 sq. ft.	100.0	100.0	100.0

7.

Future Trends

Barring any major unforeseeable changes in the world situation, the future of shopping center development will be molded by the balance of forces which, today as in the past, bear upon all commercial real estate and retail activity. The problem of trying to see into and prepare for the future, then, becomes a matter of identifying these forces, finding out where each of them is headed, judging the future balance of these forces and trends, and interpreting this balance in terms of what it means for shopping centers.

What are these forces? In looking for them, one must remember that the shopping center exists in response to a consumer demand for retail goods and services. The vitality of a shopping center depends on the continuance of this demand and on the continuance of the shopping center concept as the best response to it. One must also keep in mind that, besides the creation of new centers, the shopping center industry is involved in the careful management and operation of new and old centers, not only to maintain each center's productiveness and efficiency, but also to ensure that each center responds to changes in its trade area.

These thoughts suggest that we should look at the forces which affect three things: the trade area population's buying power and patronage of the center, the need for developers to build or alter centers to meet changes in consumer demand, and the developer's financial ability to carry out such projects. These forces and their currently discernible trends include changes in population, in population composition, and in population distribution; economic and social changes; public policy, including environment-related policy; changes in the patterns of energy use and transportation; and financing trends. These forces are interdependent, and they overlap in many areas. Along with other factors, they will determine the future of shopping centers. The shopping center developer or manager must be aware of the importance of these trends, and must be able to respond to them.[1]

Forces at Work

Demographic Changes

Few people still believe that growth is at an end in the United States. On the whole, the controversies over theories of urban growth and no-growth that arose in the early seventies have subsided. Both the public and private sectors have recognized that the best course is one of compromise, accepting the need for some growth but within a framework of more careful controls. Fundamental to this framework is predictable population change. Shopping center developers must understand current and likely future patterns of population composition, migration, and distribution in order to accurately appraise their markets and sites.[2]

Population growth is tending toward stability. In much of the United States, the birth rate continues to fall. Families are having fewer children, and many new households are composed of unmarried, nonrelated people. American couples are marrying later and divorcing more frequently. There are more elderly people. Despite the general preference for single-family detached houses, suburban sprawl —with its vastly strung-out streets and utilities— will become less affordable by greater segments of the population and less affordable for government without disproportionate increases in taxes to support required services.

These forces suggest a modification of housing types and housing locations. The demand will be for more multifamily ownership, more rental units, and higher densities. This trend, however, is not yet apparent in the housing market, because the current pattern is for people to spend a greater percentage of income on housing rather than to reduce their housing expectations. Furthermore, because of disparities between capital costs and rental achievements, rental properties are not currently an attractive investment. Nevertheless, the shift to multifamily housing and generally greater housing densities cannot be averted indefinitely.

In considering where new centers might be located and where existing centers might be expanded or modernized in the next decade, developers must recognize three current and one potential demographic trends. The three current trends are:

- The slowing down and even possible reversal of population growth in older, established suburban areas surrounding large cities.
- A reversal of out-migration from smaller cities and rural areas, with the result that the population is growing in areas removed from major metropolitan centers.
- Rapid population growth in the South and West, together with population stability or even decline in many metropolitan areas in the Northeast and Midwest.

These phenomena are major departures from longstanding population trends and are producing new opportunities for shopping center development.

The potential fourth demographic trend, which probably will be evidenced in the 1980 census, is that some central cities, particularly those where considerable residential rehabilitation is taking place, may halt the longstanding pattern of population decline and may even achieve modest net increases in population. If this change takes place, it will have been caused by the return of the middle and upper-middle-income households to the inner city, and it will therefore present new market opportunities for shopping centers.

Population will continue to grow in the second-tier suburbs. The population characteristics of more and more first-tier suburbs, however, will come to resemble those of the central city. Overall, the growth will be slow.

The more significant new population pattern will be the evolution of rural growth centers beyond the limits of metropolitan areas. Population shifts from major urban centers to smaller cities and towns, and shifts to the South, Southwest, and Far West— the "Sun Belt"—will continue.[3]

Previous patterns of continual and relatively rapid outward suburban expansion have seen shopping center development catch up with the first postwar housing boom of the late forties and early fifties; keep pace with expansion during the fifties

---

[1] See *Shopping Centers: The Next 15 Years* (New York: International Council of Shopping Centers, 1975). *The Next 15 Years* is based on a conference of industry leaders held by ICSC in April 1975. The gist of the evaluation presented in this chapter is based on a similar seminar held in May 1976 by ULI's Commercial and Office Development Council.

[2] See Robert L. Sansom, "Modern Issues Confronting Shopping Centers," in *The Next 15 Years*.

[3] See Peter A. Morrison, "The Current Demographic Context of National Growth and Development," *Environmental Comment*, July 1976.

7-1 Looking southwest at The Galleria, Houston. High intensity of land use is an important trend in present-day shopping center development.

Office
Retail
Hotel

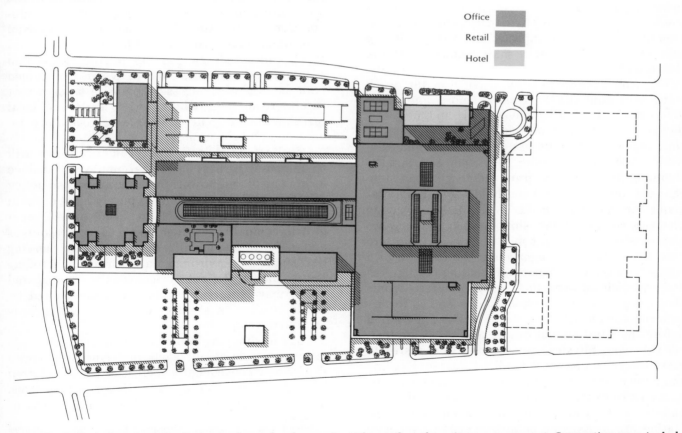

7-2 The Galleria is one of the first mixed use developments with retail as the primary component. Supporting uses include hotels and office buildings. This development is the most important focus of activity in Houston's rapidly developing western suburbs.

251

and into the sixties; and then, for a number of reasons, advance ahead of suburban expansion with the expectation that population growth would catch up. During the mid-seventies, overbuilding took place, and in many areas the end of the shopping center boom of the late sixties and early seventies is now becoming more obvious.[4] As new development slows in the coming decade, suburban shopping center expansion will also be more cautiously undertaken. Locations will be subjected to greater scrutiny, and greater emphasis will be placed on maintaining the vitality of existing centers through renovation and expansion to capture and hold new markets, rather than building new centers.

Economic and Social Changes

Long-term changes in the economy can only be surmised. Any forecast must include positive and negative variables. Informed opinion, however, offers conclusions such as these: inflation is expected to continue but will stabilize at between 2 and 5 percent per year; the domestic money supply for investment capital is expected to increase at an average annual rate of 3 percent; consumer discretionary income is expected to rise, producing an upward swing in retail sales volumes over the long term.[5]

The participation rate by women in the work force will continue to rise, as more and more divorcées and working wives seek and find employment. In itself, this social change will cause a shift in shopping habits. As more women enter the work force, more evening, weekend, and Sunday shopping hours will be provided to accommodate changed families and households. Similarly, demand for consumer goods will change, bringing about a corresponding shift in shopping center merchandise and tenant mix. Increases in leisure time have already brought about the creation of a whole new group of tenants, including craft stores and specialized sporting goods stores—tennis shops, scuba diving shops, ski shops, and so forth.

Social trends will need to be better understood before their full impact can be accurately projected. However, physical development responsive to these forces can be more readily foreseen. Existing shopping centers, except those in decaying markets, will seek to expand or modify their range of goods and services to keep pace with changes in their market areas. Existing suburban centers are now beginning to fulfill some of their potential of becoming urban subcenters and focal points of community activity. Already the range of land uses contained within the shopping center environment has begun to expand.

Economic uncertainties remain. From the developer's point of view there are two major matters of concern: availability of construction money and long-term financing, and increases in building and occupancy costs. From the consumer's point of view, four troublesome issues remain: the inflation rate, household income, availability and cost of energy (including gasoline), and availability of affordable housing.

Environmental and Other Public Policy

Environmental controls became a fact of life in the seventies, as widespread public concern about air quality and other environmental matters affected the development industry. The Clean Air Act of 1970 established the federal response to air quality control over such indirect pollutant sources as shopping centers and large parking facilities, although indirect source controls have not been activated to date. The Federal Water Pollution Control Act Amendments of 1972, the Coastal Zone Management Act (passed in 1972, amended in 1976), and a federal land use bill (introduced in a number of versions, none of which has passed both houses of Congress) comprise a series of federal regulations which add to state and local restrictions and generally increase regulatory involvement by government.

Despite federal land use regulation, states will be reluctant to pass laws that remove or reduce local control and power. Statewide land use policy affecting land development of purely local concern will favor some control to keep development growth compatible with an area's natural resources and a local municipality's capability of serving development. Environmental controls, including those aimed at saving ecologically endangered areas, may increase in intensity, accompanied by the imposition of stronger performance standards on land development.

For the shopping center developer, added regulatory controls at all levels of government mean delays and consequently increased costs, incurred by waiting for action by project approval agencies. These burdens, combined with increased costs of

[4] See David M. Elsner, "Shopping Center Boom Appears to be Fading Due to Overbuilding," The Wall Street Journal, September 7, 1976.
[5] The Next 15 Years, p. 76.

7-3 Courthouse Center, in Columbus, Indiana, is an excellent example of the new generation of downtown shopping centers. This center, with an expanded Sears store as the anchor, illustrates the combination of modest scale and dramatic architecture that can be achieved in medium-size cities.

construction and operation, mean increased occupancy costs to tenants and hence pass-through charges to customers. These new regulations will also affect the shopping center industry in other ways. Responses to them will bring innovations and refinements in all phases of retail development. Market justifications will become more important for obtaining project approval. More than ever before, location will be the strongest factor in site selection. It is likely that local public policy toward land development, even with assurances of environmental protection through federal regulations, will be more stringent. For shopping centers some key concerns will be drainage, solid waste disposal, parking, traffic, and aesthetics.

Energy and Transportation

The "energy crisis" occurred when the oil-producing countries clamped an embargo on exports in 1973, focusing the world's attention on the use of fossil fuels. The prospect of further shortages was identified, and a search was begun for alternate sources of energy. The embargo's impact was felt immediately through the reduced supply of gasoline. While the embargo has been lifted, its aftermath continues, chiefly in the form of high fuel prices.

The availability of energy and the possibility of enforced restriction of energy consumption have become critically important to the real estate industry. For shopping centers, potential curtailment of the use of natural gas and electricity, including their use for lighting and HVAC systems, must be taken into consideration.

Concern for energy conservation, if only from the standpoint of operating cost—let alone the possibility of national shortages—will likely result in some design modifications in new centers and existing centers. Computer-controlled techniques of reducing energy consumption in buildings have already been developed. These systems are being used in new and renovated centers and can be expected to become a universal element of building operation within a short time. Prospective physical modifications include elimination of skylights not related to advantageous solar orientation, and the

253

elimination of other extensive exterior glass areas along shopping malls, both popular features of centers built in the late sixties and early seventies. The large roof areas of shopping centers will present ideal opportunities for use of solar heat collectors, thus facilitating the use of solar energy as an adjunct to conventional energy sources. The use of solid wastes as a fuel source in shopping centers may emerge, since it offers the twin advantages of energy conservation and the reuse of wastes.

It is possible that the federal government will someday restrict the use of gasoline, but it is unlikely that such an action would seriously affect most shopping centers. Rather, it is the commuter —who can more readily use another form of trans-portation—who is more likely to have to stop driving his car to work:

> Even if a curtailment in the supply of gasoline were to be introduced, reductions in automobile use for other activities, such as recreation, commuting, etc., will more likely occur before there is any significant reduction in shopping trips.[6]

The smaller automobile, with its greater fuel economy, will continue to increase in popularity, although post-embargo automobile sales patterns would seem to belie that trend. The automobile industry seems to be looking for alternatives to size reduction for improving mileage.

Gasoline shortages and higher gas prices have not yet affected the demand for parking spaces

[6] Ibid., p. 84.

7-4 Most shopping centers are still designed primarily for automobile access. Shown here is Indian Springs Shopping Center in Kansas City, Kansas.

7-5 The people-mover system at Fairlane Town Center, Dearborn.

at shopping centers. But the size of parking stalls is already changing as the trend continues from larger to smaller cars. Family shopping habits may shift, but the use of automobiles for shopping will not. Therefore, the recommended parking index of 5.5 remains valid. Nevertheless, there is a growing body of information to suggest that this current standard may be excessive and that it could be reduced somewhat with only marginal reductions of service. ULI believes that the time has come to review the standards for parking space provision at shopping centers.[7]

One result of concerns about energy has been efforts to divert highway trust funds to mass transit systems. Long lead times and large amounts of capital funds are required to develop mass transportation systems. While both the San Francisco Bay area and the Washington, D.C., metro-

politan area have new heavy, fixed-rail systems in place or partially completed, most U.S. cities—particularly those newer cities that were formed largely by the automobile—are not readily suited to heavy, fixed-rail systems. A recent study by the Regional Plan Association identified only six cities —Dallas, Detroit, Houston, Los Angeles, Pittsburgh, and Baltimore—which do not have a rapid transit system but where such a system might be feasible. What is more likely is some use of light rail, greater use of buses, and development of a variety of personal rapid transit (PRT) systems that will approximate more closely the convenience of the automobile. To date, only one PRT system serving a shopping center has been constructed. As dis-

---

[7] See "It's Time to Review Industry Standard," *Shopping Center World*, Vol. 5, No. 7 (August 1976).

cussed in Chapter 6, it is the Fairlane Town Center ACT system, which connects a 1.4 million square foot super-regional center with a hotel by means of a ⅝-mile elevated track. While the system has been quite popular, capital costs appear high in terms of the increased accessibility the system has provided. Since the lead time is so long for the designing and marketing of such systems, it is probably safe to say that, in the next decade, modifications in retailing, consumer lifestyles, and general shopping habits will have a greater impact on the pattern of shopping facilities than will changes in transportation modes.

Nevertheless, the International Council of Shopping Centers reported that one-third of the centers scheduled for completion in 1976 with less than 100,000 square feet of GLA would be served by mass transit, typically bus, and that 10 percent of their customers were expected to use mass transit for access. The percentage of regional centers served by some form of mass transit is probably quite high, although ICSC reports that the percentage is lower than for smaller centers.[8] As regional centers evolve toward a role as urban subcenters, they become logical destination and transfer points for expanded transit systems. A gradual change will take place in the modes of transportation shoppers use to get to shopping centers, with more shoppers arriving by mass transit and fewer by automobile.

Public transportation service available to shopping centers will certainly be a more important factor in future site location, planning, and circulation design. To the extent that governments set requirements for transit availability or transit connections, development budgets may need to include funds to provide physical facilities for transit access and, in some instances, connecting feeder systems.

With a shift in emphasis toward mass transit, planned highway construction may be considerably delayed, reducing a center's accessibility from both present and future trade areas. It should also be noted that the introduction of publicly owned mass transit systems in densely populated areas may reduce out-migration and increase the economic potential for modernizing, expanding, or modifying the tenant mix and services of existing centers, particularly those within central areas.

Even if a significant shift in modes of transportation begins, the automobile will continue to be the primary means of transportation.

Financing Trends

Availability of investment capital and the cost of borrowing money will continue to be worrisome to the shopping center industry. High interest rates and periodic shortages of investment capital complicate the process of creating new centers and refurbishing older ones.

In the world of real estate finance, nearly all money lenders and investors look upon shopping centers as desirable investments. Shopping centers provide not only diversification of risk but also a high probability of mortgage amortization from continued income flow through lease devices which protect against inflation and against increases in operating expenses and taxes. If the high rate of inflation continues, long-term fixed loan rates will of necessity rise in response to the reduced value of future interest payments. If inflation rates continue to be high, or if they should even accelerate, we may see variable or sliding scale interest rates—such as those already used in Europe—being proposed by lenders as a more inflation-proof basis for long-term financing. Variable rates on residential loans of 20 to 30 years are already used in some areas of the United States by savings and loan associations not under federal control, but a more probable change in general financing arrangements will be the increased joint venture participation of lenders or the establishment of shorter maturities for major loans.

Like most commodities, money becomes more expensive when demand exceeds supply. This fact explains why investors, under tight money circumstances, can demand and get 9 to 12 percent when they invest in long-term debentures. Many shopping centers have leases of 20 to 25 years for key tenants, generally at the insistence of the financial institution. This has been a requirement or at least an aid in obtaining the permanent loan. It has been pointed out that shorter leases may be more often given to prime tenants and that money lenders are more flexible than is generally believed. But in any case, long-term leases tend to have relatively fixed and predetermined rents as a key feature. If variable interest rate, long-term financing were used under these circumstances, and if, after 5 years, for example, the owner were required to pay 12 percent on his mortgage instead of the 9 percent or so committed to at the time

---

[8] See "Strong Expansion Pattern Indicated," *ICSC Newsletter,* March 1976.

the center was built, he could easily face a negative cash flow. If variable interest rates are used in real estate financing, an answer to the borrower's dilemma will be found by a change in lease terms to require the tenant to pay a minimum rent that is tied to the interest rate paid by the landlord on a long-term mortgage. As the landlord meets interest rate adjustments every few years, the rent scale would slide up or down accordingly. There is precedent for such a change to meet variable interest rates, namely, the present lease clauses which specify rent payment adjustments according to changes in real estate taxes and operating expenses. The result would be an inflation-safe system for income flow to the developer. At the same time, all the burden of inflation would be borne by the tenants, possibly making occupancy prohibitively expensive. And at any rate, key tenants would vigorously resist such an arrangement.[9]

Meeting Future Needs

From the mix of influences that might affect the future of shopping center development, certain trends are already foreseeable. There will be a greater emphasis on maintaining the vitality and market of existing centers; small regional centers may appear in nonmetropolitan areas; there will be opportunities for community centers on well-located, bypassed sites in suburban areas; retail revival downtown, already apparent in many cities, can be expected to increase, often in the form of mixed use developments (MXDs), in which the shopping center development is part of a larger effort to integrate a variety of related uses into a single development.[10]

Renovation and Expansion

At today's cost levels for new shopping center construction, it makes good economic sense to begin to think in terms of "recycling" existing centers. In many cases, the developer can refinance these centers at market values significantly higher than their original base, especially in those trading areas where the market demand has been increasing and can be expected to continue to increase, thereby creating an opportunity for the developer to upgrade the tenant mix and to alter the amount of space each tenant occupies.[11]

The central aim of shopping center renovation will be to upgrade the facilities to strengthen the customer appeal by keeping merchandising in step with changing circumstances. It will be necessary for the owner to bring the architecture and general appearance to a level of taste that will appeal to the shopper. Where practical, a mall enclosure will be part of the renovation.

Where older centers are modified, attention will be focused on new storefronts, uniform, well-placed signing, and amenities such as well-maintained landscaping to provide a new image for the center. Reconstruction will also concentrate on energy conservation—minimizing heat transfer through increased use of insulation, thermal glass, and modifications in lighting and HVAC systems.

Large stores in older centers can be subdivided into a number of smaller spaces in order to increase productivity of sales spaces and to offer a greater variety of retail goods.

On-site parking, circulation, and access will be reexamined and improved where necessary. Unneeded parking space will be used for additional stores or for on-site, nonretailing facilities such as commercial recreation, offices, or municipal or social services. This diversity of use strengthens the center as a focal point of community activity. Converting parking lots to more intensive use is particularly feasible where the center benefits from access to mass transit, an arrangement which will become more common in the future. Multiuse developments are practical, and the conversion or expansion of existing centers to multiple use is likely.

As with so many aspects of development, there are no hard and fast rules governing the remodeling, renovation, and expansion of shopping centers. There is no formula for determining the time, cost, and scope of a remodeling job; no way to predict the increase (if any) in tenant sales which will result from expansion; and no step-by-step method of planning, designing, and constructing a center renovation. The absence of formal guidelines, however, does not mean that shopping center revitalization is a totally uncharted area. The following suggestions may help the developer plan a successful shopping center renovation.

- The anticipated program should be defined. The term *renovation* is used to encompass a number of activities, including mall enclosure, department store additions, expansion of the

[9] See Roy P. Drachman, "Make the Arithmetic of Shopping Centers Work," *Buildings*, Vol. 70, No. 5 (May 1976).

[10] See Robert E. Witherspoon, Jon P. Abbett, and Robert M. Gladstone, *Mixed-Use Developments: New Ways of Land Use*, ULI Technical Bulletin 71 (Washington, D.C.: ULI–the Urban Land Institute, 1976).

[11] William J. Harbeck, as quoted in *The Next 15 Years*, p. 95.

7-6 Before—an abandoned discount store and warehouse of the "plain pipe rack" era.

7-7 After—the clearly obsolete buildings in Bellevue, Washington, have been converted into an attractive neighborhood center, Evergreen Village.

mall shop area, and interior or exterior remodeling. Before the developer begins any of these activities, he must identify and undertake only those that are economically and physically feasible.

- A strong leasing team must be assembled. By using experienced personnel on the project, the developer will be able to know the expansion plans and location criteria of department stores, major chains, and franchising groups. This information can be the foundation of a renovation program.
- The tenant leases should be rewritten. It is crucially important to begin a program of modifying leases as they come up for renewal, and to deal specifically with larger tenants as

soon as possible. New leases should address remodeling mall-side storefronts, giving up an existing rear entrance, loss of exterior signing, higher pro rata common area maintenance fees, and whatever else is necessary. In a mature regional center, it may take 5 to 10 years or more for a large proportion of tenant leases to turn over, and it can take several years to pull together the research studies, financing, governmental reviews, major tenant approvals, architectural plans, and construction. It is costly and frustrating to be well into construction and then discover the lack of muscle to require the modifications that make for a smooth and profitable operation of the renovated center. In addition, as part of the tenant relations program, a developer may need to assemble market studies and other data to show the tenants that their increased cost may be more than offset by increased traffic and revenues—now and for years to come.

- The center's trade area should be evaluated. If a center was built before 1965, the size and character of its trade area may well have changed. Planning for the center would have begun in the early sixties; tenant mix, physical layout, and architectural style were all based on contemporary examples of the time. But things have changed since then, and the shopping centers of some 15 years ago may not now be in a strong competitive position. An economic or marketing consultant can examine and compare the present demographics of the trade area with the original statistics. If there has been a change, the renovation can be directed toward meeting the consumer demands of the new market.

- New revenue-producing space should be identified. When the first shopping centers were developed in the suburbs, the efficient use of space was not nearly so important as it is with today's higher costs of land, construction, and building maintenance. Early open malls were usually considerably wider than necessary for good circulation. At many renovated centers, including Lenox Square in Atlanta, Coronado Center in Albuquerque, and the Colonnade in Phoenix, there were many opportunities to convert non-revenue-producing space into high-volume shops as part of store expansions. In addition, tenant shops can be extended into malls that are too wide. While many of the earlier open malls, for example, are as wide as 60 to 80 feet and decorated with planted medians, current thinking calls for mall widths of 30 to 40 feet. Blank department store walls can also be lined with small, high-rent "wall shops." This was done successfully at Lenox Square and at South Shore Mall on Long Island. Still another method of creating new leasable area is to reconfigure tenant spaces to produce new high-traffic malls leading to a new department store or parking structure. This redivision of space can be one of the most important elements in a renovation project.

One center where new tenant space was created from old shop areas is Anaheim Plaza in Anaheim, California. Called Anaheim Center when it opened in 1957, this shopping center had two department stores, 31 shops, and an open mall. Tenants were paying an average of $3.11 per square foot. By 1970, the owners of the center felt that action would be needed to strengthen the center's merchandising mix and to improve its appearance. Ernest W. Hahn, Inc., was brought in to study the options available for conversion, to make recommendations, and to prepare a budget. The cost of enclosing the mall, building new tenant shops, and modernizing the interior storefronts and the exterior building design was estimated at $4.3 million. In a little under a year, the work was completed. There are still two department stores and the amount of new tenant space has only increased by 3,000 square feet. The real gain, however, was in the number of tenant shops, which has more than doubled, from 31 to 64. The average rent per square foot has doubled. Another such remodeling project was undertaken at the Colonnade in Phoenix. This involved a $6,000,000 expansion of a single-level, two-department-store enclosed center. The major elements of the program were the conversion of a junior department store into a two-level mall occupied by smaller tenants (including an artisans' court and food service facilities on the lower level), the addition of two freestanding buildings, redesign of the mall to reflect a Spanish architectural theme, renovation of the exterior of the center, and the creation of new tenant space by a division of existing space. Again, creation of new space from old space was a critical factor in the success of the renovation project, because it encouraged tenants with too much space to reduce their leased space while allowing others to expand. If enough revenue-producing space is recovered, a significant portion of the remodeling costs can be offset.

- Major additions should be investigated. Probably the best method of improving a center's market position, while offsetting the construction costs associated with remodeling, is the addition of a new department store and more specialty shops. Many major retailers are aggressively seeking positions in new markets and are looking for locations in established regional centers. For example, the decision by Neiman Marcus to locate at Lenox Square was a major factor in that center's expansion and renovation program. The $40 million Coronado Center expansion was possible because of The

RENOVATION—THREE EXAMPLES

This is a brief summary of events surrounding the renovation of three older shopping centers in various parts of the country:

LENOX SQUARE
Atlanta, Georgia

This shopping center opened in 1959 and was consistently the most active retail complex in its trade area.

The original open mall center had a total of 950,000 square feet of store area, including two department stores—Rich's and Davison-Paxon.

In 1971, three nearby regional centers opened, prompting the management of Lenox Square to examine enclosure and expansion.

The renovation program included the construction of a new anchor, Neiman Marcus, and 50,000 square feet of shops connecting the old mall to the new store; the enclosure of the existing open mall, highlighted by skylights, new lighting fixtures, and interior landscaping; two new parking structures to maintain the original parking ratio; and 15,000 square feet of "wall shops" added along the existing mall.

The renovation program added numerous quality specialty shop tenants, many of whom had wanted to lease space in Lenox Square for some time; created a more attractive and comfortable shopping environment; and upgraded most tenant storefronts. The average rent increase for renovated stores has been only 15 to 25 percent, and the bulk of the leases are still due for renewal.

WEST COVINA FASHION PLAZA
West Covina, California

West Covina Plaza opened in 1955 and consisted of some loosely knit freestanding and strip commercial structures, including a 200,-000 square foot Broadway. Fashion Plaza was really the central business district of West Covina.

The city had economic studies prepared in 1965 and 1971 which indicated that unless the center were expanded and modernized, downtown West Covina could become obsolete. Of particular concern was a new regional center outside the city that could siphon off shoppers.

A redevelopment agency was formed so that the city government could assist the developer with the renovation. The program included the retention of an existing Broadway department store and three strip commercial structures, while adding two department stores, 375,000 square feet of new tenant shops, a 2,000-car parking structure, and a two-level enclosed mall.

The demolition and relocation programs were scheduled to minimize inconvenience to the tenants; in fact, the J. C. Penney Company, which built a new department store as part of the project, retained its old building until the new one was completed.

CORONADO CENTER
Albuquerque, New Mexico

This open mall center started operating in 1956 with two department stores and 30 mall shops, encompassing a total of 400,000 square feet. Coronado Center was purchased from Homart, the original developer, by the Ernest W. Hahn firm in 1973, and investigation of expansion opportunities began immediately.

The renovation program involved two phases: first, a remodeling of the existing center, including enclosing the mall and increasing the tenant shop area by 20 percent through the creation of 11 "wall shops" projected into the old open mall area; second, the addition of three new department stores (two are now open) and construction of 90 new shops, all within a new two-level enclosed mall.

The renovated and expanded center now has 975,000 square feet of retail space.

7-9 While enclosure of malls has been a key part of many expansion and renovation programs, such an approach would seem less justified in areas with a pleasant climate the year around. Fashion Island, in southern California, is the largest retail complex on the Irvine Ranch.

Broadway's and Goldwater's desire to join with Sears and Rhodes at their prime Albuquerque site. A developer who is exploring the possibilities of broadening a center's merchandising mix and strengthening its market position might consider the addition of an interested mass merchandiser in a center with only full-service or high-fashion department stores, or vice versa. This was done at Mission Valley Center in San Diego, where a high-fashion Bullock's store was added to an existing May Company–Montgomery Ward complex. Conversely, at Sherman Oaks Fashion Square, in California, a Broadway store filled out the merchandise range of the existing Bullock's store. Of course, a study of the market area demographics may be necessary to justify such moves.

• A mall should be enclosed only if it makes sense. A market study will indicate factors which do and do not favor mall enclosure. The main issue is that of competition, both present and potential, and it comes down to this question: How secure is the center's share of the market? This is not an easy question in the face of the cost of a new enclosed mall, yet some developers have reported gross sales increases of 50 percent, simply as a result of mall enclosure and the addition of new storefronts, climate control, landscaping, and other aesthetics that are common ingredients in such programs. If, in a mild climate, the lack of competition and the local economics indicate that there is no need for enclosure, the mall should not be enclosed. For example, two sizable open mall additions have been undertaken recently in southern California, adding department stores and 60,000 square feet of tenant shops, respectively, to open mall centers that had well-established market positions, even though one department store (Bullock's, at Mission Valley) usually prefers to be in enclosed mall centers. Both Santa Ana Fashion Square and the Sherman Oaks Fashion Square are being expanded with additional major tenants, more developer GLA, and other improvements, but they will remain open because of the developer's preference for open malls.

- Parking changes and other site modifications should be examined. The developer will need to know whether the available land can support parking for the additional commercial area. Some questions a developer should ask: Will it make sense to spend the minimum $2,300 to $3,000 per space required to build structured parking? How much new parking will be needed? What is the best configuration? What does the local government want? Have any code requirements changed? Will the local or state government assist with funds for new parking construction? Many older centers have existing parking ratios in excess of 6.0 cars per 1,000 square feet of commercial area. Newer centers reflect developer and department store policies of 5 or 5.5 spaces per 1,000 square feet, and some current CBD redevelopments are as low as 4.0 per 1,000. The subject of parking is one of the first feasibility items a developer needs to consider.

- Zoning and planning approvals should be investigated and secured early in the process. Planning and other approvals from government agencies are no longer as routine as they were when most present candidates for renovation were built. In some cases, a proposed project may face greater restrictions on height and setback. In others, if a new department store and shops are considered for expansion into areas zoned exclusively for parking, the preparation of an environmental impact statement may be required. Building codes and utility and landscape requirements in the area will probably have also changed in the last 5 to 15 years, and these factors must be taken into consideration.

- The center should be kept fully operational during construction. It is not necessary to lose sales during remodeling; construction can be planned to minimize interference with foot traffic. The shopping center management, by creating a series of promotional events to take place during the period of enclosure or expansion, can keep shoppers coming to the center and can stimulate customers' interest and cooperation by giving them a sense of participation. The open, visible acknowledgment of construction activity is now a frequent practice in shopping center renovations and often results in increased mall traffic and sales.

In summary, there are at least four advantages a developer can capitalize on in renovating an existing shopping center:

- A very good to superior location.
- An established identity among shoppers.
- Fewer zoning, environmental, and permit problems.
- Lower average costs and mortgage rates than are typical of new construction.

New Shopping Centers

Slow growth in the suburbs will reduce the opportunities for new shopping centers. If current trends in suburban growth continue, then after 1980 the opportunity for new suburban centers will arise only in especially advantageous locations, such as areas where a gap is left between the trade areas of existing centers, or where unusual conditions call for specialized shopping center development. Longer development times, higher construction costs, and greater restriction on land use by environmental regulations and local land use controls will tend to diminish the feasibility of new center development but will reinforce the position of existing centers, as suggested earlier.

It will be increasingly difficult to build superregional centers. Higher predevelopment and construction costs will require higher rent payments from tenants. Financing criteria and permit approvals will also be more difficult to satisfy. It will be essential to keep the small independent local merchants in business and to encourage their entering the shopping center field. National merchants will be more cautious about new investments where a long-term market future is unclear. While they will be willing to participate in new centers with good evidence of quality and high potential sales volumes, their reluctance to expand in less sure circumstances may plague the industry for some time.

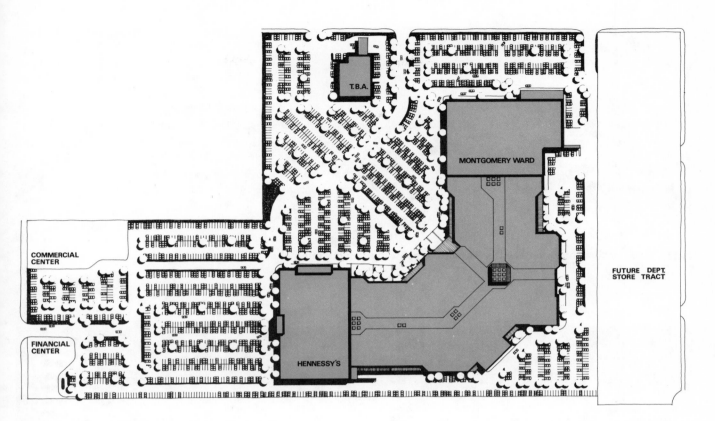

7-10 Site plan—Rimrock Mall, Billings, Montana.

Smaller regional centers designed to function in the same manner as the large regionals, by virtue of their multiple full-line department store tenantry, will account for an increasing share of the total shopping center development business. The smaller centers will be designed for bypassed sites and the unserved markets of lightly populated regions surrounding small cities where customers are drawn from vast distances. An example of this type of center is Rimrock Mall in Billings, Montana. The wide market area, which extends into 23 counties and portions of three states, has a total population of 275,000. Some of the special operational requirements that have been identified at Rimrock include a very high Saturday shopping peak, a high demand for food and food service, and a high demand for public restrooms and waiting rooms. The center in effect has replaced Billings' Main Street as a gathering place for the ranchers and farmers in the surrounding area on their periodic visits to "town." [12]

The smaller center of the future will be less monumental in design. Interior and exterior finishes of walls, ceilings, and floors will be carefully chosen to allow lower costs without significantly reducing aesthetics or maintainability. Air conditioning and heating tolerances will be broadened by a few degrees to reduce equipment installation, operating costs, and use of energy. Simplified lighting will be used, with lower level lighting in the mall but with heightened lighting at the storefronts to attract shoppers to the merchandise displays. These new centers will typically have lower actual traffic counts than customary today, but the sales volumes will be satisfactory because people will spend more per trip. Because of distances shoppers will travel, they will stay longer at the center. Hence such centers' need for good food service and restrooms.

It will take less time to develop these mid-market centers. But the time differential is difficult to quantify because of regional variables in permitting procedures. Nevertheless, these smaller, mid-market centers, enclosed and weather-conditioned, will probably be the greatest focus of development activity in the near future.

[12] See Eric Peterson, "Trend to Smaller Centers: They're Less Complicated, Cheaper, Faster to Build," *Shopping Center World*, Vol. 5, No. 3 (April 1976).

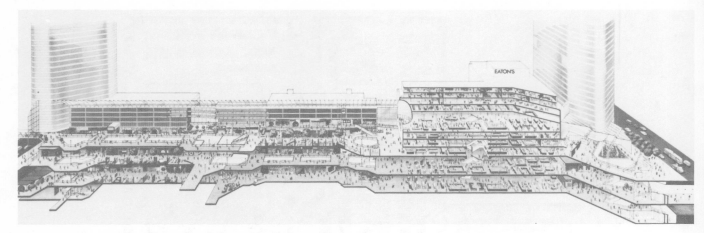

7-11 Cross section of Eaton Centre, Toronto, graphically depicts internal spatial relationships.

7-12 Eaton Centre under construction in August 1976. The first phase of this important CBD development includes a million-square-foot Eaton's store, a 26-story office building, and a multilevel, glass-covered retail mall.

Centers in CBDs

Central areas of large cities are once again becoming desirable locations for major building projects. Most noteworthy in this respect has been the evolution of MXDs—large-scale, high-density urban projects characterized by physical integration of mutually supportive land uses.[13] Between 1965 and 1975, mixed use developments began to transform the skylines of many North American cities. Retail is one of four key project components typically found in MXDs; the others are office, hotel-motel, and residential uses. Both office and retail functions appear with equal frequency, although office uses tend to dominate most such projects in terms of square footage. In several projects, most notably The Galleria in Houston, the retail use is the centerpiece of the MXD. The more common arrangement, however, is for retail to fulfill a supportive function, even though it is still a significant revenue-producing use.

The downtown shopping center without all the elements of an MXD is also a new form of CBD revitalization. Such projects, which accounted for more than 10 percent of the centers opened in 1976, are characterized by the introduction of suburban shopping center design techniques into the high-density CBD environment. This approach affords great promise for broadly based downtown revival. Two projects illustrate the point. One is The Gallery at Market East, in Philadelphia, where a 215,000 square foot multilevel retail mall is being built to connect Strawbridge and Clothier's flagship store with a new 500,000 square foot Gimbels department store. The Rouse Company, developers of The Gallery, report that it will open in mid-1977. Another example is Eaton Centre, Toronto, where Cadillac Fairview is building a 1 million square foot Eaton's store at the opposite end of a three-level, multiblock, enclosed shopping mall from an existing Simpson's store. The project occupies a strategically located 14.5-acre downtown site with direct subway access at two points. Two office towers are also part of Eaton Centre, scheduled to open during 1977.

Other evidence of retail revival downtown includes the replacement of obsolete department stores with modern construction, and the remodeling and renovation of older flagship stores to maintain their economic health.

In smaller cities, downtown often remains an active commercial center. In such cities, there are opportunities for merchandising in a trade area still having a downtown focus, one that has not been fragmented by the development of suburban shopping centers. Such communities tend to be homogeneous, and social conflicts are absent. Buses provide mass transportation, utilities are in place, and environmental problems are rarely complex. Zoning is established, and a market exists. These advantages allow a downtown shopping center to be feasible in many cities. A good example of such a situation is Courthouse Center in Columbus, Indiana, where the community developed a 113,000 square foot retail mall, anchored by a Sears department store, a block from the Bartholomew County courthouse, which remains the visible focal point of community life.

For weaker retail districts, the principles of suburban shopping center development can still be applied, but with important differences. Close cooperation will be required among the participants in the development process, including the city, special authorities, the developer and his team of consultants, and prospective tenants. Retail malls incorporating multiple uses can be expected to spark other downtown revitalization. However, a legal framework which permits redevelopment is essential. Progressive redevelopment enabling acts have already been passed in California, Utah, Missouri, Oregon, Minnesota, and Ohio.

Among the best of these laws is the one in California, which grants cities the power of eminent domain and authority to issue tax increment bonds, which are retired by the increased taxability of the new development. One of the early examples of the use of this tool to create a new shopping center was Central City Mall in San Bernardino, California, opened in 1972.[14] As mentioned in the discussion of Hawthorne Plaza in Chapter 6, the California Community Redevelopment Law is designed to promote revitalization of blighted urban areas through a partnership of public and private interests, including "planning, redevelopment, replanning, redesign, clearance, reconstruction or rehabilitation or any combination of these as may be appropriate or necessary in the interest of the general welfare." The law allows developers to purchase inner city land at prices competitive with

---

[13] See *Mixed-Use Developments* (footnote 10 above). Also see Louis G. Redstone, *The New Downtowns: Rebuilding Business Districts* (New York: McGraw-Hill, 1976).

[14] See "Central City Mall," *Project Reference File*, Vol. 3, No. 9 (April–June 1973).

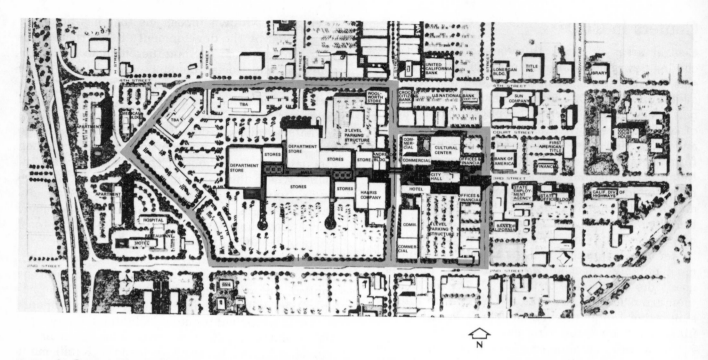

N

7-13 At Central City Mall in San Bernardino, California, a new suburban-style, two-level shopping center has been joined to another super-block where a new city hall is the central focus. In this unique project, the covered mall and both structured and unstructured parking areas are owned by the city. Only the store sites were sold to the developer.

suburban locations. Eminent domain is used to buy the identified properties at fair market value, and to pay for relocation and redevelopment through tax anticipation bonds and tax increment financing.[15]

In addition to public-private cooperation through enabling legislation for financing retail redevelopment, such centers will require a change in the traditional suburban shopping center configuration. These changes are already apparent in a number of centers on sites of 30 acres and often much less: different orientation to streets; subterranean or multideck parking structures, with extensive use of ramps, bridges, escalators, and other systems for moving people from their cars to the department stores and mall shops. Unusual mall patterns and multilevel malls will be used to adapt the facilities to the limited site and its structure. Vertical, two-level malls and two or three-level department stores will require ingenuity in design for compatibility with an urban scene and the community atmosphere.

New urban retail developments will be limited but, as developers break away from past formulas and, with extensive cooperation from government, move toward the implementation of new center design, they will be responding effectively to the needs of cities and their commercial cores. The key requirement will be a greater willingness by government, retailers, developers, and the public to change traditional attitudes and set the stage for future actions that will make the new urban centers work.

In the future, more than ever before, the shopping center development industry will be a highly sophisticated business with little room for error and with a high degree of emphasis on professionalism.

---

[15] See Russell Keith Peterson, "Development of Retail Facilities in Redevelopment Project Areas," a report issued by Charles Kober Associates, Los Angeles.

APPENDICES
AND
INDEX

APPENDIX A

Selected References & Information Sources

Books

Applebaum, William. *Shopping Center Strategy: A Case Study of the Planning, Location, and Development of the Del Monte Center, Monterey, California.* New York: International Council of Shopping Centers, 1970.

—— and S. O. Kaylin. *Case Studies in Shopping Center Development and Operation.* New York: International Council of Shopping Centers, 1974.

Balachandran, M. *Malls and Shopping Centers: A Selected Bibliography (1970-1975).* Exchange Bibliography no. 1123. Monticello, Illinois: Council of Planning Librarians, 1976.

Bell, Curtis C. *Shopping Center Development Guide.* Washington: National Association of Home Builders, 1975.

Callahan, William W. *Shopping Center Promotions: A Handbook for Promotion Directors.* New York: International Council of Shopping Centers, 1972.

Carpenter, Horace, Jr. *Shopping Center Management. Principles and Practices.* New York: International Council of Shopping Centers, 1974.

Garrett, Robert L., Hunter A. Hogan, Jr., and Robert M. Stratton. *The Valuation of Shopping Centers.* Philadelphia: Ballinger Publishing Co., 1976.

Gruen, Victor, and Larry Smith. *Centers for the Urban Environment: Survival of the Cities.* New York: Van Nostrand Reinhold, 1973.

——. *Shopping Towns USA.* New York: Reinhold, 1960.

Hornbeck, James S., ed. *Stores and Shopping Centers.* New York: McGraw-Hill, 1962.

International Council of Shopping Centers. *Enclosed Mall Shopping Centers.* New York: International Council of Shopping Centers, 1965.

——. *Shopping Centers: The Next 15 Years.* New York: International Council of Shopping Centers, 1975.

Levin, Michael S. *Measuring the Fiscal Impact of a Shopping Center on Its Community.* New York: International Council of Shopping Centers, 1975.

Lion, Edgar. *Shopping Centers: Planning, Development and Administration.* New York: John Wiley & Sons, 1976.

McKeever, J. Ross. *Shopping Center Zoning.* Technical Bulletin 69. Washington: Urban Land Institute, 1973.

Nelson, Richard L. *The Selection of Retail Locations.* New York: McGraw-Hill, 1966.

Nyburg, Robert S. *Shopping Center Merchants Associations.* New York: International Council of Shopping Centers, 1959.

Practicing Law Institute. *Shopping Centers 1976.* New York: Practicing Law Institute, 1976.

Rams, Edwin M., ed. *Analysis and Valuation of Retail Location.* Reston, Virginia: Reston Publishing Company, 1976.

Redstone, Louis G. *New Dimensions in Shopping Centers and Stores.* New York: McGraw-Hill, 1973.

——. *The New Downtowns: Rebuilding Business Districts.* New York: McGraw-Hill, 1976.

Telchin, Charles S. *How to Improve Developer/Tenant Planning and Construction Coordination.* New York: International Council of Shopping Centers, 1977.

Touche Ross & Co. *Depreciable Lives of Shopping Centers.* New York: International Council of Shopping Centers, 1973.

Urban Land Institute. *Parking Requirements for Shopping Centers.* Technical Bulletin 53. Washington: Urban Land Institute, 1965.

——. *Standard Manual of Accounting for Shopping Center Operations.* Washington: Urban Land Institute, 1971.

Periodicals

Appraisal Journal (quarterly). American Institute of Real Estate Appraisers, 430 North Michigan Avenue, Chicago, Illinois 60611.

Chain Store Age Executive (monthly). Lebhar-Friedman, Inc., 425 Park Avenue, New York, New York 10022.

Directory of Shopping Centers in the United States and Canada (annual, with quarterly updates). National Research Bureau, 424 North Third Street, Burlington, Iowa 52601. The 17th edition, 1976, was issued in five separate sections: Eastern States, Midwestern States, Southern States, Western States, and Canada.

Dollars and Cents of Shopping Centers (triennial, 6th edition 1975). Urban Land Institute, 1200 18th Street, N.W., Washington, D.C. 20036.

Downtown Idea Exchange (twice monthly). Downtown Research and Development Center, 555 Madison Avenue, New York, New York 10022.

ICSC Newsletter (monthly). International Council of Shopping Centers, 445 Park Avenue, New York, New York 10022.

National Mall Monitor (bimonthly). National Mall Monitor, One Cherry Hill, Suite 806, Cherry Hill, New Jersey 08034.

Percentage Leases (Commercial Rental Survey, irregular; 13th edition 1973, 14th edition scheduled for 1977). Realtors National Marketing Institute, 430 North Michigan, Chicago, Illinois 60611.

Shopping Center Leasing Opportunities (annual). International Council of Shopping Centers, 445 Park Avenue, New York, New York 10022.

Shopping Center World (monthly). Communication Channels, Inc., 461 Eighth Avenue, New York, New York 10001.

Stores (monthly). National Retail Merchants Association, Inc., 100 West 31st Street, New York, New York 10001.

Survey of Buying Power (annual). Sales and Marketing Management, 633 Third Avenue, New York, New York 10017.

Urban Land (monthly). Urban Land Institute, 1200 18th Street, N.W., Washington, D.C. 20036.

U.S. Bureau of the Census Reports:
Census of Business—taken every five years (years ending in 2 and 7). Covers establishments in retail trade, wholesale trade, and selected service industries.
Current Business Reports: Retail Trade. A number of separate reports are issued:
Weekly Retail Sales
Advance Monthly Retail Sales
Monthly Department Store Sales in Selected Areas
Final Weekly Sales Estimates
Monthly Retail Trade
Annual Report, Retail Trade
Current Economic Reports: County Business Patterns (annual, issued in separate reports by state).

Organizations

Downtown Research and
Development Center
555 Madison Avenue
New York, New York 10022

International Council
of Shopping Centers
665 5th Avenue
New York, New York 10022

National Retail Merchants
Association, Inc.
100 West 31st Street
New York, New York 10001

Urban Land Institute
1200 18th Street, N.W.
Washington, D.C. 20036

APPENDIX B

TENANT CLASSIFICATIONS

Categories from Dollars and Cents of Shopping Centers: 1978; code
numbers from Dollars and Cents: 1978 and from the
Standard Industrial Classification (SIC) Manual

TENANT CATEGORY	$ & ¢ CODE	SIC CODE	TENANT CATEGORY	$ & ¢ CODE	SIC CODE
GENERAL MERCHANDISE			Art gallery	M-03	5999
Department store	A-01	5311	Cameras	M-04	5946
Junior department store	A-02	5311	Toys	M-05	5945
Variety store	A-03	5311	Bike shop	M-06	5941
Discount department store	A-04	5311	Arts and crafts	M-07	5999
Showroom catalog store	A-05	5399	**GIFTS/SPECIALTY**		
FOOD			Imports	N-01	5999
Supermarket	B-01	5411	Luggage and leather	N-02	5948
Convenience market	B-02	5411	Cards and gifts	N-03	5947
Meat, poultry, fish	B-03	5423	Candles	N-04	5999
Specialty food	B-04	5499	Books and stationery	N-05	5942/3
Delicatessen	B-05	5411	**JEWELRY AND COSMETICS**		
Bakery	B-06	5463	Credit jewelry	P-01	5944
Candy, nuts	B-07	5441	Costume jewelry	P-02	5999
Dairy products	B-08	5451	Jewelry	P-03	5944
Health food	B-09	5499	Cosmetics	P-04	5999
FOOD SERVICE			**LIQUOR**		
Restaurant without liquor	C-01	5812	Liquor and wine	Q-01	5921
Restaurant with liquor	C-02	5812	Wine and cheese	Q-02	5921/5451
Cafeteria	C-03	5812	**DRUGS**		
Fast-food/carryout	C-04	5812	Super-drug (over 10,000 sq. ft.)	R-01	5912
Cocktail lounge	C-05	5813	Drug	R-02	5912
Doughnut shop	C-06	5812	**OTHER RETAIL**		
Ice cream parlor	C-07	5812	Yard goods	S-01	5949
Yogurt store	C-08	5812	Tobacco	S-02	5993
Pretzel shop	C-09	5812	Pet shop	S-03	5999
CLOTHING			Flowers	S-04	5992
Ladies' specialty	D-01	5631	Plant store	S-05	5992
Ladies' ready-to-wear	D-02	5621	Other retail	S-06	5999
Bridal shop	D-03	5621	**PERSONAL SERVICES**		
Maternity	D-04	5621	Beauty	T-01	7231
Hosiery	D-05	5631	Barber	T-02	7241
Millinery	D-06	5631	Shoe repair	T-03	7251
Children's wear	D-07	5641	Cleaner and dyer	T-04	7212
Menswear	D-08	5611	Laundry	T-05	7212
Family wear	D-09	5651	Figure salon	T-06	7299
Furs	D-10	5681	Photographer	T-07	7221
Unisex/jean shop	D-11	5699	Formal wear/rental	T-08	7299
Leather shop	D-12	5699	Interior decorator	T-09	7399
SHOES			Travel agent	T-10	4722
Family shoe	E-01	5661	Key shop	T-11	7699
Ladies' shoe	E-02	5661	**RECREATION/COMMUNITY**		
Men's and boys' shoe	E-03	5661	Post office	W-01	7399
Children's shoe	E-04	5661	Music studios and dance	W-02	7911/8299
HOME FURNISHINGS			Bowling alley	W-03	7933
Furniture	F-01	5712	Cinemas	W-04	7832
Lamps	F-02	5719	Ice/roller skating	W-05	7999
Floor coverings	F-03	5713	Community hall	W-06	—
Curtains and drapes	F-04	5714	Arcade, amusement	W-07	7993
Upholstering	F-05	5714	Day care and nursery	W-08	8351
China and glassware	F-06	5719	**FINANCIAL**		
HOME APPLIANCES/MUSIC			Bank	X-01	602
Appliances	G-01	5722	Savings and Loan	X-02	612
Radio, TV, hi-fi	G-02	5732	Finance company	X-03	6145
Sewing machines	G-03	5722	Small loans	X-04	6145
Records and tapes	G-04	5733	Brokerage	X-05	6211
Musical instruments	G-05	5733	Insurance	X-06	63
BUILDING MATERIALS/GARDEN			Real estate	X-07	6531
Garden	H-01	5261	**OFFICE (other than financial)**		
Paint and wallpaper	H-02	5231	Optometrist	Y-01	8042
Hardware	H-03	5251	Medical and dental	Y-02	8011/8021/8031
Home improvements	H-04	5211	Legal	Y-03	8111
AUTOMOTIVE SUPPLIES/SERVICE STATION			Accounting	Y-04	8131
Automotive (TBA)	K-01	5531	Architect	Y-05	8911
Auto dealer	K-02	5511	Employment agency	Y-06	7361
Service station	K-03	5541	Other office	Y-07	—
Car wash	K-04	7542	**OTHER**		
Cycle shop	K-05	5571	Vacant space	Z-01	—
HOBBY/SPECIAL INTEREST			Miscellaneous income	Z-02	—
Sporting goods	M-01	5941	Warehouse	Z-03	4225
Hobby	M-02	5945			

APPENDIX C

Sample Lease Agreement

Note: This document is presented to suggest the detail and complexity of typical lease agreements. Its use is neither endorsed nor recommended; on the contrary, its duplication in any form is specifically prohibited under the terms of the copyright covering this publication. Each shopping center developer must look to his own legal counsel to devise appropriate legal documents for the particular center under consideration.

CONTENTS

LEASE AGREEMENT

THIS LEASE AGREEMENT (hereinafter called "Lease") made as of the ____ day of _____, 19____, by and between:

(hereinafter called "Landlord"); and_____

_____

(hereinafter called "Tenant").

WITNESSETH

FOR AND IN CONSIDERATION OF the sum of One Dollar ($1.00) in hand paid by each of the parties to the other, and other good and valuable consideration, receipt and sufficiency of which is hereby acknowledged, the parties agree as follows:

DATA SHEET

(1) PREMISES: That area outlined in red on Exhibit A-2 hereto, and further described as approximately _____ square feet.

(2) TERM: ____ years ____ months and ____ days, but in no event ending later than _____.

(3) PERMITTED USE: The Premises shall be used by the Tenant solely for the display and sale:

(4) TENANT NAME: Tenant shall operate and do business in the Premises, and all signs and advertising shall be under the trade name _____

(5) TOTAL ANNUAL MINIMUM RENT: $_____ payable in twelve (12) equal monthly installments of $_____.

(6) ANNUAL BASE ELECTRICAL COST: $_____ included in (5) above.

(7) PERCENTAGE RENT:

(8) CONSTRUCTION AND FIXTURING DAYS: _____.

(9) Notice Address for Landlord: Tenant:

(10) RADIUS CLAUSE: ____ Miles ____ Years.

The exhibits listed below are incorporated in this Lease by this reference and are to be construed as part of this Lease:

Exhibit A consisting of:

A-1—Site Plan
A-2—Shopping Center Building
A-3—Premises
Exhibit B—Description of Landlord's Work and Tenant's Work.
Exhibit C—Architectural Standards.

ARTICLE 1: PREMISES

Landlord hereby leases to Tenant and Tenant hereby leases from Landlord, subject to and with the benefit of the terms, covenants, conditions and provisions of this Lease, the Premises, extending to the center line of the party walls and to the exterior faces of all other walls, situated within the Shopping Center Tract. The Premises are as shown outlined in red on Exhibit A-2, together with the appurtenances specifically granted in this Lease, but reserving and excepting to Landlord the use of the exterior walls (other than store fronts), the roof and the right to install, maintain, use, repair and replace pipes, ducts, conduits, wires and appurtenant fixtures leading through the Premises in locations which will not materially interfere with Tenant's use thereof. The Premises are located on a tract of land owned by Landlord as shown on Exhibit A-1 (hereinafter called "Shopping Center Tract"). The "Shopping Center Tract" together with adjacent tracts of land owned by others which may be developed as department stores as shown on Exhibit A-1 shall constitute the "Shopping Center."

Tenant is also granted the right of non-exclusive use, in common with others, of the automobile parking areas and other Common Areas (as hereinafter defined) from time to time existing within the Shopping Center described in this Lease.

After the commencement date of the Term has been established, Landlord shall furnish to Tenant a written statement in recordable form specifying the commencement date, the termination date and the actual as-built number of square feet of Gross Leasable Area in the Premises as certified to by Landlord's architect or engineer, the exact amount of the Total Annual Minimum Rent computed thereon and, if there shall have been any change

in Exhibits A-2 or A-3 with respect to the Premises, the same shall be modified to reflect such change. Such statement when so executed by both Landlord and Tenant, shall be deemed to be incorporated in and become a part of this Lease.

ARTICLE 2: LANDLORD WARRANTIES

Landlord hereby warrants that it and no other person, firm or corporation has the right to lease the Premises hereby demised. So long as Tenant shall perform each and every covenant to be performed by Tenant hereunder, Tenant shall have peaceful and quiet use and possession of the Premises without hindrance on the part of Landlord, and Landlord shall defend Tenant in such peaceful and quiet use and possession under Landlord. Tenant's rights under this Lease are and shall always be subordinate to the operation and effect of any mortgage, deed of trust, trust deed, or other security instrument now or hereafter placed upon the Shopping Center Tract, or any part or parts thereof by Landlord. This clause shall be self-operative, and no further instrument of subordination shall be required. In confirmation thereof, Tenant shall execute such further assurances as may be required by Landlord or any person, firm or corporation claiming through, by or under Landlord.

ARTICLE 3: TERM

TO HAVE AND TO HOLD for a Term beginning at the earlier of (a) the expiration of the number of days shown as "Construction and Fixturing Days" on the Data Sheet after Tenant has received written notice from Landlord that the work to be performed by Landlord pursuant to Exhibit B has been substantially completed (hereinafter called the "Delivery Date") or (b) the opening by Tenant of its business in the Premises, and continuing for the Term unless sooner terminated as hereinafter provided. The term "substantially completed" as used herein shall mean that the work to be performed by Landlord pursuant to Exhibit B has been completed with the exception of minor items which can be fully completed prior to completion of Tenant's Work without material interference with Tenant.

ARTICLE 4: IMPROVEMENTS

Performance of Landlord's Work and Approval of Landlord's Work. Landlord shall cause to be performed the work, if any, described in Exhibit B as "Landlord's Work". All such work shall be done in a good and workmanlike manner employing good materials and so as to conform to all governmental requirements. Tenant agrees that Landlord may make any changes in Landlord's Work which may become reasonably necessary or advisable (other than substantial changes), without the written approval of Tenant. A certification from Landlord that Landlord has completed its work shall be binding and conclusive evidence of the completion of Landlord's Work.

Performance of Tenant's Work. Tenant agrees that it will, after receipt from Landlord of notice that Landlord has substantially completed Landlord's Work, proceeding with all reasonable dispatch, perform the work described in Exhibit B as "Tenant's Work" in accordance with the provisions of Exhibit C: Architectural Standards so as to ready the Premises for opening not later than the Grand Opening Date. No work shall be done or fixtures or equipment installed by Tenant (a) without the express prior written approval of Landlord, or (b) thereafter in such manner as to interfere with Landlord or Landlord's other tenants. During the period of occupancy of the Premises by Tenant from the Delivery Date until the commencement date of the Term, no Total Annual Minimum Rent or other charges payable by Tenant shall accrue, but otherwise such occupancy shall be subject to all the terms, covenants and conditions contained in this Lease, including but not limited to insurance and the payment for all utilities, heat, air conditioning, electricity, water, telephone, sanitary sewer, and trash removal. Tenant agrees to employ for such work one or more bondable, responsible contractors whose labor will work in harmony with other labor working in the Shopping Center, and to cause such contractors employed by Tenant to carry Workmen's Compensation Insurance in accordance with statutory requirements and Comprehensive Public Liability Insurance covering such contractors on or about the Premises and Shopping Center in amounts at least equal to the limits set forth in Article 18: Tenant Insurance, and to submit certificates evidencing such coverage to Landlord prior to the commencement of such Tenant Work.

ARTICLE 5: PLANS

Tenant shall prepare, at its sole cost and expense, and in full compliance with the provisions of Exhibits B and C hereof, complete plans and specifications for all Tenant Work, whether original and/or alterations, including store front, signs and/or advertising matter, and shall submit such plans and specifications in accordance with Exhibit C to Landlord, or Landlord's designated representative, for approval prior to commencement of any work.

All such plans and specifications shall meet the requirements of this Lease, and all applicable local, state and federal regulations, rules, codes and ordinances. Tenant agrees that Tenant shall not employ Landlord's general contractor or subcontractors without the express written consent of Landlord first obtained.

ARTICLE 6: USE

Tenant shall occupy the Premises upon the commencement of the Term, and thereafter will continuously conduct in all of the Premises only the business expressly set forth in the Data Sheet, for such hours of operation as shall be determined by Landlord. Tenant shall at all times conduct its business in a reputable manner as a quality establishment in accordance with the standards of the Shopping Center, and shall not conduct any fire, bankruptcy, going out of business or auction sales, either real or fictitious. The Premises shall not be used in such manner that in accordance with any requirement of law or of any public authority, Landlord shall be obliged on account of the purpose or manner of said use to make any addition or alteration to or in the building. All sales from vending machines must be approved in advance in writing by Landlord, other than vending machines for the sole use of Tenant's employees.

Tenant will at all times during the Term of this Lease maintain displays of merchandise in the show windows of the Premises. All articles and the arrangement, style, color and general appearance thereof, in the interior of the Premises which shall be visible from the exterior thereof, including, without limitation, window displays, advertising matter, signs, merchandise and store fixtures, shall be maintained in keeping with the character and standards of the Shopping Center.

ARTICLE 7: RENT

Tenant covenants and agrees to pay to Landlord at the address set out in Article 46 for the payment of rents, or at such other place as Landlord may designate in writing to Tenant, rent at the following rates and times:

A. Total Annual Minimum Rent at the rate set out in the Data Sheet, in advance, on the first day of each calendar month, or part thereof, during the Term. The Total Annual Minimum Rent for any portion of a calendar month at the beginning of or end of the Term shall be proportioned on the basis of 360-day year.

B. Percentage Rent shall be determined and payable quarterly, on or before the fifteenth (15th) day of May, August, November and within thirty (30) days of the conclusion of each Lease Year for the complete Lease Year based on "Gross Sales" (as hereinafter defined) for the preceding three calendar month period or Lease Year, as the case may be, or portion thereof falling within the Term, by dividing the figures set out in Section 7 of the Data Sheet referring to Gross Sales by four (4) (the resultant figure hereinafter called the "Quarterly Percentage Rent") and applying the Percentage Rent percentage found in Section 7 of the Data Sheet to the amount of Gross Sales of the quarter annual period in question which exceeds the Quarterly Percentage Rent. The first payment of Percentage Rent shall include the period, if any, from the date of the commencement of the Term to the first day of the first full calendar month in the first full three calendar month period in the Term. As soon as practicable after the end of each Lease Year (as hereinafter defined) but in no event later than March 1, the Percentage Rent paid or payable for such preceding Lease Year shall be adjusted between Landlord and Tenant, each party hereby agreeing to make such adjustment and to pay to the other, on demand, such amount as may be necessary to effect adjustment to the agreed Percentage Rent.

C. Tax on Rentals. Tenant shall pay, as additional rent, before any fine, penalty, interest or cost may be added thereto for nonpayment, any tax that may be levied, assessed or imposed upon or measured by the rents reserved hereunder or upon a commercial lease by any governmental authority acting under any present or future law.

D. Tenant covenants to pay all rents when due and payable without any setoff, deduction or demand whatsoever. Any monies paid or expenses incurred by Landlord to correct violations of any of Tenant's obligations hereunder shall be additional rent. Any additional rent provided for in this Lease becomes due with the next installment of Total Annual Minimum Rent due after receipt of notice of such additional rent from Landlord.

ARTICLE 8: GROSS SALES

As used herein the term "Gross Sales" shall mean the recognition of the entire amount of the actual sales price at the time of purchase whether wholly or partially for cash or on credit of all merchandise and services sold and all other receipts by sale, barter, or otherwise of all business conducted in or from the Premises including, without limiting the foregoing, all sales to employees or agents of Tenant, all orders taken in or from the Premises although said orders may be received by telephone or mail, or filled elsewhere, or procured from the Premises by house to house or other canvassing, all sales by any sublessee, licensee or concessionaire in or from the Premises, all without credit to Tenant for cash discounts (other than normal employee discounts) or uncollected or uncollectible credit accounts. Sales to customers on a layaway or lay-by basis shall be recognized within ninety (90) days of the layaway or lay-by transaction and in any event must be fully recognized when the merchandise leaves the Premises. The term "Gross Sales" shall also include without limitation, all deposits not refunded to purchasers, all service charges for layaway or lay-by sales and all commissions received for vending machines on the Premises for use by the general public and other cash receipts resulting from sales transactions on the Premises.

All sales are to be recorded on cash registers equipped with a transaction number control or recorded on sales checks which are numerically controlled. There shall be no adjustment to Gross Sales for cash shortages. There shall be excluded from Gross Sales any sum collected and paid out for any sales or excise tax based upon all taxable sales in this definition of Gross Sales as required by law whether now or hereafter in force, to be paid by Tenant or collected from its customers, to the extent that such taxes have been included in the Gross Sales price. The term "Gross Sales" shall not include the exchange or transfer of merchandise between the stores of Tenant, if any, where such exchange or transfers of merchandise are made solely for the convenient operation of the business of Tenant and not for the purpose of consummating a sale made in, from, or upon the Premises or for the purpose of depriving Landlord of the benefit of a sale; the amount of returns to shippers or manufacturers, nor the amount of any cash credit refunds upon any sale where the merchandise sold, or some part thereof is thereafter returned by the purchaser to and accepted by Tenant, nor sales of fixtures. There shall also be excluded from the term "Gross Sales" all fees or service charges for delivery fees and C.O.D. fees. The term "Gross Sales" shall also exclude finance charges resulting from Tenant's Accounts Receivable.

ARTICLE 9: RECORDS AND REPORTS

Tenant shall and hereby agrees that it and its subtenants will keep in the Premises or at its headquarters, a permanent, accurate set of books and records, in accordance with generally accepted accounting methods and principles, of all sales of merchandise and all revenue derived from other departments of the business conducted in said Premises during each day of the Term hereof, and all supporting records including cash register tapes, sales checks, state sales and use tax reports, and business and occupation tax reports. Tenant further agrees that it and its subtenants will so keep, retain, and preserve these records for at least two (2) years after the expiration of each Lease Year.

Tenant further covenants and agrees (a) that not later than the fifteenth (15th) day of each calendar month it will deliver to Landlord an informal, unaudited statement signed by Tenant or by an authorized officer or agent of Tenant showing the Gross Sales made in the preceding calendar month; (b) that not later than the fifteenth (15th) day of May, August, and November, it will deliver to Landlord a written statement signed by Tenant or by an authorized officer or agent of Tenant, showing the Gross Sales made in the preceding three calendar month period; and (c) that not later than thirty (30) days after the close of each Lease Year, and after the completion of the Term or any renewal thereof, or earlier termination, it will deliver to Landlord a statement of Gross Sales for the preceding Lease Year accompanied by the signed opinion of an independent Certified Public Accountant stating specifically that he has examined the report of Gross Sales of the preceding Lease Year, that his examination included such tests of Tenant's books and records as he considered necessary under the circumstances, and that such report presents fairly Gross Sales of the preceding Lease Year. If Tenant shall fail to deliver the foregoing to Landlord within said thirty (30) day period, Landlord shall have the right thereafter to employ an independent Certified Public Accountant to examine such books and records as may be necessary to certify the amount of Tenant's Gross Sales for such Lease Year, and Tenant shall promptly pay to Landlord the cost thereof.

In the event Landlord is not satisfied with the annual statement of Gross Sales as submitted by Tenant and its subtenants, then and in that event after ten (10) days written notice, Landlord shall have the right to have its employees, mortgagees or outside auditors make a special audit of Tenant's and its subtenant's books and records pertaining to sales on or in connection with the Premises leased herein. If such audit shall disclose a discrepancy of more than one percent (1%) of Gross Sales, Tenant shall promptly pay to Landlord the cost of said audit in addition to the deficiency in rent, which shall be payable in any event. Landlord shall have the right to audit Tenant's books and records for a period of two years after the close of each Lease Year, except where an audit of Tenant's books and records finds a discrepancy of more than three percent (3%), then Landlord shall have the right to audit the books and records back to the inception date of this Lease.

ARTICLE 10: TAXES

Tenant shall pay in each Tax Year (as hereinafter defined), during the Term of this Lease and as additional rent, a proportionate share of the real estate and all ad valorem taxes (including but not limited to special assessments) due and payable with respect to the Shopping Center Tract and improvements thereon imposed by any state, county, school district, municipal, or other government authority.

Tenant's proportionate share for any Tax Year shall be determined by dividing the total number of square feet of Gross Leasable Area (as hereinafter defined) within the Shopping Center Tract into the total taxes payable on the Shopping Center Tract for the tax year in question and multiplying the resulting quotient times the number of square feet of Gross Leasable Area in the Premises.

Upon receipt of the tax bills in each Tax Year or partial Tax Year in the event the taxing authority having jurisdiction over the Shopping Center Tract shall require payment of taxes in two or more equal installments, Landlord will certify to Tenant the amount of taxes per square foot of Gross Leasable Area and the amount due from Tenant, if any. Within thirty (30) days after receipt of such certification from Landlord, Tenant will pay to Landlord any amount stated therein to be due.

In addition to the foregoing, Tenant at all times shall be responsible for and shall pay, before delinquency, all municipal, county, state or federal taxes levied, assessed or unpaid on any leasehold interest, any right of occupancy, any investment of Tenant in the Premises, or any personal property of any kind owned, installed, or used by Tenant including Tenant's leasehold improvements, or on Tenant's right to occupy the Premises.

For the Tax Year in which this Lease commences or terminates, the provisions of this Section shall apply, but Tenant's liability for its proportionate share of any taxes for such year shall be subject to a pro rata adjustment, based upon the number of full calendar months of said Tax Year during which Tenant is obligated under this Lease to occupy the Premises and pay Total Annual Minimum Rent.

In the event Landlord shall contest the amount of real estate taxes due and payable under this provision and shall be successful and receive a refund, Tenant shall receive credit for its pro rata share of such refund less the cost of such appeal. Tenant's pro rata share shall be determined in accordance with the provisions of this Lease.

For the purpose of this Lease, the term "Tax Year" shall mean the twelve (12) month period established as the real estate tax year by the taxing authorities having lawful jurisdiction over the Shopping Center Tract and the term "Gross Leasable Area" shall be deemed to mean the area within the Shopping Center Tract designated by Landlord for tenant occupancy and use.

ARTICLE 11: LEASE YEAR

The term "Lease Year" shall mean, in the case of the first Lease Year, that period from the commencement of the Term as determined in accordance with the provisions of Article 3 hereof to the first succeeding January 31; thereafter, "Lease Year" shall mean each successive twelve (12) calendar month period following the expiration of the first Lease Year, in each case commencing on February 1 and ending the next succeeding January 31, except that in the event of the termination of this Lease on any day other than the last day of a Lease Year, then the last Lease Year shall be the period from the end of the preceding Lease Year to such date of termination.

ARTICLE 12: COMMON AREA

The term "Common Area" means the entire areas designed for common use or benefit within the Shopping Center, including, but not by way of limitation, parking lots, landscaped and vacant areas, passages for trucks and automobiles, elevators, areaways, roads, walks, curbs, corridors, courts and arcades, together with facilities such as washrooms, comfort rooms, lounges, drinking fountains, toilets, stairs, ramps, elevators, escalators, shelters, community rooms, porches, bus stations and loading docks, with facilities appurtenant to each and water filtration and treatment facilities, including, but not limited to, treatment plant(s) and settling ponds whether located within or outside of the Shopping Center. The Common Areas shall at all times be subject to the exclusive control and management of Landlord and may be expanded, contracted or changed by Landlord from time to time as deemed desirable. Subject to reasonable, nondiscriminatory rules and regulations to be promulgated by Landlord, the Common Area is hereby made available to Tenant and its employees, agents, customers and invitees for their reasonable non-exclusive use in common with other tenants, their employees, agents, customers, invitees and Landlord for the purposes for which constructed. Landlord shall have the right to change the areas, location and arrangement of parking areas and other Common Areas; to enter into, modify and terminate easements and other agreements pertaining to the use and maintenance of the Common Area; to restrict parking by tenants, their officers, agents, and employees to designated areas within the Common Area; to construct surface or elevated parking areas and facilities; to establish and change the level of parking surfaces; to close all or any portion of the Common Area to such extent as may, in the opinion of Landlord's counsel, be necessary to prevent a dedication thereof or the accrual of any rights to any person or to the public therein; to close temporarily any or all portions of the Common Areas; to discourage noncustomer parking; and to do and perform such other acts in and to said areas and improvements as, in the exercise of good business judgment, Landlord shall determine to be advisable with a view to the improvement of the convenience and use thereof by tenants, their officers, agents, employees and customers. Landlord may require the payment to it of a reasonable fee or charge by the public for the use of all or part of the Common Areas, which may be by meter or otherwise; in such event all fees or charges so derived shall be applied in reduction of the costs and expenses of operation and maintenance of the parking areas before such costs and expenses are apportioned among the occupants.

The Shopping Center may be constructed in stages and construction of later stages may necessitate the rearrangement and alteration of some or all of the Common Areas. Landlord, therefore, reserves the right in its sole discretion to change, rearrange, alter, modify or supplement any or all of the Common Areas designed for the common use and convenience of all tenants so long as adequate facilities in common are made available to the Tenant herein.

Tenant and its employees shall park their cars only in those portions of the Common Areas designated from time to time for that purpose by Landlord. Tenant shall furnish Landlord with State automobile license numbers assigned to Tenant's car or cars and cars of its employees within five (5) days after taking possession of the Premises and shall thereafter notify Landlord of any changes within five (5) days after such changes occur. If Tenant or its employees fail to park their cars in the designated Common Areas, Landlord shall have the right in its sole discretion to (a) charge Tenant Ten Dollars ($10.00) per day per car parked in any Common Area other than those designated, and/or (b) have such car(s) physically removed from the Shopping Center at Tenant's expense without any liability whatsoever to Landlord.

Tentative Monthly Operating Charge. Tenant shall pay as additional rent Tenant's proportionate share of the cost and expenses of maintaining and operating the Common Area. In respect of each calendar month falling wholly within the Term of this Lease, Tenant shall pay, in advance, on the first of the month a tentative Common Area monthly operating charge, which initially shall be an amount estimated by Landlord prior to the beginning of the Term hereof. If the rents hereinabove reserved shall commence on a date other than the first of a month, Tenant shall pay on said rental commencement date a tentative Common Area monthly operating charge for the balance of such month equal to one-thirtieth of the tentative monthly operating charge multiplied by the remaining number of days in such month. If the rents commence on a date other than February 1, then Landlord may elect to adjust the initial tentative monthly operating charge to be effective for each calendar month in the following first operating year, based upon reasonably anticipated increases or decreases in Common Area costs and expenses. In respect of each full calendar month in the second operating year and in each subsequent operating year and in any terminal fractional operating year, Tenant shall pay in advance a tentative Common Area monthly operating charge on the first day of the month (or as soon thereafter as Landlord shall have notified Tenant of the amount of the tentative monthly Common Area operating charge) based upon reasonably anticipated increases or decreases in Common Area costs and expenses. In respect to any fractional calendar month at the end of a terminal fractional operating year, Tenant shall pay in advance on the first day of such month an amount equal to one-thirtieth of the tentative monthly operating charge for the next preceding calendar month multiplied by the remaining number of days in the Term of this Lease.

Total Final Operating Charge. Within sixty (60) days after the end of the first operating year falling wholly within the Term of this Lease and each succeeding operating year, Landlord shall compute the total final annual Common Area charge for the operating year allocable to all occupants in respect of the operation of said Common Area for such year and shall allocate to Tenant the same proportion thereof that the sum of the tentative monthly operating charges to Tenant for such operating year bears to the sum of the tentative monthly operating charges to all occupants for the same operating year. Tenant shall be furnished a copy in reasonable detail of such final computation and allocation. If the amount thus allocable to Tenant exceeds the sum of the tentative monthly operating charges for the same operating year already paid by Tenant, Tenant shall pay such excess to Landlord on demand. If the amount thus allocated to Tenant is less than the sum of the tentative monthly operating charges for the same operating year already paid by Tenant, Landlord shall refund the difference. The sum of the tentative monthly operating charges for any initial fractional operating year shall be adjusted and any deficiency or excess shall be paid by or refunded to Tenant, as the case may be, after the end of the first operating year falling wholly within the Term of this Lease (or if Landlord so elects after the end of said initial fractional operating year) on the basis of the same proportionate increase or decrease as shall result from the determination of Tenant's share of the total final operating charge in the manner hereinabove provided. Within sixty (60) days after the end of the Term, the sum of the tentative monthly operating charges for any terminal fractional operating year shall be adjusted and any deficiency or excess shall be paid by or refunded to Tenant.

Definitions. For the purposes of this Article, the following definitions shall apply: Each period of twelve (12) consecutive calendar months ending January 31, if all of such period shall fall within the Term of this Lease, shall constitute a "Common Area operating year", herein referred to as "operating year". Any fraction of an operating year between the date when the rents hereinabove reserved commence and the beginning of the first full operating year shall constitute an initial fractional operating year and any fraction of any operating year within the Term hereof beginning after the end of the last full operating year shall constitute a terminal fractional operating year. Landlord shall have annual certified public accountant audits made of operating expenses of the Common Area which shall be open to inspection of Tenant. Such costs and expenses shall be those of maintaining and operating the Common Area (whether located within or outside the Shopping Center) in a manner deemed by Landlord reasonable and appropriate and for the best interests of the tenants of the Shopping Center including without limitation, all costs and expenses of operating, repairing, lighting, cleaning, painting, insuring (including liability insurance for personal injury, death and property liability and insurance against fire, theft or other casualties), removing of snow, ice, debris and surface water, sewer, striping, security police (including cost of uniforms, equipment and all employment taxes), electronic intrusion and fire control devices and telephonic alert system devices, inspecting, equipment and fixture depreciation, Workmen's Compensation, insurance covering personnel, fidelity bonds for personnel, insurance against liability for defamation and claims of false arrest occurring in and about the Common Area, plate glass insurance for glass exclusively serving the Common Area, regulation of traffic, fees for permits, licenses, or use taxes, cost and expense for the rental of music program services, and loudspeaker systems, and all costs and expenses (other than those of a capital nature) of replacement of paving, curbs, sidewalks, walkways, roadways, parking surfaces, landscaping, drainage, utilities and lighting facilities, to the sum total of all of the above shall be added a sum equal to fifteen percent (15%) thereof for administration of the Common Area. Such costs and expenses shall not include any initial construction costs of a capital nature, profit or interest in Landlord's investment, rent and insurance or depreciation other than as specified herein.

ARTICLE 13: UTILITY SERVICES

A. **Gas, Water and Sewer.** Landlord agrees to construct and maintain facilities designated to supply gas, water and sewer to the Premises or to nearby places. Tenant, at its own cost, shall provide the extensions, facilities and other work related thereto. Tenant shall pay, when billed, for all gas, water and sewer service used in the Premises. If Tenant shall use gas, water and sewer service for any purpose in the Premises and if Landlord shall elect to supply the service or services used, or if said services are invoiced to Tenant through Landlord, Tenant shall accept and use the same as tendered by Landlord and pay therefor, when billed, as additional rent, at the appropriate rates filed with the proper regulating authority and in effect, or if not required to be so filed or if not in effect, then at rates prevailing in the nearby vicinity for similar service. Without Landlord's written consent in advance, gas shall not be used by Tenant for water heaters for domestic water. Tenant, at its own expense and with equipment installed in accordance with specifications approved in writing by Landlord, shall heat or chill the water to meet its own requirement, if any, and for that purpose shall use electricity.

B. **Electricity.** Landlord shall provide electrical service for conducting Tenant's business in the Premises. The sum as set out in the Data Sheet shall hereinafter be referred to as the "base electrical cost". At the expiration of each full or initial fractional Lease Year, Landlord shall estimate the cost of the electricity which will be used in serving the Premises occupied by Tenant for the ensuing Lease Year. Should said cost for electricity as determined by Landlord for any ensuing Lease Year be more or less than the "base electrical cost", then Tenant's Total Annual Minimum Rent for such ensuing Lease Year shall be increased or decreased by the same amount.

However, should an increase or decrease in the "base electrical cost" be occasioned by either (1) a change in the rates charged by the local public utility power company, or (2) an increase or decrease in the number of hours of use by Tenant, or (3) a change in the usage of the Premises, then on each such occasion a proportionate adjustment shall be made in Tenant's Total Annual Minimum Rent, upward or downward as the case may be, effective as of the first day of the ensuing calendar month.

Such adjustments in the amount of the Total Annual Minimum Rent for the Premises by Tenant for the ensuing Lease Year shall not exceed the estimated cost where electric service provided to such Premises directly by the local public utility.

Any changes in Tenant's Total Annual Minimum Rent as aforesaid shall be adjusted to a monthly basis as to payment.

C. **Heating, Air Conditioning and Ventilating.** Landlord agrees at its own cost to construct, operate and maintain a system designed to heat, air condition and ventilate the Premises and other occupied areas, in accordance with the criteria set out in the Description of Landlord's Work and Tenant's Work attached hereto as Exhibit B. Tenant shall perform such work and pay such amounts as are required of it under Exhibit B. Tenant agrees to accept and use such heating, air conditioning and ventilating in the Premises and to pay for such use, as additional rent, its pro rata share of the costs of operating the heating, air conditioning and ventilating system (herein referred to as the "Operating Charge") as hereinafter provided.

1. *Tentative Monthly Operating Charge.* In respect of each calendar month the first day of which shall fall on or after the beginning of the Term hereof but prior to the end of the first operating year falling wholly within the Term of this Lease, Tenant shall pay, in advance, on the first of the month a tentative monthly operating charge, which initially shall be an amount estimated by Landlord prior to the beginning of the Term hereof. If the rents hereinabove reserved shall commence on a date other than the first of a month, Tenant shall pay on the first day that rents commence a tentative operating charge for the balance of such month equal to one-thirtieth of the tentative monthly operating charge hereinabove stated in this paragraph, multiplied by the remaining number of days in such month. If the rents commence on a date other than February 1, then Landlord may elect to adjust the initial tentative monthly operating charge to be effective for each calendar month in the following first operating year, based upon reasonably anticipated increases in operating costs and expenses. In respect of each full calendar month in the second operating year and in each subsequent operating year and in any terminal fractional operating year, Tenant shall pay, in advance, on the first day of the month (or as soon thereafter as Landlord shall notify Tenant of the amount of the tentative monthly operating charge applicable to such operating year or period) a tentative monthly operating charge based upon reasonably anticipated increases or decreases in operating costs and expenses. In respect of any fractional calendar month at the end of a terminal fractional operating year, Tenant shall pay, in advance, on the first day of such month an amount equal to one-thirtieth of the tentative monthly operating charge for the next preceding calendar month multiplied by the remaining number of days in the Term of this Lease.

2. *Total Final Annual Operating Charge.* Within sixty (60) days after the end of the first operating year falling wholly within the Term of this Lease and of each succeeding operating year, Landlord shall compute the total final annual operating charge for the operating year allocable to all occupants in respect to the operation of the heating, air conditioning and ventilating system for such year and shall allocate to Tenant the same proportion thereof that the sum of the tentative monthly operating charges to Tenant for such operating year bears to the sum of the tentative monthly operating charges to all occupants for the same operating year. Tenant shall be furnished a copy in reasonable detail of such final computation and allocation. If the amount thus allocated to Tenant exceeds the sum of the tentative monthly operating charges for the same operating year already paid by Tenant, Tenant shall pay such excess to Landlord on demand. If the amount thus allocated to Tenant is less than the sum of the tentative monthly operating charges for the same operating year already paid by Tenant, Landlord shall refund the difference. The sum of the tentative monthly operating charges for any initial fractional operating year shall be adjusted and any deficiency or excess shall be paid by or refunded to Tenant, as the case may be, after the end of the first operating year falling wholly within the Term of this Lease (or if Landlord so elects, after the end of said initial fractional operating year) on the basis of the same proportionate increase or decrease as shall result from the determination of Tenant's share of the total final annual operating charge in the manner hereinabove provided. Within sixty (60) days after the end of the Term, the sum of the tentative monthly operating charges for any terminal fractional operating year shall be adjusted and any deficiency or excess shall be paid by or refunded to Tenant.

3. *Determination of Total Final Annual Operating Charge.* Operating charges for each operating year shall include all items of cost and expense which in usual accounting practice are treated as operating costs or expenses, including, but not limited to, fuel, water, electricity, supplies, wages and other compensation (including those of supervisory personnel), depreciation of maintenance equipment, Workmen's Compensation Insurance, payroll taxes, boiler, compressor and other insurance and ordinary maintenance and repairs, to the sum total of which shall be added fifteen (15%) thereof, together with the depreciation of the original cost to Landlord of constructing, erecting and installing the heating, ventilating and air conditioning equipment, and the resulting amount shall constitute the total final annual operating charge. Operating charges shall not, however, include real and personal property taxes (other than personal property taxes on equipment used in Common Area maintenance), maintenance of the four outer walls and roof of the central plant, or any major replacement, or repairs of the type ordinarily charged as capital improvements in good accounting practice. Operating charges shall reflect all costs and expenses of full operation during hours when the Shopping Center is open, which hours shall be determined by Landlord, and all costs and expenses of operation on a reasonably curtailed basis, which shall be applicable to the service furnished generally to tenants and occupants during off-hours when the Shopping Center is not open.

4. *Definitions.* For the purposes of this Article the following definitions shall apply: Each period of twelve (12) consecutive calendar months ending January 31, if all of such period shall fall within the Term of this Lease, shall constitute a heating, air conditioning and ventilating operating year, herein referred to as an "operating year". Any fraction of an operating year between the date when the rents hereinabove reserved commence and the beginning of the first full operating year shall constitute an initial fractional operating year and any fraction of an operating year with the Term hereof beginning immediately after the end of the last full operating year shall constitute a terminal fractional operating year.

5. *Audit.* Landlord shall have annual certified public accountant audits made of operating charges in connection with said heating, air conditioning and ventilating system, and such audit reports shall be open to inspection by Tenant.

D. Discontinuance of Service. Landlord reserves the right with ten (10) days' prior notice to Tenant to cut off and discontinue gas, water, electricity, air conditioning, heating, ventilating, antenna service and any or all other service, without liability to Tenant, whenever and during any period for which bills for the same or for rent are not promptly paid by Tenant, and where necessary to make repairs or alterations (except for emergency repairs in which case no prior notice shall be required). No such action by Landlord, or notice thereof, shall be construed as an eviction or disturbance of possession or as an election by Landlord to terminate this Lease.

E. Interruption of Service. Landlord shall not be liable in damages or otherwise if the furnishing by Landlord or by any other supplier of any utility service or other service to the Premises shall be interrupted or impaired by fire, accident, riot, strike, Act of God, the making of necessary repairs or improvements or by any causes beyond Landlord's control.

ARTICLE 14: MERCHANTS ASSOCIATION
Tenant will, upon commencement of the Term, promptly become a member of, participate fully in, and remain in good standing in the existing Shopping Center Merchants Association organized to promote the activities of the Shopping Center, and will abide by the rules and regulations of such Association. Tenant agrees to pay to such Association such annual dues and/or special assessments as shall be fixed by the Association's Board of Directors payable in the manner prescribed by the Merchants Association. In the event the Shopping Center Merchants Association shall be disbanded, Tenant agrees to pay to Landlord, in lieu of dues to the Merchants Association, a "Promotional Charge" equal to the amount being formerly paid to the Merchants Association to be utilized by Landlord for the advertising, promotion, public relations and administrative expenses of the Shopping Center. The Promotional Charge payable by Tenant to Landlord will be subject to adjustment by a percentage equal to the percentage of increase or decrease from the "base period" (as hereinafter defined) of the Consumer Price Index (U.S. City Average) of the United States Bureau of Labor Statistics or a similar or successor index published by the United States government. The "base period" for the purposes of such adjustment shall be deemed to be _____, and the Promotional Charge shall be adjusted on the third (3rd) anniversary of such month and every three (3) years thereafter on such anniversary date.

In addition to any other dues and/or special assessments, Tenant agrees to pay to such Association and/or Landlord in the event such Association has been disbanded, a single "Grand Opening" assessment equal in amount to the regular annual dues, for the promotion of the Grand Opening of that portion of the Shopping Center in which the Premises are located. Tenant agrees to pay such Grand Opening Assessment within thirty (30) days of the date of receipt of a bill for such payment from the Association and/or Landlord.

ARTICLE 15: FIXTURES
All trade fixtures, merchandise, supplies, decorative light fixtures and movable apparatus owned by Tenant and installed in the Premises shall remain the property of Tenant and shall be removable from time to time and also at the expiration of the Term or any renewal or extension thereof, or other termination thereof, provided Tenant shall not at such time be in default under any covenant or agreement contained herein; and provided further that Tenant repair any damage to the Premises caused by the removal of said fixtures; and, if in default, Landlord shall have a lien on said fixtures and apparatus as security against loss or damage resulting from any such default by Tenant and said fixtures and apparatus shall not be removable by Tenant until such default is cured. All leasehold improvements installed within the Premises by Tenant (including but not limited to light fixtures and carpeting) shall be the property of Tenant until Tenant shall vacate the Premises, at which time title to such leasehold improvements shall vest in Landlord, and in addition any trade fixtures, merchandise, supplies and movable apparatus left in the Premises by Tenant shall become the property of Landlord.

ARTICLE 16: CARE OF THE PREMISES
A. Tenant will (a) keep the inside and outside of all glass in the doors and windows of the Premises clean; (b) keep all exterior store front surfaces of the Premises clean; (c) replace promptly, at its expense, any broken door closers and any cracked or broken glass of the Premises with glass of like kind and quality; (d) maintain the Premises at its expense in a clean, orderly and sanitary condition and free of insects, rodents, vermin and other pests; (e) keep any garbage, trash, rubbish or refuse removed at its expense on a regular basis and temporarily stored in the Premises in accordance with local codes; (f) keep all mechanical apparatus free of vibration and noise which may be transmitted beyond the Premises; (g) comply with all laws, ordinances, rules and regulations of governmental authorities and all recommendations of the Fire Underwriters Rating Bureau now or hereafter in effect; (h) light the show windows of the Premises and exterior signs during all business hours of the Shopping Center and replace promptly all light bulbs when burned out; and (i) conduct its business in all respects in a dignified manner in accordance with high standards of the store operation in the Shopping Center existing at the time of execution of this Lease. Tenant will not, without the written consent of Landlord, place or maintain any merchandise or other articles in any vestibule or entry of the Premises, on the footwalks adjacent thereto or elsewhere on the exterior of the Premises or common facilities; use or permit the use of any loud speakers, phonographs, public address systems, flashing, moving and/or rotating lights, sound amplifiers, musical instruments, television or radio broadcasts within the Shopping Center which is in any manner audible or visible outside the Premises; permit undue accumulations of garbage, trash, rubbish or other refuse within or without the Premises; cause or permit odors to emanate or be dispelled from the Premises; solicit bills or other advertising matter to the public outside the Premises, in or upon any automobiles parked in the parking areas or in any other Common Areas; permit the parking of delivery vehicles so as to interfere with the use of any driveway, walk, parking area, mall or other Common Areas in the Shopping Center; or receive or ship articles of any kind except through service facilities designated by Landlord.

B. Landlord shall keep the foundations, the four outer walls, the roof, downspouts and gutters of the building of which the Premises are a part and, to the extent not located on the Premises of tenants or other occupants, the plumbing, sewage and heating, air conditioning and ventilating systems in good repair, ordinary wear and tear excepted, provided Tenant shall have given Landlord written notice of the necessity for such repairs, but shall not be required to make any other repairs, whether or not due to the negligence of Tenant, its agents or employees. Except as otherwise provided in this Article, the Premises including but not limited to plumbing, electrical and other mechanical equipment, shall at all times be kept in good order, condition and repair of equal quality and class with the original work by Tenant at Tenant's own cost and expense and in accordance with all laws, directions, rules and regulations of regulatory bodies or officials having jurisdiction in that regard. If Tenant refuses or neglects to commence repairs within ten (10) days after written demand, or adequately to complete such repairs within a reasonable time thereafter, Landlord may make the repairs without liability to Tenant for any loss or damage that may accrue to Tenant's stock or business by reason thereof, and if Land-lord makes such repair, Tenant shall pay to Landlord, on demand, as additional rent, the costs thereof with interest at the maximum interest permitted by law from the date of commencement of said repairs. Tenant will not alter the exterior of the Premises (including the store front and/or signs, lettering, and advertising matter on any windows or doors) and will not make any structural alterations to the exterior or interior of the Premises or any part thereof or do any exterior decoration or build any fences or install any radio or television antennae, loud speakers, sound amplifiers or similar devices on the roof or exterior walls of the buildings without first obtaining Landlord's written approval of such alterations. Tenant will not overload the electrical wiring serving the Premises or within the Premises, and will install at its expense, but only after obtaining Landlord's written approval, any additional electrical wiring which may be required in connection with Tenant's apparatus.

C. Tenant will not paint or decorate any part of the exterior of the Premises, including store fronts, or any part of the interior visible from the exterior thereof or paste any signs to any portion of the Premises, or display any signs attached to show windows or within twelve (12) inches of the mall lease line of the Premises without obtaining Landlord's written approval. Landlord shall have the right, in Landlord's sole discretion, to require Tenant to remove any sign visible from the Common Area which is not in keeping with the standards of the Shopping Center.

D. Tenant will repair promptly, at its expense, any damage to the Premises or any other improvement within the Shopping Center caused by bringing into the Premises any property for Tenant's use, or by the installation or removal of such property, regardless of fault or by whom such damage shall be caused, unless caused by Landlord, its agents, employees or contractors; and in default of such repairs by Tenant, Landlord may make the same and Tenant agrees to pay, as additional rent, the cost thereof to Landlord promptly upon Landlord's demand therefor.

E. Landlord shall have the exclusive right to use all or any part of the roof of the Premises or any additions thereto for any purpose; to erect additional stories or other structures over all or any part of the Premises; to erect in connection with the construction thereof temporary scaffolds and other aids to construction on the exterior of the Premises, provided that access to the Premises shall not be denied; and to install, maintain, use, repair and replace within the Premises pipes, ducts, conduits, wires and all other mechanical equipment serving other parts of the Shopping Center, the same to be in locations within the Premises as will not materially interfere with Tenant's use thereof.

Landlord may make any use it desires of the side or rear walls of the Premises, provided that such use shall not encroach on the interior of the Premises.

ARTICLE 17: ADVERTISING
Tenant shall use as its advertised business address the name and address of the Shopping Center. Tenant's trade name set out in the Data Sheet shall not be changed without Landlord's prior written approval. Tenant agrees that Landlord's name or the name of the Shopping Center shall not be used in any confusing, detrimental or misleading manner, and upon termination of this Lease, Tenant will cease to use Landlord's name or the name of the Shopping Center, or any part thereof, in any manner.

ARTICLE 18: TENANT INSURANCE
A. **Public Liability Insurance.** Prior to its entry into the Premises and thereafter during the Term of this Lease, Tenant shall keep in full force and effect, at its expense, a policy or policies of public liability insurance with respect to the Premises and the business of Tenant and any approved subtenant, licensee, or concessionaire, with companies licensed to do business in _____, in which both Tenant and Landlord shall be adequately

covered under reasonable limits of liability not less than: $_____ for injury or death to any one person; $_____ for injury or death to more than one person, and $_____ with respect to damage to property. Tenant shall furnish Landlord with certificates or other evidence acceptable to Landlord that such insurance is in effect, which evidence shall state that Landlord shall be notified in writing thirty (30) days prior to cancellation, material change or nonrenewal of insurance. At any time after the first two (2) years of the Term, Landlord shall have the option to require Tenant to increase the amount of such insurance coverage.

B. **Boiler Insurance.** If Tenant operates a pressure boiler or other pressure vessels in the Premises, Tenant will place and carry boiler insurance with companies licensed to do business in _____ in adequate amounts approved by Landlord, but not less than $_____ property damage per occurrence, and will comply fully with all applicable laws, statutes and regulations with reference to the operation and inspection of boilers and steam vessels. Tenant shall furnish Landlord with certificates or other evidence acceptable to Landlord that such insurance is in effect, which evidence shall state that Landlord shall be notified in writing thirty (30) days prior to cancellation, material change or nonrenewal of insurance.

C. **Workmen's Compensation.** If the nature of Tenant's operation is such as to place any or all of its employees under the coverage of local Workmen's Compensation or similar statutes, Tenant shall also keep in force, at its expense, so long as this Lease remains in effect and during such other time as Tenant occupies the Premises or any part thereof, Workmen's Compensation or similar insurance affording statutory coverage and containing statutory limits. At the written request of Landlord, Tenant agrees to furnish to Landlord evidence of Workmen's Compensation coverage. If Tenant shall not comply with its covenants made in this Section, Landlord may cause insurance as aforesaid to be issued, and in such event Tenant agrees to pay, as additional rent, the premium for such insurance upon Landlord's demand.

D. **Waiver of Subrogation.** Landlord hereby waives any and all right that it may have to recover from Tenant damages for any loss occurring to property of Landlord by reason of any act or omission of Tenant; provided, however, that this waiver is limited to those losses for which Landlord is compensated by its insurers and then only to the extent that Landlord's policies of insurance permit it to waive the insurer's right of subrogation.

Tenant hereby waives any and all right that it may have to recover from Landlord damages for any loss occurring to property of Tenant by reason of any act or omission of Landlord; provided, however, that this waiver is limited to those losses for which Tenant is compensated by its insurers and then only to the extent that Tenant's policies of insurance permit it to waive the insurer's rights of subrogation.

E. **Landlord's Insurance.** Landlord will during the Term of this Lease keep in force a standard form of life insurance policy with extended coverage endorsement added as from time to time issued in _____, covering the shell of the building of which the Premises are a part as initially constructed by Landlord. All fixtures, merchandise, supplies, goods, and leasehold improvements made by Tenant, shall be the sole responsibility of Tenant to insure as Tenant desires.

F. **Tenant Covenants.** Tenant will not do or suffer to be done, or keep or suffer to be kept, anything in, upon or about the Premises which will contravene Landlord's policies insuring against loss or damage by fire or other hazards (including, without limitation, public liability) or which will prevent Landlord from procuring such policies in companies acceptable to Landlord. If anything done, omitted to be done or suffered to be done by Tenant, or kept or suffered by Tenant to be kept, in,

upon or about the Premises shall cause the rate of fire or other insurance on the Premises or other property of Landlord in companies acceptable to Landlord to be increased beyond the minimum rate from time to time applicable to the Premises for the use permitted under this Lease or to any other property for the use or uses made thereof, Tenant will pay, as additional rent, the amount of any increase upon Landlord's demand.

ARTICLE 19: TENANT INDEMNITY
Tenant will indemnify Landlord and save it harmless from and against any and all claims, actions, damages, liability and expense in connection with loss of life and/or personal injury arising from or out of the occupancy or use by Tenant of the Premises or any part thereof or any other part of Landlord's property, occasioned wholly or in part by any negligent act or omission of Tenant, its officers, agents, contractors or employees.

ARTICLE 20: MECHANICS LIENS
Tenant agrees. . . .

ARTICLE 21: ASSIGNMENT OR SUBLETTING
Tenant agrees not to sell, assign, mortgage, pledge, franchise or in any manner transfer this Lease or any estate or interest thereunder and not to sublet the Premises or any part or parts thereof and not to permit any licensee or concessionaire therein without the previous written consent of Landlord in each instance first obtained. Consent by Landlord to one assignment of this Lease or to one subletting, sale, mortgage, pledge or other transfer including licensing or the grant of a concession shall not be a waiver of Landlord's rights under this Article as to any subsequent similar action. This prohibition includes any subletting, assignment or transfer which would otherwise occur by operation of law.

If, at any time during the Term of this Lease, Tenant (and/or the guarantor, if any) is

(i) a corporation or a trust (whether or not having shares of beneficial interest) and there shall occur any change in the identity of any of the persons then having power to participate in the election or appointment of the directors, trustees, or other persons exercising like functions and managing the affairs of Tenant; or

(ii) a partnership or association or otherwise not a natural person (and is not a corporation or a trust) and there shall occur any change in the identity of any of the persons who then are members of such partnership or association or who comprise Tenant;

Tenant shall so notify Landlord and Landlord may terminate this Lease by notice to Tenant given within ninety (90) days thereafter. This Section shall not apply if Tenant (and/or guarantor, if any) named herein is a corporation and the outstanding voting stock thereof is listed on a recognized securities exchange or is wholly owned by another corporation whose outstanding voting stock is so listed.

Notwithstanding the foregoing, Tenant shall have the right, without the consent of Landlord first obtained, to assign this Lease to its parent company or to an affiliate or subsidiary corporation or a corporation into which Tenant shall be merged, provided, however, Tenant shall not be released from any obligation hereunder, and provided further that such assignee shall agree in writing to assume all of Tenant's obligations.

Landlord's rights to assign this Lease are and shall remain unqualified. Upon any sale of the Premises and provided the purchaser assumes all obligations under this Lease, Landlord shall thereupon be entirely freed of all obligations of Landlord hereunder and shall not be subject to any liability resulting from any act or omission or event occurring after such conveyance, except that any covenant or obligation of Landlord hereunder affecting land owned by Landlord shall continue for its term during such ownership, but no longer. Upon the sale or other transfer of Landlord's interest in this Lease, Tenant agrees to recognize and attorn to such transferee as Landlord, and Tenant further agrees to execute

and deliver a recordable instrument setting forth the provisions of this paragraph.

ARTICLE 22: CONDEMNATION
If the whole or any part of the Premises shall be taken under the power of eminent domain, this Lease shall terminate as to the part so taken on the date Tenant is required to yield possession thereof to the condemning authority. Landlord shall make such repairs and alterations as may be necessary in order to restore the part not taken to useful condition and the Total Annual Minimum Rent and Percentage Rent shall be reduced proportionately as to the portion of the Premises so taken. If the amount of the Premises so taken substantially impairs the usefulnes of the Premises for the use permitted in the Data Sheet, either party may terminate this Lease on the date when Tenant is required to yield possession. All compensation awarded for any taking of the fee and the leasehold shall belong to and be the property of Landlord provided, however, that Landlord shall not be entitled to any award made to Tenant for loss of business, fair value of, and cost of removal of stock and fixtures.

The term "eminent domain" shall include the exercise of any governmental power and any purchase or other acquisition in lieu of condemnation.

ARTICLE 23: FIRE
If the Premises shall be damaged by fire, the elements, unavoidable accident or other casualty insurable under full standard extended risk insurance offered at the time in _____, but are not thereby rendered untenantable, in whole or in part, Landlord shall promptly at its expense cause such damage to be repaired, without abatement of rent; if, however, the Premises shall be rendered untenantable in part, Landlord shall at its expense cause the damage to be repaired, and the Total Annual Minimum Rent and Percentage Rent meanwhile shall be abated proportionately as to the portion of the Premises rendered untenantable. If by reason of such occurrence the Premises shall be rendered wholly untenantable, Landlord shall at its expense cause such damage to be repaired, and the Total Annual Minimum Rent meanwhile shall be abated, unless within sixty (60) days after said occurrence Landlord shall notify Tenant in writing that it has elected not to reconstruct the Premises, whereupon this Lease and the tenancy hereby created shall cease as of the date of said occurrence, the Total Annual Minimum Rent and Percentage Rent to be adjusted as of such date. In no event shall Landlord be liable for damage to or replacement or repair of fixtures, floor coverings, furniture and equipment owned by Tenant nor leasehold improvements made or accepted by Tenant or the previous occupants of the Premises, but shall be limited to the shell of the building of which the Premises form a part as initially constructed by Landlord. It is understood and agreed that Landlord's reconstruction obligations shall be limited to the work originally performed by Landlord under Exhibit B hereof.

ARTICLE 24: SURRENDER OF PREMISES
This Lease shall terminate at the end of the original Term hereof, or any extension or renewal thereof, without the necessity of any notice from either Landlord or Tenant to terminate the same, and Tenant hereby waives notice to vacate the Premises and agrees that Landlord shall be entitled to the benefit of all provisions of law respecting the summary recovery of possession of premises from a tenant holding over to the same extent as if statutory notice had been given. For the period of six (6) months prior to the expiration of the Term or any renewal or extension thereof, Landlord shall have the right to display on the exterior of the Premises (but not in any window or doorway thereof) the customary sign "For Rent", and during such period Landlord may show the Premises and all parts thereof to prospective tenants during normal business hours.

On the last day of the Term or on the sooner termination thereof, Tenant shall peaceably surrender the Premises in good order, condition and repair, broom-clean, fire and other unavoidable casualty and reasonable wear and tear only excepted. Tenant shall, at its expense, remove its trade fixtures, (not including floor covering and lighting equipment) and signs from the Premises and any property not removed shall be deemed abandoned. Any damage caused by Tenant in the removal of such items shall be repaired by and at Tenant's expense. All alterations, additions, improvements and fixtures (other than Tenant's trade fixtures and signs) which shall have been made or installed by either Landlord or Tenant upon the Premises and all hard surface bonded or adhesively affixed flooring and all lighting fixtures shall remain upon and be surrendered with Premises as a part thereof, without disturbance, molestation or injury, and without charge, at the expiration or termination of this Lease and shall then become property of Landlord. If the Premises be not so surrendered, Tenant shall indemnify Landlord against loss, liability or expense resulting from delay by Tenant in so surrendering the Premises, or failure to leave the Premises in the condition required hereunder including, but not limited to, claims made by any succeeding tenant founded on such delay. Tenant shall promptly surrender all keys for the Premises to Landlord at the place then fixed for payment of rent and shall inform Landlord of combinations on any locks and safes on the Premises. The provisions of this Article 24 shall survive termination of this Lease.

ARTICLE 25: DEFAULT

If Tenant shall violate: (a) the covenant to pay rent and/or any other monetary charge within ten (10) days after the time such rent and/or monetary charge is due and payable to Landlord; (b) any other covenant made by it in this Lease and shall fail to comply or begin and diligently prosecute compliance within fifteen (15) days after being sent written notice of such violation by Landlord; or (c) file or have filed against it any bankruptcy or other creditors action, then, in any of such events, it shall be optional for Landlord to enter the Premises and do such things as may be permitted hereunder in the manner set out herein and Landlord shall have no liability to Tenant for any loss or damages resulting in any way from such action by Landlord. Tenant agrees to pay promptly upon demand any expense incurred by Landlord in taking such action, and it shall be optional for Landlord to declare this Lease forfeited and the Term ended, and to re-enter the Premises, with or without process of law, using such force as may be necessary to remove all persons or chattels therefrom, and Landlord shall not be liable for damages by reason of such re-entry or forfeitures; but notwithstanding such re-entry by Landlord, the liability of Tenant for all rents provided for herein shall not be relinquished or extinguished for the balance of the Term of this Lease. Tenant will pay, in addition to the rents and other sums agreed to be paid hereunder, such additional sums as the court may adjudicate reasonable as attorneys' fees in any suit or action instituted by Landlord to enforce the provisions of this Lease, or the collection of the rents due Landlord hereunder. Tenant shall also be liable to Landlord for the payment of interest at the maximum interest permitted by law on all rents and other sums due Landlord hereunder not paid within ten (10) days from the date same became due and payable, such interest to accrue from the date such payment is due and payable.

Notwithstanding such re-entry and termination, Tenant shall pay an amount of money equal to the total rent which but for termination would have become payable during the remainder of the Term, less the amount of rent, if any, which Landlord may receive during such period from others to whom the Premises may be rented on such terms and conditions and at such rents as Landlord, in its sole discretion, shall deem proper. If such termination shall take place after the expiration of two or more Lease Years of this Lease,

the Percentage Rent payable, if any, in each Lease Year after such termination, shall be conclusively presumed to be equal to the average Percentage Rent payable during such expired Lease Years. If such termination shall take place before the expiration of two Lease Years of this Lease, the Percentage Rent payable in each Lease Year after such termination shall be conclusively presumed to be equal to twelve (12) times the average monthly payment of Percentage Rent due and payable prior to such termination, based upon Gross Sales during each such month. Such liquidated damages shall be payable in monthly installments, in advance, on the first day of each calendar month following such termination, and continuing until the date originally fixed herein for the expiration of the then current Term of this Lease, and any suit or action brought to collect the amount of any deficiency for any month shall not in any manner prejudice the right of Landlord to collect any deficiency for any subsequent month by a similar proceeding.

ARTICLE 26: CHANGES TO CENTER

Landlord hereby reserves the absolute right at any time and from time to time to: (a) make changes or revisions in the Site Plan as shown on Exhibit A, including but not limited to additions to, subtractions from, or re-arrangements of the building areas and/or Common Areas (both interior and/or exterior) indicated on Exhibit A; and (b) construct additional or other buildings or improvements in or on the Shopping Center Tract and to make alterations thereof or additions thereto and to build additional stores on any such building or buildings and to build adjoining same. In the event Landlord shall elect to construct any additional buildings, all easement rights granted herein to Tenant shall automatically terminate as to the land upon which such additional buildings are constructed.

ARTICLE 27: GRAND OPENING AND NON-INTERFERENCE

The Grand Opening Date of that portion of the Shopping Center in which the Premises are located shall be fixed by Landlord.

Tenant recognizes that the Shopping Center is open for business and that any construction work to be done in, at or upon the Premises by Tenant may interfere with the operation of the Shopping Center. Therefore, Tenant agrees to use its best efforts during the performance of any construction work to cause no interference to the Shopping Center, or any person, firm or corporation doing business in the Shopping Center.

ARTICLE 28: EXPANSION OF TENANT'S PREMISES: RENT ADJUSTMENT

In the event of any expansion of the Rentable Floor Area of the Premises by the addition of a mezzanine floor or addition of other usable space so that the total number of square feet of Rentable Floor Area of the Premises is greater than that set out on the Data Sheet, adjustment shall be made in the application of the formulas for the computation of Tenant's additional rents payable under this Lease where such additional rent is calculated on Rentable Floor Area in the Premises, including payments under Article 10: Taxes, Article 12: Common Area, Article 13: Utility Services, and Article 14: Merchants Association.

ARTICLE 29: NON-LIABILITY

Landlord shall not be responsible or liable to Tenant for any loss or damage that may be occasioned by or through the acts or omissions of persons occupying adjoining premises or any part of the premises adjacent to or connected with the Premises or any part of the building of which the Premises are a part, or any persons transacting any business in the Shopping Center or present in the Shopping Center for any other purpose or for any loss or damage resulting to Tenant or its property from burst, stopped or leaking water, gas, sewer, sprinkler or steam pipes or plumbing fixtures or from any failure of or defect in any electric line, circuit or facility.

ARTICLE 30: HOLDING OVER

In the event Tenant remains in possession of the Premises after the expiration of this Lease and without the execution of a new lease, it shall be deemed to be occupying the Premises as a tenant from month to month, subject to all the conditions, provisions and obligations of this Lease in so far as the same can be applicable to month-to-month tenancy cancellable by either party upon thirty (30) days written notice to the other.

ARTICLE 31: UNDERSTANDING OF THE PARTIES

This Lease shall be binding from the date hereof until the commencement of the Term as provided herein and thereafter according to its terms; provided, however, that in consideration of the sums of money previously expended by Landlord in connection with the Shopping Center Tract, and the sum of One Dollar ($1.00) in hand paid by Landlord to Tenant, the receipt and sufficiency of which is hereby acknowledged, Landlord shall have the option to cancel this Lease if Tenant shall fail to open for business on or before the twentieth (20th) day following the date set out in Article 3 hereof, by giving Tenant written notice. If this Lease is cancelled pursuant to such option, Tenant will execute an instrument in recordable form containing a release and surrender of all right, title and interest in and to the Premises under this Lease or otherwise and Tenant appoints Landlord its attorney-in-fact to execute such a document.

This Lease represents the full and complete agreement of the parties and any and all warranties, representations or understandings made by either party prior to the execution of this Lease shall be deemed to have been merged into this Lease.

If Landlord shall fail to deliver to Tenant possession of the Premises within one (1) year of the date Tenant executes this Lease, this Lease shall be null and void.

ARTICLE 32: INSPECTION
Tenant will permit. . . .

ARTICLE 33: SHORT FORM
The parties. . . .

ARTICLE 34: NON-WAIVER
No reference. . . .

ARTICLE 35: CAPTIONS
The captions. . . .

ARTICLE 36: APPLICABLE LAW
This Lease. . . .

ARTICLE 37: SUCCESSORS
This Lease. . . .

ARTICLE 38: FORCE MAJEURE
The time. . . .

ARTICLE 39: BROKERS
Each of the parties. . . .

ARTICLE 40: NO PARTNERSHIP
Any intention to create a joint venture or partnership relation between the parties hereto is hereby expressly disclaimed. The provisions of this Lease in regard to the payment by Tenant and the acceptance by Landlord of a percentage of Gross Sales of Tenant and others is a reservation of rent for the use of the Premises.

ARTICLE 41: LIABILITY
If two or more individuals. . . .

ARTICLE 42: AUTHORITY
Landlord warrants. . . .

ARTICLE 43: COPIES
This Lease is executed. . . .

ARTICLE 44: EXAMINATION
The submission of this Lease. . . .

ARTICLE 45: ESTOPPEL
Tenant agrees that. . . .

ARTICLE 46: NOTICES
Any notice desired. . . .

ARTICLE 47: RADIUS CLAUSE
Should Tenant, in its sole discretion, elect, during the years and radius set out in the Data Sheet, to directly or indirectly operate, manage or have any interest in any store for

a business in competition with the business permitted under the provisions of the Data Sheet entitled "Permitted Use", then, in that event, Landlord shall have the option to either:

a. increase the Total Annual Minimum Rent by an amount equal to the sum of Two Dollars ($2.00) times the number of square feet in the Premises; or

b. include the Gross Sales of the store so opened in the calculations for Percentage Rent due under this Lease.

In the event Landlord shall elect a., there shall be no adjustment in the figures set out in the Data Sheet relative to the determination of Percentage Rent.

This Lease and the exhibits thereto constitute the full and complete agreement between the parties and each party represents to the other that there are no other terms, obligations, covenants, representations, warranties or conditions other than as contained herein.

IN WITNESS WHEREOF, Landlord and Tenant have caused this Lease to be signed, sealed and delivered as of the day first above written.

(Tenant)

By _____

Its _____

By _____

Its _____

(Seal)

(Landlord)

By _____

Vice President

By _____

Assistant Secretary

(Seal)

EXHIBIT A

(not shown)

EXHIBIT B

LANDLORD'S AND TENANT'S WORK

Landlord shall hereinafter be defined as including Landlord and Landlord's Architect. Tenant shall hereinafter be defined as including Tenant, Tenant's Architect/Designer, Tenant's Contractor and Tenant's Subcontractors.

I. DESCRIPTION OF LANDLORD'S WORK

A. STRUCTURE

Landlord shall provide a two level structural shell designed in accordance with all governing building codes.

1. *Framing.* Columns shall be structural steel covered by three layers of fire code gypsum board. Overhead structures shall be steel beams or steel bar joists with fireproofing provided by Landlord.

2. *Roof.* Roof shall be insulated built-up twenty (20) year bondable type.

3. *Exterior Walls.* Exterior walls below grade shall be damp-proofed masonry or concrete. Above grade walls shall be masonry.

4. *Space Height.* Landlord shall maintain minimum clear height of not less than 12'-0" from the finished floor slab to overhead obstructions.

B. PARTITIONS AND WALLS

1. *Partitions.* Landlord shall provide exposed metal stud demising partitions between adjacent mercantile tenant spaces. Metal studs shall extend from Tenant's finished floor slab to underside of Landlord's overhead structure. Calculations for the area of Tenant's Premises shall be made to the center of the demising partitions.

2. *Service Corridors.* Landlord shall provide exposed concrete block service corridor and exit core demising partitions. Exposed concrete block shall extend from finished floor slab to underside of Landlord's overhead structure. Calculations for the area of Tenant's Premises shall be made to the center of the concrete block demising partitions.

3. *Exterior Walls.* Landlord shall provide poured concrete exterior walls below grade. Landlord shall provide insulated brick and concrete block walls above grade. Calculations for the area of Tenant's Premises shall be made to the outside edge of exterior walls.

C. INTERIOR FINISHES

1. *Lower Level Floor.* Landlord shall provide a 4" slab on grade with troweled concrete surface ⅝" below the finished mall elevation. A portion of Tenant's slab as designated by Landlord shall be "blocked-out" to facilitate connection of Tenant's underslab utilities. Should Tenant desire location in area other than designated, Tenant shall remove existing concrete and replace with material specified herein.

2. *Upper Level Floor.* Landlord shall provide a structural slab designed for a 100 lb. live load with a troweled finish surface to within ⅝" below the finished mall elevation.

3. *Service Door.* Landlord shall provide a 3'-8" x 10'-10" x 1¾" hollow metal, "B" label door and frame for Premises adjacent to Landlord's service corridors as governed by applicable building codes. Locksets will be the mortise type and each door leaf shall have not less than 1½ pair of butts. Service door and hardware shall be installed by Landlord at a location designated by Landlord.

4. *Neutral Strips.* Landlord shall provide vertical and overhead horizontal neutral strips at the store front lease line between Premises and adjacent tenant spaces, exit or service corridors and/or department stores.

D. UTILITIES

1. *Electricity.* Landlord shall furnish and install empty electrical conduit from Landlord's secondary distribution system, containing a switch and fuse, to a point designated by Landlord within Tenant's Premises. Conduits shall be sized to carry sufficient conductor capacity for an electric load of 10 watts per square foot. Tenant's service shall be 208 volt, 3 phase, 60 HZ, 4 wire.

2. *Domestic Water.* Landlord shall provide a cold water line in the ceiling space of the lower level. A valve connection shall be provided for each premise at a point designated by Landlord. If in the judgment of Landlord, Tenant is deemed to be a large consumer of water, Tenant shall be required to furnish and install a water meter in an area easily accessible by Landlord and within Tenant's Premises.

3. *Sanitary Sewer.*
a.) Lower Level. Landlord shall provide a sanitary sewer branch line with plugged connection within the "blocked-out" portion of Tenant's slab designated by Landlord.
b). Upper Level. Landlord shall provide sanitary sewer branch lines with plugged connections at various locations designated by Landlord.

4. *Plumbing Vent Riser.* Landlord shall pentrate roof membrane with vent risers and provide plugged vent branch connections at strategic points designated by Landlord.

5. *Heating, Ventilating and Air Conditioning.* Landlord shall construct a heating, ventilating and air conditioning system with delivery facilities brought to a point designated by Landlord within Tenant's Premises.

6. *Toilet Exhaust.* Landlord shall provide common toilet exhaust ducts at locations designated by Landlord.

7. *Gas.* Gas service from the gas utility company shall be made available for Tenant's domestic use, other than water heating, at a point designated by Landlord.

8. *Telephone.* Landlord shall provide empty conduit for telephone service from the boundary of Tenant's Premises to a telephone terminal panel in a location designated by Landlord.

9. *Fire Protection.* Landlord shall provide a sprinkler branch line with suitable connection device at a point designated by Landlord within Tenant's Premises.

II. DESCRIPTION OF TENANT'S WORK

Tenant shall at its sole cost and expense perform all work set forth in this section necessary to prepare the Premises to a condition which permits therein the conduct of Tenant's stated business.

A. PREPARATION OF DRAWINGS

Tenant shall prepare and submit to Landlord for approval preliminary design drawings, working drawings, specifications and calculations as specified in Exhibit C. All structural, mechanical and electrical drawings shall be prepared and stamped by an engineer or architect licensed to do business within the State of _____.

B. CONSTRUCTION

1. *Structural.* Any modification, revision or addition to Landlord's structure shall be designed by Tenant's structural engineer and shall be subject to the separate written approval of Landlord.

2. *Interior Finishes.*
a.) Floors.
1.) Lower level tenants shall install compacted back fill and slab on grade in "blocked-out" areas after completion of Tenant's underslab utility connections. All slab grade concrete installed by Tenant shall be 3000 PSI/28 day/reinforced with 6 x 6 - 10 x 10 WW mesh.
2.) Upper level tenants shall make all floor penetrations necessary to facilitate Tenant's utility connections. All such penetrations must be sealed in accordance with Landlord's standard design details.
3.) All finish floor covering materials must be selected or adapted in thickness to correspond exactly with the level of the finish mall floor, which will be ⅝" above the troweled concrete floor of Premises.
b.) Walls. Tenant shall install one layer of ⅝" fire code gypsum board, taped with spackled joints, tight to the underside of the structure above on Tenant's side of the demising partitions other than at Landlord's service corridors. Tenant shall furnish and install all interior wall finish materials.
c.) Store Front. Tenant shall be responsible for all store front construction in an area extending horizontally on the store front lease line between Landlord's neutral strips and vertically from Tenant's finished floor 12'-0" to the underside of soffit element provided by Landlord.
d.) Ceiling. Tenant shall provide a finished ceiling in all nonstorage areas wihtin Premises.

3. *Sign.* Tenant shall furnish and install an illuminated sign at the store front of the Premises in accordance with the criteria established in Exhibit C.

4. *Utilities.*
a.) Electricity. Tenant shall furnish and install conductors from Landlord's secondary distribution panel to within the Premises, as well as all interior distribution equipment within Premises.
b.) Domestic Water. Tenant shall design and install all facilities and extensions of service within Premises. If Tenant desires hot domestic water, Tenant shall provide an electric water heater.
c.) Sanitary Sewer.
1.) Lower Level. Tenant shall design and install all sanitary waste facilities and extensions of service within Premises. In the event Tenant desires sewer facilities in locations other than in "blocked-out" areas designated by Landlord, it shall be the responsibility of Tenant to remove the existing slab in accordance with accepted construction practices and to install plumbing, replace back fill materials and concrete in accordance with Landlord's standard design details.
2.) Upper Level. Tenant shall design and install all sanitary waste facilities and extensions of service for Premises. Tenant shall provide all required floor penetrations for

connection to sanitary sewer tap provided by Landlord. All floor penetrations shall be completed in accordance with Landlord's standard design details and in such a manner to prevent permeations of odors or liquids to the space below. All horizontal sanitary waste lines installed in the attic space of the lower level tenants shall be insulated to prevent condensation damage.

    3.) Tenant shall provide floor drains in toilet areas.

    4.) Tenant shall provide accessible clean-outs in toilet areas.

    d.) Plumbing Vent Riser. Tenant shall design and install all extensions of vent lines to Landlord's plugged connection. Tenant shall provide an additional plugged connection for future Tenant use at Landlord's vent riser location.

    e.) Heating, Ventilating and Air Conditioning. Tenant shall design and install internal distribution within Premises. Any special exhaust and/or make-up air equipment shall be provided and installed by Tenant.

    f.) Toilet Exhaust. Tenant shall design and install extension of toilet exhaust system from Premises to common toilet exhaust duct provided by Landlord.

    g.) Gas. Tenant shall design and install extensions of service from truck court location to Premises in accordance with governing codes and subject to Landlord's written approval.

    h.) Telephone. Tenant shall make provisions for all telephone equipment within Premises as well as extensions of conductors to telephone equipment room in accordance with local utility practices.

    i.) Fire Protection. Tenant shall design and install an automatic wet fire sprinkler system within Tenant's Premises. This system shall be designed on an ordinary hazard basis and shall be in accordance with all requirements of Landlord's Fire Insurance Underwriter.

    5. Special Equipment. Tenant shall design and install all mechanical equipment, elevators, escalators, conveyors or other equipment related to the operation of Tenant and located within Premises.

    6. Fixtures and Furniture. Tenant shall provide and install all furniture and fixtures within Premises.

C. GENERAL PROVISIONS

    1. Approvals.

      a.) Landlord. Tenant shall secure Landlord's written approval of all designs, plans, specifications and contractors performing Tenant's Work prior to the commencement of construction.

      b.) Utilities. Tenant shall secure approval of utility installations where required.

    2. Permits, Licenses, Codes. Tenant shall obtain all necessary licenses and permits to complete Tenant's Work. All Tenant Work shall conform to all applicable statutes, ordinances, regulations and codes and to the requirements of all other regulatory authorities.

    3. Public Safety. Tenant shall confine the construction work to within the Premises as much as possible and shall work in an orderly manner removing trash and debris from the project on a daily basis. At no time will pipes, wires, boards or other construction materials cross public areas where harm could be caused to the public. The requirements of "Occupational Safety and Health Administration" (OSHA) prepared by the Department of Labor will govern. If Tenant fails to comply with these requirements Landlord will cause remedial action (at Tenant's cost) as deemed necessary by Landlord to protect the public.

    4. Tenant Damages to Construction. Tenant will be required to furnish the necessary ramps, chutes, coverings, etc., to protect Landlord's and adjoining premises from damage. All repair of damage to Landlord's facilities and to adjoining premises will be at the cost of the tenant causing the damage. Actual repair work will be accomplished by Landlord's original installer of work damaged.

    5. Temporary Signs. Tenant shall install temporary store name signs in the event Tenant does not have permanent, approved signs installed at the time Tenant commences business. Such signs shall be of a material and color harmonious with the store front. Paper signs and signs painted directly on store front or show windows are not permitted.

III. WORK FOR TENANT BY LANDLORD, TENANT TO REIMBURSE LANDLORD FOR COST OF SUCH WORK

A. UNDERSLAB WORK

At Tenant's written request and prior to Landlord's scheduled concrete pour, Landlord shall install Tenant's underslab electrical and utility extensions in accordance with plans and specifications provided by Tenant and approved by Landlord. Tenant shall reimburse Landlord for all direct costs of such installation.

B. TEMPORARY SERVICES

    1. Temporary Heat. It shall be the responsibility of Tenant to provide temporary heat for the construction of Tenant's Premises if deemed necessary by Tenant.

    2. Temporary Power. During construction, Landlord shall cause temporary electrical service to be made available in areas designated by Landlord. It shall be Tenant's responsibility to provide and maintain temporary lines from Landlord's designated service area to the Premises and to distribute this power within the Premises. For providing this service, Tenant shall reimburse Landlord on a monthly basis at a rate of _____¢ per square foot of Premises per month or a minimum of $_____ per month, whichever is greater. Payment is to be remitted by the first of each month after service is connected and in no case later than the store opening date. Tenant shall be charged for this service during Tenant's Construction and Fixturing Days whether this service is used or not.

    3. Trash Removal. During the initial construction, fixturing and merchandise stocking of Tenant's Premises, Landlord shall provide trash removal service at areas designated by Landlord. It shall be the responsibility of Tenant and Tenant's contractors to remove all trash and debris from Premises on a daily basis and to break down all boxes and place all such trash and debris in the containers supplied for that purpose by Landlord. For providing this service, Tenant shall reimburse Landlord on a single quoted basis at a rate of _____¢ per square foot of Premises or a minimum charge of $_____, whichever is greater. Payment is to be remitted at the commencement of the construction of Tenant's Premises. Tenant shall be charged for this service during Tenant's Construction and Fixturing Days whether this service is used or not. In the event Tenant's trash is allowed to accumulate for a 24 hour period or longer within Tenant's Premises or in the arcades, mall or service corridors adjacent to the Premises, Landlord shall remove Tenant's or Tenant's contractor's trash at a charge of 1.5 times Landlord's cost.

    4. Temporary Barricades. Landlord shall furnish temporary barricades at the store front lease line for those tenants who in Landlord's judgment will not have completed their store front by the Grand Opening Date. For providing this service, Tenant will reimburse Landlord at a rate of $_____ per lineal foot of store front barricade. Tenant shall be responsible for removal and relocation of Tenant's temporary barricade upon completion of Tenant construction.

C. ROOF PENETRATIONS

All roof penetrations required by Tenant shall be performed by Landlord's roofing contractor at the direction of Landlord. Tenant shall request, in writing, approval to penetrate roof. Upon approval of such request, Landlord will direct roofing contractor to proceed with installation, the cost of installation shall be reimbursed by Tenant.

D. STRUCTURAL REVISIONS

Any modification, revision or addition to Landlord's structure when designed by Tenant and approved by Landlord shall be constructed by Landlord's contractor. Tenant shall reimburse Landlord for all costs of such installation. Structural supports, curbing and flashing shall be in accordance with standard project details.

E. MECHANICAL, ELECTRICAL OR HVAC REVISIONS

In the event Tenant's store design standards exceed the Mechanical, HVAC or Electrical Design Standards established by this Lease, Tenant shall request, in writing, approval to exceed Landlord's standards. If approved by Landlord, Landlord shall make the necessary revisions to Landlord's Mechanical, HVAC, or Electrical System to accommodate Tenant's design standards. Tenant shall reimburse Landlord for all Landlord's direct costs involved in modifying Landlord's systems.

IV. GENERAL REQUIREMENTS

A. LANDLORD INTRUSION

Landlord, Tenant or an authorized utility company, as the case may be, shall have the right, subject to Landlord's written approval, to run utility lines, pipes, conduits or ductwork where necessary or desirable, through attic space, column space or other parts of the Premises, and to repair, alter, replace or remove the same, all in a manner which does not interfere unnecessarily with Tenant's use thereof.

B. LANDLORD'S CONTRACTORS

Tenant shall not use any general contractor or subcontractor that is under contract to the Landlord in the construction of Landlord's building and improvements without Landlord's written approval. Upon Tenant's written request, Landlord will furnish to Tenant a list of the contractors or subcontractors so restricted.

C. COMMENCEMENT OF TENANT CONSTRUCTION

A minimum of five (5) days prior to the commencement of Tenant construction, Tenant shall submit the following items to Landlord via registered or certified mail:

    1. A certificate setting forth the name and address of Tenant's general, mechanical, electrical and sprinkler contractor involved in the completion of Tenant's Work portion of Premises.

    2. A certificate setting forth the proposed commencement date of construction and the estimated completion dates of construction work, fixturing work and projected opening date.

    3. Certificates of Insurance as called for herein. Tenant's contractors shall not be permitted to commence any work until all required insurance has been obtained and certificates have been received by Landlord.

Tenant shall secure, pay for and maintain or cause its contractor(s) to secure, pay for and maintain during the preparation of the Premises, the following insurance in the following amounts, which shall be endorsed in all policies to include Landlord and its beneficiaries and their employees and agents as insured parties, and which shall provide in all policies that Landlord shall be given ten (10) days prior written notice of any alteration or termination of coverage, in the amounts as set forth below:

Tenant's General Contractor's and Subcontractor's Required Minimum Coverages and Limits of Liability.

    a. Workmen's Compensation. Employer's Liability Insurance with limits of not less than $_____ and as required by State law and any insurance required by any Employee Benefit Acts or other statutes applicable where the work is to be performed as will protect the contractor and subcontractors from any and all liability under the aforementioned Acts.

    b. Comprehensive General Liability Insurance (including Contractor's Protective Liability) in an amount not less than $_____ per person and $_____$ per occurrence whether involving personal injury liability (or death resulting therefrom) or property damage liability or a combination thereof with a minimum aggregate limit of $_____$. Such insurance shall provide for explosion and collapse coverage and contractual liability coverage and shall insure the general contractor and/or subcontractors against any and all claims for personal injury, including death resulting therefrom, and damage to the property of others and arising from his operations under the Contract and whether such operations are performed by the general contractor, subcontractors or any of their subcontractors, or by anyone directly or indirectly employed by any of them.

c. Comprehensive Automobile Liability Insurance, including the ownership, maintenance and operation of any automotive equipment, owned, hired and non-owned in the following minimum amounts:

    (i) Bodily injury,
       each person $\_\_\_\_\_$
    (ii) Bodily injury,
       each occurrence $\_\_\_\_\_$
    (iii) Property Damage,
       each occurrence $\_\_\_\_\_$
    (iv) Property Damage,
       Aggregate $\_\_\_\_\_$

d. Tenant's Protective Liability Insurance. Tenant shall provide Owner's Protective Liability Insurance as will insure Tenant against any and all liability to third parties for damage because of bodily injury liability (or death resulting therefrom) and property damage liability of others or a combination thereof which may arise from work in the completion of the Premises, and any other liability for damages which the general contractor and/or subcontractors are required to insure under any provisions herein. Said insurance shall be provided in minimum amounts as follows:

    (i) Bodily injury,
       each person $\_\_\_\_\_$
    (ii) Bodily injury,
       each occurrence $\_\_\_\_\_$
    (iii) Property Damage,
       each occurrence $\_\_\_\_\_$
    (iv) Property Damage,
       Aggregate $\_\_\_\_\_$

e. Tenant's Builders Risk Insurance. Tenant shall provide a completed Value Form "All Physical Loss" Builder's Risk coverage on its work in the Premises as it relates to the building within which the Premises is located, naming the interests of the Landlord, its general contractor and all subcontractors, as their respective interest may appear, within a radius of 100 feet of the Premises.

D. TENANT CONTRACTORS

All contractors engaged by Tenant shall be bondable, licensed contractors, having good labor relations, capable of performing quality workmanship and working in harmony with Landlord's contractors and other contractors on the job. In the event Tenant's contractor willfully violates the requirements of this Lease, Landlord may order Tenant's contractor to remove himself, his equipment and his employees from Landlord's property.

E. MATERIALS AND WARRANTIES

Tenant shall use only new, first class materials in the completion of Tenant's Work. All work and equipment shall be warranted for a minimum of one year from installation.

F. PROOF OF PAYMENT

Tenant shall provide Landlord with proof of payment that all costs of construction of Tenant's Work have been paid. Such proof shall include Waivers of Lien and sworn statements from Tenant's contractors or such other proof as may be required by Landlord in special instances.

G. CONFLICTS

Where conflict between building codes, utility regulations, statutes, ordinances or other regulatory authority requirements and Landlord's requirements, as set forth herein exist, the more stringent of the two shall govern.

EXHIBIT C
ARCHITECTURAL STANDARDS

It is the desire of Landlord to give Tenant the greatest practical freedom in design, but such design must offer a pleasant, orderly appearance and must harmonize with the design of the Shopping Center itself and the design of the surrounding stores. All Tenant Work shall conform to the following standards.

I. ARCHITECTURAL DESIGN CRITERIA

A. FLOORS

1. Landlord has depressed Tenant slab ⅝"; Tenant finish materials must be selected so as to cause Tenant's finish floor elevation to correspond exactly with Landlord's finish mall floor elevation.

2. Waterproofing. All kitchen and food handling areas on the upper level shall be waterproofed with regular asphalt sprinkle mopping, 3 layers of No. 15 asphalt felt with regular asphalt moppings between layers and on top surface.

3. Carpeting shall be used in all sales areas except in such instances where other equivalent types of floor covering materials are specifically approved by Landlord. Vinyl tile and vinyl asbestos tile are not considered acceptable finish materials.

4. Should an expansion joint occur in Premises, Tenant is responsible for the construction of the floor affected by that joint in a manner consistent with standard project details.

5. If Tenant elects to set the base of Tenant's store front back from lease line, Tenant shall furnish and install flooring material identical in quality, color and pattern to the mall flooring within the area extending from lease line to such new store front line.

6. All exposed concrete within Premises must be sealed.

B. STORE FRONTS

1. A minimum of 50% of the Tenant's store front shall be open for pedestrian circulation. Those tenants having, in the judgment of Landlord, an inordinate proportion of store front to floor area will be considered exempt from this requirement. However, in no case will excessive blind wall sections be permitted.

2. Integral with the store front design shall be an air relief opening of not less than 0.5 square feet per one hundred (100) square feet of Tenant's Premises.

3. No store front or any part thereof shall project beyond the lines describing the Premises with the exception that signs may project beyond the store front lease line as described in Exhibit C.

4. All store front work requiring structural support, including sliding door tracks and housing boxes for grilles shall be supported at their head sections by a welded structural steel framework which, in turn, shall be securely attached and braced to the existing building structure.

5. Aluminum store front construction shall employ extruded anodized sections and/or sliding aluminum and glass doors, with pockets to receive sliding doors, open type rolling aluminum curtains or ornamental metal grilles. All sliding door or rolling grille tracks must be recessed into their respective soffit or floor elements to maintain flush elevations.

6. All wood, if permitted by code, employed in conjunction with store front work shall be kiln-dried, mill quality finish.

7. All glass used in conjunction with store front work shall be tempered plate glass.

8. Integral with the store front design shall be a one-hour rated draft curtain extending twenty-four inches (24") down from the finished ceiling elevation.

C. WALLS

1. All interior partitions shall be metal stud or noncombustible wood frame construction with taped and spackled fire code gypsum board finish on all sides. Interior partitions

shall not exceed the ceiling height of Premises.

2. Metal stud demising partition walls by Landlord between adjacent tenant spaces shall be covered by Tenant with one layer of ⅝" fire code gypsum board from the floor to the underside of Landlord's structure.

3. Exposed concrete block walls will not be permissible in sales area of Tenant's Premises. Block walls not concealed by fixtures must be covered with gypsum board by Tenant.

4. If finished ceiling is to be omitted in Tenant's storage area, then the partition wall dividing remainder of Premises from storage area must be one-hour rated construction and extend from the floor slab to the underside of Landlord's overhead structure.

D. CEILINGS

1. Maximum ceiling height will be 12'-0" unless otherwise specifically allowed by Landlord.

2. Exposed wood framing and combustible materials will not be allowed above Tenant's finished ceiling.

3. Should an expansion joint occur in the Premises, Tenant is responsible for the construction of the ceiling affected by that joint in a manner consistent with acceptable construction design practices.

II. MECHANICAL-ELECTRICAL DESIGN CRITERIA

A. HEATING, VENTILATING AND AIR CONDITIONING DESIGN

1. *Landlord's HVAC Design Criteria*
  a.) Heating
    1.) Outside dry bulb temperature: −19°F.
    2.) Inside dry bulb temperature: Prevailing temperature of 68°F dry bulb in merchandising areas and 60°F dry bulb in service areas during occupied hours.
  b.) Cooling
    1.) Outside dry bulb: 80°F.
    2.) Outside wet bulb: 75°F.
    3.) Inside dry bulb: Prevailing 78°F. dry bulb in merchandising areas.
  c.) Total electrical heat producing load: Total heat gains from the electrical wattage of lighting, appliances and miscellaneous electrical items shall be based on a total of 6 watts of electrical heat producing load per square foot of Premises or the equivalent maximum of 21 BTU per hour per square foot of Premises.
  d.) Internal Sensible and Latent Heat Gains: Internal sensible and latent heat gains shall be based on 60 square feet of Premises per person.
  e.) Air Supply: Total cool air supply to Tenant's Premises shall be based on the total internal sensible heat load calculated from the Design Criteria established by paragraphs b, c and d above and where applicable, based on exposed outside wall "U" value of 0.10, a roof assembly "U" value of 0.10 and a supply air diffusion temperature difference of 20°F ± 3°F.

2. *Landlord's Central System*
  a.) Cooling: Landlord shall provide large packaged roof top air conditioning units (variable volume type) complete with air cooled refrigeration, condensing units, DX coils, supply fans, filters, all automatic dampers and controls. These units shall furnish 55°F ± 3°F supply air to the Premises via common low pressure air distribution duct systems during occupied Shopping Center hours on a year round basis. Landlord shall provide a supply duct outlet for each tenant's premises at a point designated by Landlord.
  b.) Heating: Landlord's units do not have heating coils. However, Landlord will provide heaters above upper level tenant ceiling plenums which shall operate from night set back thermostats to offset roof heat losses primarily during unoccupied hours. Landlord shall also provide heaters in public mall and service areas to operate during occupied and unoccupied hours to maintain the space temperature. Landlord shall provide hot water

valved connections, at a point designated by Landlord, for those premises having an exposed outside wall. The supply hot water temperature shall vary from 190°F @ −20°F outside ambient temperature to 90°F @ 70°F outside ambient temperature.

c.) Ventilation: Outside fresh air shall be provided at the central A.C. units with economizer cycle and enthalpy controls and with not more than 5 CFM per person as required by code during occupied cycle.

d.) Tenant Toilet Exhaust: Landlord will furnish a central toilet exhaust duct system at both levels including the fan(s) with a connection for each tenant's toilet exhaust.

3. *Additional HVAC Demand*

If Tenant's HVAC design requirements exceed Landlord's Design Criteria of a total heat producing load of 21 BTU per hour per square foot of Premises or an equivalent of 6 watts per square foot of Premises, Tenant shall submit the proper load calculations and request, in writing, the required additional cooling capacity. If approved by Landlord, Landlord shall make the necessary revisions to accommodate Tenant's request. Tenant shall pay for the necessary revisions and the increased cooling capacity in the form of an increased monthly HVAC Operating Charge.

4. *Tenant's System*

a.) Description: Tenant shall design and install a complete supply air system within Tenant's Premises from the supply air duct(s) furnished and installed in Tenant's ceiling space by Landlord. Tenant's system shall be a variable volume type complete with variable volume terminal units, insulated ductwork, supply diffusers, temperature control devices and associated wiring.

b.) Tenant Cooling-Heating System: Tenant shall design and provide 100% shut-off variable volume terminal units of sizes and quantities needed to satisfy cooling load and temperature control zone requirements based on actual heat gain calculation for the Premises.

Landlord's furnished air supply to the space has no heating capability. Reheating of conditioned air or duct heaters will not be permitted. Variable volume units shall be capable of modulating air supply to the space to maintain space temperature. However, space hot water unit heaters, cabinet heaters or baseboard heaters in Tenant service areas or in Tenant areas with an exterior wall exposure will be permitted to offset the winter heat loss load.

c.) Variable Volume Terminal Units and Temperature Control: Units shall have a capability to adjust in the field from 0 to 100% of minimum air flow (normally set at 20% minimum). Discharge air volume from the units shall not be affected by the upstream duct pressure variations. Units shall be insulated to minimize noise to the space. Variable volume terminal units may be controlled by solid state electronic, or electric motors and space thermostat.

d.) Return Air: All lower and upper level tenants shall relieve air to mall through store front or other acceptable means. The store front relief air opening shall be not less than 0.5 square feet per one hundred (100) square feet of Tenant's Premises. Grille type doors are an acceptable alternate to this requirement.

e.) Tenant Duct System Static Pressure Design: Tenant's air distribution system including ductwork, variable volume air control devices, diffusers, grilles and registers shall be designed such that the static pressure loss in Tenant distribution system does not exceed 0.75″ W.G.

f.) Ductwork: Tenant's ductwork shall be designed, furnished and installed in strict accordance with the standards described in the latest edition of the ASHRAE Guide and Data Book and in the latest editions of the Duct Manual and Sheet Metal Construction for Ventilating and Air Conditioning Systems, published by SMACNA and/or local codes. Supply, return and exhaust duct work shall be galvanized steel except kitchen range exhaust duct work which shall be minimum 18 gauge welded steel and shall comply with local code requirements.

g. Diffusers, registers, grilles: Shall be of adjustable type for volume and direction control.

h.) Thermostat: Shall be located in an accessible location and not obstructed by any merchandising or appliances nor shall it have light fixtures or other similar heat producing elements adjacent to it. Thermostat shall act to control variable volume units as well as any space heating devices used.

i.) Ceiling Access Panels: Tenant shall provide access panels for service to Landlord's and/or Tenant's equipment and/or facilities, and all connections to Landlord's services and facilities above the ceiling level within the Premises at locations designed by Landlord.

j.) Tenant Toilet Exhaust: Tenant shall design and provide exhaust from Tenant's toilet facilities as per code requirements. Toilet exhaust duct from Tenant's Premises shall be connected to Landlord's main toilet exhaust duct system at ceiling level as designated by Landlord.

k.) Miscellaneous Exhaust System:

1.) All odor and moisture producing areas and high heat producing equipment and appliances must be exhausted by special mechanical exhaust systems to atmosphere. Special exhaust systems shall be designed to prevent odors, heat and/or moisture from entering the mall and to Landlord's air conditioning system. Exhaust air quantities shall be in an adequate amount and shall be no less than required by code.

2.) It is required that totally enclosed, highly illuminated show windows be ventilated by means of positive air supply or exhaust. Such exhaust system may be discharged into the false ceiling space, if and at such location as approved by Landlord.

3.) Special exhaust systems including fans, ductwork, registers, grilles, controls and accessories shall be provided by Tenant. Exhaust discharge openings directly to the exterior will not be allowed without permission of Landlord. In all cases, exhaust ductwork shall connect directly to exhaust hoods, if provided, or registers or grilles mounted in ceiling in ventilated area.

4.) Air quantities in excess of ten percent (10%) of total air supplied to the Premises, which are exhausted to atmosphere through Tenant's special exhaust system(s), require Landlord's approval.

l.) Make-up Air System: Tenant shall provide a complete make-up air system if Tenant requires exhaust air quantities in excess of ten percent (10%) of total air allowed to the Premises upon approval of Landlord. Energy equipment and distribution for make-up air system shall be provided by Tenant.

m.) Location of equipment serving special exhaust and make-up air systems and special heating and cooling systems shall be designated and/or approved by Landlord. Engineering and designs showing structural loads added and all supports shall be furnished and installed by Tenant. Routing of ductwork serving special exhaust and make-up air systems shall be designated and/or approved by Landlord. Tenant's ducts passing through the roof shall have motorized shut-off damper(s).

n.) Special cooling and heating equipment, such as required for refrigerated display cases, walk-in coolers, steam presses, etc., shall be provided by Tenant.

o.) Openings through roof: At Tenant's written request and for Tenant's equipment, based upon approved plans, Landlord's roofing contractor will, at Tenant's costs, provide the openings, anchoring devices, curbs, flashings, patching, etc., necessary to maintain the integrity and guarantee of the roof.

p.) Sheet metal supply duct work shall be insulated with 1″ thick, ½ lb. density insulation. Hot water piping for space heating shall be insulated with a minimum of 1″ thick insulation not exceeding a flame spread rating of 25 and a Smoked Developed rating of 50.

q.) Hot water piping shall be Schedule 40 black steel; 2½″ and above shall use standard weight welded fittings; 2″ and smaller shall use 125 pound black cast iron screwed fittings. The system shall be designed to a 125 pound working pressure. All valves shall be ball type. Unions or flanges shall be installed for the removal of automatic control valves.

B. PLUMBING DESIGN

1. *Tenant's Plumbing Design Requirements*

a.) Tenant's sanitary, vent and domestic water piping shall adhere to all local code requirements.

b.) Water supplies to fixtures shall be valved at fixtures.

c.) Domestic hot and cold water piping shall be insulated with minimum ¾″ fiberglass insulation having an average thermal conductivity not exceeding .22 BTU in. per sq. ft. per °F per hour at mean temperature of 75°F.

d.) Piping shall be supported from hangers at an adequate distance with adequate supporting hanger rods fastened to building framing whenever possible.

e.) Water heaters shall be equipped with UL approved temperature and pressure relief valves.

f.) Tenant water closets shall be flush tank type.

2. *Gas Piping Requirements*

a.) Gas piping 1¼″ and over shall be Schedule 40 black steel pipe with welded joints and fittings on all sizes.

b.) Gas piping 1″ and under may be Schedule 40 black steel with screwed fittings if permitted by local code.

c.) Gas cocks and unions shall be installed ahead of each appliance.

C. FIRE PROTECTION

Tenant, at its expense, shall design (on an ordinary hazard basis), furnish and install a complete automatic wet sprinkler system throughout the Premises in accordance with the following requirements:

1. All work related to the sprinkler system shall be in accordance with the requirements of Landlord's Fire Insurance Underwriter.

2. Landlord shall provide a suitable connection on Landlord's sprinkler distribution main at Tenant's Premises. Tenant's Work starts on the downstream side of the test blank. The test blank shall not be removed by Tenant or by Tenant's contractor until Tenant's system has been pressure tested by Tenant's contractor in presence of Landlord's representative.

3. Before proceeding with any installation work, Tenant shall forward a set of reproducible engineered sprinkler plans for the Premises to Landlord. Such plans shall bear the written approval of Landlord's Fire Insurance Underwriter.

4. Tenant's sprinkler system shall be tested at water pressure of 200 psig for a period of two (2) hours in the presence of Landlord's representative.

5. Tenant's system shall have all facilities for proper drainage and any necessary test valves, orifices or equipment required.

6. Landlord's sprinkler main will become active on a schedule established by Landlord. Any damage caused by Tenant to Landlord's sprinkler system will be repaired by Landlord's contractor at Tenant's expense.

7. Upon completion of the system, and on possession of Premises, Tenant shall submit a written certificate to Landlord from the Underwriter stating that the system was inspected and approved.

D. ELECTRIC DESIGN CRITERIA

1. *Landlord's Work*

a.) Landlord shall furnish and install a main fusible disconnect switch in Landlord's distribution panel.

b.) Landlord shall cause electrical conduits (without conductors) to be provided to a boundary line of the Premises from Landlord's distribution panel located at a point designated by Landlord.

c.) Conduit and switch shall be sized to carry sufficient conductor capacity for an electrical load of ten (10) watts per square foot of the Premises area. If Tenant's design requirements exceed the installed electrical load of ten (10) watts per square foot of Premises area, Tenant shall request the required additional electrical capacity. If it is approved by Landlord, Landlord will make a provision for additional electrical capacity and Tenant shall pay an additional amount in the monthly electrical charges and reimburse Landlord for all Landlord's direct costs for furnishing additional capacity.

d.) Landlord's electrical service to Tenant: 208Y/120 volt, 3 phase, 60 HZ, 4 wire.

e.) Landlord shall cause suitable empty telephone conduit to be provided to a boundary line of Tenant's Premises from main telephone terminal backboard located at a point designated by Landlord.

2. *Tenant's Work*

Tenant, at its cost, shall provide all work which shall include, but not be limited to, furnishing and installing the following electrical equipment and services in the Premises.

a.) Fuse(s) and conductors from Landlord's switchboard location to Tenant's distribution panel. For the purpose of periodic check-metering of electrical energy consumption, Tenant shall provide sufficient slack at Landlord's main distribution panel gutters prior to making connection to fuse-switch terminals to permit the use of clamp-on check meters.

b.) Panelboard(s), with twenty percent (20%) spare capacity, transformers, conduits and branch wiring, outlet boxes, and final connection to electrical devices including equipment.

c.) Lighting fixtures and lamps, time clocks, clocks and signs.

d.) Telephone equipment, phone alert system, conduit and outlet boxes.

e.) Security equipment with conduit and outlets if desired.

f.) Exit lights and emergency lighting as required by local codes and ordinances.

3. *Electrical Material Standards for Tenant's Premises*

a.) Electrical materials shall be new, shall meet National Electrical Code Standards, shall bear the Underwriter's Laboratories label, and shall be compatible with the general architectural design.

b.) All transformers shall be dry-type with low sound level.

c.) Wire and cable shall be insulated copper wire with fire resistant outer covering. It shall be properly coded with a neutral, according to N.E. Code. All conductors shall be type THW or THWN and shall not be smaller than No. 12 "AWG".

d.) Panelboards shall be 208Y/120 volt, 3 phase, 4 wire, solid neutral. Cabinets shall be constructed of code gauge sheet steel with hinged steel door and trim.

e.) Lighting fixtures shall bear Underwriter's label. Recessed fixtures installed in furred spaces shall be connected by means of flexible conduit and "AF" wire run to a branch circuit outlet box which is independent of the fixture.

f.) Electric motors shall be designed to latest NEMA standards. Motors rated at ½ horse power and above shall be 3 phase.

III. SIGN CRITERIA

It is intended that the signing of the Premises be developed in an imaginative and varied manner. Although previous and current signing practices of tenants will be considered, all signs shall conform to the criteria set forth hereafter.

A. Exterior Signs

No exterior signs will be permitted unless Tenant's Premises as shown on Exhibit A is in excess of ____ square feet.

B. Interior Signs

1. Tenant shall be required to identify Premises by an illuminated sign contained wholly within limitations of Premises and subject to requirements as outlined hereafter.

a.) Signs shall not project beyond the store front line more than two (2) inches if less than eight (8) feet above finish mall floor or more than six (6) inches if greater than (8) feet above finish mall floor.

b.) Wording of sign shall be limited to store name as indicated on this Lease.

c.) The use of a corporate crest, logo, or insignia shall be permitted provided such crest, logo or insignia meet all criteria described herein.

d.) Multiple or repetitive signing on store fronts shall not be permitted.

e.) Sign letter or components shall not have exposed neon or other lamps. All light source shall be concealed by translucent material. Sign letters or components may be back-illuminated with lamps contained wholly within the depth of the letter. Maximum brightness in any event shall not exceed 100 foot lamberts. Light leaks in sign letters will not be permitted and must be repaired promptly by Tenant.

f.) The average height of sign letters or components on stores shall not exceed 18 inches.

g.) The extreme outer limits of sign letters or components shall fall within a rectangle each of the two short sides of which shall not fall closer than 24 inches to the side lease line of the Premises; the top side of which shall not fall closer than 12 inches to the soffit of the mall facia element. No part of the sign letters shall hang free of the background when such background is provided.

h.) Signs of box or cabinet type construction will be permitted only if cabinet is recessed flush with store front, the illuminated surface is limited to letters and/or other minimum decorative surfaces and the non-illuminated portions of the cabinet are covered by the store front finish material.

2. The following types of signs or sign components shall be PROHIBITED:

a.) Signs employing moving or flashing lights.

b.) Signs employing exposed raceways, ballast boxes or transformers.

c.) Sign manufacturer's names, stamps or decals.

d.) Signs employing painted non-illuminated letters.

e.) Signs employing luminous-vacuum formed type plastic letters.

f.) Signs employing unedged or uncapped plastic letters or letters with no returns and exposed fastenings.

g.) Paper or cardboard signs, stickers or decals hung around, on or behind store front (including glass doors and/or windows).

h.) Signs purporting to identify leased department or concessionaires contained within the Premises.

IV. DRAWING SUBMISSIONS, REVIEWS AND APPROVALS

Landlord's written approval of Design Drawings, Working Drawings and Sign Shop Drawings is required prior to the commencement of Tenant construction.

A. Tenant Information Package

Within ten (10) days from the execution of this Lease, Landlord will forward the Tenant Information Package for the Premises to Tenant. The Tenant Information Package shall contain Landlord's technical and design information appropriate for the design and construction of Tenant's Premises.

B. Design Drawings

1. Within a maximum of thirty (30) days from either the date Tenant receives the Tenant Information Package or from the date Lease is executed, whichever is the latter, Tenant shall submit one (1) sepia and two (2) print sets of Design Drawings to Landlord for review and approval.

2. Tenant's Design Drawings shall include, but not be limited to the following:

a. Floor Plan at ⅛"=1'-0" scale.

b. Store Front Elevation at ⅛"=1'-0" scale including finish materials and colors as well as proposed sign location, size and color.

c. Longitudinal Section at ⅛"=1'-0" scale.

d. Rendering may be required for unusual store designs.

3. As soon as possible after receipt of Design Drawings, Landlord shall return to Tenant one (1) set of prints of Design Drawings with suggested modifications and/or approval. If, upon receipt of approved Design Drawings bearing Landlord's comments, Tenant wishes to take exception thereto, Tenant may do so in writing by certified or registered mail addressed to Landlord, within ten (10) days from date of receipt of Design Drawings. Unless such action is taken, it will be deemed that all comments made by Landlord on Design Drawings are acceptable to and approved by Tenant.

4. If Design Drawings are returned to Tenant with comments, but not bearing approval of Landlord, said Design Drawings shall be immediately revised by Tenant and resubmitted to Landlord for approval within ten (10) days of their receipt by Tenant.

C. Working Drawings

1. A maximum of sixty (60) days from the date of receipt by Tenant of Landlord's approval of Tenant's Design Drawings or a minimum of thirty (30) days prior to the commencement date of Tenant's Construction and Fixturing Days, whichever is the shorter, Tenant shall submit one (1) sepia and two (2) print sets of Working Drawings to Landlord for review and approval.

2. Tenant's Working Drawings shall include, but not be limited to, the following:

a.) Architectural Drawings

(1) Key Plan showing location of Premises within the Shopping Center.

(2) Floor Plan at ⅛"=1'-0" scale.

(3) Longitudinal Section at ⅛"=1'-0" scale.

(4) Interior Elevations at ⅛"=1'-0" scale.

(5) Store Front Plan, Section, Elevation at ¼"=1'-0" scale.

(6) Reflected Ceiling Plan at ⅛"=1'-0" scale.

(7) Partition Wall Sections at ½"=1'-0" scale.

(8) Door, Finish and Color Schedules and samples.

(9) Specifications.

b.) Electrical Drawings

(1) Circuitry Plan at ⅛"=1'-0" scale.

(2) Panelboard schedules.

(3) Riser Diagrams.

(4) Electric Load Tabulation.

(5) Specifications.

c.) Mechanical Drawings

(1) HVAC Distribution Plan at ⅛"=1'-0" scale.

(2) Mechanical/Electrical Data Tabulation Sheet.

(3) Plumbing Plan at ⅛"=1'-0".

(4) Specifications.

D. SPRINKLER SUBCONTRACTOR SHOP DRAWINGS

1. Tenant's sprinkler subcontractor shall submit Shop Drawings directly to Landlord's Fire Insurance Underwriter for approval. Submission shall include one (1) sepia transparency and two (2) blueline prints.

2. Drawings shall include:

a.) Reflected Ceiling Plan with sprinkler head locations dimensioned at a minimum scale of ⅛"=1'-10".

b.) Automatic Sprinkler details.

c.) Specifications

E. SIGN FABRICATORS SHOP DRAWING

1. Tenant's sign fabricator shall submit Shop Drawings directly to Landlord for approval. All submissions to include one (1) sepia transparency and two (2) blueline prints unless otherwise noted.

2. Shop drawing must include full dimensions, letter style and type, face (color, material and thickness), returns (color, material and thickness), type of lighting, brightness, mounting hardware and transformer location and access.

APPENDIX D

Sample Merchants Association Bylaws

Note: This sample set of merchants association bylaws is presented to provide a general understanding of the organization of a typical merchants association. It is not endorsed as a model. Rather, each association should develop documents appropriate to the particular center.

ARTICLE I

Purpose, Members and Dues

Section 1. Purpose and General Statement: The purpose of the Association shall be to promote _____ (hereinafter referred to as the "Mall") through the sponsorship of commercial, cultural, educational, community and other programs; and, in furtherance of such purpose, to engage in and conduct promotional programs and publicity, special events, decorations, cooperative advertising in the general interest and for the benefit of the Mall. The Association does not own any of the common areas of the Mall and the use of the same is in the absolute control of the landlord of the Mall. The rights and obligations of the tenants of the Mall that are members shall in no way be diminished or enhanced by their membership in the Association and said rights and obligations shall be governed solely by the respective leases entered into wih the landlord of the Mall. The Association shall be conducted as a non-profit organization, and no part of the profits (if any) shall inure to the benefit of any member or be used for any other purpose.

Section 2. Members: Each and every business, doing business in the Mall as a tenant and any owner of property doing business in the Mall as a merchant, upon payment of dues shall be a member of the Association and as such shall be entitled to one vote. The owner of the Mall shall be a full member of the Association and in such capacity shall be entitled to one vote and shall have the right to attend and participate in all meetings of the members. Membership in the Association shall continue so long as the respective member (or associate member) continues to conduct business in the Mall as a merchant; provided, however, that membership in the Association may be terminated by a two-thirds vote of the Board of Directors upon the occurrence of either of the following events: (1) The member (or associate member) has failed to pay its dues when same have become due and payable; and (2) The member has failed to comply with the rules, regulations, resolutions and By-Laws of the Association.

Section 3. Associate Membership: Associate membership is open to all persons or businesses doing business in the area adjacent to or contiguous with the Mall. Associate membership must be sponsored and approved by the owner of the Mall and be ratified by a majority vote of the Board of Directors, provided, however, that an associate member shall have no right to vote at Association member's meetings or become a member of the Board of Directors. Associate members shall pay $_____ to the Association in initial assessments (payable when approved for membership by the Board of Directors) as well as annual dues to the Association of $_____. In addition, associate members shall be subject to increases in dues in the same manner in which regular members shall be subject.

Section 4. Dues: An initial assessment and regular monthly dues shall be paid by the members of the Association as provided by Lease or other Agreement. Such monthly payments shall commence on the date provided by Lease or other Agreement and shall be subject to adjustments, increasing said monthly dues to the extent required by increases in the cost of promotional, public relations and advertising services as provided in such Lease or other Agreement.

Section 5. Annual Meetings: The Association shall hold each year, during the second week within the month of March, an annual meeting of the members for the election of directors and the transaction of any business within the powers of the Association. Failure to hold an annual meeting at the designated time shall not, however, invalidate the corporate existence of the Association or affect otherwise valid corporate acts.

Section 6. Special Meetings: At any time in the interval between annual meetings, special meetings of the members may be called by the President or by the Board of Directors or by members having one-third of the votes entitled to be cast at such meeting.

Section 7. Place of Meetings: All meetings of the members shall be held at a place designated by the Board of Directors.

Section 8. Notice of Meetings: Not less than ten (10) days nor more than fifty (50) days before the date of every meeting of members, the Secretary-Treasurer shall give to each member written or printed notice stating the specific time and place of the meeting and, in the case of a special meeting, the purpose or purposes for which the meeting is called, either by mail or by presenting it to him personally or by leaving it at his place of business in the Shopping Center. If mailed, such notice shall be deemed to be given when deposited in the United States mail addressed to the member at his post office address as it appears on the records of the Association, with postage thereon prepaid. Notwithstanding the foregoing provision a waiver of notice in writing, signed by the person or persons entitled to such notice and filed with the records of the meeting, whether before or after the holding thereof, or actual attendance at the meeting in person or by proxy, shall be deemed equivalent to the giving of such notice to such person. Any meeting of members, annual or special, may adjourn from time to time to reconvene at the same or some other place, and no notice need be given of any such adjourned meeting other than by announcement.

Section 9. Quorum: One-third of the members in good standing present, in person or by proxy, shall constitute a quorum. In the absence of a quorum, the members present or by proxy, by majority vote and without notice other than by announcement, may adjourn the meeting from time to time until a quorum shall attend. At any such adjourned meeting at which a quorum shall be present, any business may be transacted which might have been transacted at the meeting as originally notified.

Section 10. Votes Required: A majority of the votes cast at a meeting of members, duly called and at which a quorum is present, shall be sufficient to take or authorize action upon any matter which may properly come before the meeting, unless more than a majority of votes cast is required by statute or by these By-Laws.

Section 11. Proxies: Any member may vote either in person or by proxy or representative designated in writing by such member, provided, however, no person may serve as a proxy or representative for more than one (1) member.

Section 12. Voting: In all elections for directors every member of the Association shall have the right to vote, in person or by proxy, or by representative. Votes may not be cumulated.

ARTICLE II

Board of Directors

Section 1. Powers: The business and affairs of the Association shall be managed by its Board of Directors. The Board of Directors may exercise all the powers of the Association, except such as are conferred upon or reserved to the members by the Articles of Incorporation or the By-Laws. The Board of Directors may enforce the rules, regulations, resolutions and By-Laws of the Association by whatever means it deems appropriate, except such as are specifically prohibited by statute, Lease or other Agreement, or the By-Laws of the Association. The Board of Directors shall keep full and fair accounts of its transactions.

Section 2. Number of Directors: The number of Directors of the Association shall be nine (9); all of whom shall be members (not associate members) of the Association; provided, however, that at all times the Mall management, _____, and the _____, department stores, shall be represented on the Board of Directors.

Section 3. Election of Directors: Directors shall be elected at each annual meeting of the members and shall hold office until the next annual meeting when the new Directors are elected. Notwithstanding the foregoing, at all times the Mall management, _____, and the _____, department stores, shall have their respective designated representatives on the Board of Directors. The first Board of Directors shall be elected at the Formation meeting held in February and shall hold office until the first annual meeting in March. Election of a director shall be by a majority vote of all members in good standing present at such meeting either in person or by proxy.

Section 4. Nominating Committee: A nominating committee of not less than three (3) representatives of active members of this Association shall be appointed by the President not less than thirty (30) days prior to the election, whose duty it shall be to nominate from the representatives of the active members of this Association as many members as may be voted on for members of the Board of Directors as there are vacancies to be filled. Said committee shall file a list of nominees recommended with the Secretary-Treasurer of this Association not later than fifteen (15) days before the election.

The Secretary-Treasurer of this Association shall mail to all members of this Association ten (10) days prior to the election a list of the nominees recommended by the nominating committee.

All other nominations shall be submitted to the Secretary-Treasurer in writing with five (5) signatures of members in good standing at least three (3) days prior to the annual meeting. No nominations shall be accepted from the floor. If additional nominations are submitted, ballots will be prepared and voting will be by ballot. Members will vote for as many members as there are vacancies to be filled. Voting shall not be cumulative.

Section 5. Vacancies: Any vacancy, except those of Mall management, occurring in the

Board of Directors for any cause shall be filled by a candidate receiving a majority of the votes of the remaining members of the Board of Directors. A director so elected shall hold office until the next annual meeting of members or until his successor is elected and qualifies.

Section 6. Regular Meetings: Regular meetings of the Board of Directors shall be held at least ten (10) times annually, but not more often than once each month, at such place or places as shall be designated by the Board.

Section 7. Special Meetings: Special meetings of the Board of Directors may be called at any time by the President or by a majority vote of the members of the Board of Directors. Such meetings shall be held at a place or places as shall be designated by the Board of Directors. The notice with respect to any such special meetings may but need not contain a statement of the purpose or purposes of such meeting.

Section 8. Members Attending Meetings: Any member in good standing of the Association shall be allowed to attend either regular or special meetings of the Board of Directors. The Board of Directors shall have the right, however, to move into executive session by a majority vote of the quorum at any duly constituted meeting.

Section 9. Notice of Meetings: Except as provided in Section 6, notice of the place, day and hour of every regular and special meeting shall be given to each director two (2) days (or more) before the meeting, by delivering the same to him personally, or by sending the same to him by telegraph, or by leaving the same at his residence or usual place of business, or in the alternative, by mailing such notice three (3) days (or more) before the meeting, postage prepaid and addressed to him at his last known post office address, according to the records of the Association. Unless required by these By-Laws or by resolution of the Board of Directors, no notice of any meeting of the Board of Directors need state the business to be transacted thereat. No notice of any meeting of the Board of Directors need be given to any director who submits a signed waiver of notice before or after the meeting, or who attends and does not object thereat to the transaction of any business because of the lack of or tardy notice. Any meeting of the Board of Directors, regular or special, may adjourn from time to time to reconvene at the same or some other place, and no notice need be given of any such adjourned meeting other than by announcement of such meeting.

Section 10. Quorum: At all meetings of the Board of Directors, a majority of the entire Board of Directors shall constitute a quorum for the transaction of business. Except in cases in which it is by statute, by the Articles of Incorporation or by the By-Laws otherwise provided, the vote of a majority of such quorum at a duly constituted meeting shall be sufficient to elect and pass any measure. In the absence of a quorum, the directors present by majority vote and without notice other than by announcement at such meeting may adjourn the meeting from time to time until a quorum shall be present, any business may be transacted which might have been transacted at the meeting as originally scheduled.

Section 11. Removal of Directors: At any meeting of the members of the Association called for the purpose of removing any director, such director may be removed from office for cause or without cause, and another be elected in the place of the director removed by a majority of vote of members in good standing present at such meeting either in person or by proxy.

Section 12. Compensation: Directors, as such, shall not receive any stated compensation for their services, but by resolution of the Board, their expenses of attendance, if any, may be allowed for attendance at each regular or special meeting of the Board; provided, however, that nothing herein contained shall be construed to preclude any director from serving the Association in any other capacity and receiving compensation therefor.

ARTICLE III
Officers

Section 1. Executive Officers: The executive officers of this Association shall be a President, Vice President and Secretary-Treasurer. The President and Vice President shall be active members or representatives of active members of this Association, elected by the Board of Directors from their own number at the first meeting after the annual election of directors, and they shall hold office for one (1) year and until their successors are elected. The Secretary-Treasurer shall be an employee of the Mall management and shall be appointed by the Mall management representative on the Board of Directors, and shall hold such position until his successor is appointed by the Mall management representative on the Board of Directors.

Section 2. President: It shall be the duty of the President to preside at all meetings of the Association and of the Board of Directors. He shall have general supervision over the affairs of this Association, subject to the direction and control of the Board of Directors. Standing committees shall be appointed by the President, with the consent and approval of the Board of Directors. Emergency or special committees may be appointed by the President.

Section 3. Vice President: In the absence of the President or in the event of his inability to act, the Vice President shall exercise all powers and perform all duties of the President.

Section 4. Secretary-Treasurer: The Secretary-Treasurer shall perform all the duties incident to the offices of a secretary and treasurer of a corporation, and such other duties as, from time to time, may be assigned to him by the Board of Directors or the President. The Secretary-Treasurer shall cause to be kept minutes of the meetings of the members and of the Board of Directors in books provided for that purpose; he shall see that all notices are duly given in accordance with the provisions of the By-Laws or as required by law; he shall be custodian of the records of the Association; he shall have charge of and be responsible for all funds, securities, receipts and disbursements of the Association, and shall deposit, or cause to be deposited in the name of the Association, all monies or other valuable effects in such banks, trust companies or other depositories as shall, from time to time be selected by the Board of Directors; he shall render to the President and to the Board of Directors, whenever requested, an account of the financial condition of the Association. Within thirty (30) days of the annual election for Board of Directors, the Secretary-Treasurer shall tender to the new Board of Directors an audited statement of the accounts for the preceding fiscal year.

Section 5. Assistant Officers: The Board of Directors may appoint such assistant officers as it deems advisable which assistant officers shall have such duties as from time to time may be assigned to them, or any one of them, by the Board of Directors or the President. Assistant officers shall be active members or representatives of the members of the Association.

Section 6. Removal: Any officer or agent of the Association may be removed by the Board of Directors whenever, in its judgment, the best interests of the Association will be served thereby.

Section 7. Compensation: Officers shall serve without salary; however, they shall be reimbursed for expenses incurred in the execution of their office, as approved by the Board of Directors.

ARTICLE IV
Sundry Provisions

Section 1. Fiscal Year: The fiscal year of the Association shall commence February 1st and terminate January 31st of the following year.

Section 2. Annual Reports: The Secretary-Treasurer shall cause to be prepared annually a full and correct statement of the affairs of the Association, including a balance sheet and a financial statement of the operations for the preceding fiscal year, which shall be submitted at the annual meeting of the members and mailed to all members, and filed within twenty (20) days thereafter at the principal office of the Association in the State of _____.

Section 3. Disbursements: All checks, drafts and orders for the payment of money, notes and other evidences of indebtedness, issued in the name of the Association, shall unless otherwise provided by resolution of the Board of Directors, be signed by any two (2) of the following three (3) officers: President, Vice President or Secretary-Treasurer. These persons shall be bonded to the extent deemed necessary by the Board of Directors.

Section 4. Bonds: The Board of Directors may require any officer, agent or employee of the Association to give bond to the Association, conditioned upon the faithful discharge of his duties, with one or more sureties and in such amount as may be satisfactory to the Board of Directors.

Section 5. Insurance: The Board of Directors shall purchase such insurance as it and the Mall management deem necessary to protect the Association and indemnify the owner of the Mall from any claims arising from the promotional or other activities of the Association.

Section 6. Dividends: No dividends shall be paid to any member of the Association.

Section 7. Meeting Agenda: No member may introduce at any meeting of members of the Board of Directors any topic for discussion not directly related to the purpose of the Association as defined in Article I, Section 1, of the By-Laws.

Section 8. Amendments: A unanimous vote of the members is required to adopt new By-Laws or to amend the following sections:

Article I, Sections 1, 2 and 11
Article II, Sections 2 and 3
Article IV, Sections 1 and 7

All other sections may be amended at any annual meeting of the members by a majority of members present at such meeting either in person or by proxy, or at any special meeting called for that purpose.

APPENDIX E

Sample Zoning Ordinance Provisions

Note: Zoning for shopping centers can be handled in any of a variety of ways. In this sample the shopping center is treated as a conditional use, thus allowing for flexibility in the approval requirements for each center. These ordinance provisions are not endorsed as a model but rather are given as an example of one of several suitable methods.

8. Shopping Centers

The purpose of these regulations is to encourage the effective and timely development of land for commercial purposes in accordance with the objective and policies of the _____ _____ Land Use Plan; to assure suitable design in order to protect the property values and the residential environment of adjacent neighborhoods; and to minimize traffic congestion on the public streets.

a. **Application**—In addition to the general application requirements provided in Sub-section A of this Section, the applicant shall furnish the following information and exhibits to the Zoning Board of Appeals concerning his proposed development:

1) *Ownership*—All land in the proposed shopping center shall be held in either single ownership or in unified control and shall contain no public streets or alleys. A shopping center site can not lie on two sides of a public street or alley.

2) *Existing Conditions*—
a) Boundary line of proposed shopping center, and the total acreage encompassed thereby;
b) The size and location of existing sewers, water mains, culverts, manholes, and other underground facilities within the tract.

3) *Proposed Conditions* — Preliminary sketches showing the following:
a) Location, general layout, and dimensions of principal and accessory buildings;
b) Traffic circulation within the confines of the shopping center;
c) Location, arrangement, and dimensions of automobile parking bays, aisles, and loading spaces;
d) Location and dimensions of vehicular drives, entrances, exits, acceleration and deceleration lanes;
e) Location and dimensions of pedestrian entrances, exits, walks, and walkways;
f) Location, arrangement, and dimensions of truck loading and unloading spaces and docks;
g) Architectural sketches of the proposed buildings;
h) Drainage and sanitary systems.

4) *Market Analysis*—A market analysis, prepared and signed by a recognized independent market analyst acceptable to the Planning Commission, containing the following determination:
a) Trade area of proposed shopping center;
b) Population of the trade area, present and projected;
c) Effective buying power in the trade area, present and projected;
d) Net potential customer buying power for stores in the proposed shopping center, and on the basis of such buying power, the recommended store types and store floor area;
e) Residual amount of buying power and how it may be expected to be expended in existing business areas serving the proposed trade area.

5) *A statement of financial responsibility.*

b. **Procedure**—A public hearing shall be held in accordance with Article Six, Section V-A and the Council shall pass a resolution accepting or rejecting the application. If the application is accepted, the Planning Commission shall have the administrative power and duty, in accordance with the requirements of this Ordinance to review the preliminary and final site plans for proposed shopping centers and make a written report to the Council. The Council shall then act upon the accepted application in accordance with the provisions of Article Six, Section V-A. The Building and Zoning Officer shall grant no building permit or certificate of occupancy except for construction and occupancy in strict compliance with a conditional use permit and a final site plan approved by the Council. Such building permits must be requested within one (1) year of the date of approval of the conditional use permit.

1) *Preliminary Site Plan Submission*—A preliminary site plan for the development of such property shall be presented to the Planning Commission for review. The preliminary site plan shall show the following, together with appropriate dimensions:
a) Proposed name of the shopping center;
b) Location by legal description;
c) Names and addresses of applicant and designer who made the plan;
d) Scale of plan, 1" to 100';
e) Date;
f) North arrow;
g) Contours at two (2) foot intervals;
h) Boundary line of proposed shopping center, indicated by a solid line, and the total acreage encompassed thereby;
i) Location, widths, and names of all existing or prior platted streets, railroad and utility rights-of-way, parks, and other public open spaces, permanent buildings and structures, houses or permanent easements, and section and municipal boundary lines, within five hundred (500) feet of the tract;
j) Existing sewers, water mains, culverts and other underground facilities within the tract, indicating pipe sizes, grades, manholes and location;
k) Location, arrangement, and dimensions of automobile parking space, width of aisles, width of bays, angle of parking;
l) Location, arrangement, and dimensions of truck loading and unloading spaces and docks;
m) Location and dimensions of vehicular drives, entrances, exits, acceleration and deceleration lanes;
n) Location and dimensions of pedestrian entrances, exits, walks;
o) Drainage system and sanitary sewer;
p) Location, height, and materials of walls, fences, and screen plantings;
q) Ground cover, finished grades, slopes, banks, and ditches;
r) Location and general exterior dimensions of principal and accessory buildings;
s) Location, size, height, and orientation of all signs other than signs flat on building facades;
t) Preliminary architectural drawings for all buildings;
u) If it is proposed to restrict signs or to establish an association of merchants by means of lease provisions or covenants, the text of such provisions;
v) The stages, if any, to be followed in the construction of the shopping center;
w) A traffic flow chart showing circulation patterns within the confines of the shopping center.

2) *Action on Preliminary Site Plan*—Not more than sixty (60) days after receipt of the preliminary site plan, the Planning Commission shall determine whether the proposed shopping center would comply with all requirements of this Ordinance, and on such basis, shall:
a) Approve the preliminary plan. The applicant may then proceed to file a final site plan; or,

b) Notify the applicant in writing how the plan must be amended to comply with the requirements of this Ordinance. The applicant may, within thirty (30) days thereafter or within such further period as may be agreed to by the Planning Commission, submit an amended preliminary plan containing the required changes. If an amended preliminary plan is not filed within the prescribed period, the original preliminary plan shall be considered disapproved. If an amended preliminary plan is filed within the prescribed period, the Planning Commission shall approve or disapprove the plan within thirty (30) days after the date of filing, or within such further period as may be agreed to by the applicant; or,

c) Notify the Council and the applicant in writing that the plan does not comply with the requirements of this Ordinance and is not susceptible to amendment. The applicant may then apply to the Council for a review of the decision of the Planning Commission.

3. *Final Site Plan Submission*—Within one (1) year after approval of the preliminary site plan, the applicant shall submit to the Planning Commission a final site plan of either (1) the entire shopping center, or (2) the first stage of such center that is to be constructed. Such plan shall be drawn to scale, shall include appropriate dimensions, shall contain all information required by this Ordinance for a preliminary plan, shall contain final architectural drawings for all buildings included in the final site plan, and shall contain any additional information required by the Planning Commission at the time of the preliminary plan.

a) Stage Construction—If development of the shopping center is to be carried out in progressive stages, each stage shall be so planned that the requirements and intent of this Ordinance shall be fully complied with at the completion of each stage. No final plan for the initial stage of development of any shopping center shall be approved unless such stage comprises a total ground floor area of at least twenty-five thousand (25,000) square feet and at least three (3) of the designated principal uses.

b) Action on Final Site Plan—Compliance with Preliminary Site Plan—Not more than thirty (30) days after receipt of a final site plan for a shopping center or for any stage thereof, the Planning Commission shall determine whether such final plan is in compliance with the preliminary plan as approved by the Commission. If the final plan is determined to be in compliance and if all applicable requirements of this Sub-section are also complied with, the Commission shall recommend to the Council approval of the final plan. In all other instances, the Commission shall recommend disapproval of the final plan and shall so notify the applicant in writing. The applicant may then apply to the Council for a review of the decision of the Planning Commission. If the final plan is disapproved because of noncompliance with the preliminary plan, the final plan may thereafter be submitted to the Commission as an amended preliminary plan. The procedure for the consideration of such amended preliminary plan shall be the same as that for the consideration of an original preliminary plan.

c) Change of Final Site Plan—If the applicant wants to make any amendment to an approved final plan, a written request shall be submitted to the Commission. If, in the opinion of the Commission, a requested change is sufficiently substantial, the Commission shall require the submission of an amended final plan. The procedure for the consideration of such written request or of such amended final plan shall be the same as that for the consideration of a final plan.

c. **Standards for Development—**

1) *Permitted Uses*—Any use permitted in the CB zone except dwellings and dwelling units is permitted as a principal use of land in a shopping center.

2) *Site Area*—A shopping center shall be located on a zoning lot having an area of at least ten (10) acres.

3) *Floor Area Ratio*—The combined floor area ratio for all principal buildings, together with all accessory buildings, shall not exceed 0.35 on any zoning lot.

4) *Maximum Lot Coverage* — The total ground area, occupied by all principal buildings, together with all accessory buildings, shall not exceed twenty-five (25) per cent of the total area of the zoning lot.

5) *Building Setback Line*—Each zoning lot shall have a building setback from all street rights-of-way of at least eighty (80) feet. A strip twenty (20) feet deep along the front line shall be maintained as a landscaped buffer strip. The remaining area may be used for parking.

6) *Side and Rear Yards*—Each zoning lot shall have side and rear yards of at least fifty (50) feet in width. A strip twenty (20) feet in width or depth along side and rear lot lines shall be maintained as a landscaped buffer strip. The remainder of the area may be used for parking.

7) *Height Restriction*—No principal building shall exceed five (5) stories or fifty-five (55) feet in height; no accessory building or other structure shall exceed one (1) story or twenty (20) feet in height.

8) *Special Buffer Requirement Adjacent to Residential Areas*—Along any boundary line adjacent to a residential area, a buffer yard shall be provided which shall be at least one hundred (100) feet in depth, measured from the property line.

9) *Access and Traffic Control*—

a) *Access Barrier*—Each zoning lot, with its buildings, other structures, and parking and loading areas, shall be physically separated from each adjoining street by a curb or other suitable barrier against unchanneled motor vehicle ingress and egress. Such barrier shall be located at the edge of or within, a twenty (20) feet deep strip along the property line. Except for the access ways permitted by (b) below, the barrier shall be continuous for the entire length of the property line.

b) *Access Ways*—Each zoning lot shall have not more than two (2) access ways to any one street unless unusual circumstances demonstrate the need for additional access points. Each access way shall comply with the following requirements:

The width of any access way leading to a public street shall not exceed twenty-five (25) feet at its intersection with the property line. Curb returns shall have a minimum radius of thirty (30) feet.

At its intersection with the property line, no part of any access way shall be nearer than one hundred (100) feet to the intersection of any two (2) street right-of-way lines, nor shall any such part be nearer than fifty (50) feet to any side or rear property line.

The location and number of access ways shall be so arranged that they will reduce traffic hazards as much as possible.

10) *Off-Street Parking Areas*—All off-street parking spaces and servicing drives shall be located within the boundaries of the property being developed as a shopping center. Off-street parking spaces shall be provided at the rate of at least three (3) square feet of parking area to one (1) square foot of gross floor area. Spaces provided behind the stores or shops shall not be considered usable by the public and shall not be considered in calculating the minimum space required; provided however, that if the shopping center is so designed that all of the shops and stores face

upon a central mall and all sections of the parking area are provided with adequate connecting internal drives, the location of parking areas may completely surround such shops and stores.

11) *Off-Street Loading Areas*—Each shop or store shall have a rear or side entrance that is accessible to a loading area and service drive. Service drives shall be a minimum of twenty-six (26) feet in width and shall be in addition to and not part of the drives or circulation system used by the vehicles of shoppers. The arrangement of truck loading and unloading facilities for each shop or store shall be such that in the process of loading or unloading no truck will block or extend into any other private or public drive or street used for vehicular circulation. Loading and delivery zones shall be clearly marked.

12) *Lighting*—All parking areas and access ways shall be flood lighted at night during business hours. All outside lighting shall be arranged and shielded to prevent glare or reflection, nuisance, inconvenience, or hazardous interference of any kind on adjoining streets or residential properties.

13) *Waste Pens*—Each building shall be provided with an enclosed waste pen of sufficient size to accommodate all trash and waste stored on the premises.

14) *Trash Burners and Incinerators*—There shall be no trash burner or incinerators, or any burning of trash or rubbish on the premises.

8.1 Regional Shopping Centers

These regulations are to apply to the development of shopping centers containing a wide range of retail business and accessory uses serving a trade area embracing a large segment of the community.

a. **Application**—In addition to the general application requirements provided in Sub-section A of this Section, the applicant shall furnish the following information and exhibits to the Zoning Board of Appeals concerning his proposed development:

1) *Ownership*—All land in the proposed shopping center shall be held in either single ownership or in unified control and shall contain no public streets or alleys. A shopping center site cannot lie on two sides of a public street or alley.

2) *Existing Conditions*—

a) Boundary line of proposed shopping center, and the total acreage encompassed thereby;

b) The size and location of existing sewers, water mains, culverts, manholes, and other underground facilities within the tract.

3) *Proposed Conditions* — Preliminary sketches showing the following:

a) Location, general layout, and dimensions of principal and accessory buildings;

b) Traffic circulation within the confines of the shopping center;

c) Location, arrangement, and dimensions of automobile parking bays, aisles, and loading spaces;

d) Location and dimensions of vehicular drives, entrances, exits, acceleration and deceleration lanes;

e) Location and dimensions of pedestrian entrances, exits, walks, and walkways;

f) Location, arrangement, and dimensions of truck loading and unloading spaces and docks;

g) Architectural sketches of the proposed buildings;

h) Drainage and sanitary systems.

4) *Market Analysis*—A market analysis, prepared and signed by a recognized independent market analyst acceptable to the Planning Commission, containing the following determination:

a) Trade area of proposed shopping center;

b) Population of the trade area, present and projected;

c) Effective buying power in the trade area, present and projected;

d) Net potential customer buying power for stores in the proposed shopping center,

and on the basis of such buying power, the recommended store types and store floor area;

e) Residual amount of buying power and how it may be expected to be expended in existing business areas serving the proposed trade area.

5) A statement of financial responsibility.

b. **Procedure**—A public hearing shall be held in accordance with Article Six, Section V-A, and, in addition the Planning Commission shall review the application in accordance with the requirements of this Ordinance and shall prepare a written recommendation to the Council. The Council shall act upon the application in accordance with the provisions of Article Six, Section V-A. The Planning Commission shall have the further administrative power and duty to review the final plans for compliance with the standards of this Ordinance and the conditions set forth in the conditional use permit and no building permit shall be issued except in compliance with such standards and conditions.

1) *Preliminary Site Plan Submission*—A preliminary site plan for the development of such property shall be presented to the Planning Commission for review. The preliminary site plan shall show the following, together with appropriate dimensions:

a) Proposed name of the shopping center;

b) Location by legal description;

c) Names and addresses of applicant and designer who made the plan;

d) Scale of plan, 1″ to 100′;

e) Date;

f) North arrow;

g) Contours at two (2) foot intervals;

h) Boundary line of proposed shopping center, indicated by a solid line, and the total acreage encompassed thereby;

i) Location, widths, and names of all existing or prior platted streets, railroad and utility rights-of-way, parks, and other public open spaces, permanent buildings and structures, houses or permanent easements, and section and municipal boundary lines, within five hundred (500) feet of the tract;

j) Existing sewers, water mains, culverts and other underground facilities within the tract, indicating pipe sizes, grades, manholes and location;

k) Location, arrangement, and dimensions of automobile parking space, width of aisles, width of bays, angle of parking;

l) Location, arrangement, and dimensions of truck loading and unloading spaces and docks;

m) Location and dimensions of vehicular drives, entrances, exits, acceleration and deceleration lanes;

n) Location and dimensions of pedestrian entrances, exits, walks;

o) Drainage system and sanitary sewer;

p) Location, height, and materials of walls, fences, and screen plantings;

q) Ground cover, finished grades, slopes, banks, and ditches;

r) Location and general exterior dimensions of principal and accessory buildings;

s) Location, size, height, and orientation of all signs other than signs flat on building facades;

t) Preliminary architectural drawings for all buildings;

u) If it is proposed to restrict signs or to establish an association of merchants by means of lease provisions or convenants, the text of such provisions;

v) The stages, if any, to be followed in the construction of the shopping center. The preliminary site plan shall show any areas reserved for future development even though specific plans for such areas have not been developed.

w) A traffic flow chart showing circulation patterns within the confines of the shopping center.

2) *Action on Preliminary Site Plan*—Not more than sixty (60) days after receipt of the preliminary site plan, the Planning Commission shall determine whether the proposed shopping center would comply with all require-

ments of this Ordinance, and on such basis, shall:

a) Approve the preliminary plan and recommend to the Council that the conditional use permit be granted stating any special conditions which should in the opinion of the Planning Commission be a part of such permit. Such recommendation shall cover height of buildings, staging of construction, and the development of reserved areas shown on the preliminary site plan. The applicant may then proceed to file a final site plan; or,

b) Notify the applicant in writing how the plan must be amended to comply with the requirements of this Ordinance. The applicant may, within thirty (30) days thereafter or within such further period as may be agreed to by the Planning Commission, submit an amended preliminary plan containing the required changes. If an amended preliminary plan is not filed within the prescribed period, the original preliminary plan shall be considered disapproved. If an amended preliminary plan is filed within the prescribed period, the Planning Commission shall approve or disapprove the plan within thirty (30) days after the date of filing, or within such further period as may be agreed to by the applicant; or,

c) Notify the Council and the applicant in writing that the plan does not comply with the requirements of this Ordinance and is not susceptible to amendment. The applicant may then apply to the Council for a review of the decision of the Planning Commission.

3) *Final Site Plan Submission*—Within one (1) year after approval of the preliminary site plan, the applicant shall submit to the Planning Commission a final site plan of either (1) the entire shopping center, or (2) the first stage of such center that is to be constructed. Such plan shall be drawn to scale, shall include appropriate dimensions, shall contain all information required by this Ordinance for a preliminary plan, shall contain final architectural drawings for all buildings included in the final site plan, and shall contain any additional information required by the Planning Commission at the time of the preliminary plan.

a) *Stage Construction*—If development of the shopping center is to be carried out in progressive stages, each stage shall be so planned that the requirements and intent of this Ordinance shall be fully complied with at the completion of each stage. No final plan for the initial stage of development of any shopping center shall be approved unless such stage comprises a total ground floor area of at least twenty-five thousand (25,000) square feet and at least three (3) of the designated principal uses.

b) *Action on Final Site Plan*—Compliance with Preliminary Site Plan—Not more than thirty (30) days after receipt of a final site plan for a shopping center or for any stage thereof, the Planning Commission shall determine whether such final plan is in compliance with the preliminary plan as approved by the Commission. If the final plan is determined to be in compliance and if all applicable requirements of this Sub-section are also complied with or if the Planning Commission shall determine that modifications, if any, and the proposed development of the reserve areas, if any, contained in the final site plan are in harmony with the general purposes and intent of the approved preliminary plan,

and not in conflict with the comprehensive plan for development, the Commission shall so notify the Council. The applicant may then apply for a Building Permit. In all other instances, the Commission shall recommend disapproval of the final plan and shall so notify the applicant in writing. The applicant may then apply to the Council for a review of the decision of the Planning Commission. If the final plan is disapproved because of noncompliance with the preliminary plan, the final plan may thereafter be submitted to the Commission as an amended preliminary plan. The procedure for the consideration of such amended preliminary plan shall be the same as that for the consideration of an original preliminary plan.

c) *Change of Final Site Plan*—If the applicant wants to make any amendment to an approved final plan, a written request shall be submitted to the Commission. If, in the opinion of the Commission, a requested change is sufficiently substantial, the Commission shall require the submission of an amended final plan. The procedure for the consideration of such written request or of such amended final plan shall be the same as that for the consideration of a final plan.

c. **Standards for Development—**

1) *Permitted Uses*—Any use permitted in the CB zone is permitted as a principal use of land in a shopping center except that the Planning Commission shall have the power to recommend and the Council to approve as part of the conditional use permit uses which are not permitted in the CB zone and in addition shall have the power to exclude certain specific uses not compatible with a regional shopping center.

2) *Site and Floor Area*—A Regional Shopping Center shall contain 500,000 square feet of gross leasable area and be located on a zoning lot of at least 50 acres.

3) *Floor Area Ratio*—The combined floor area ratio for all buildings shall not exceed 0.50 on any zoning lot.

4) *Maximum Lot Coverage*—The total ground area, occupied by all principal buildings together with all accessory buildings, shall not exceed twenty-five (25) per cent of the total area of the zoning lot.

5) *Building Setback Line*—Each zoning lot shall have a building setback from all street rights-of-way of at least eighty (80) feet. A strip fifty (50) feet deep along the front line shall be maintained as a landscaped buffer strip. The remaining area may be used for parking.

6) *Side and Rear Yards*—Each zoning lot shall have side and rear yards of at least fifty (50) feet in width. A strip twenty (20) feet in width or depth along side and rear lot lines shall be maintained as a landscaped buffer strip. The remainder of the area may be used for parking.

7) *Height Restriction*—The height of any building in the Regional Shopping Center shall not exceed the limit as specified in the conditional use permit recommended by the Planning Commission and approved by the Council.

8) *Special Buffer Requirement Adjacent to Residential Areas*—Along any boundary line adjacent to a residential area, a buffer yard shall be provided which shall be at least one hundred (100) feet in depth, measured from the property line.

9) *Access and Traffic Control—*

a) Access Barrier—Each zoning lot, with its buildings, other structures, and parking and loading areas, shall be physically separated from each adjoining street by a curb or other suitable barrier against unchanneled motor vehicle ingress and egress. Such barrier shall be located at the edge of or within, a twenty (20) foot deep strip along the property line. Except for the access ways permitted by (b) below, the barrier shall be continuous for the entire length of the property line.

b) Access Ways—Each zoning lot shall have not more than two (2) access ways ot any one street unless unusual circumstances demonstrate the need for additional access points. Each access way shall comply with the following requirements:

The width of any access way leading to a public street which exceeds 25 feet shall have a median between the entrance and exit lanes. Curb returns shall have a minimum radius of thirty (30) feet.

At its intersection with the property line, no part of any access way shall be nearer than one hundred (100) feet to the intersection of any two (2) street right-of-way lines, nor shall any such part be nearer than fifty (50) feet to any side or rear property line.

The location and number of access ways shall be so arranged that they will reduce traffic hazards as much as possible.

10) *Off-Street Parking Areas*—All off-street parking spaces and servicing drives shall be located within the boundaries of the property being developed as a shopping center. Off-street parking spaces shall be provided at the rate of at least two (2) square feet of parking area to one (1) square foot of gross floor area. Spaces provided behind the stores or shops shall not be considered usable by the public and shall not be considered in calculating the minimum space required; provided however, that if the shopping center is so designed that all of the shops and stores face upon a central mall and all sections of the parking area are provided with adequate connecting internal drives, the location of parking areas may completely surround such shops and stores.

11) *Off-Street Loading Areas*—Each shop or store shall have a rear or side entrance that is accessible to a service entrance. Further, any loading dock shall be enclosed within the building. The arrangement of truck loading and unloading facilities for each shop or store shall be such that in the process of loading or unloading no truck will block or extend into any drive or street used for vehicular circulation. Loading and delivery zones shall be clearly marked.

12) *Lighting*—All parking areas and access ways shall be flood lighted at night during busines hours. All outside lighting shall be arranged and shielded to prevent glare or reflection, nuisance, inconvenience, or hazardous interference of any kind on adjoining streets or residential properties.

13) *Waste Pens*—Each building shall be provided with an enclosed waste pen of sufficient size to accommodate all trash and waste stored on the premises.

14) *Trash Burners and Incinerators*—There shall be no trash burner or incinerators, or any burning of trash or rubbish on the premises.

APPENDIX F

Metric Conversions

meters = feet × 0.305
kilometers = miles × 1.609
square meters = square feet × 0.093
hectares = acres × 0.405
(1 hectare = 10,000 square meters)

INDEX